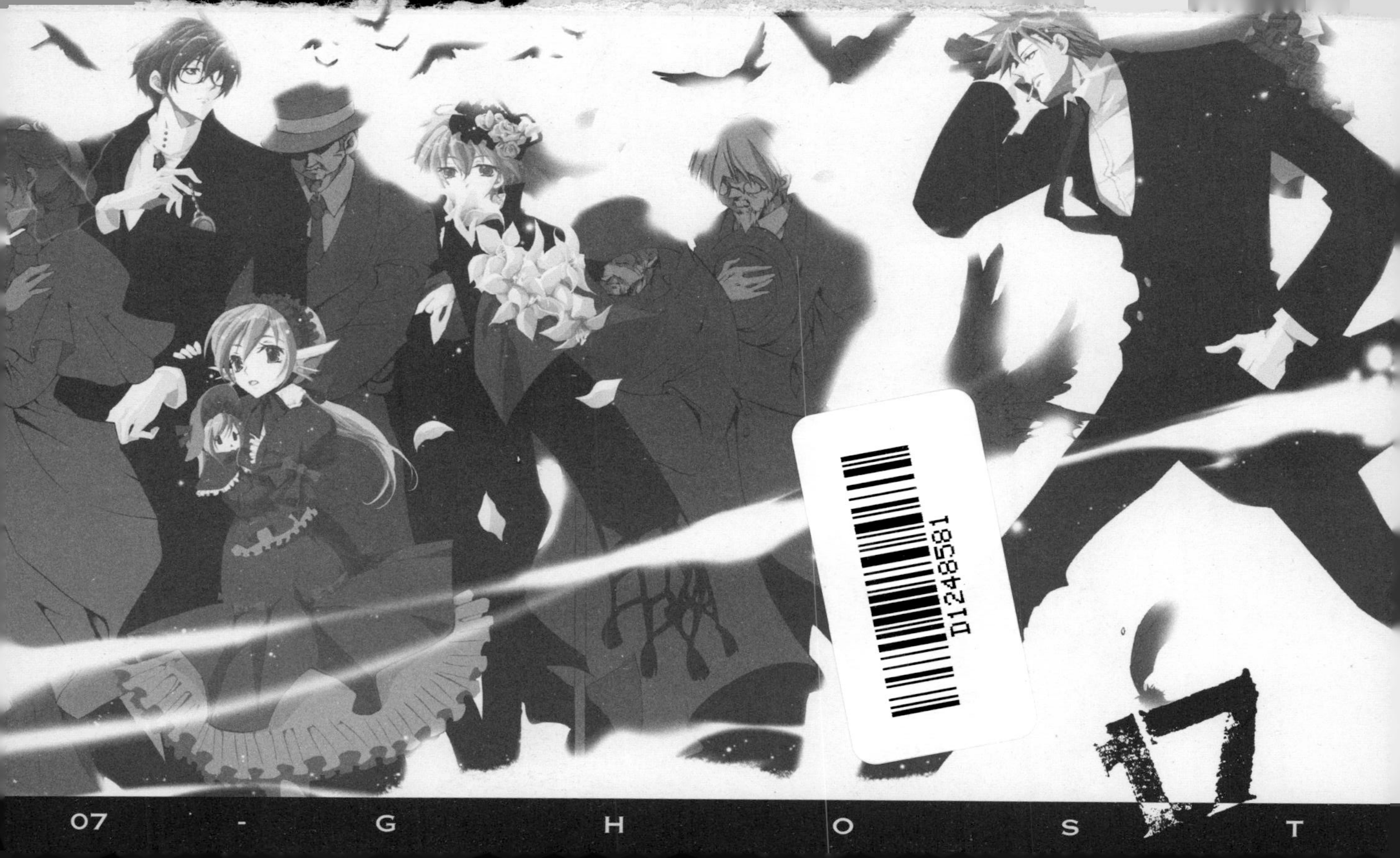
17
07 - G H O S T

-GHOST
ONTENTS

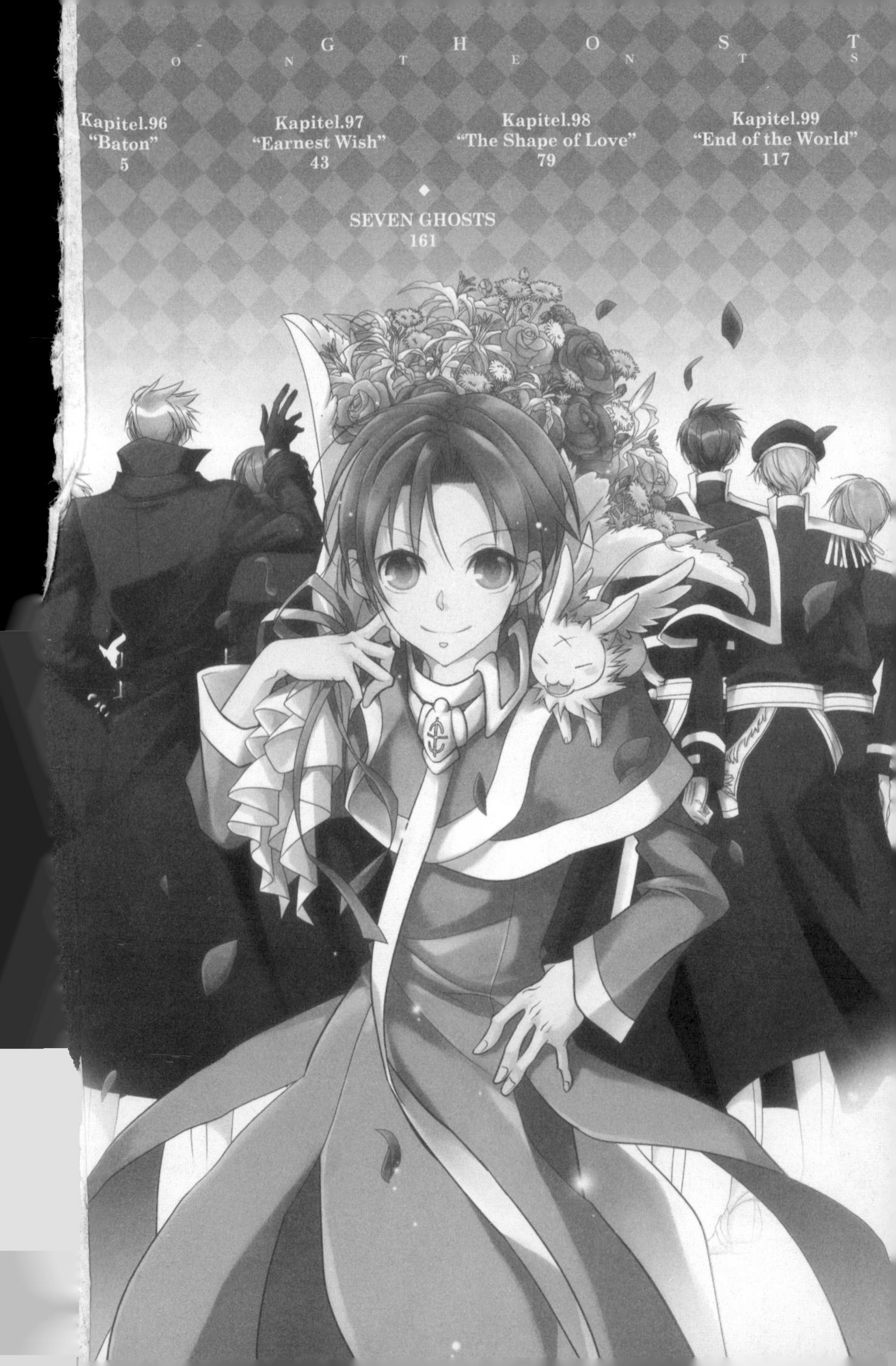

07-GHOST

YUKINO ICHIHARA
YUKI AMEMIYA

17

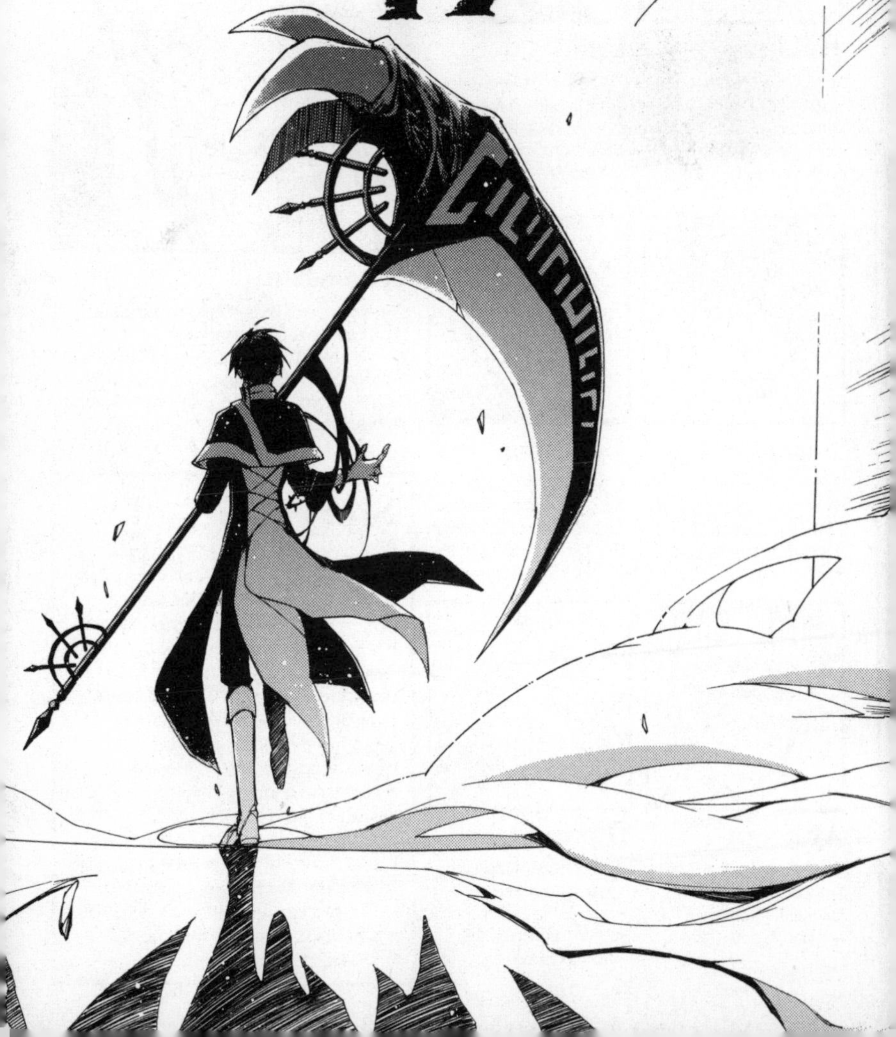

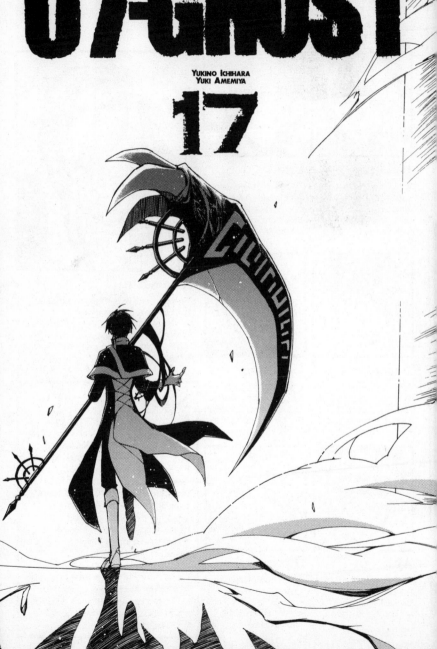

Characters

One thousand years ago, two equally powerful nations coexisted. One was the Barsburg Empire, protected by the Eye of Rafael. The other was the Raggs Kingdom, protected by the Eye of Mikael. Now that the Raggs Kingdom has been destroyed, things have changed...

Hakuren

Teito's friend from the prestigious Oak family. Aimed to be a bishop, but is now the princess's tutor. Not fond of women.

Frau

Bishop who saved Teito. Companion on his journey. He is Zehel of the Seven Ghosts. Bearer of Verloren's scythe.

Teito Klein

Born a prince of Raggs, Teito was stripped of his memories and raised as a soldier by the military academy's chairman. For most of his life, he was unaware that he was a living Pandora's Box, the vessel that contains Verloren's body.

Ayanami

Bishop who can manipulate puppets. He is Fest of the Seven Ghosts. Just escaped the empire's imprisonment.

Labrador

Flower-loving bishop with the power of prophecy. He is Prophe of the Seven Ghosts. Just escaped the empire's imprisonment.

Ayanami

Imperial Army's Chief of Staff. Pursuing Pandora's Box inside Teito. He is the evil death god, Verloren.

Ouka

First princess of the Barsburg Empire. Vessel of the Eye of Rafael. Replica of the actual princess.

Story

Teito is a student at the Barsburg Empire's military academy until the day he discovers that his father was the king of Raggs, the ruler of a kingdom the Barsburg Empire destroyed. He runs away, but loses his best friend to the diabolical Ayanami. As a first step in avenging Mikage's death, Teito becomes an apprentice bishop to obtain special privileges. He then embarks on a journey through the God Houses to the "Land of Seele," which holds the key to his past and the truth about the fall of Raggs. He is swallowed by Verloren, but not fully consumed—Frau becomes one with the scythe to protect him. Now Teito must convince Frau's soul to return.

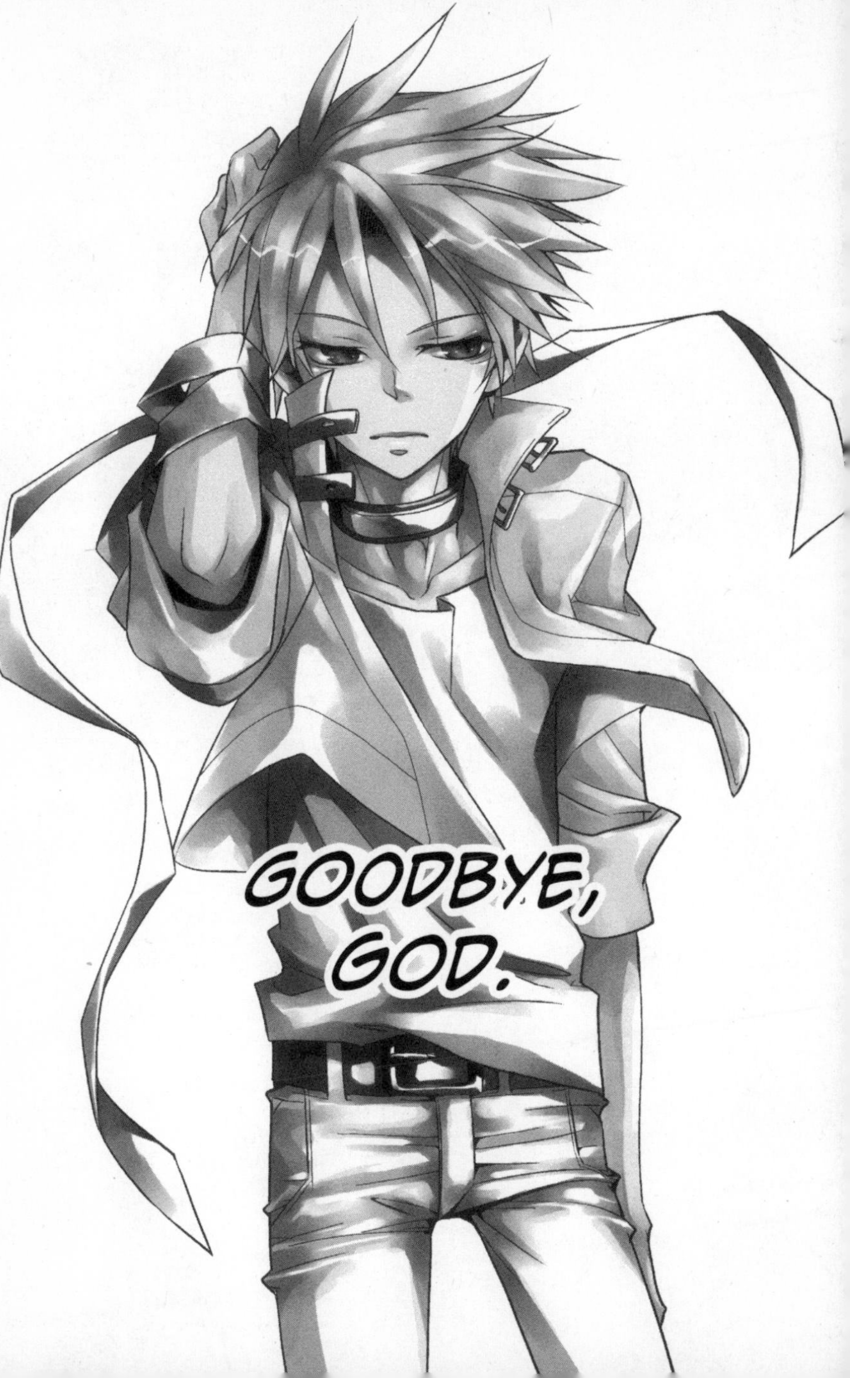
GOODBYE, GOD.

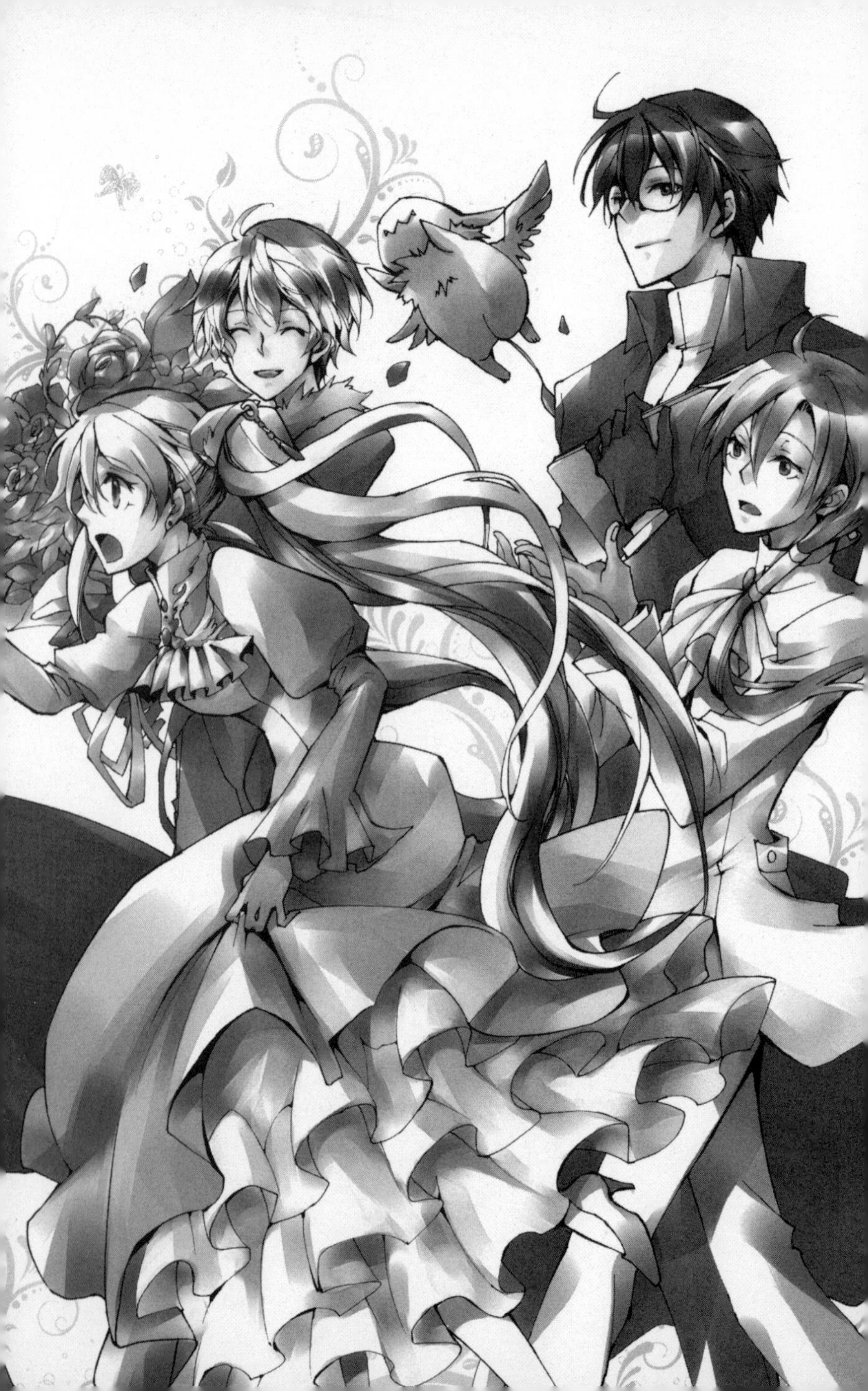

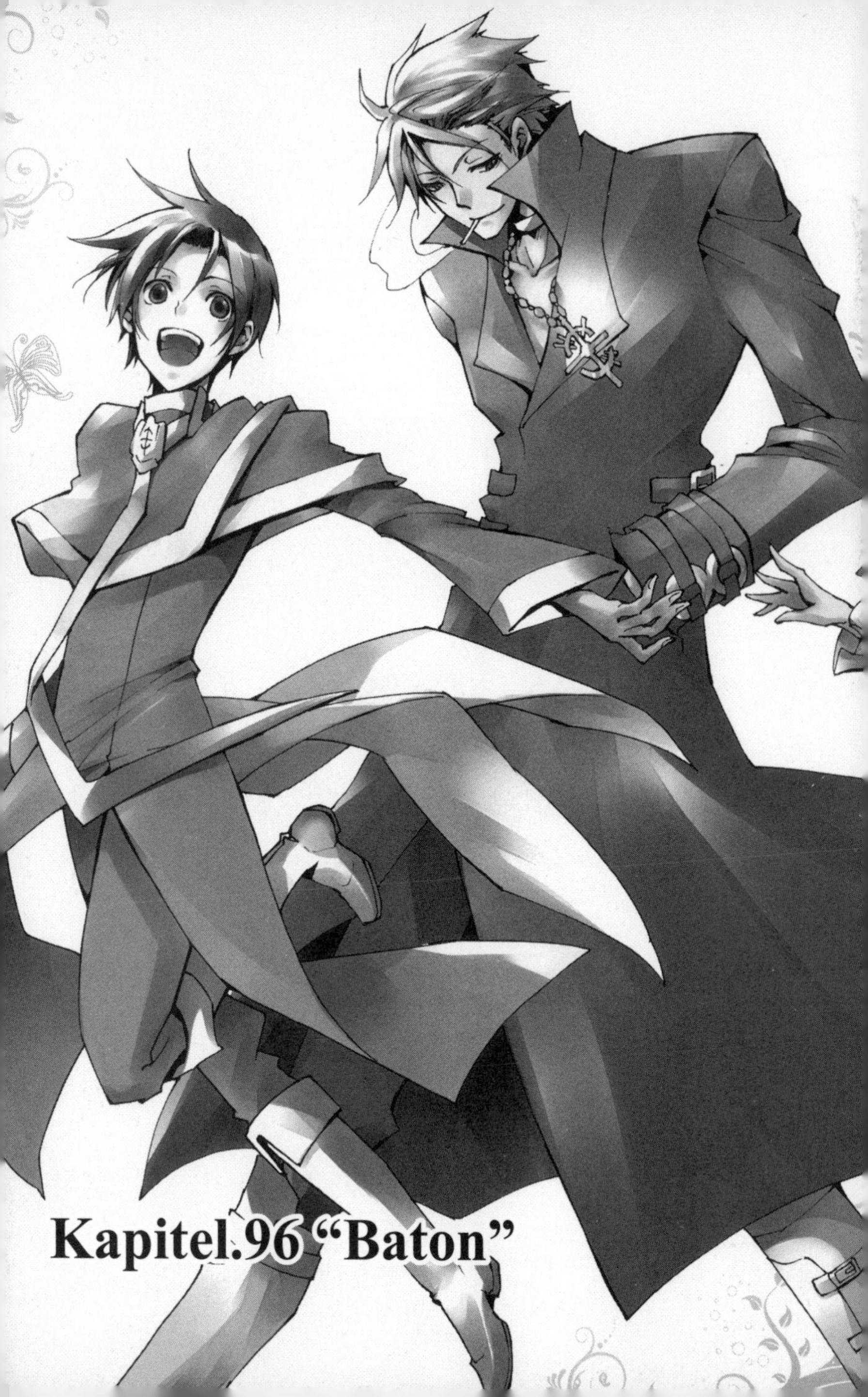
Kapitel.96 "Baton"

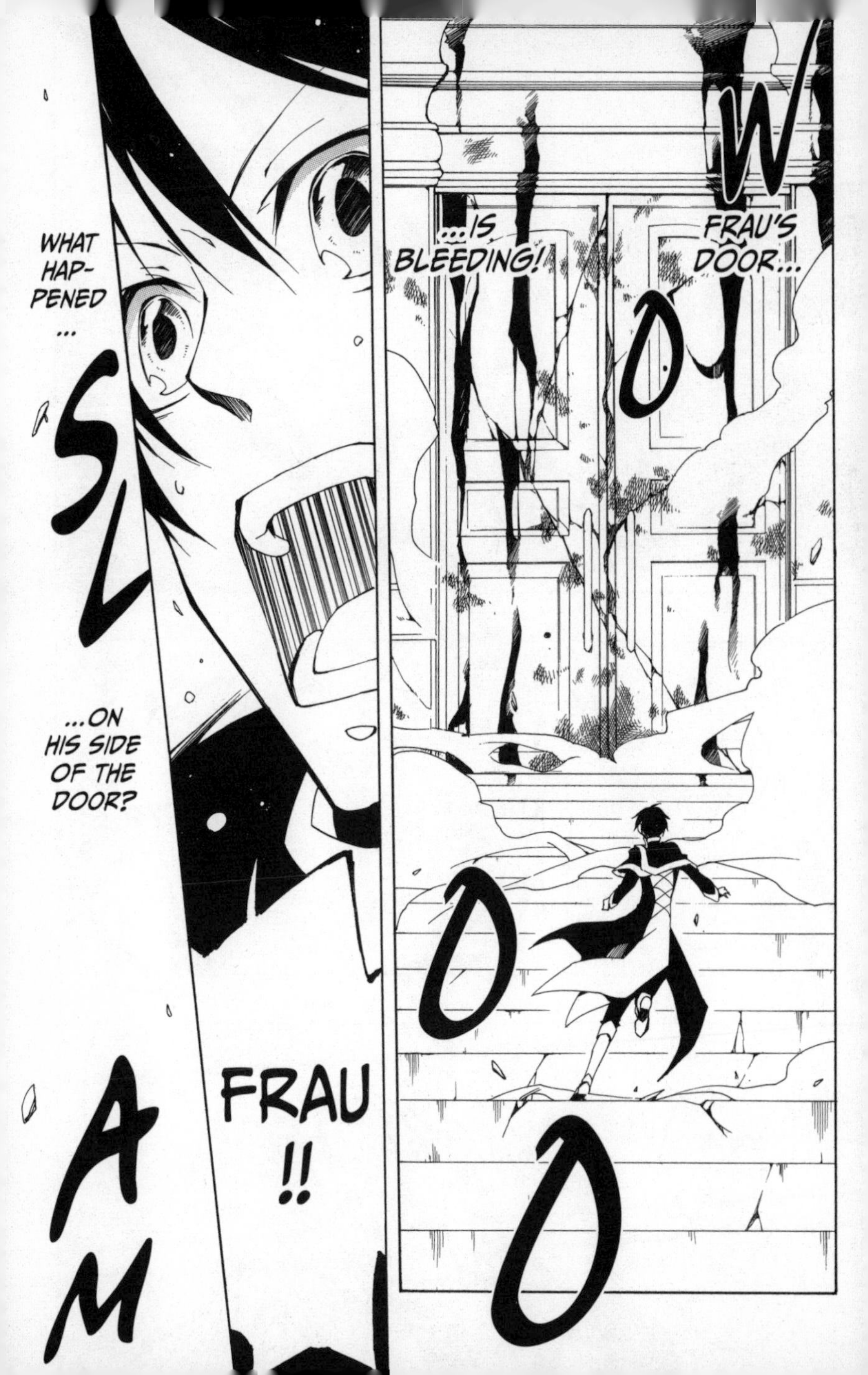
FRAU'S DOOR...
...IS BLEEDING!
FRAU !!
WHAT HAP-PENED ...
...ON HIS SIDE OF THE DOOR?

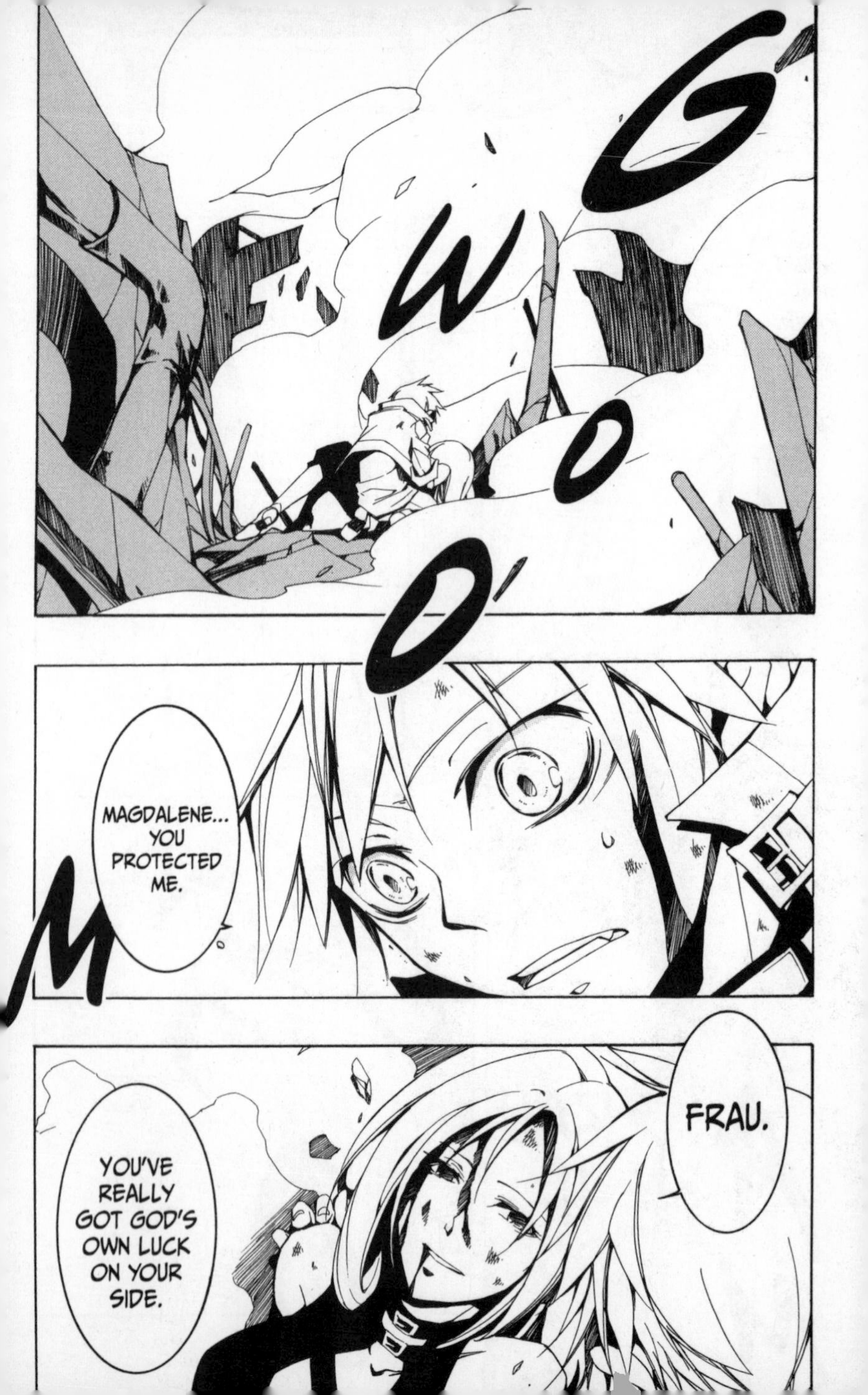
GWOOOM
MAGDALENE... YOU PROTECTED ME.
FRAU.
YOU'VE REALLY GOT GOD'S OWN LUCK ON YOUR SIDE.

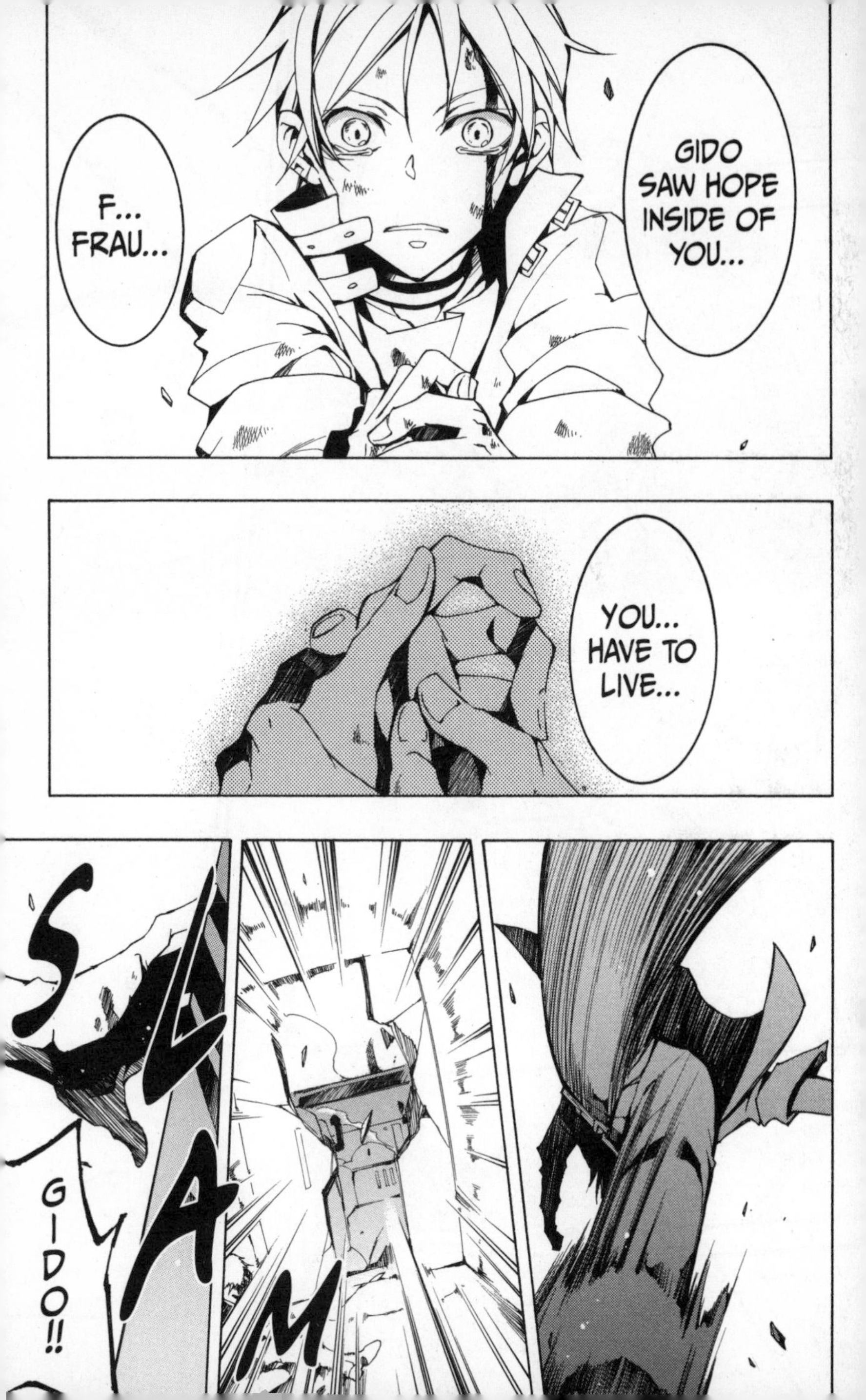
GIDO SAW HOPE INSIDE OF YOU...
F... FRAU...
YOU... HAVE TO LIVE...
SLAM
GIDO!!

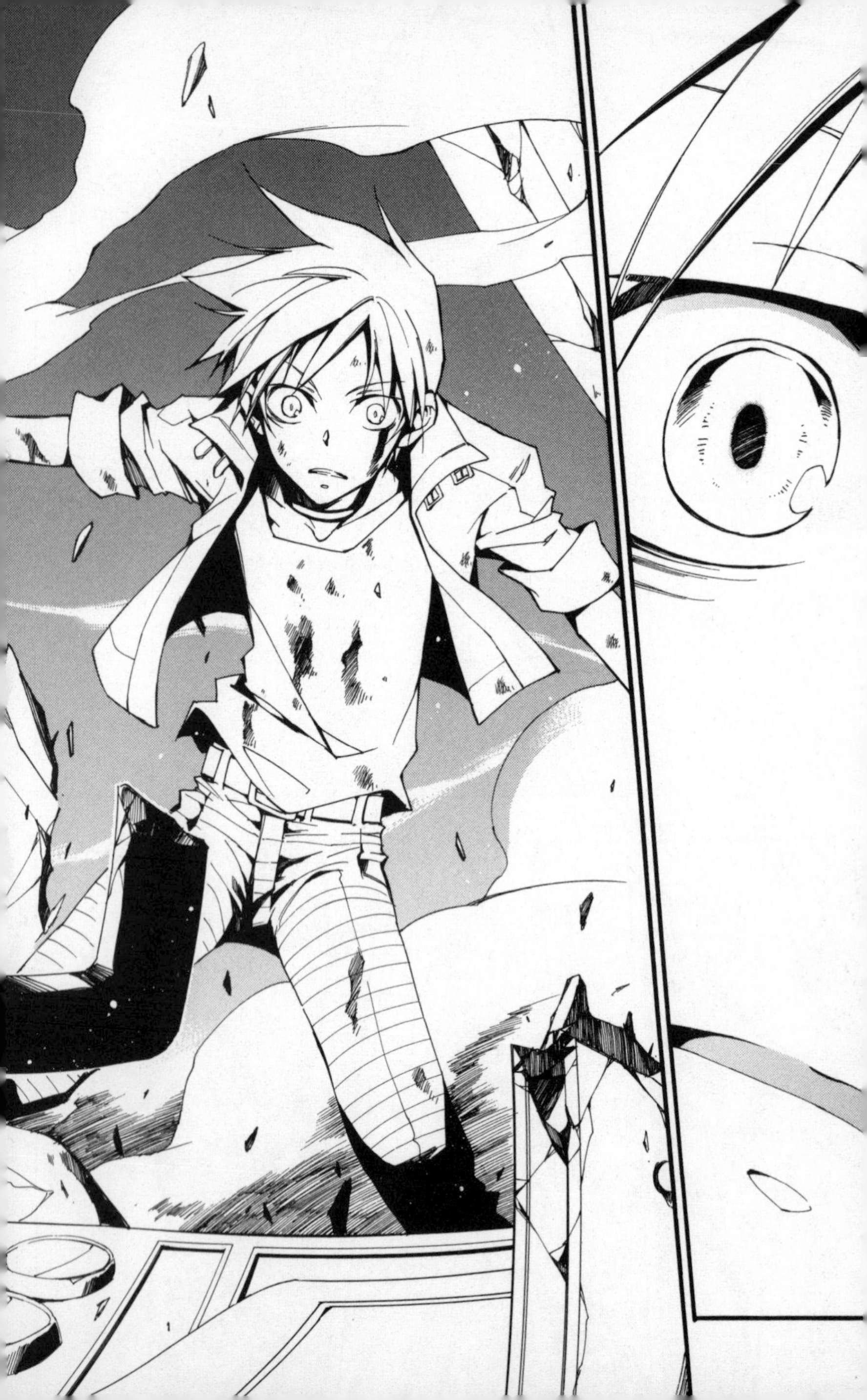

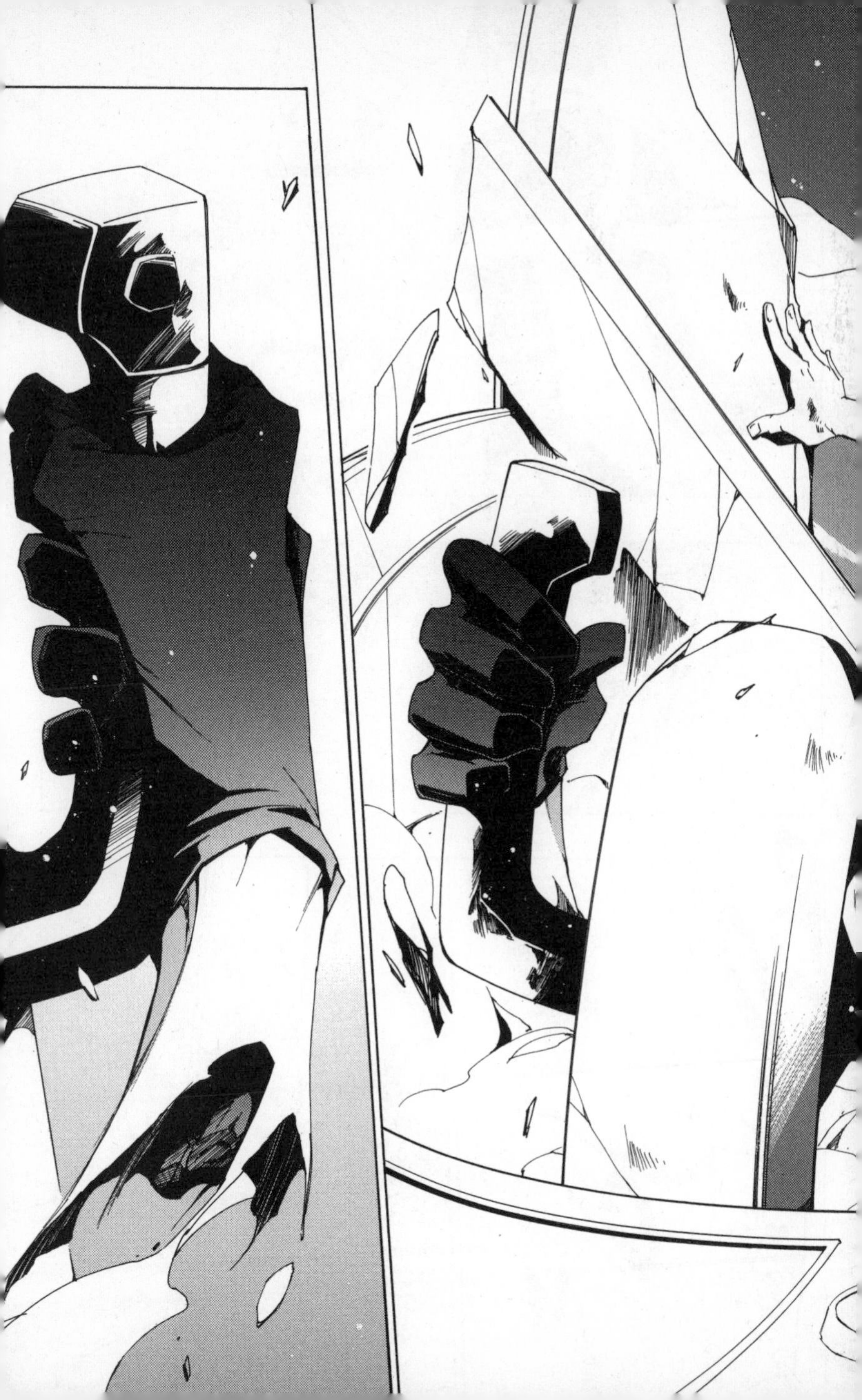

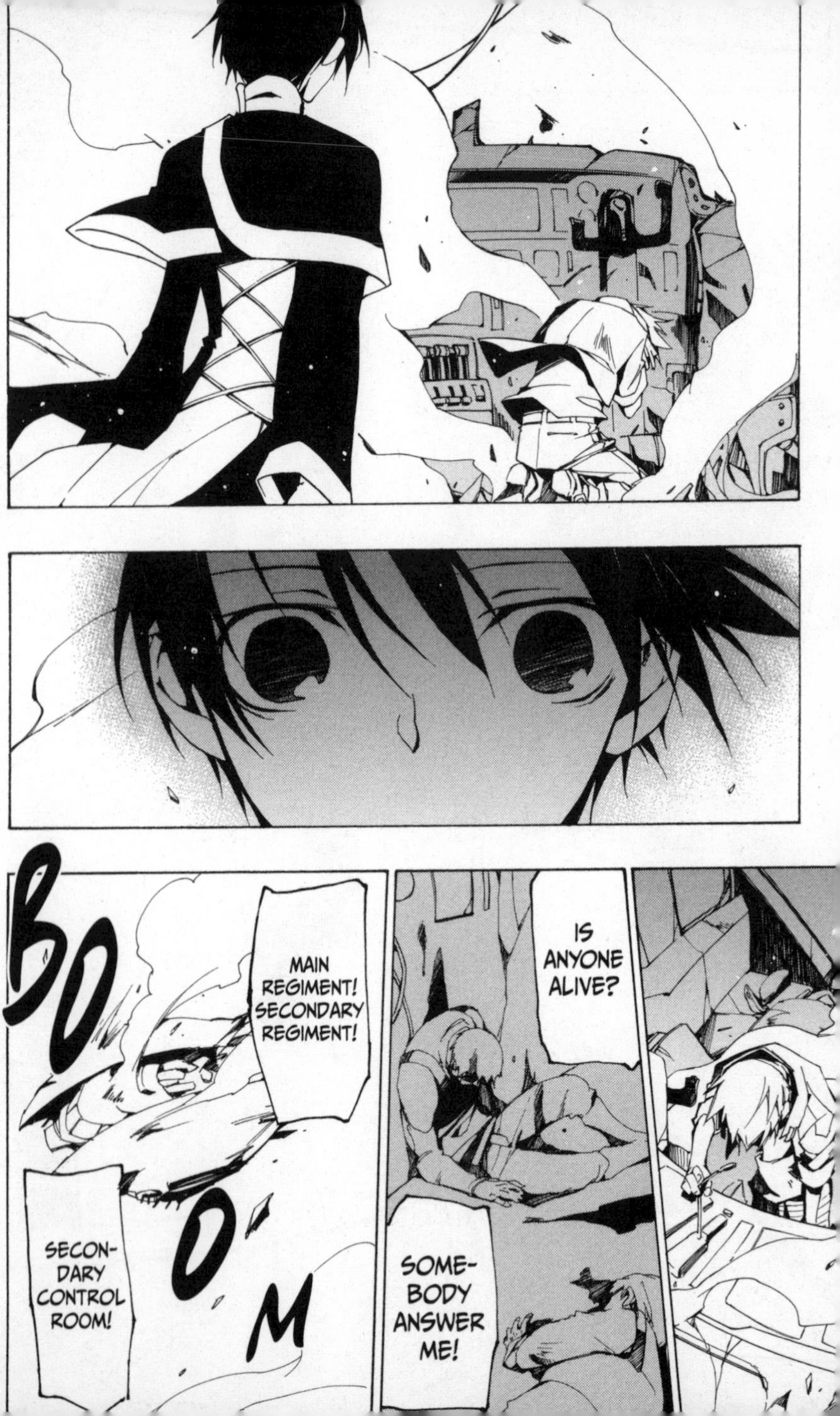
IS ANYONE ALIVE?
SOME-BODY ANSWER ME!
MAIN REGIMENT! SECONDARY REGIMENT!
BOOM
SECON-DARY CONTROL ROOM!

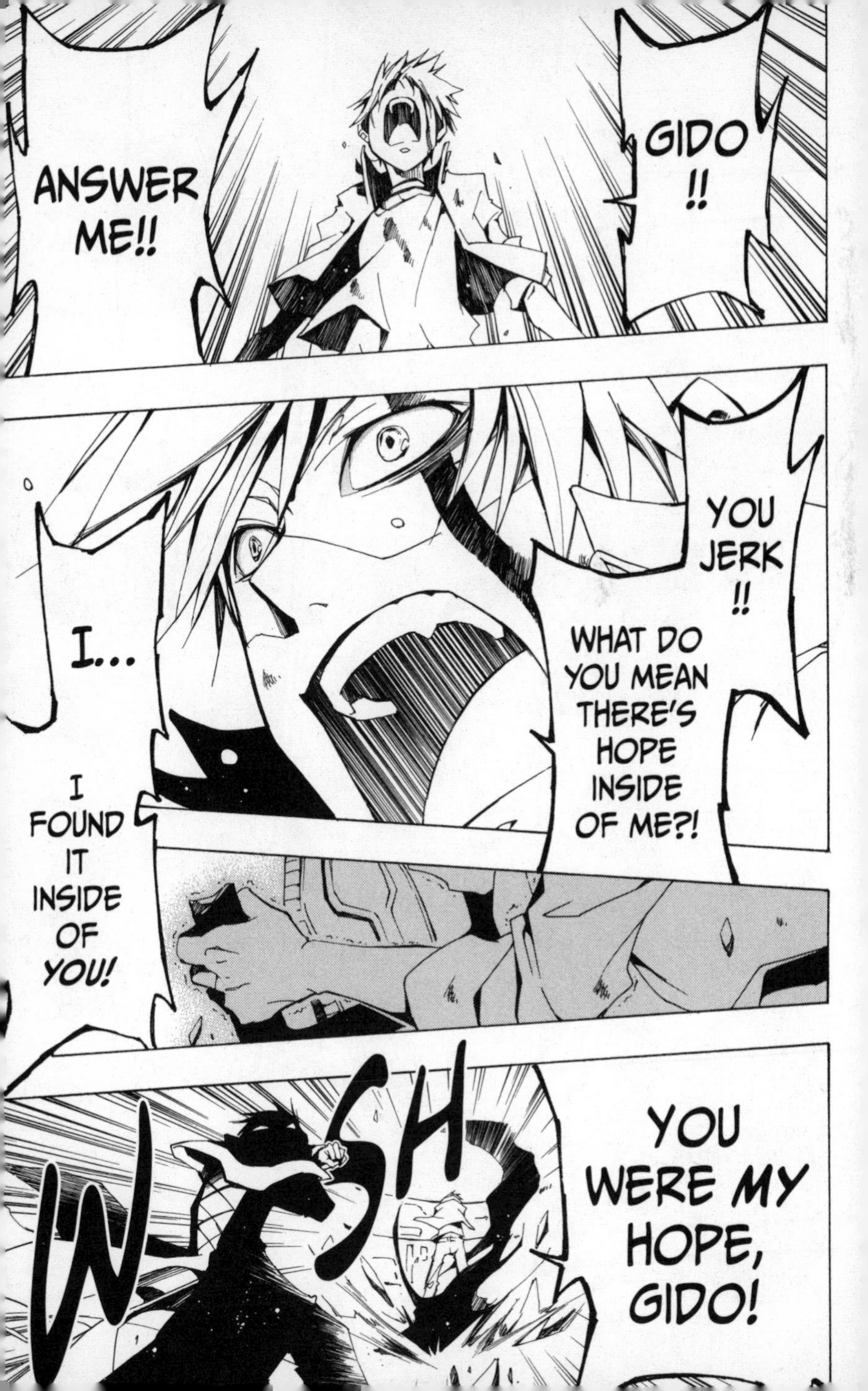
GIDO !!
ANSWER ME!!
YOU JERK !!
WHAT DO YOU MEAN THERE'S HOPE INSIDE OF ME?!
I...
I FOUND IT INSIDE OF YOU!
YOU WERE MY HOPE, GIDO!
WSH

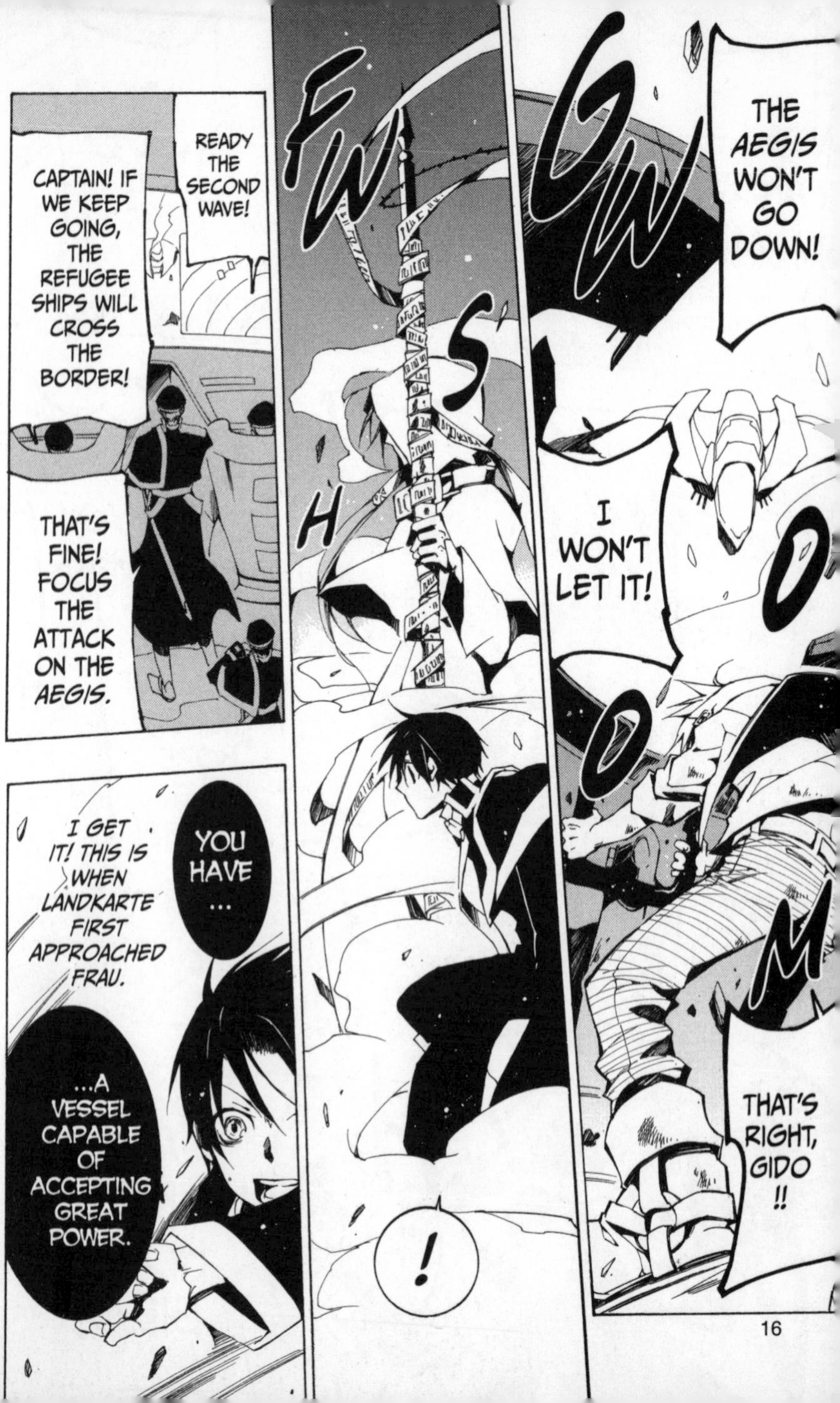
THE AEGIS WON'T GO DOWN!
I WON'T LET IT!
THAT'S RIGHT, GIDO!!
FWISH
!
READY THE SECOND WAVE!
CAPTAIN! IF WE KEEP GOING, THE REFUGEE SHIPS WILL CROSS THE BORDER!
THAT'S FINE! FOCUS THE ATTACK ON THE AEGIS.
YOU HAVE...
I GET IT! THIS IS WHEN LANDKARTE FIRST APPROACHED FRAU.
...A VESSEL CAPABLE OF ACCEPTING GREAT POWER.

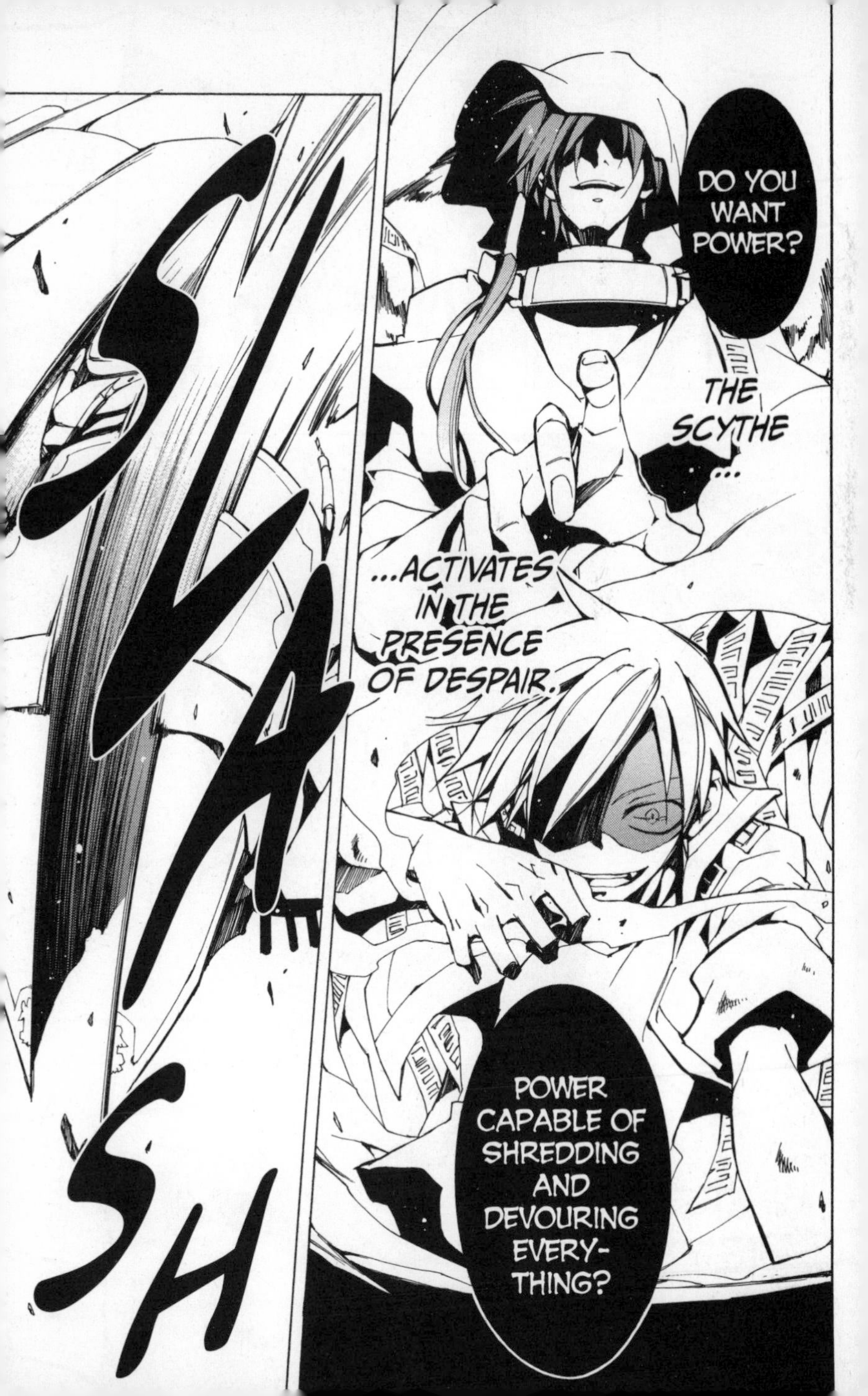
DO YOU WANT POWER?
THE SCYTHE...
...ACTIVATES IN THE PRESENCE OF DESPAIR.
POWER CAPABLE OF SHREDDING AND DEVOURING EVERY-THING?
SH

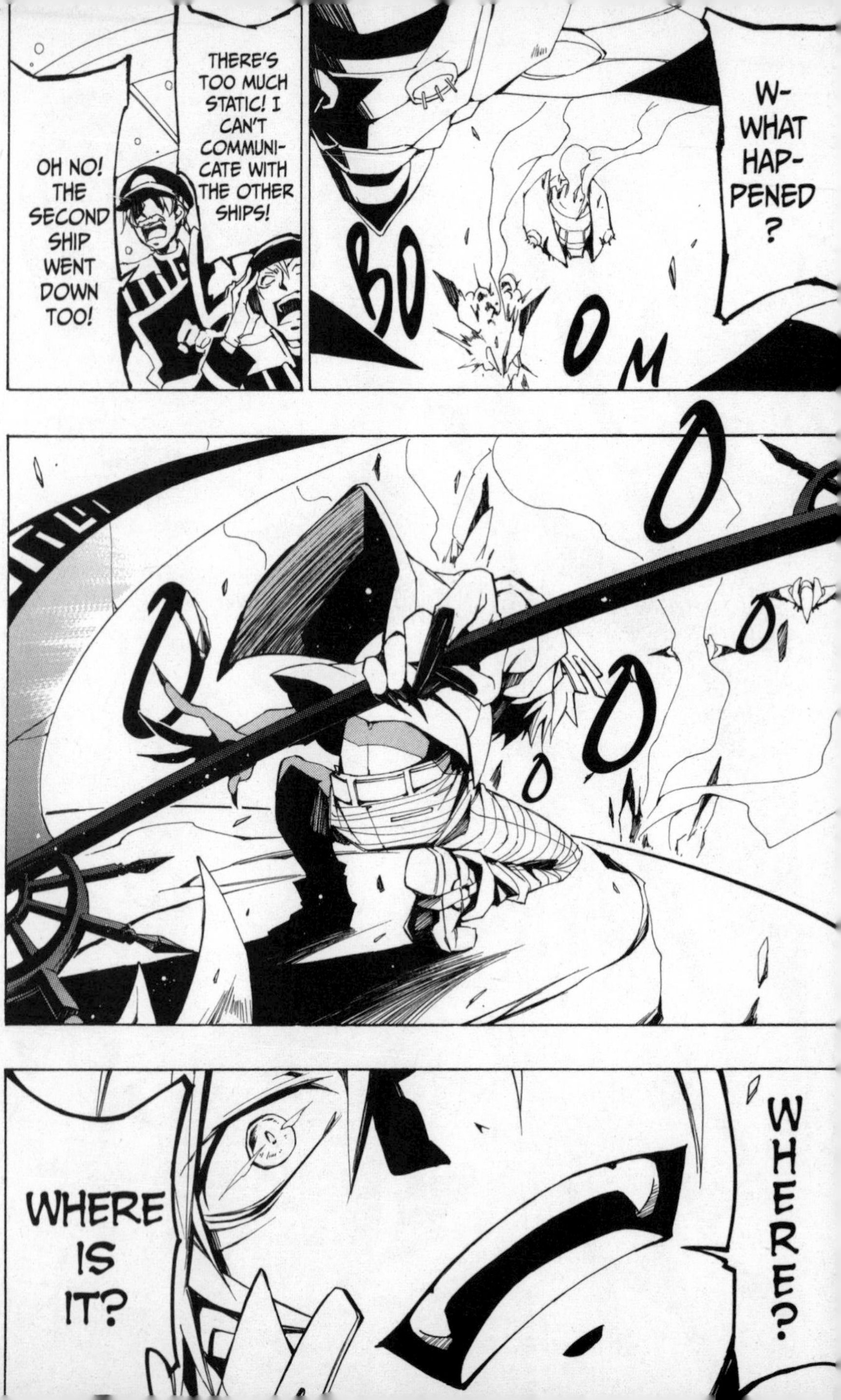
W-WHAT HAP-PENED?
BOOM
THERE'S TOO MUCH STATIC! I CAN'T COMMUNI-CATE WITH THE OTHER SHIPS!
OH NO! THE SECOND SHIP WENT DOWN TOO!
OOOOOO
WHERE?
WHERE IS IT?

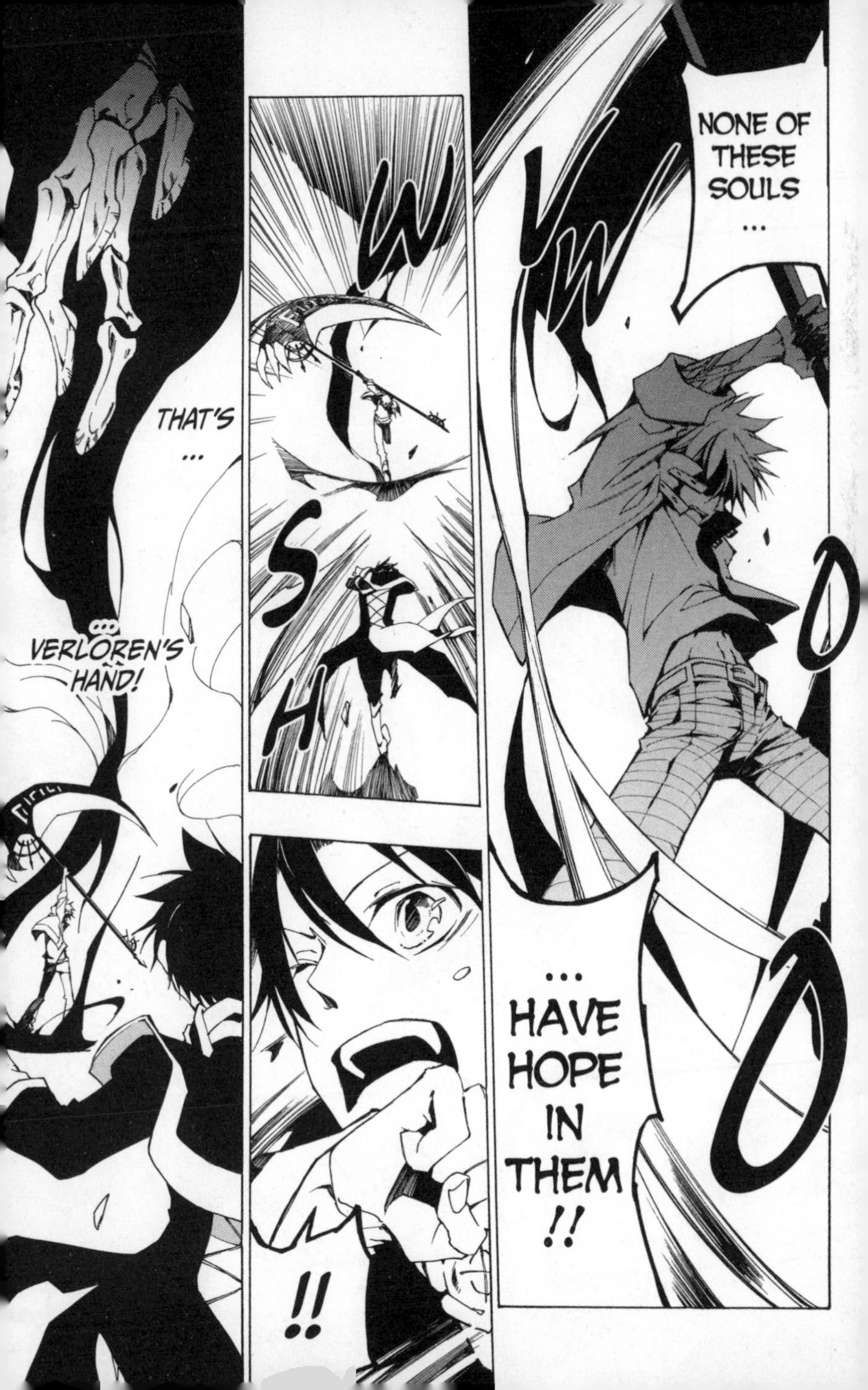
NONE OF THESE SOULS ...
... HAVE HOPE IN THEM !!
!!
THAT'S ...
... VERLOREN'S HAND!

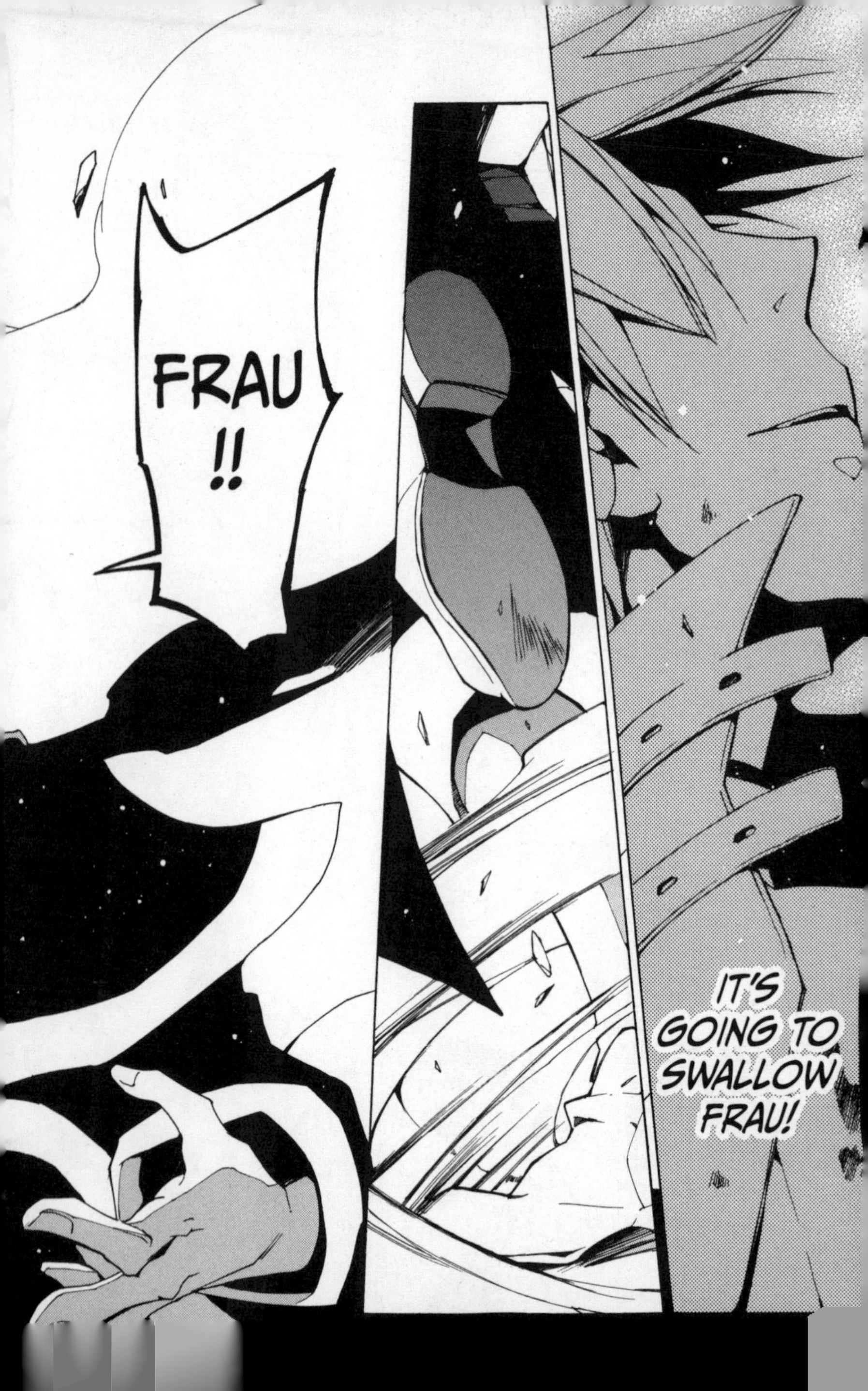
IT'S GOING TO SWALLOW FRAU!
FRAU!!

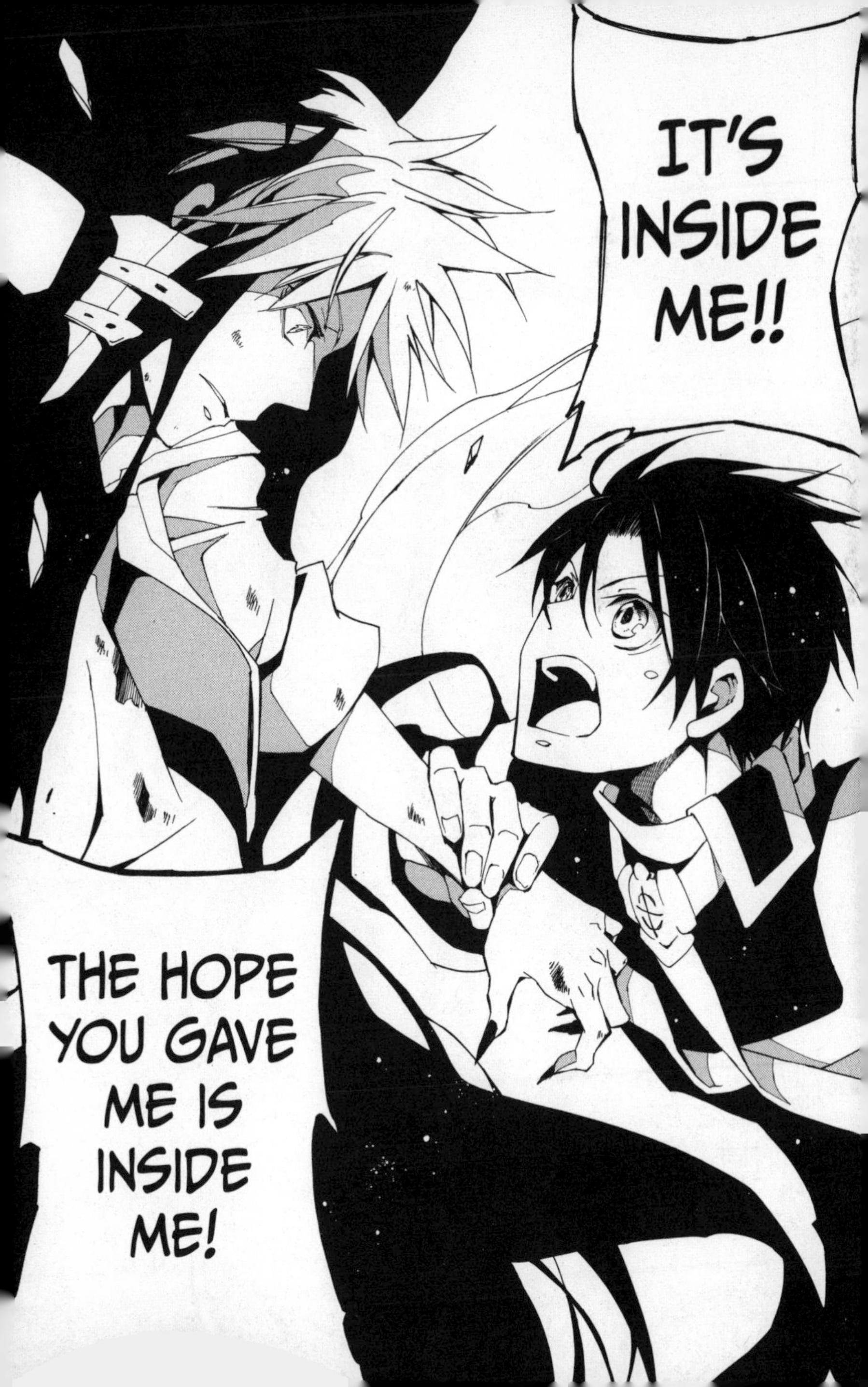
IT'S INSIDE ME!!
THE HOPE YOU GAVE ME IS INSIDE ME!

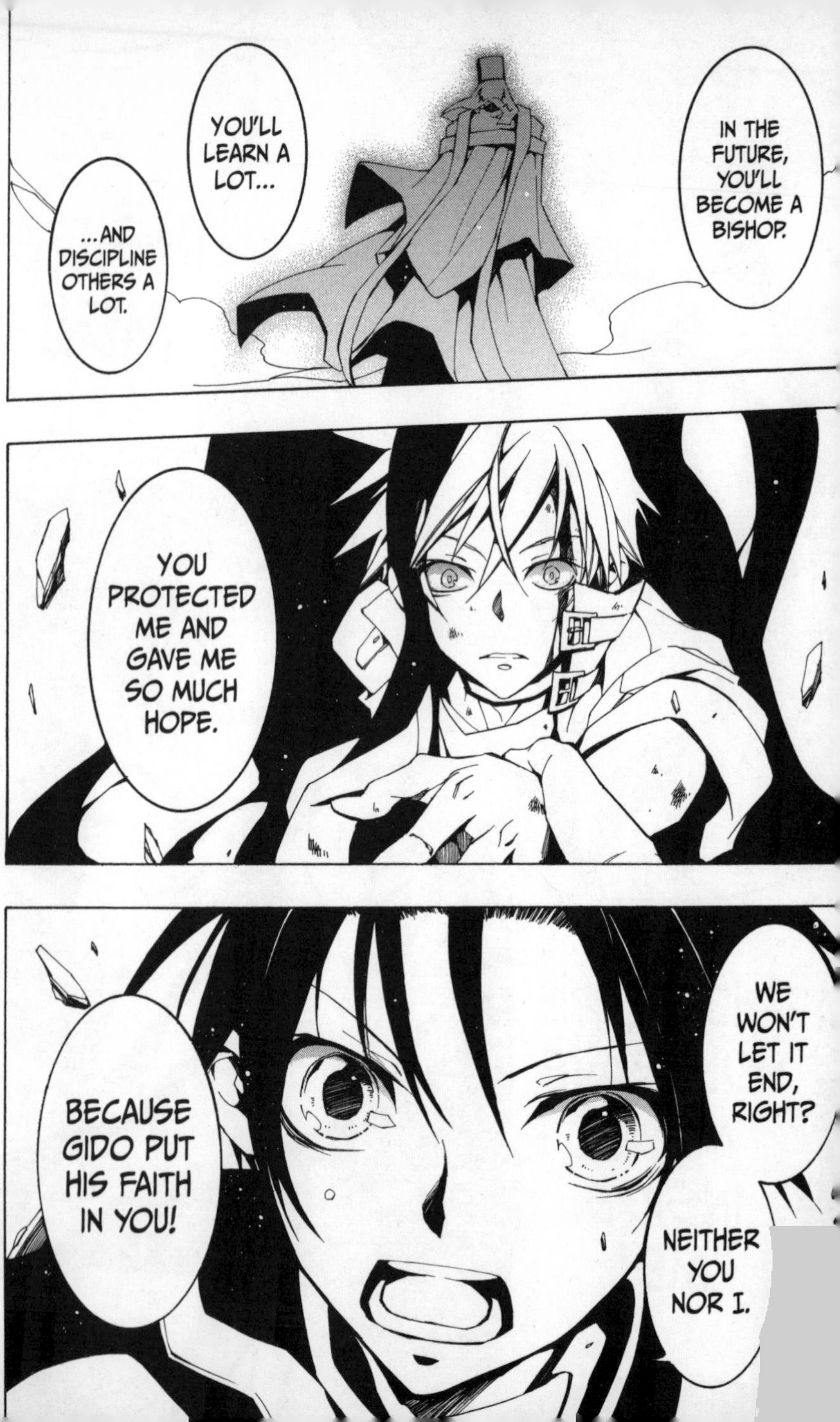
IN THE FUTURE, YOU'LL BECOME A BISHOP.
YOU'LL LEARN A LOT...
...AND DISCIPLINE OTHERS A LOT.
YOU PROTECTED ME AND GAVE ME SO MUCH HOPE.
WE WON'T LET IT END, RIGHT?
NEITHER YOU NOR I.
BECAUSE GIDO PUT HIS FAITH IN YOU!

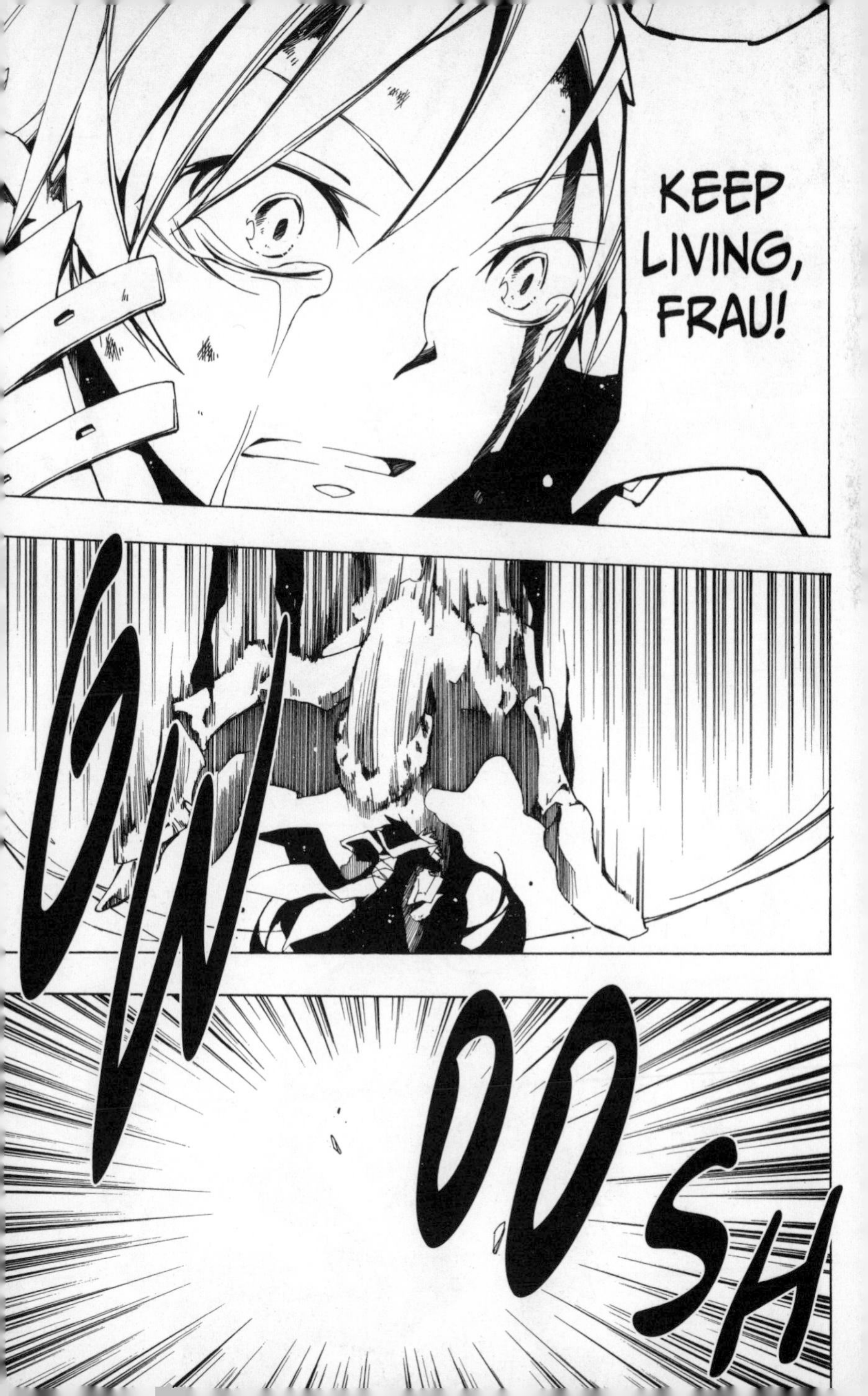
KEEP LIVING, FRAU!
SWOOSH

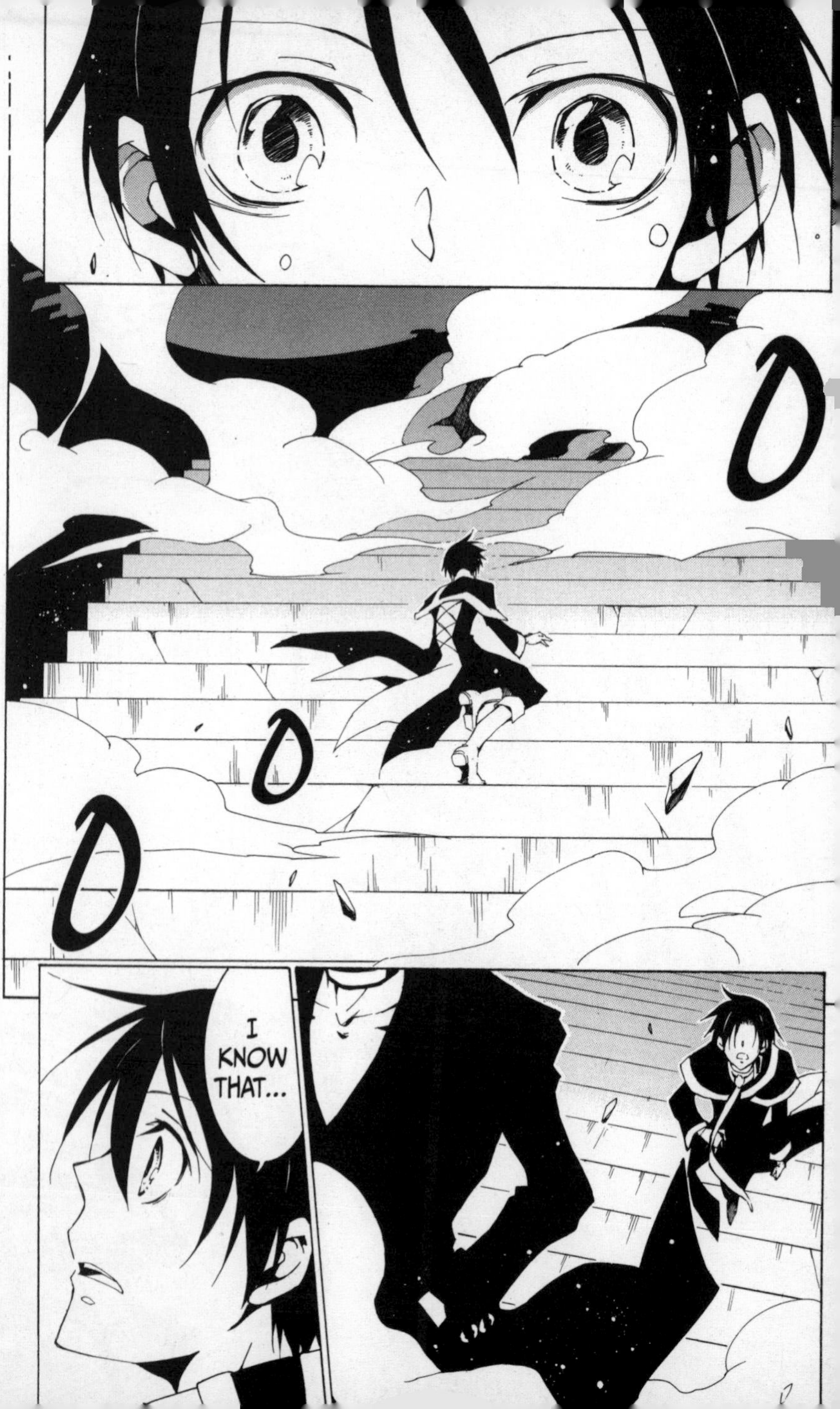
D
D
D
I KNOW THAT...

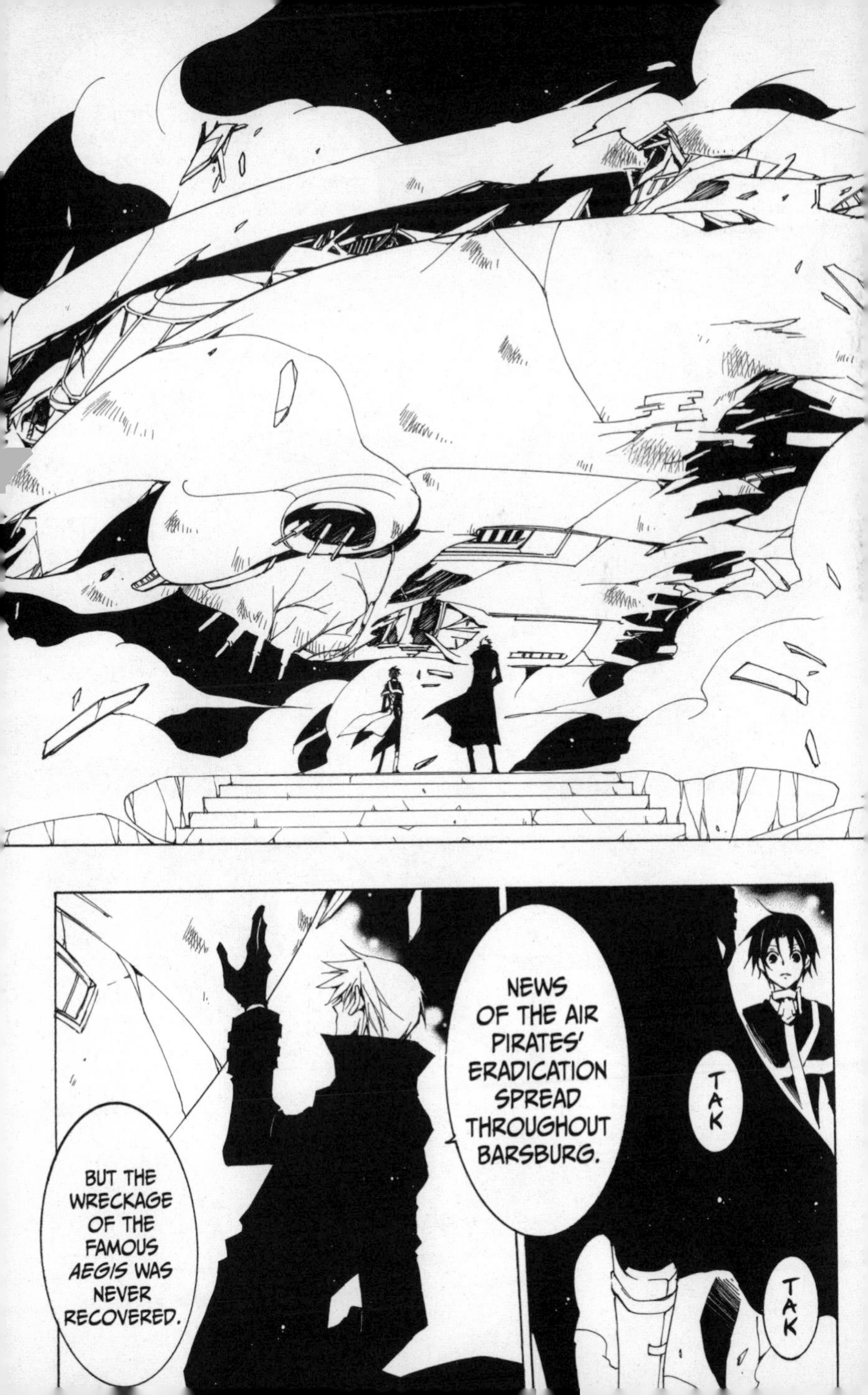
TAK
NEWS OF THE AIR PIRATES' ERADICATION SPREAD THROUGHOUT BARSBURG.
TAK
BUT THE WRECKAGE OF THE FAMOUS AEGIS WAS NEVER RECOVERED.

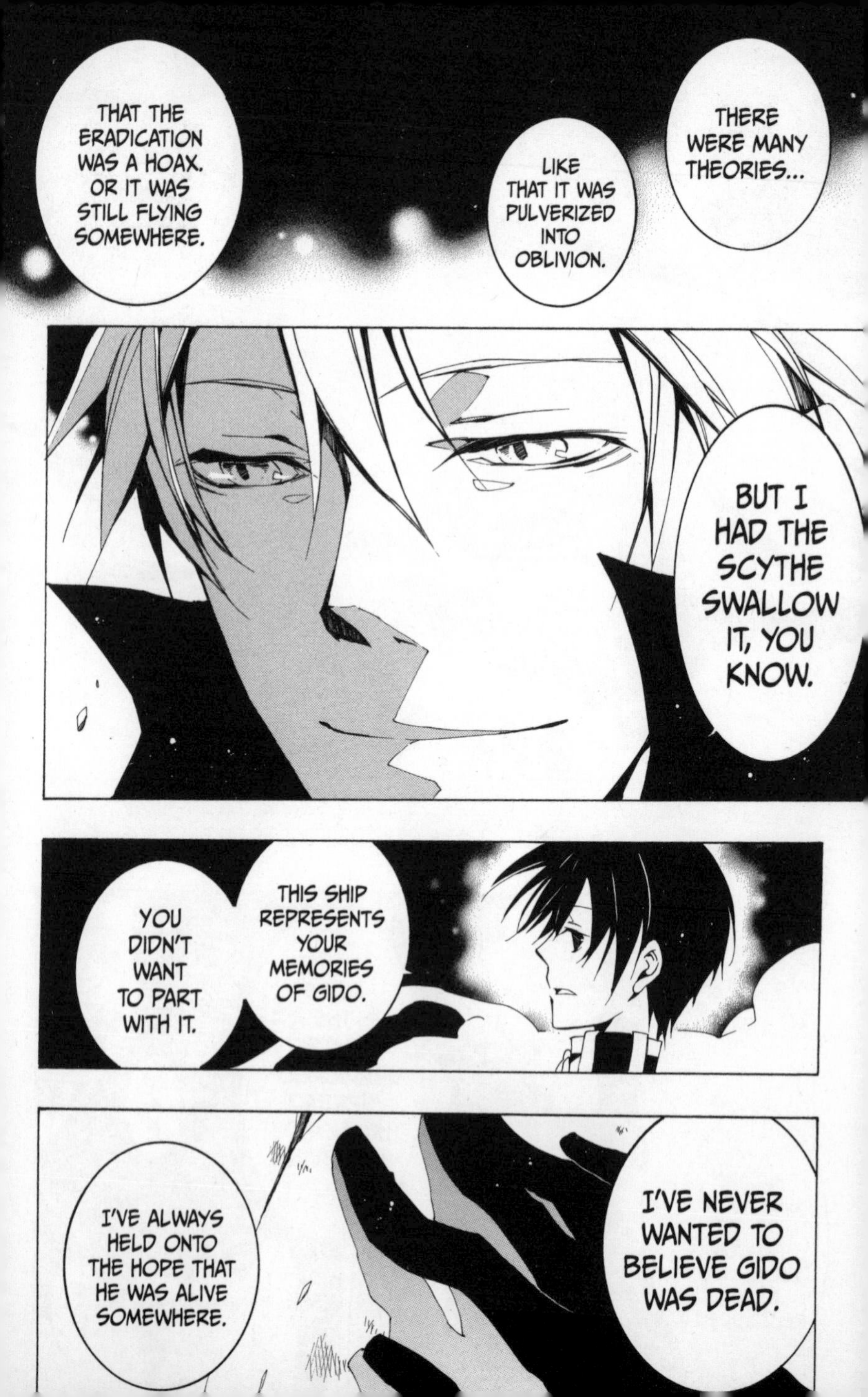
THERE WERE MANY THEORIES...
LIKE THAT IT WAS PULVERIZED INTO OBLIVION.
THAT THE ERADICATION WAS A HOAX. OR IT WAS STILL FLYING SOMEWHERE.
BUT I HAD THE SCYTHE SWALLOW IT, YOU KNOW.
THIS SHIP REPRESENTS YOUR MEMORIES OF GIDO.
YOU DIDN'T WANT TO PART WITH IT.
I'VE NEVER WANTED TO BELIEVE GIDO WAS DEAD.
I'VE ALWAYS HELD ONTO THE HOPE THAT HE WAS ALIVE SOMEWHERE.

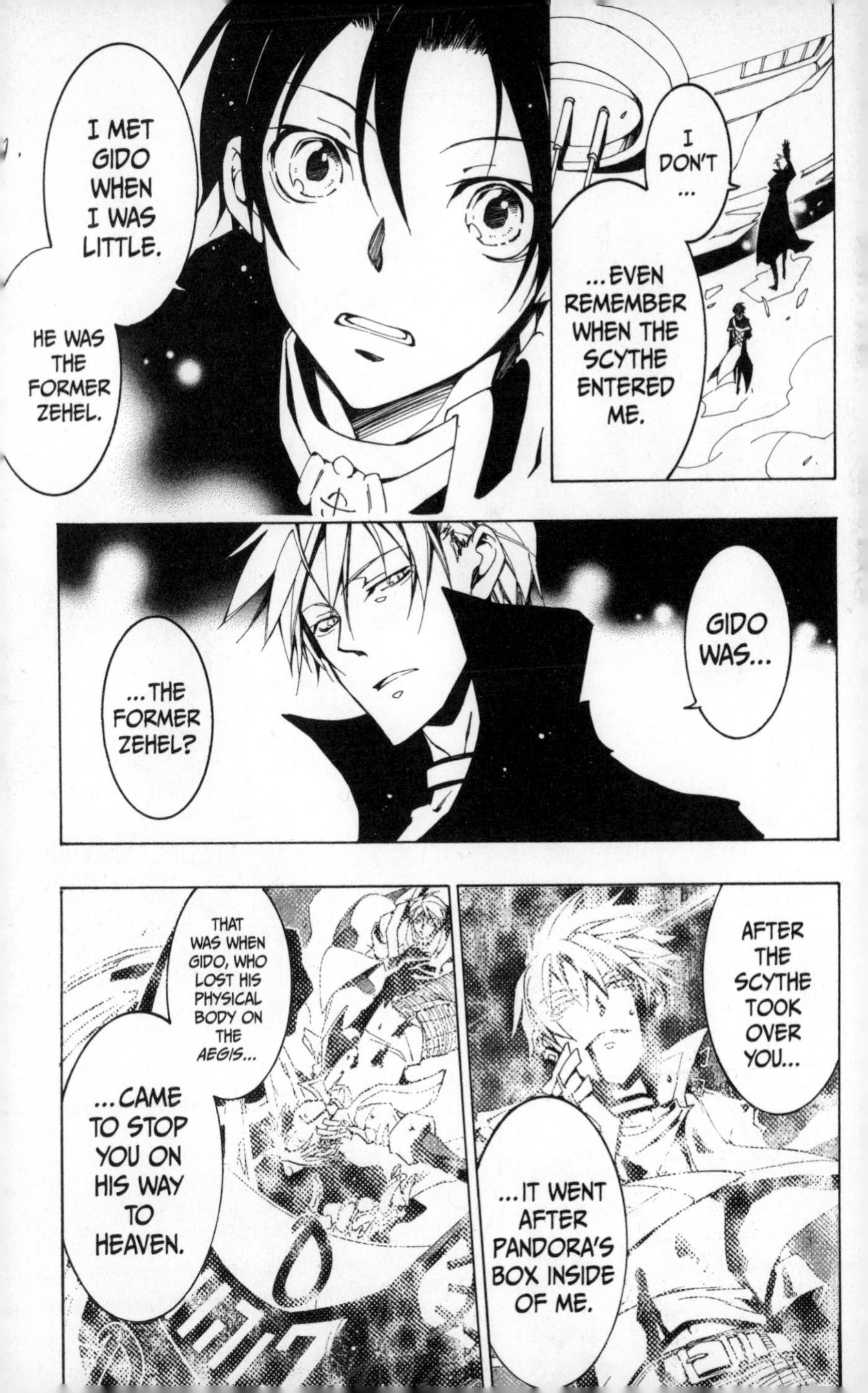
I DON'T ...
...EVEN REMEMBER WHEN THE SCYTHE ENTERED ME.
I MET GIDO WHEN I WAS LITTLE.
HE WAS THE FORMER ZEHEL.
GIDO WAS...
...THE FORMER ZEHEL?
AFTER THE SCYTHE TOOK OVER YOU...
...IT WENT AFTER PANDORA'S BOX INSIDE OF ME.
THAT WAS WHEN GIDO, WHO LOST HIS PHYSICAL BODY ON THE *AEGIS*...
...CAME TO STOP YOU ON HIS WAY TO HEAVEN.

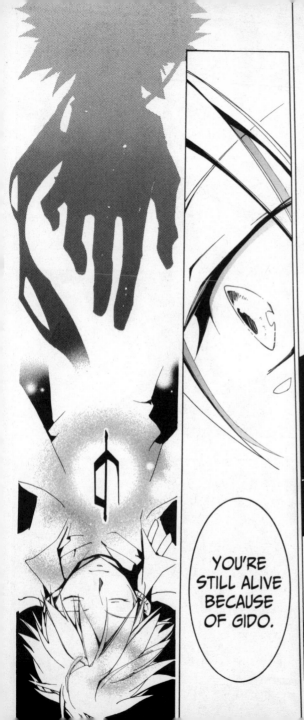

THANKS TO ZEHEL'S POWER...

...YOU WERE ABLE TO CONTROL THE SCYTHE.

YOU'RE STILL ALIVE BECAUSE OF GIDO.

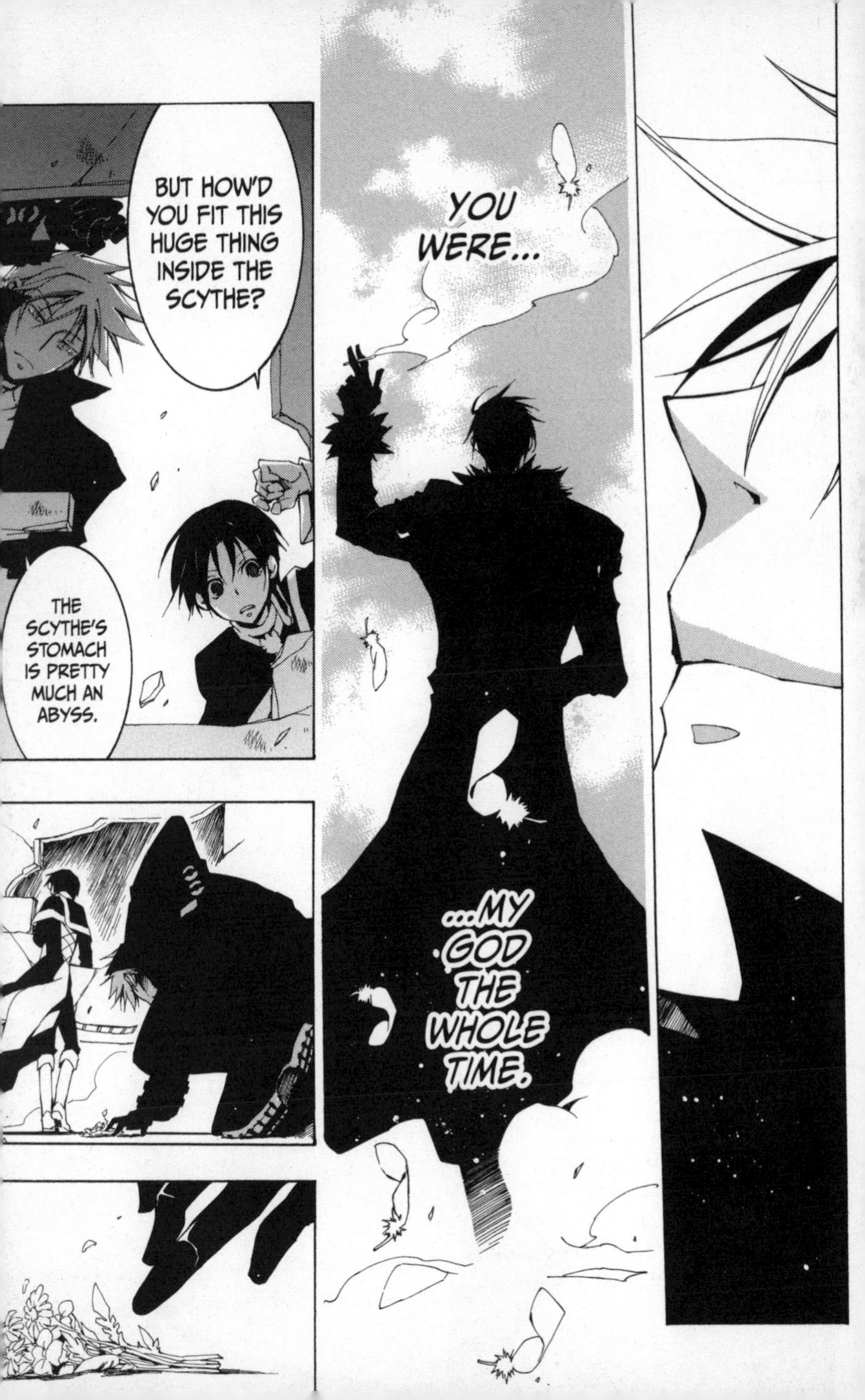
YOU WERE...
...MY GOD THE WHOLE TIME.
BUT HOW'D YOU FIT THIS HUGE THING INSIDE THE SCYTHE?
THE SCYTHE'S STOMACH IS PRETTY MUCH AN ABYSS.

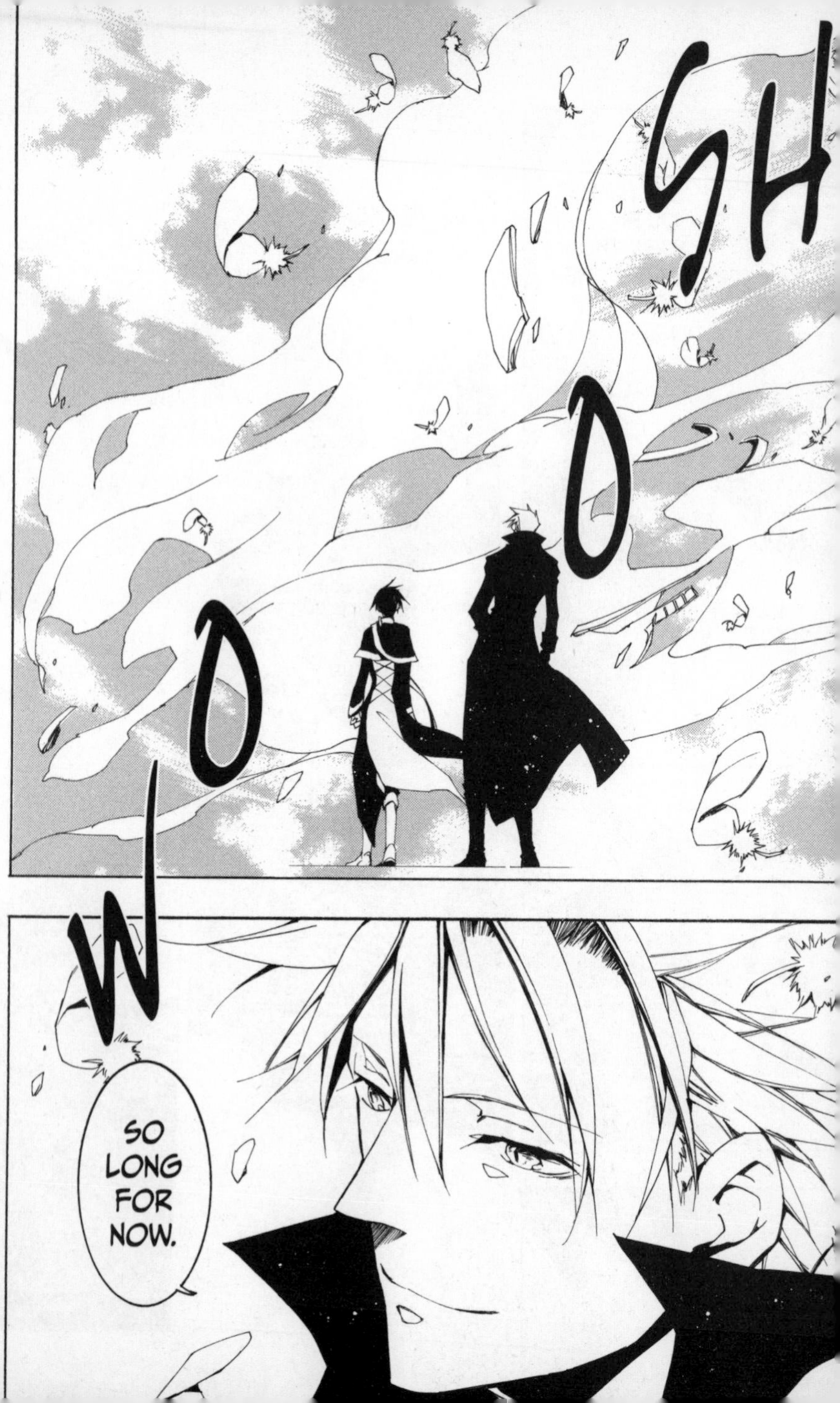
SH
WOOO
SO LONG FOR NOW.

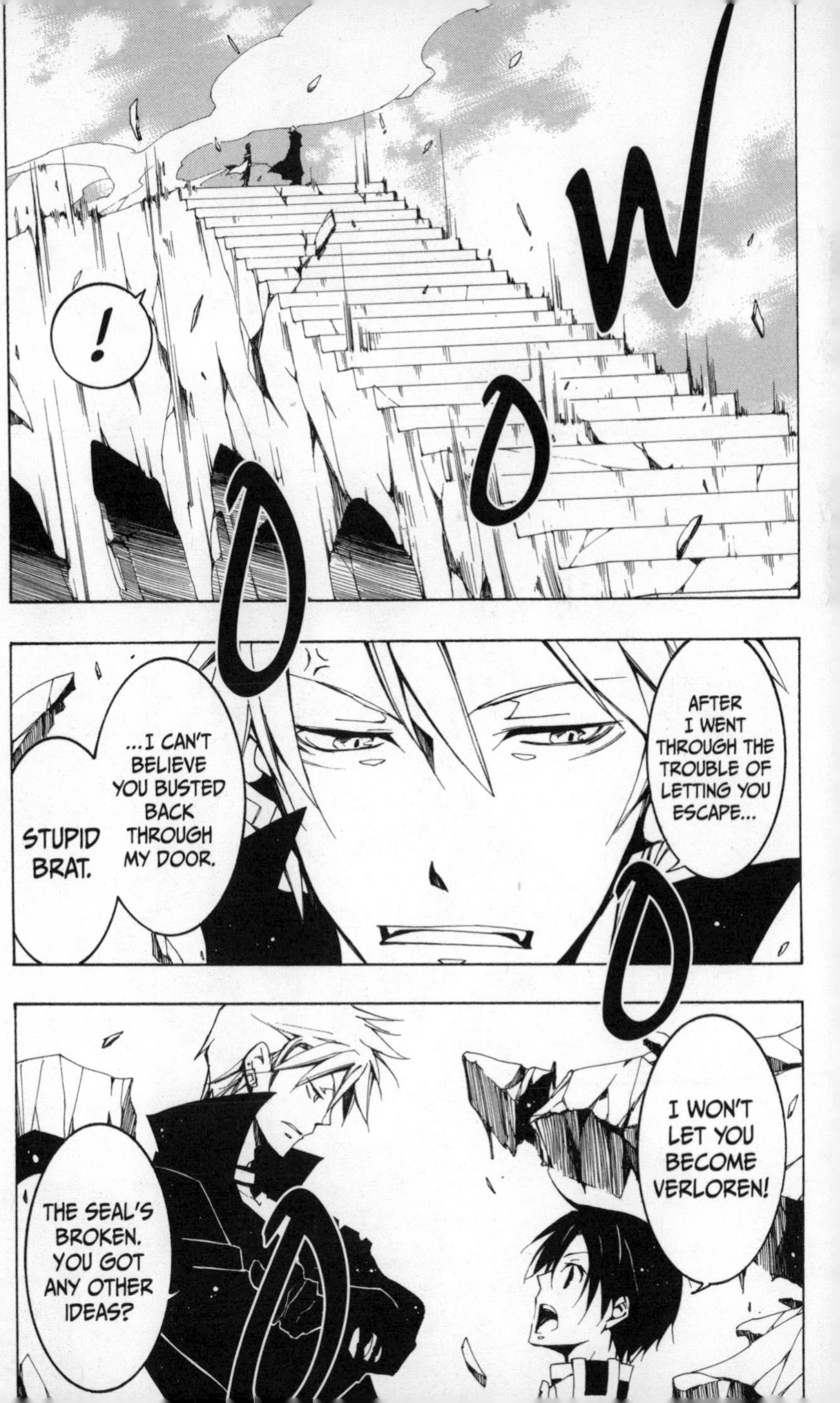
W
D
D
!
AFTER I WENT THROUGH THE TROUBLE OF LETTING YOU ESCAPE...
...I CAN'T BELIEVE YOU BUSTED BACK THROUGH MY DOOR.
STUPID BRAT.
D
D
I WON'T LET YOU BECOME VERLOREN!
THE SEAL'S BROKEN. YOU GOT ANY OTHER IDEAS?

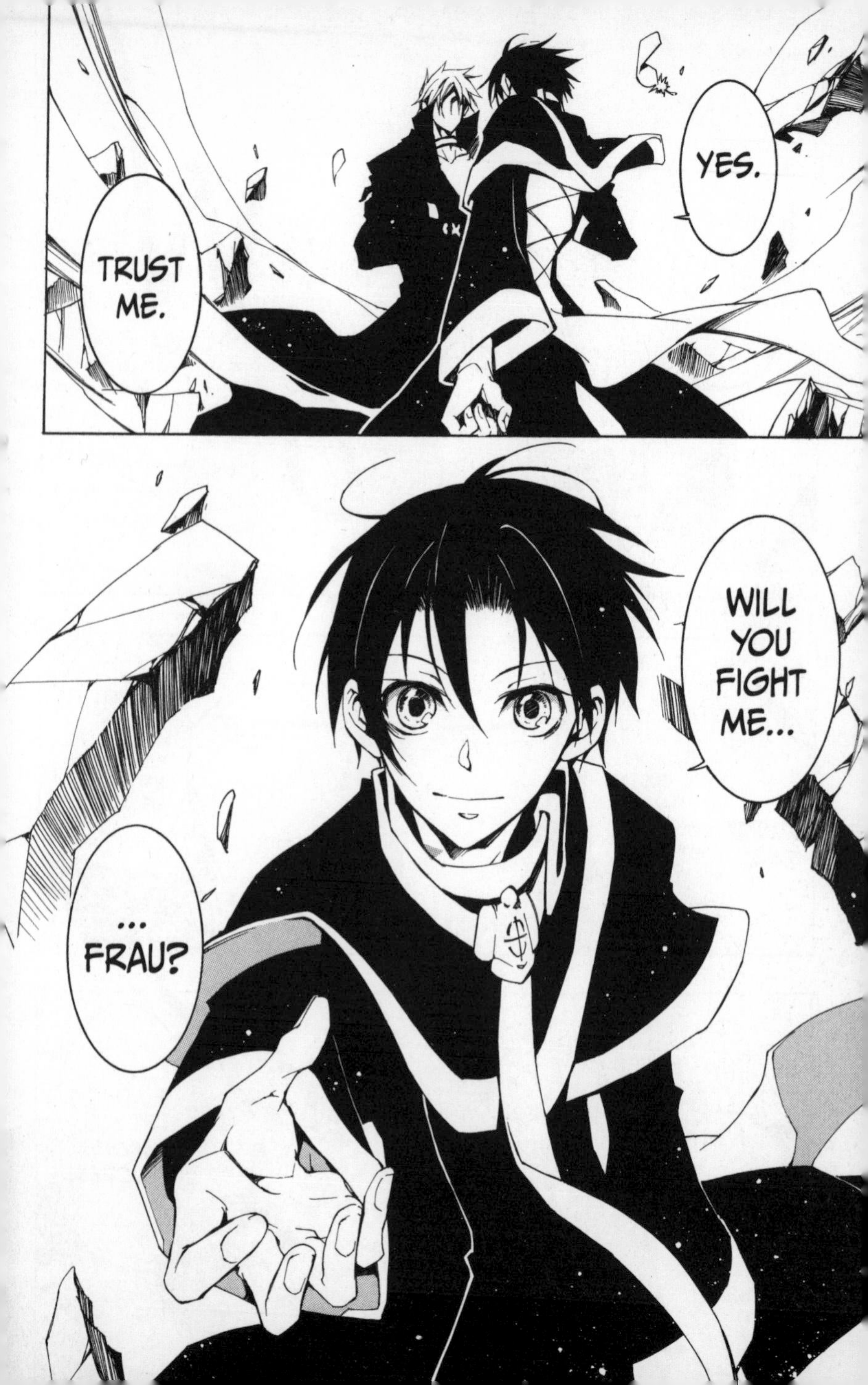
YES.
TRUST ME.
WILL YOU FIGHT ME...
... FRAU?

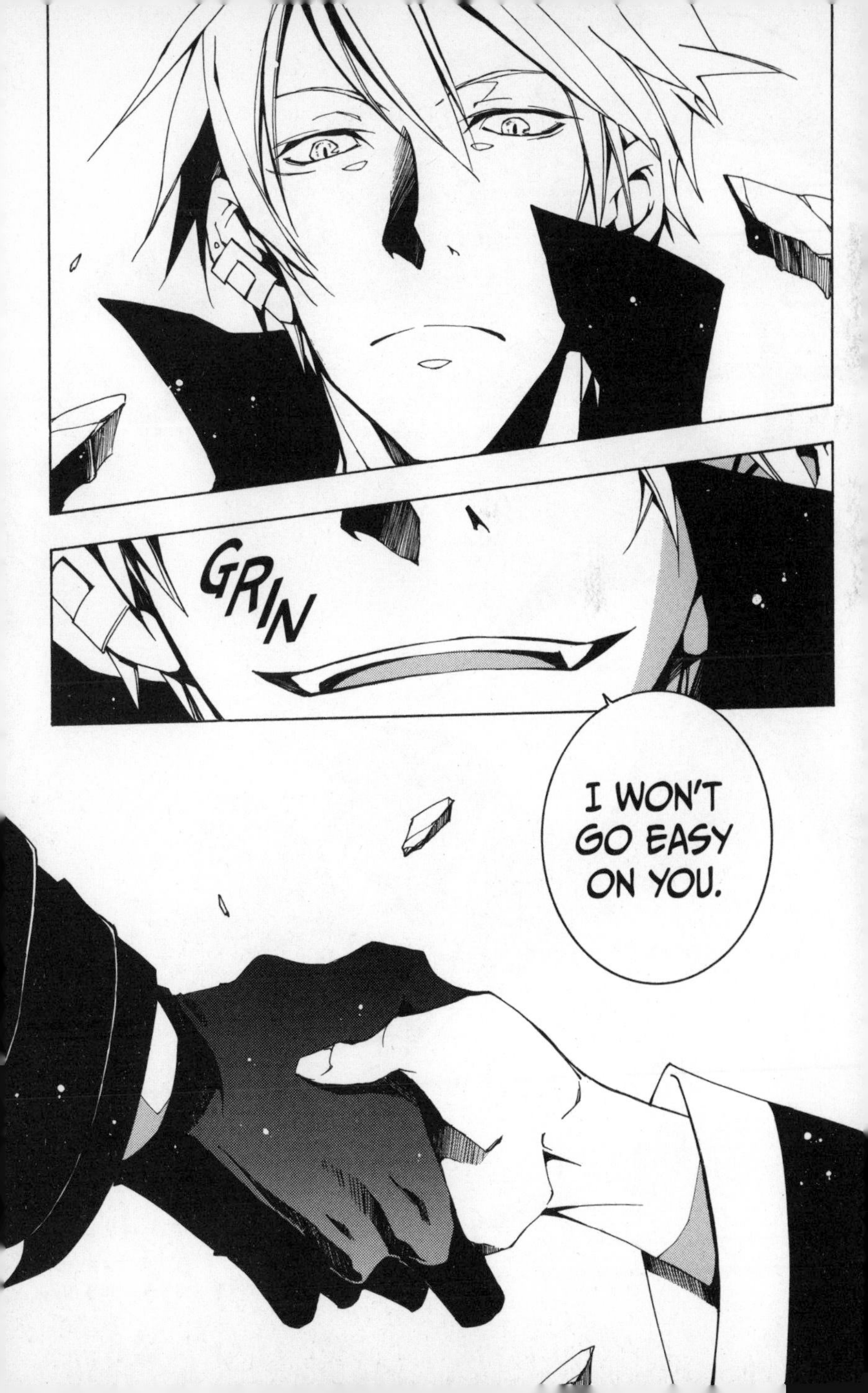
GRIN
I WON'T GO EASY ON YOU.

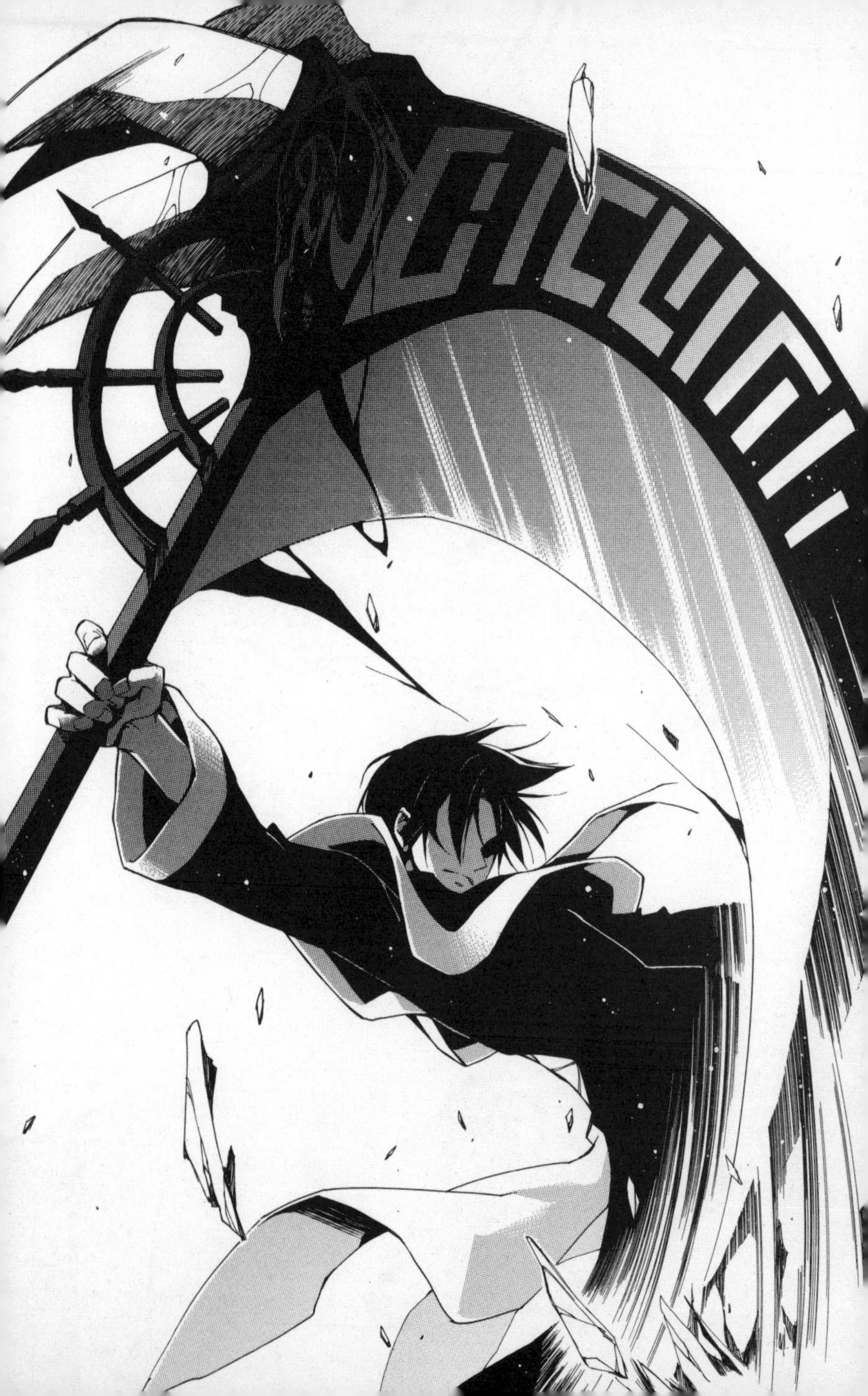

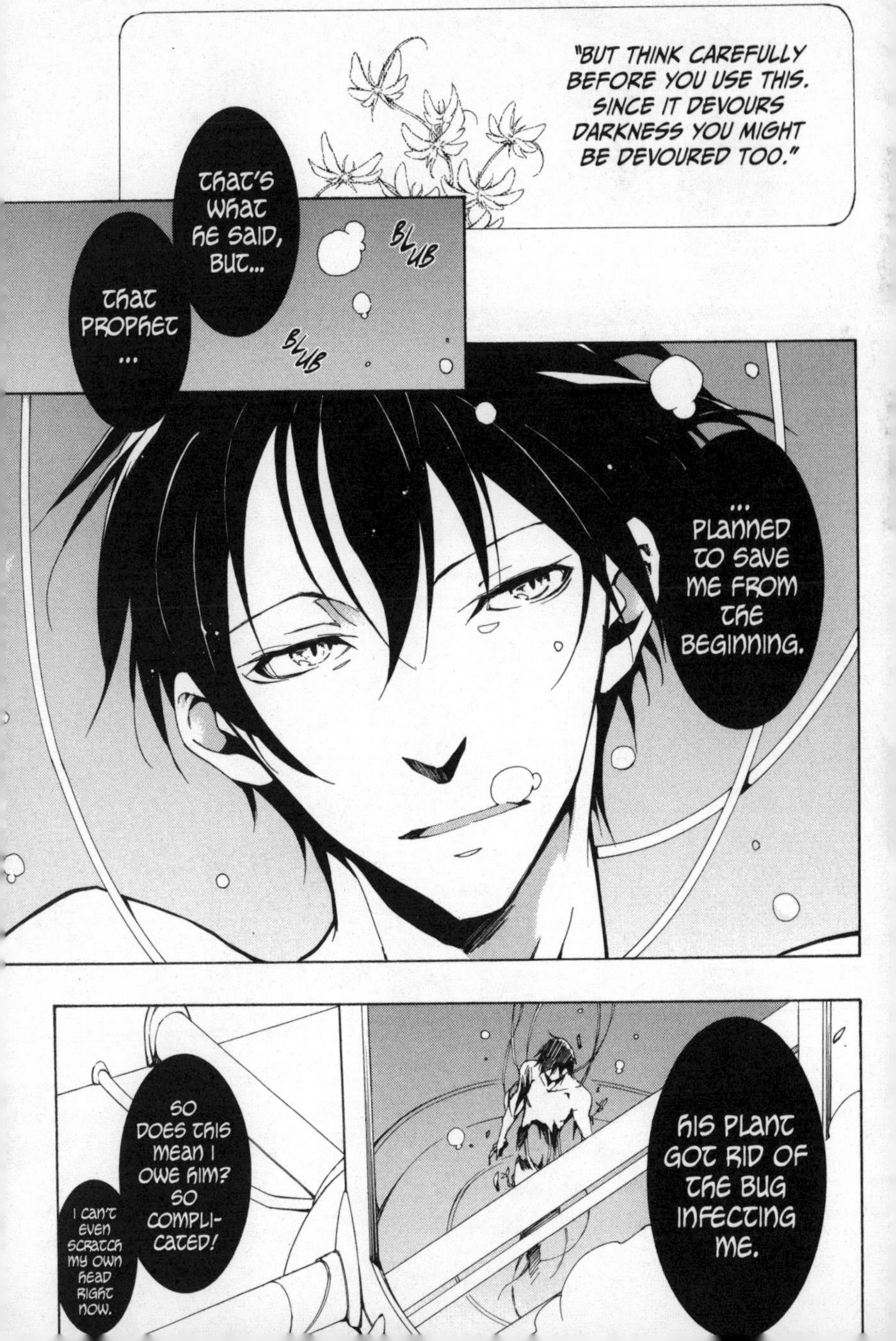
"BUT THINK CAREFULLY BEFORE YOU USE THIS. SINCE IT DEVOURS DARKNESS YOU MIGHT BE DEVOURED TOO."
THAT'S WHAT HE SAID, BUT...
BLUB
BLUB
THAT PROPHET ...
... PLANNED TO SAVE ME FROM THE BEGINNING.
HIS PLANT GOT RID OF THE BUG INFECTING ME.
SO DOES THIS MEAN I OWE HIM? SO COMPLI-CATED!
I CAN'T EVEN SCRATCH MY OWN HEAD RIGHT NOW.

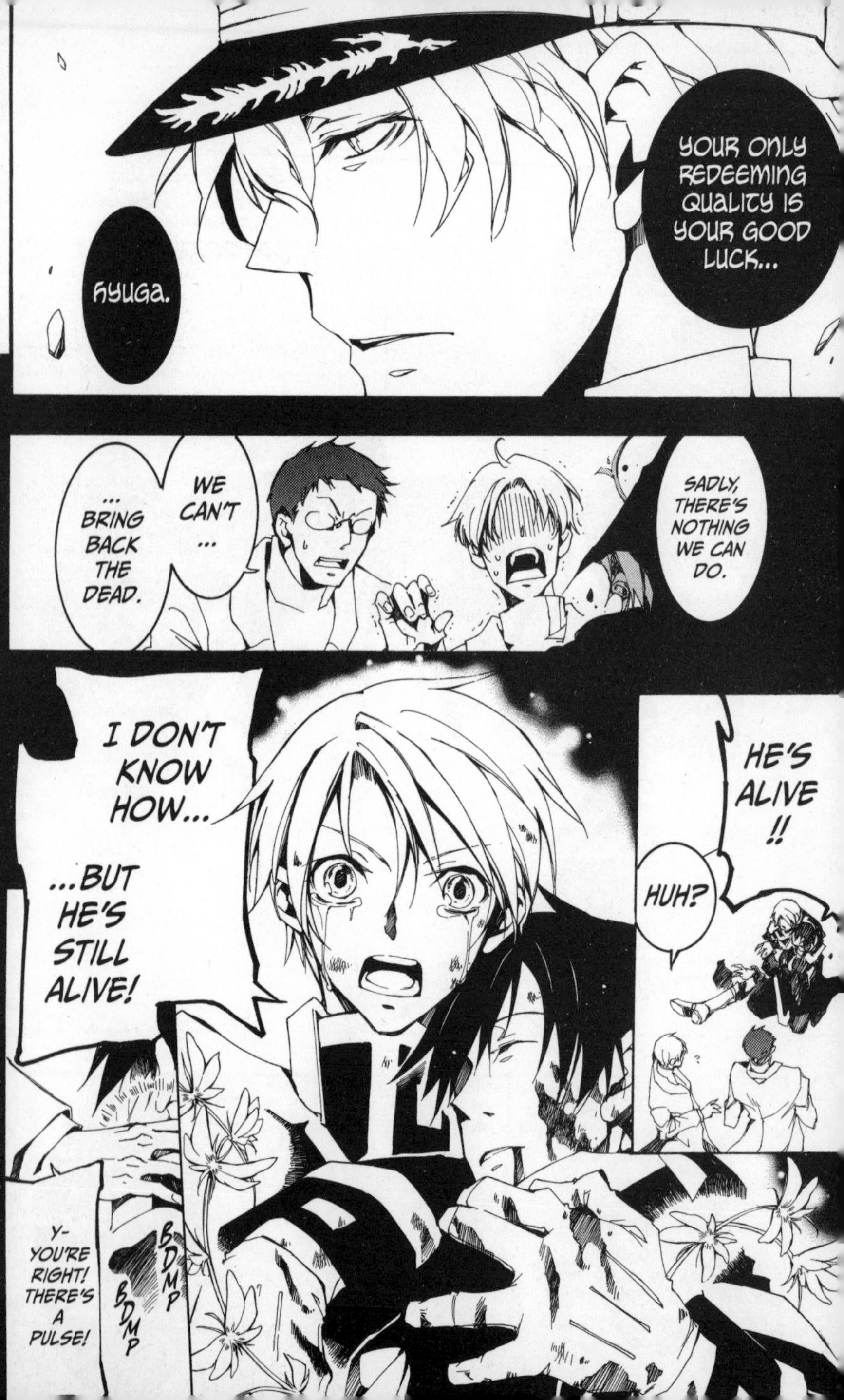
YOUR ONLY REDEEMING QUALITY IS YOUR GOOD LUCK...
HYUGA.
SADLY, THERE'S NOTHING WE CAN DO.
WE CAN'T ...
... BRING BACK THE DEAD.
HE'S ALIVE !!
HUH?
I DON'T KNOW HOW...
...BUT HE'S STILL ALIVE!
BDMP
BDMP
Y-YOU'RE RIGHT! THERE'S A PULSE!

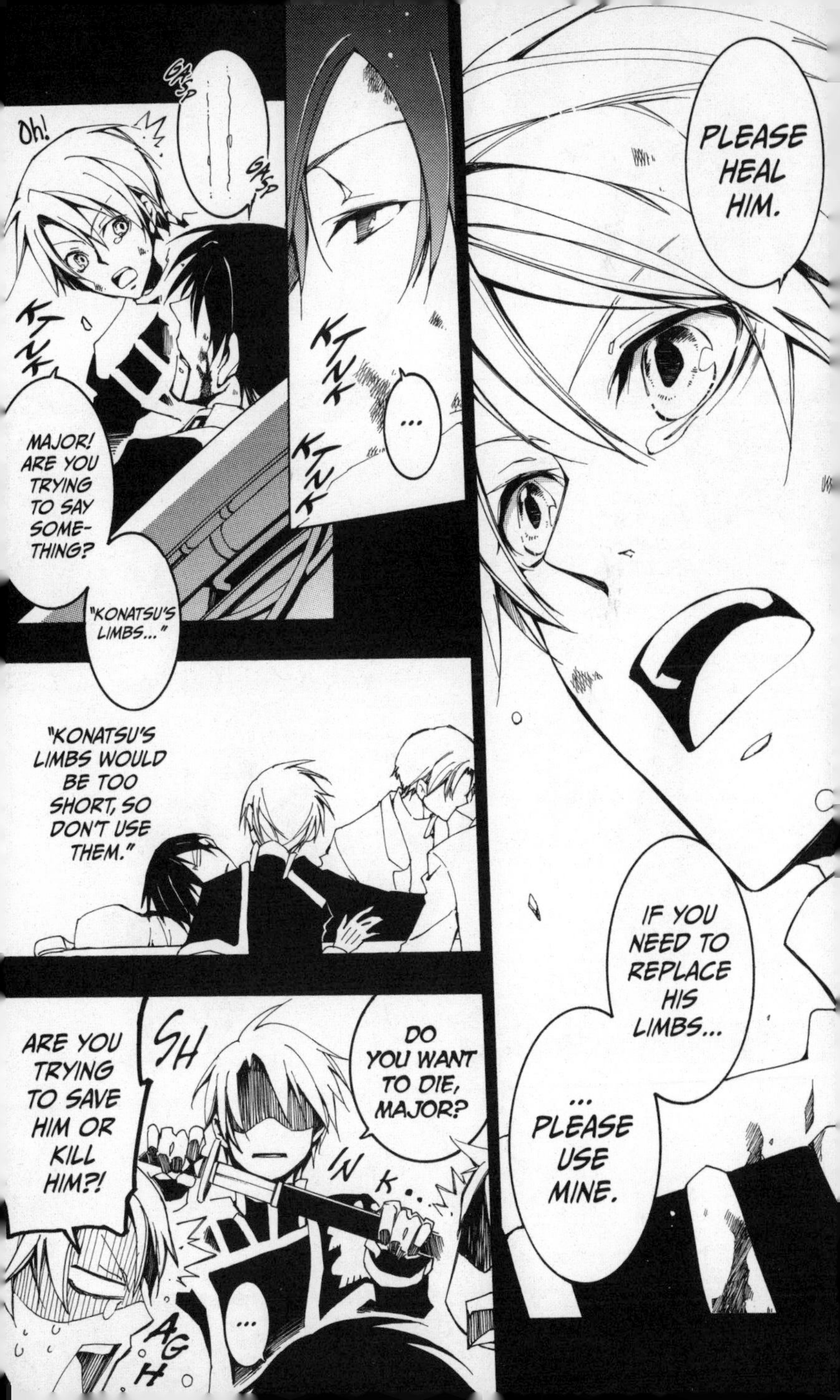
PLEASE HEAL HIM.
IF YOU NEED TO REPLACE HIS LIMBS...
... PLEASE USE MINE.
KINK KINK
...
GASP
...
GASP
Oh!
KINK
MAJOR! ARE YOU TRYING TO SAY SOME-THING?
"KONATSU'S LIMBS..."
"KONATSU'S LIMBS WOULD BE TOO SHORT, SO DON'T USE THEM."
DO YOU WANT TO DIE, MAJOR?
SHINK...
ARE YOU TRYING TO SAVE HIM OR KILL HIM?!
...
AGH

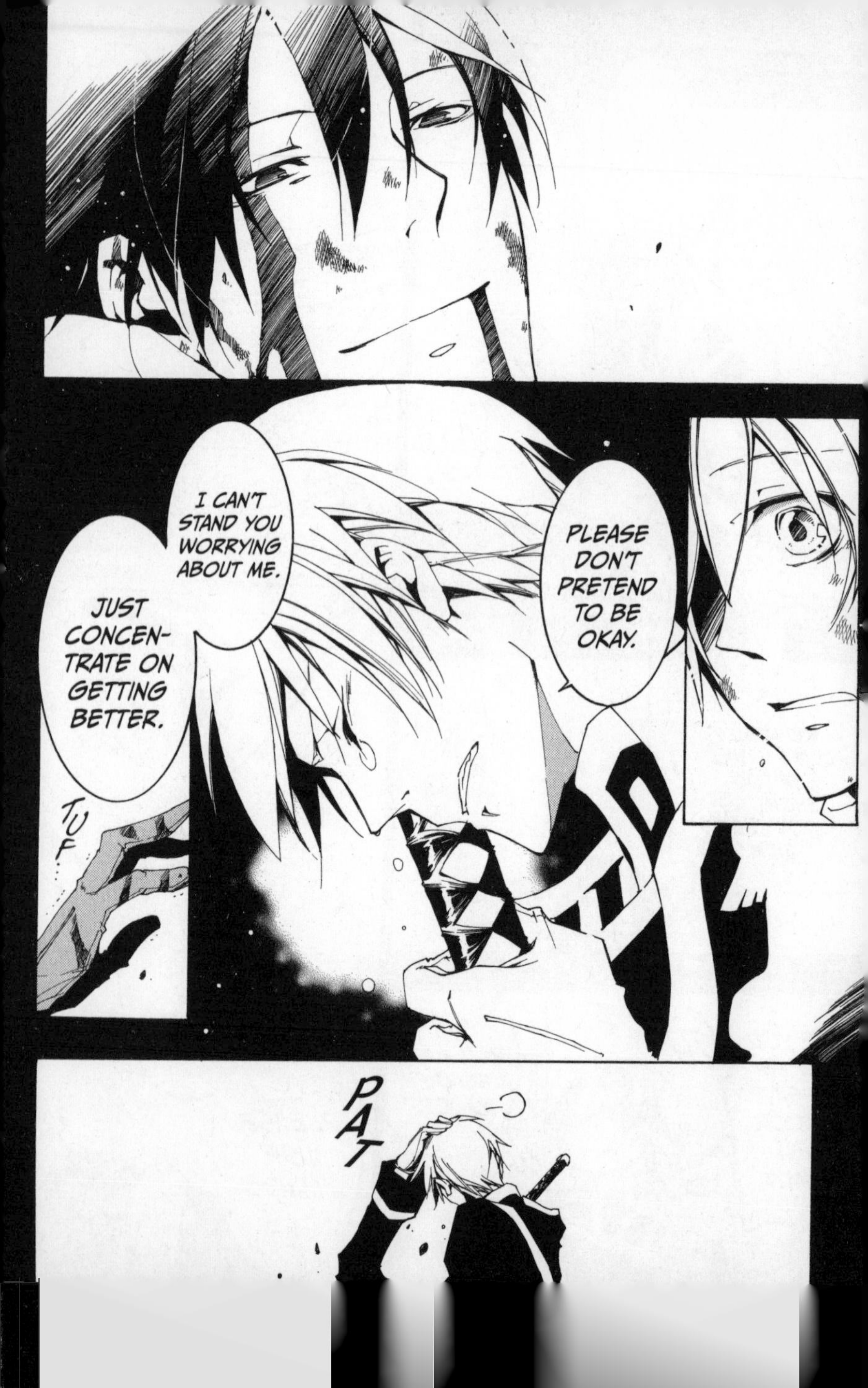
PLEASE DON'T PRETEND TO BE OKAY.
I CAN'T STAND YOU WORRYING ABOUT ME.
JUST CONCENTRATE ON GETTING BETTER.
TUF
PAT

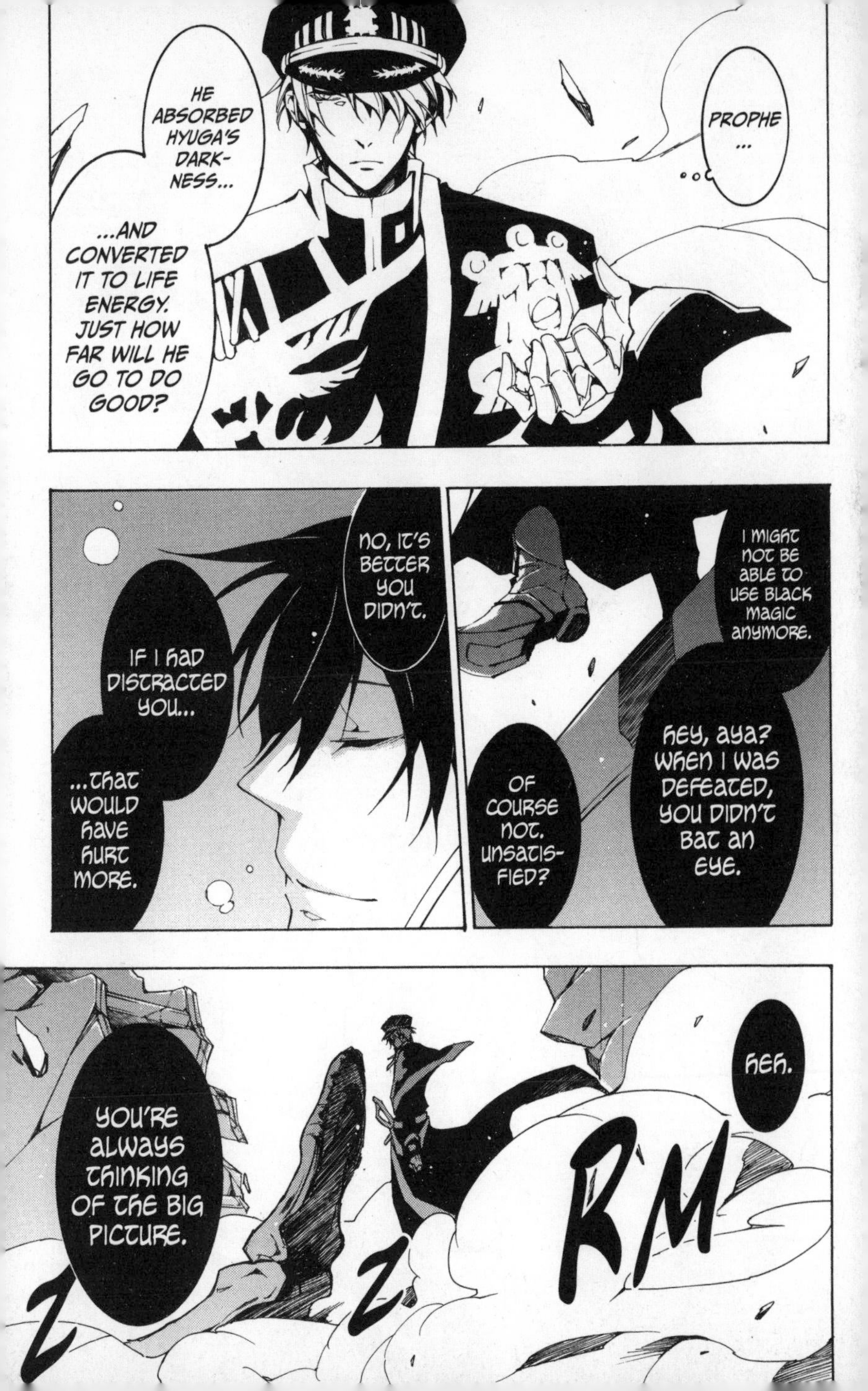
PROPHE ...
HE ABSORBED HYUGA'S DARK-NESS...
...AND CONVERTED IT TO LIFE ENERGY. JUST HOW FAR WILL HE GO TO DO GOOD?
I MIGHT NOT BE ABLE TO USE BLACK MAGIC ANYMORE.
HEY, AYA? WHEN I WAS DEFEATED, YOU DIDN'T BAT AN EYE.
OF COURSE NOT. UNSATIS-FIED?
NO, IT'S BETTER YOU DIDN'T.
IF I HAD DISTRACTED YOU...
...THAT WOULD HAVE HURT MORE.
HEH.
RM
YOU'RE ALWAYS THINKING OF THE BIG PICTURE.
Z
Z

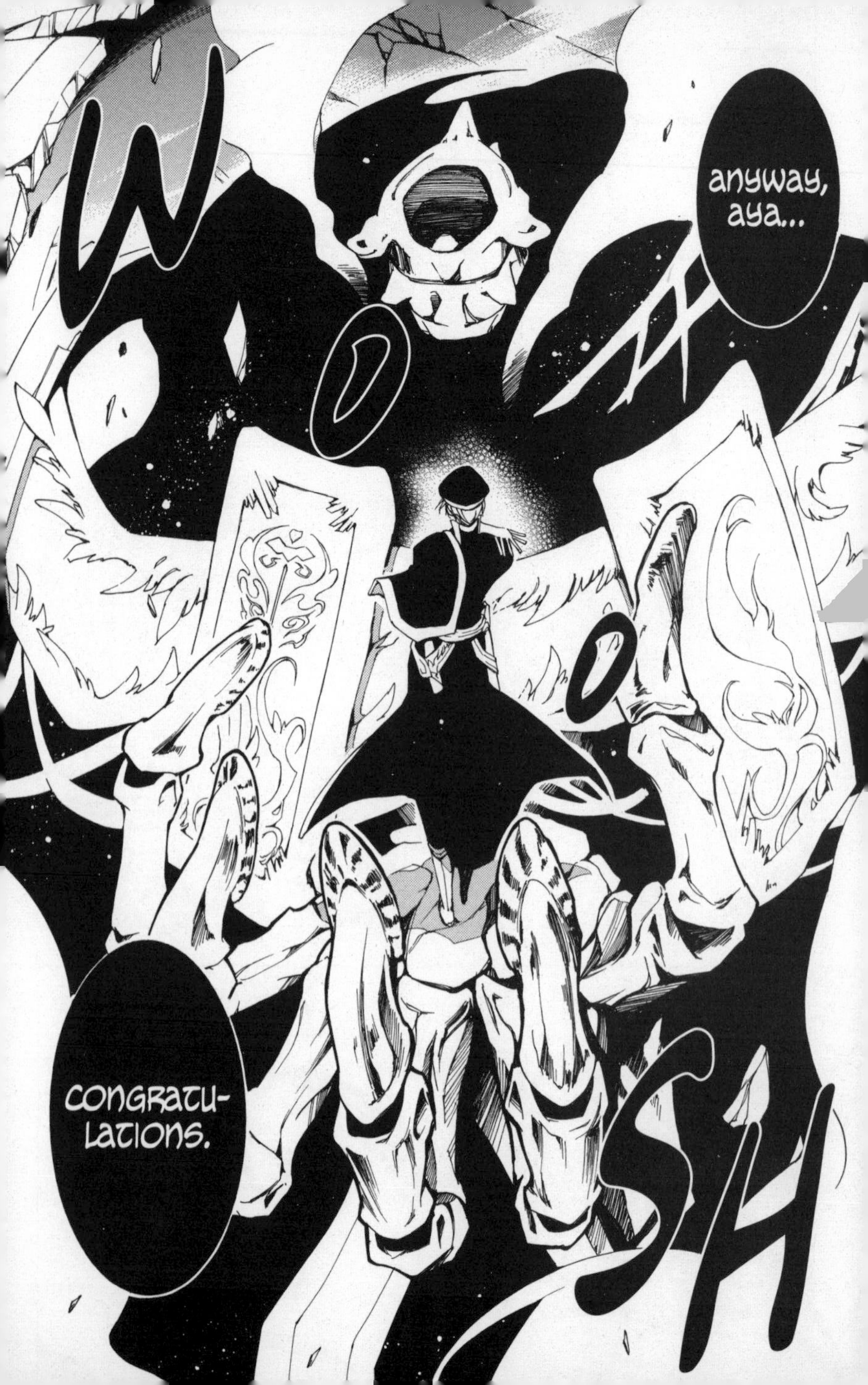
anyway, aya...
WOOSH
CONGRATU-LATIONS.

07-GHOST

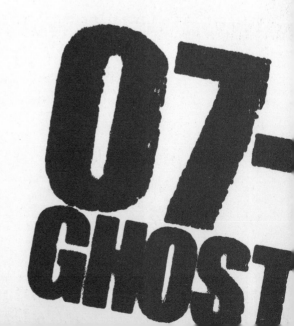

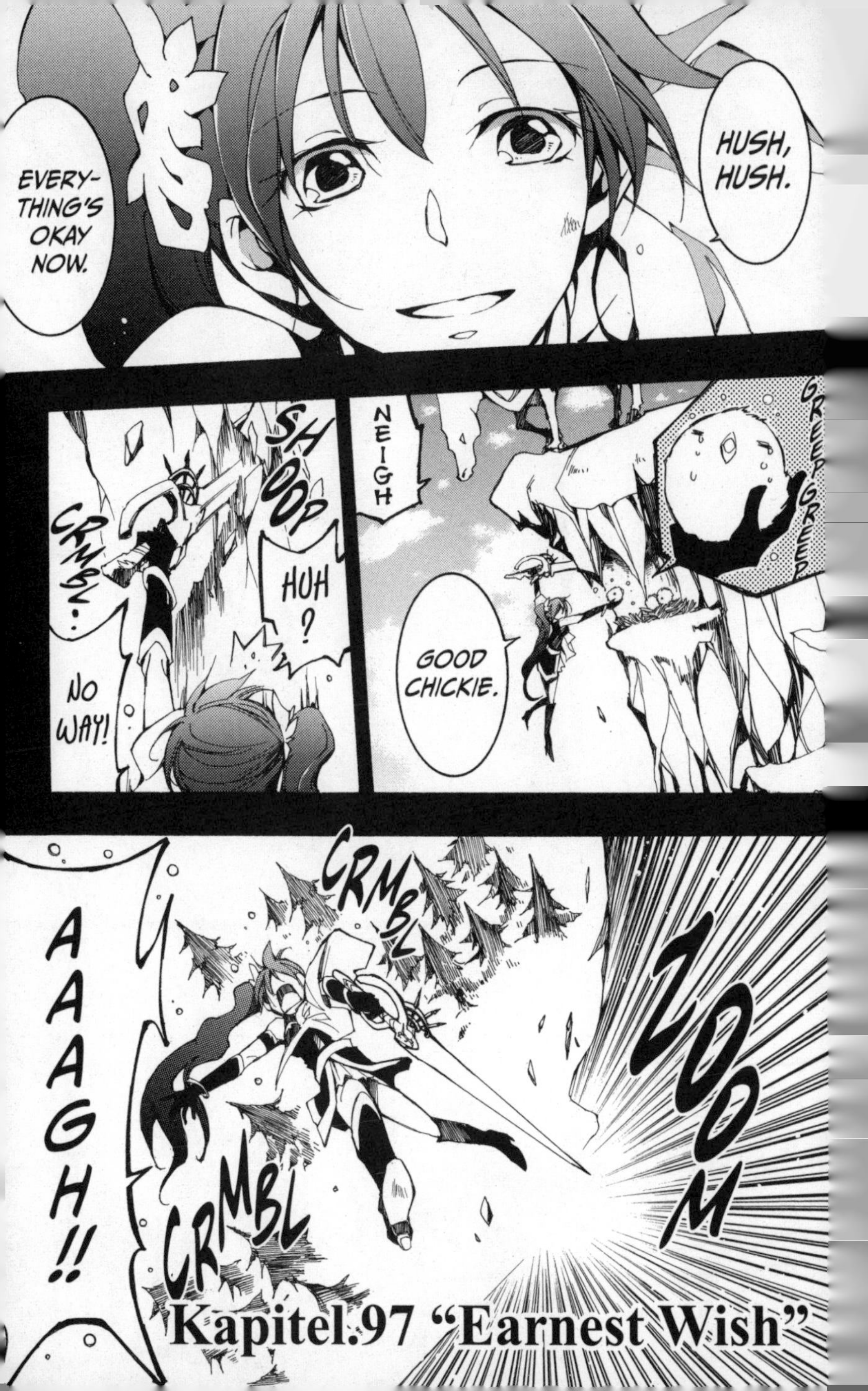
HUSH, HUSH.
EVERY-THING'S OKAY NOW.
GREEP GREEP
NEIGH
GOOD CHICKIE.
SHOOOP
HUH?
CRMBL...
NO WAY!
ZOOOM
CRMBL
AAAAGH!!
CRMBL

Kapitel.97 "Earnest Wish"

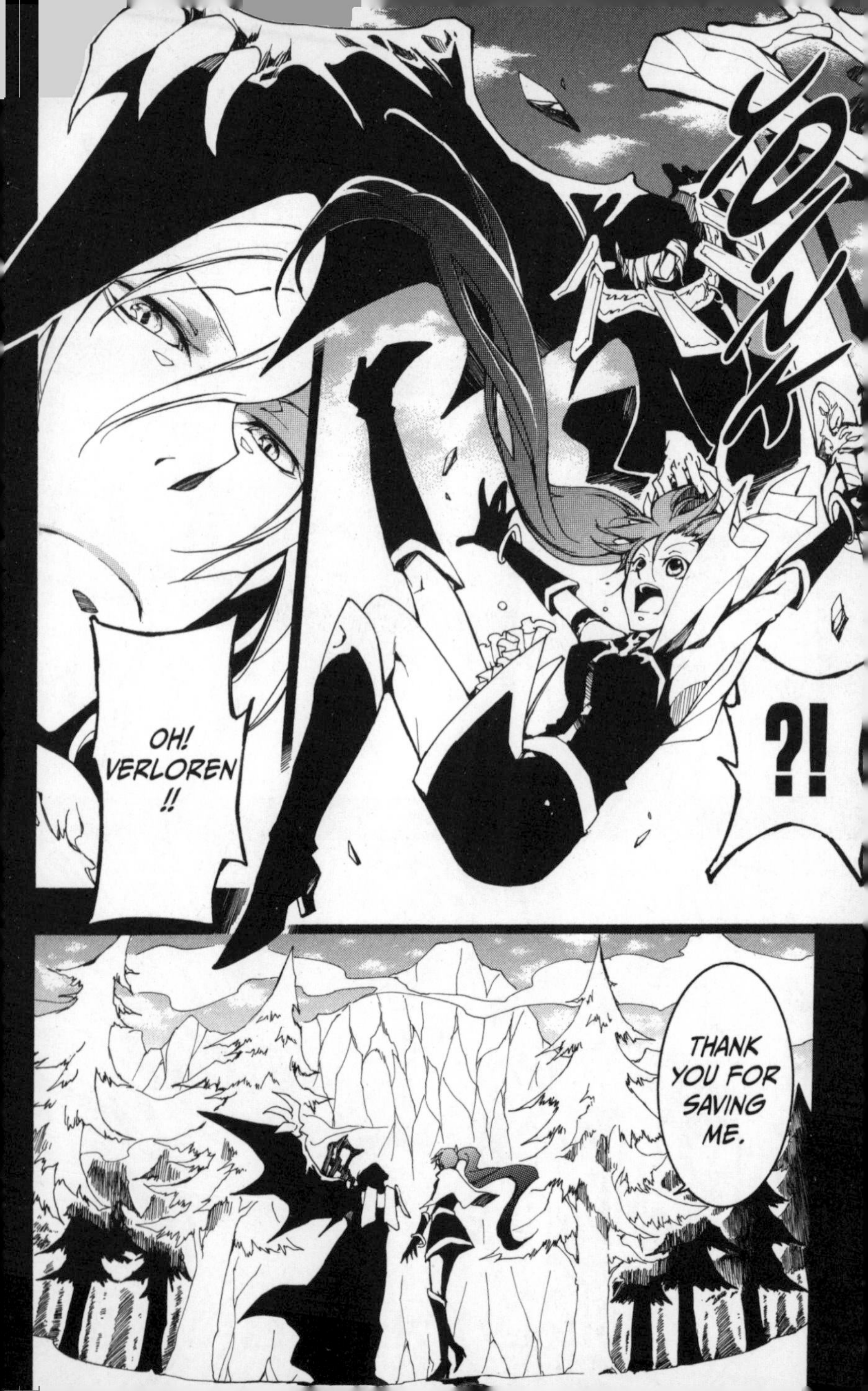
YOINK
?!
OH! VERLOREN !!
THANK YOU FOR SAVING ME.

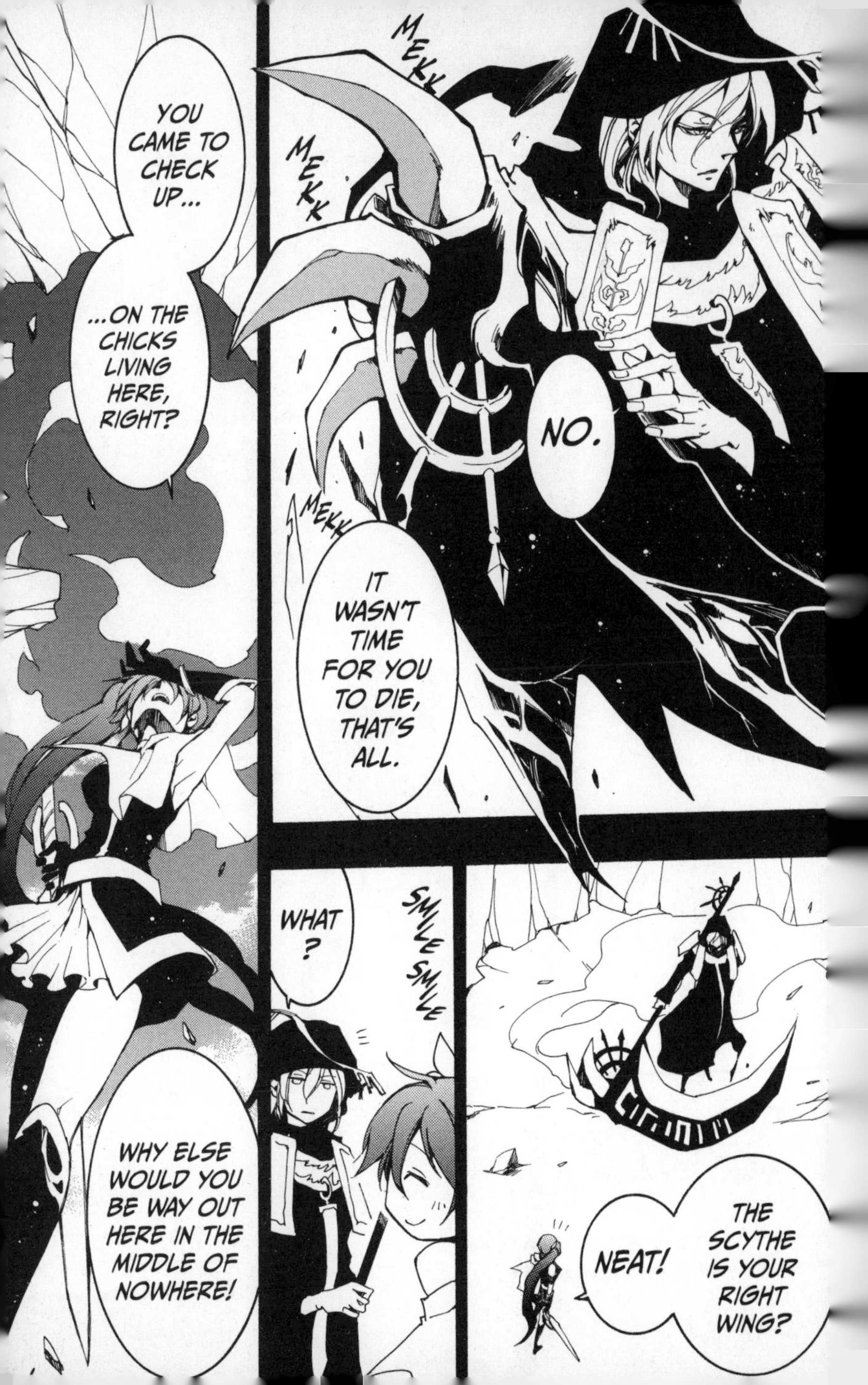
MEKK
MEKK
NO.
MEKK
IT WASN'T TIME FOR YOU TO DIE, THAT'S ALL.
THE SCYTHE IS YOUR RIGHT WING?
NEAT!
SMILE SMILE
WHAT?
YOU CAME TO CHECK UP...
...ON THE CHICKS LIVING HERE, RIGHT?
WHY ELSE WOULD YOU BE WAY OUT HERE IN THE MIDDLE OF NOWHERE!

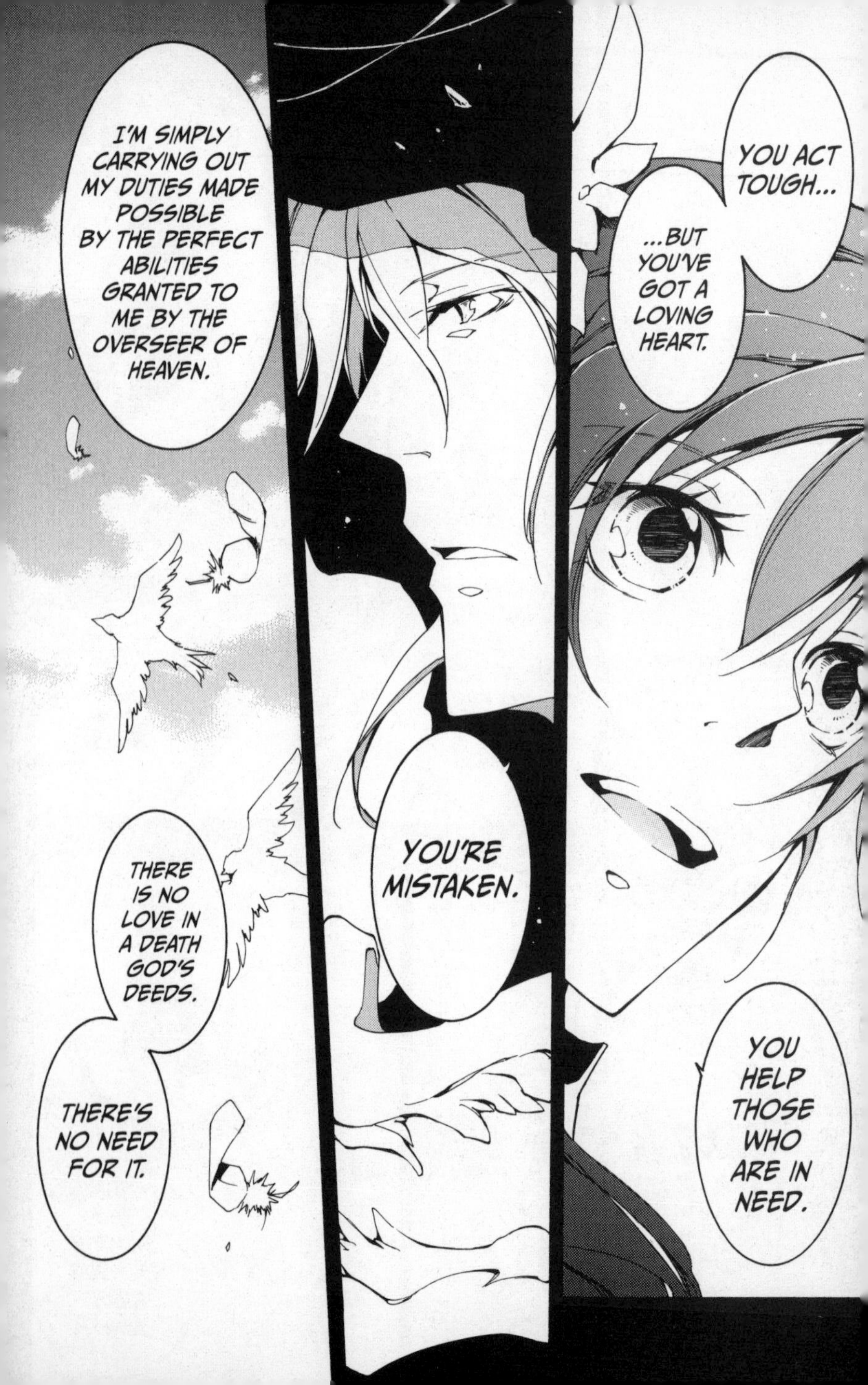
YOU ACT TOUGH...
...BUT YOU'VE GOT A LOVING HEART.
YOU HELP THOSE WHO ARE IN NEED.
YOU'RE MISTAKEN.
I'M SIMPLY CARRYING OUT MY DUTIES MADE POSSIBLE BY THE PERFECT ABILITIES GRANTED TO ME BY THE OVERSEER OF HEAVEN.
THERE IS NO LOVE IN A DEATH GOD'S DEEDS.
THERE'S NO NEED FOR IT.

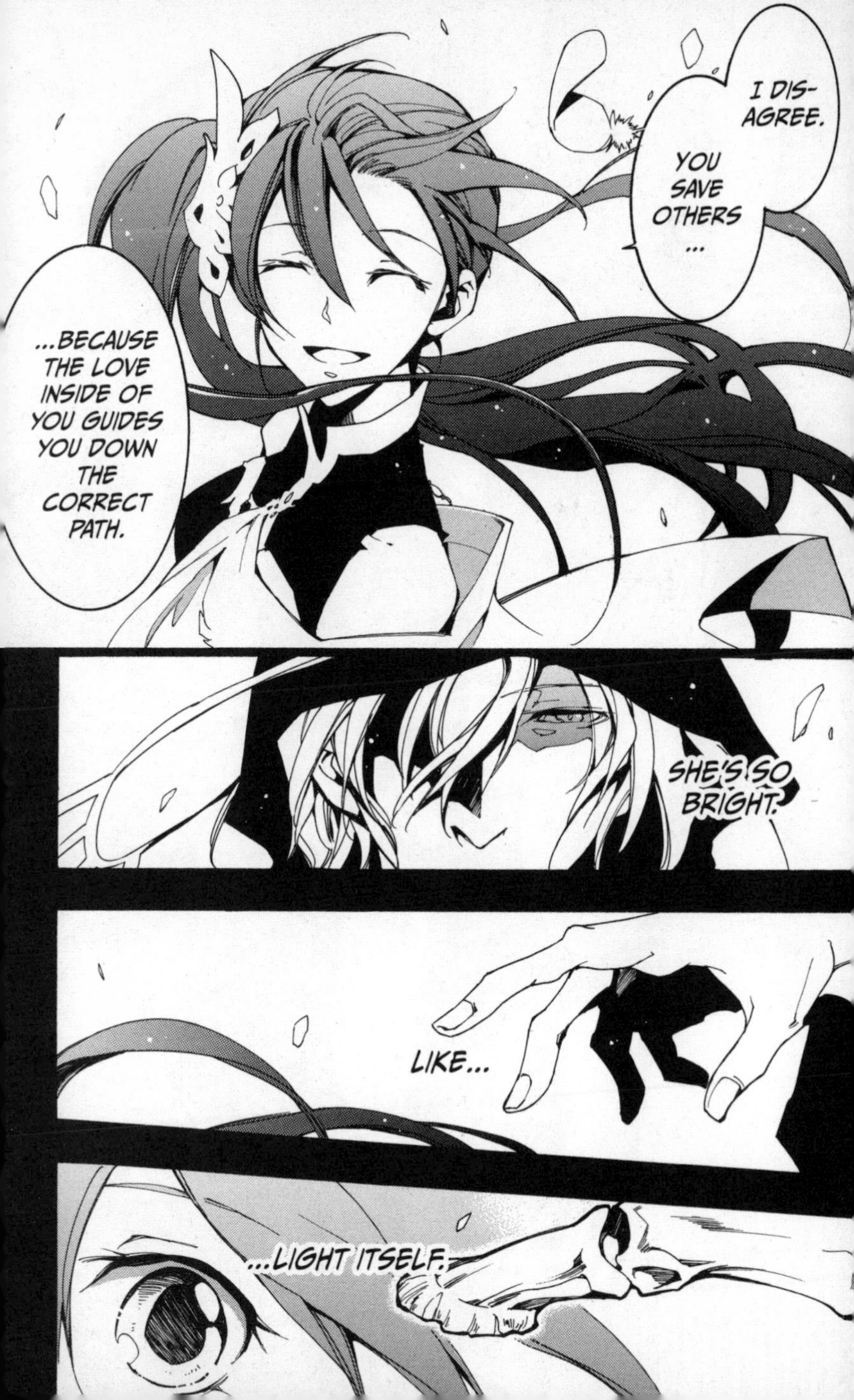
I DIS-AGREE.
YOU SAVE OTHERS ...
...BECAUSE THE LOVE INSIDE OF YOU GUIDES YOU DOWN THE CORRECT PATH.
SHE'S SO BRIGHT.
LIKE...
...LIGHT ITSELF.

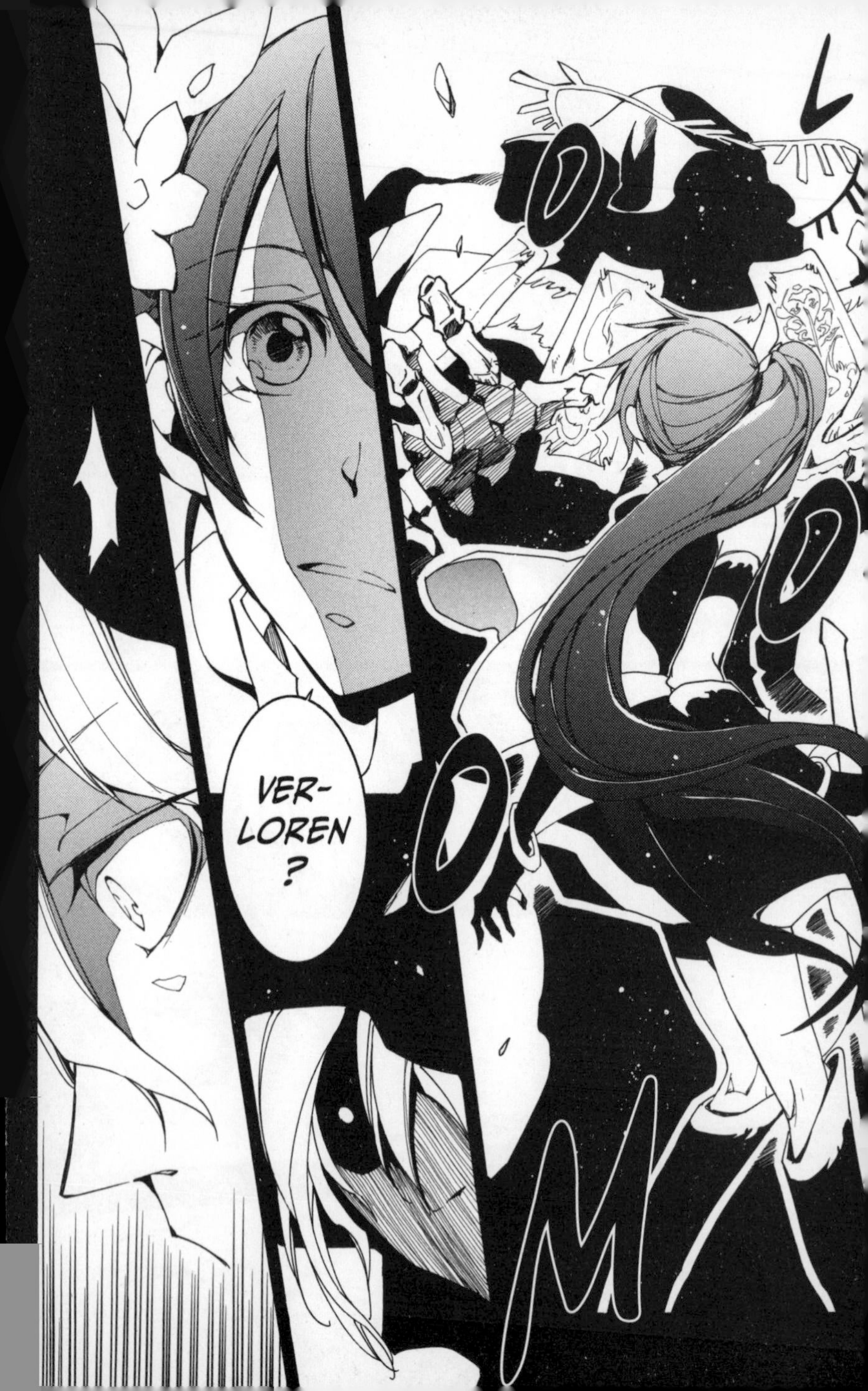
VER-LOREN?

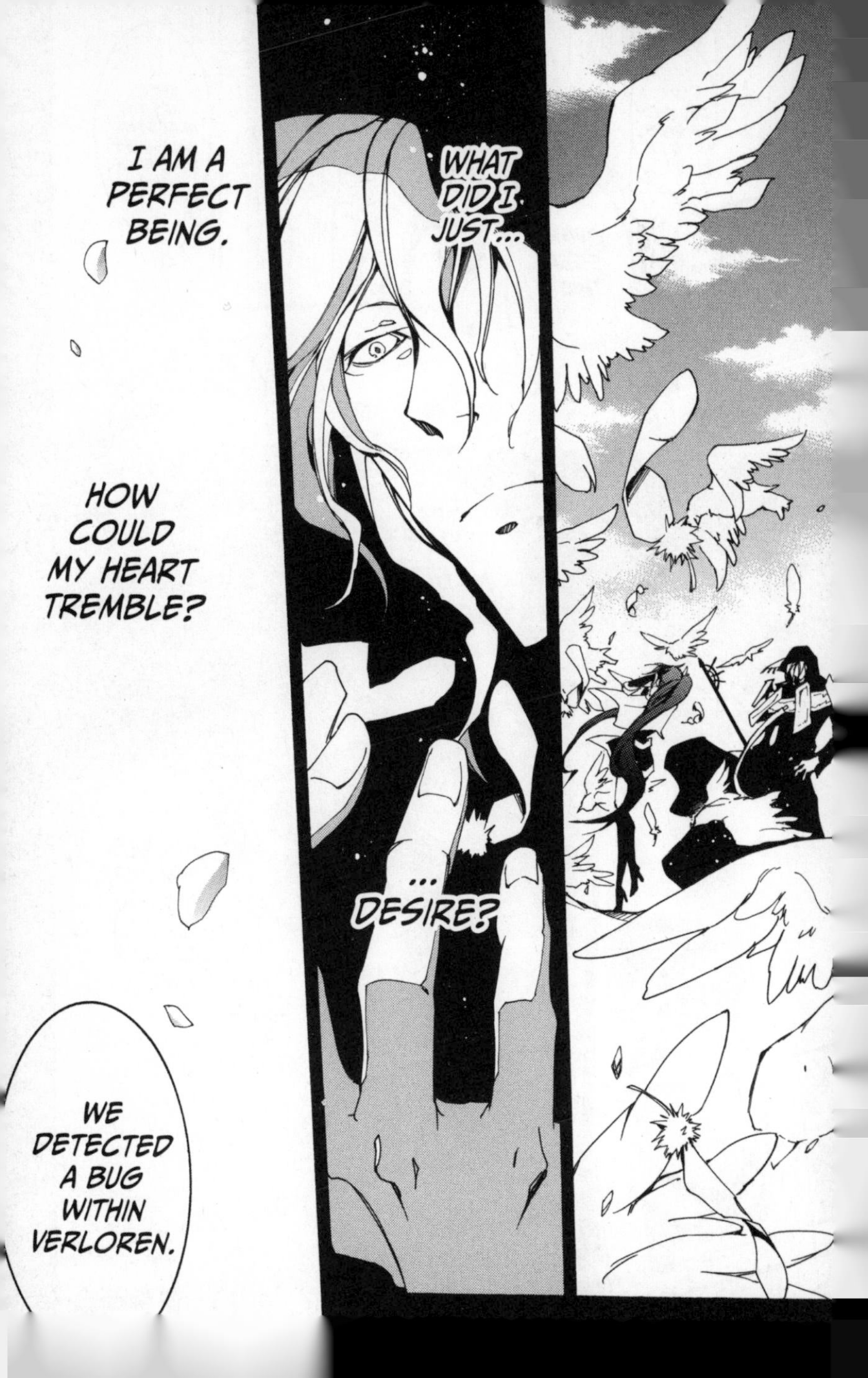
WHAT DID I JUST...
... DESIRE?
I AM A PERFECT BEING.
HOW COULD MY HEART TREMBLE?
WE DETECTED A BUG WITHIN VERLOREN.

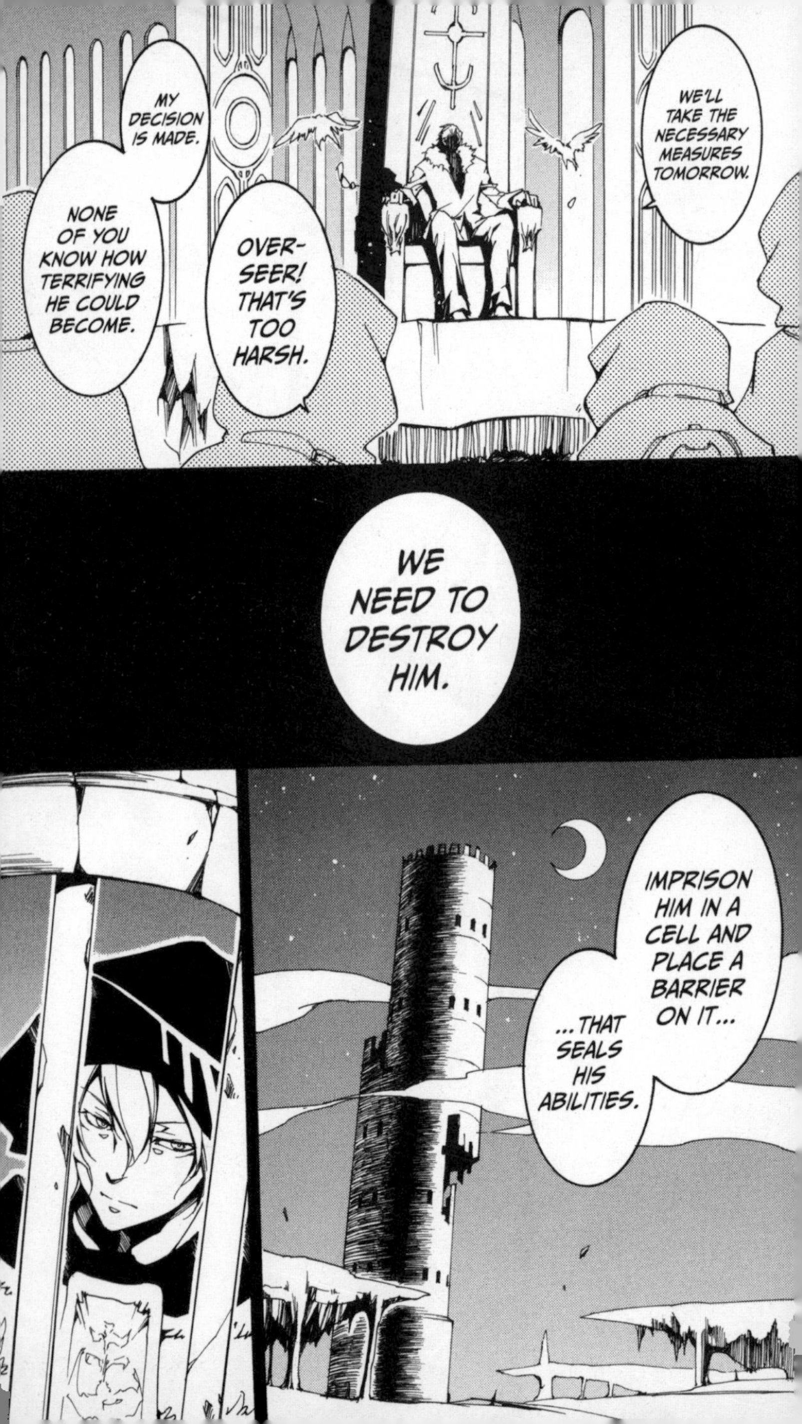
WE'LL TAKE THE NECESSARY MEASURES TOMORROW.
OVER-SEER! THAT'S TOO HARSH.
MY DECISION IS MADE.
NONE OF YOU KNOW HOW TERRIFYING HE COULD BECOME.
WE NEED TO DESTROY HIM.
IMPRISON HIM IN A CELL AND PLACE A BARRIER ON IT...
...THAT SEALS HIS ABILITIES.

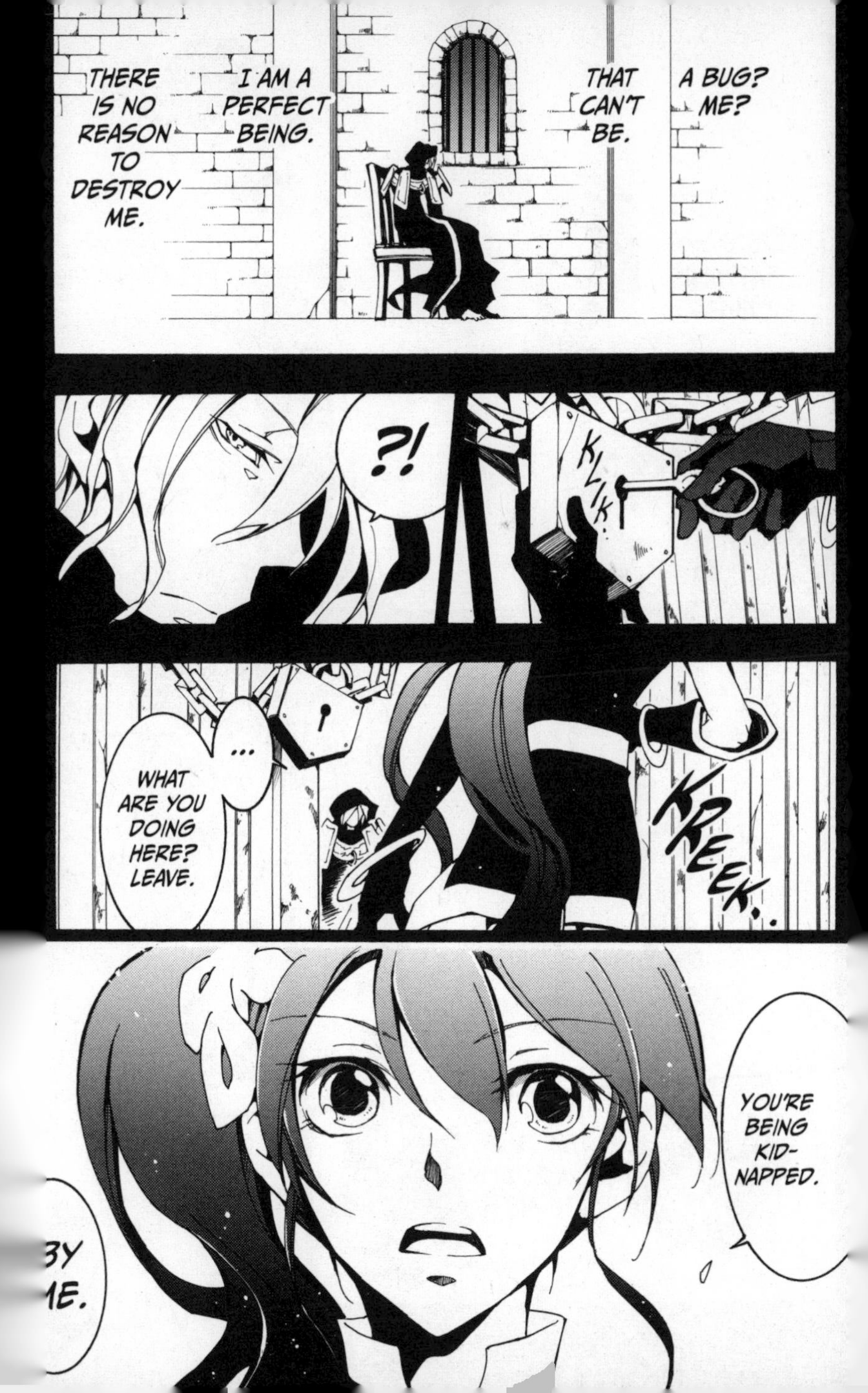
A BUG? ME?
THAT CAN'T BE.
I AM A PERFECT BEING.
THERE IS NO REASON TO DESTROY ME.
KLIK
?!
KREEK..
...
WHAT ARE YOU DOING HERE? LEAVE.
YOU'RE BEING KID-NAPPED.
BY ME.

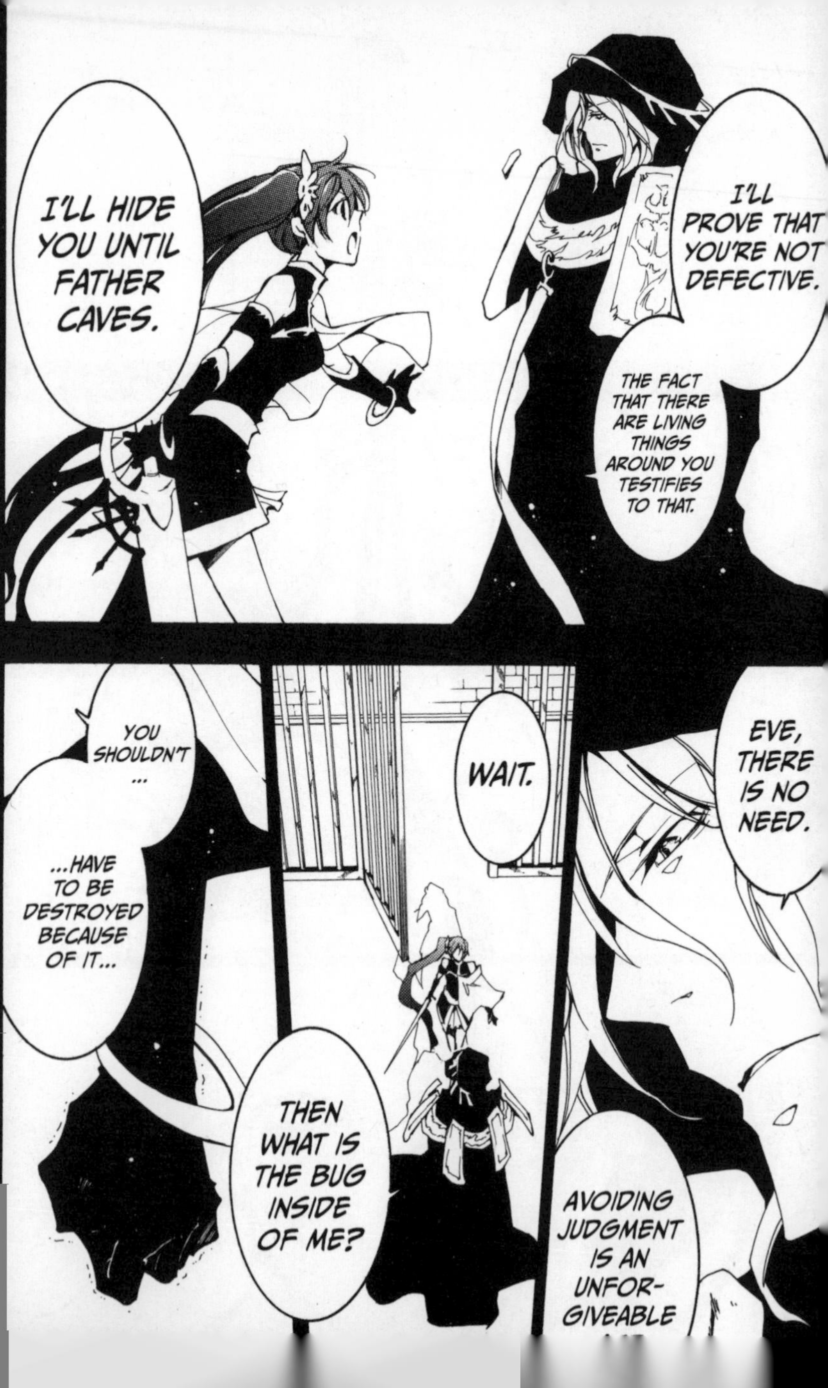
I'LL PROVE THAT YOU'RE NOT DEFECTIVE.
THE FACT THAT THERE ARE LIVING THINGS AROUND YOU TESTIFIES TO THAT.
I'LL HIDE YOU UNTIL FATHER CAVES.
EVE, THERE IS NO NEED.
AVOIDING JUDGMENT IS AN UNFORGIVEABLE
WAIT.
THEN WHAT IS THE BUG INSIDE OF ME?
YOU SHOULDN'T ...
...HAVE TO BE DESTROYED BECAUSE OF IT...

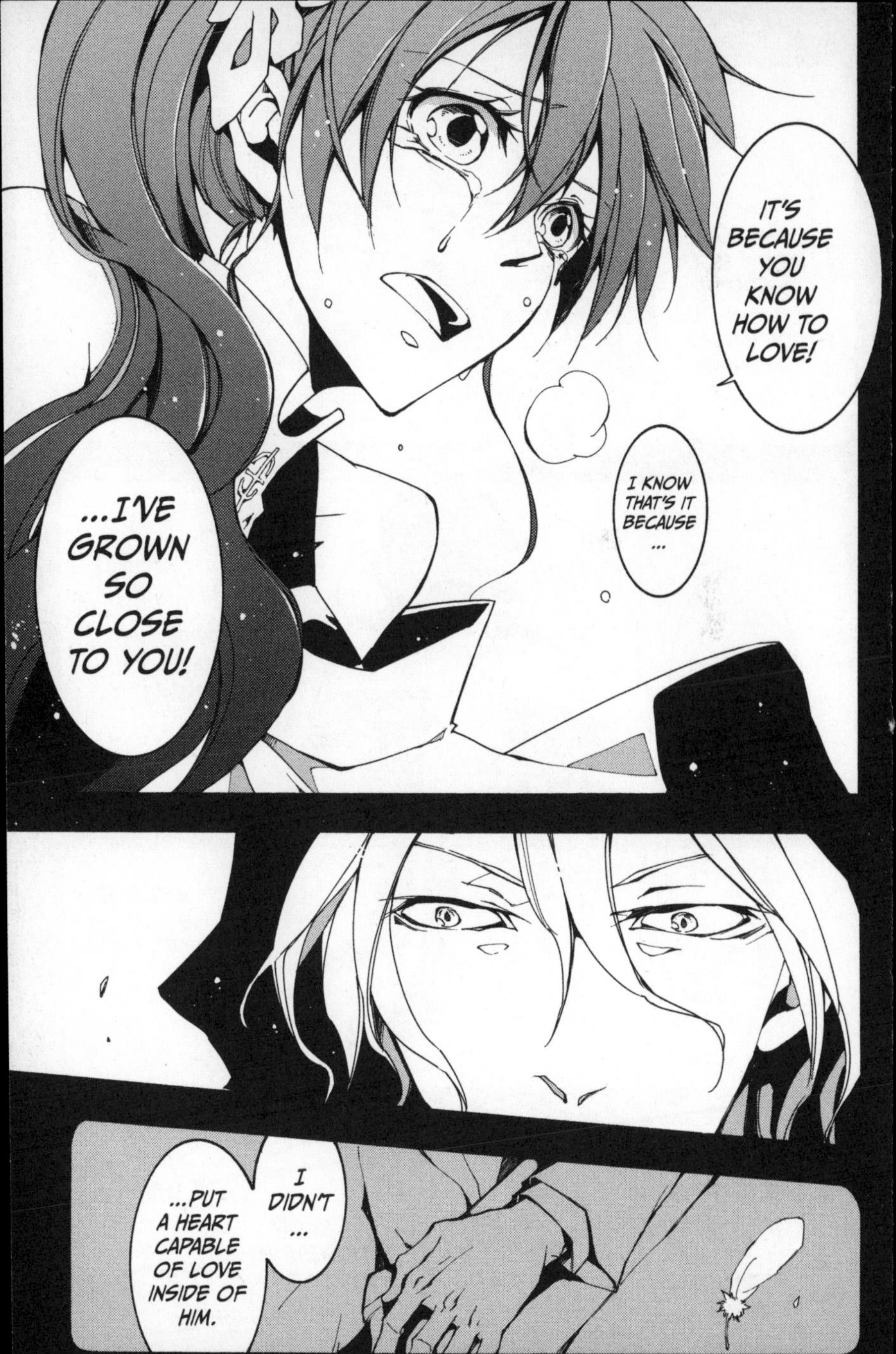
IT'S BECAUSE YOU KNOW HOW TO LOVE!
I KNOW THAT'S IT BECAUSE ...
...I'VE GROWN SO CLOSE TO YOU!
I DIDN'T ...
...PUT A HEART CAPABLE OF LOVE INSIDE OF HIM.

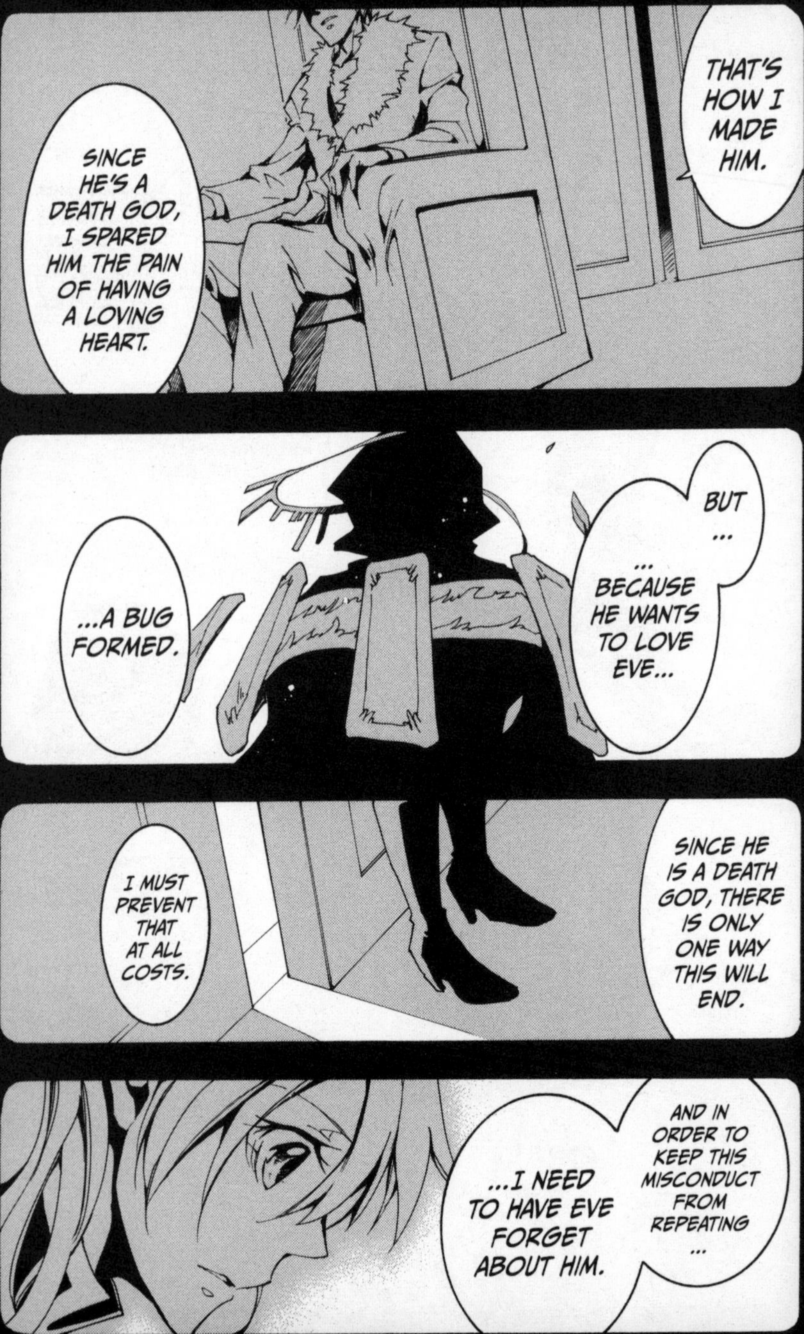
THAT'S HOW I MADE HIM.
SINCE HE'S A DEATH GOD, I SPARED HIM THE PAIN OF HAVING A LOVING HEART.
BUT ...
... BECAUSE HE WANTS TO LOVE EVE...
...A BUG FORMED.
SINCE HE IS A DEATH GOD, THERE IS ONLY ONE WAY THIS WILL END.
I MUST PREVENT THAT AT ALL COSTS.
AND IN ORDER TO KEEP THIS MISCONDUCT FROM REPEATING ...
...I NEED TO HAVE EVE FORGET ABOUT HIM.

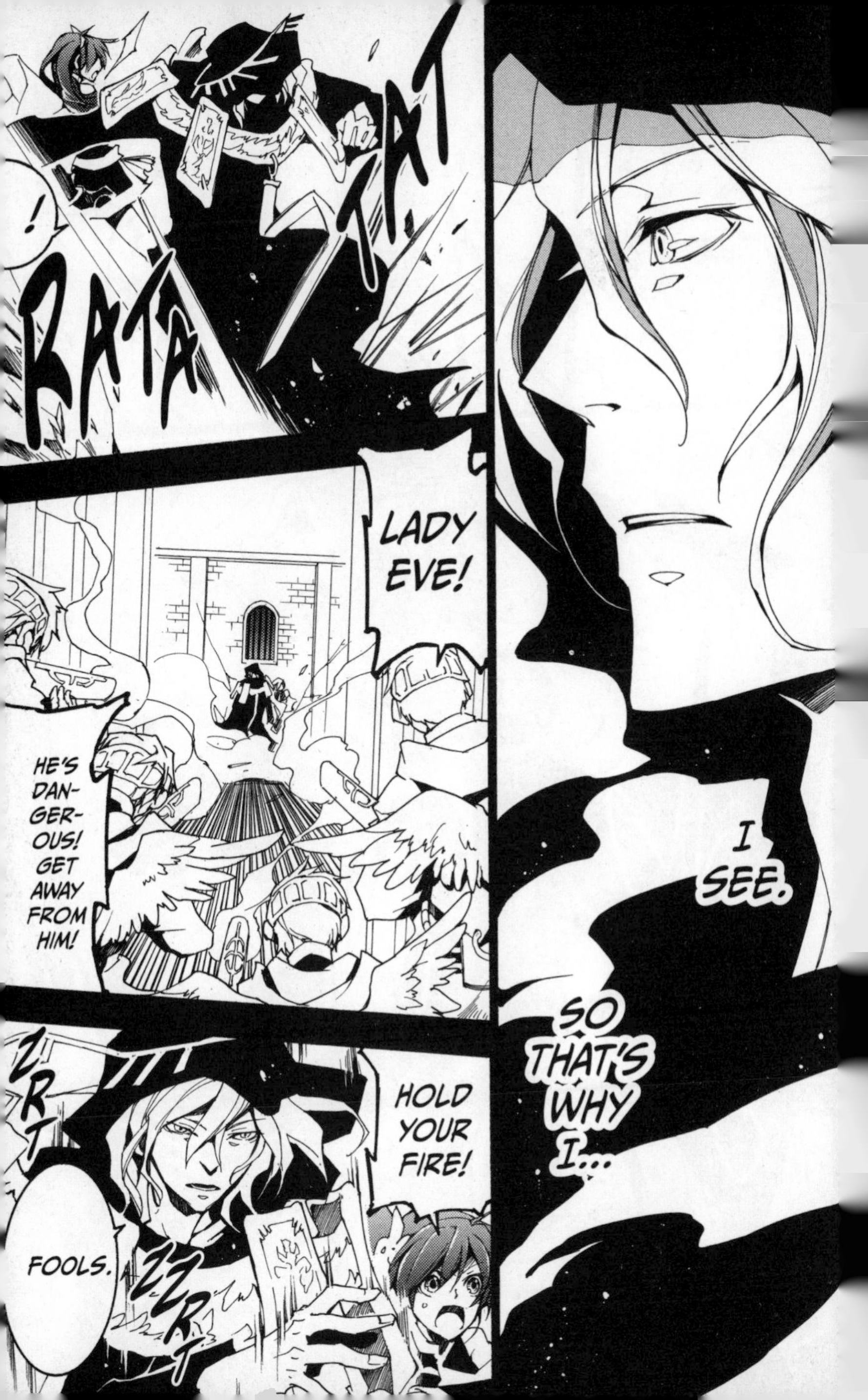
I SEE.
SO THAT'S WHY I...
!
RATA
TAT
LADY EVE!
HE'S DANGEROUS! GET AWAY FROM HIM!
ZRT
HOLD YOUR FIRE!
FOOLS.
ZZZRT

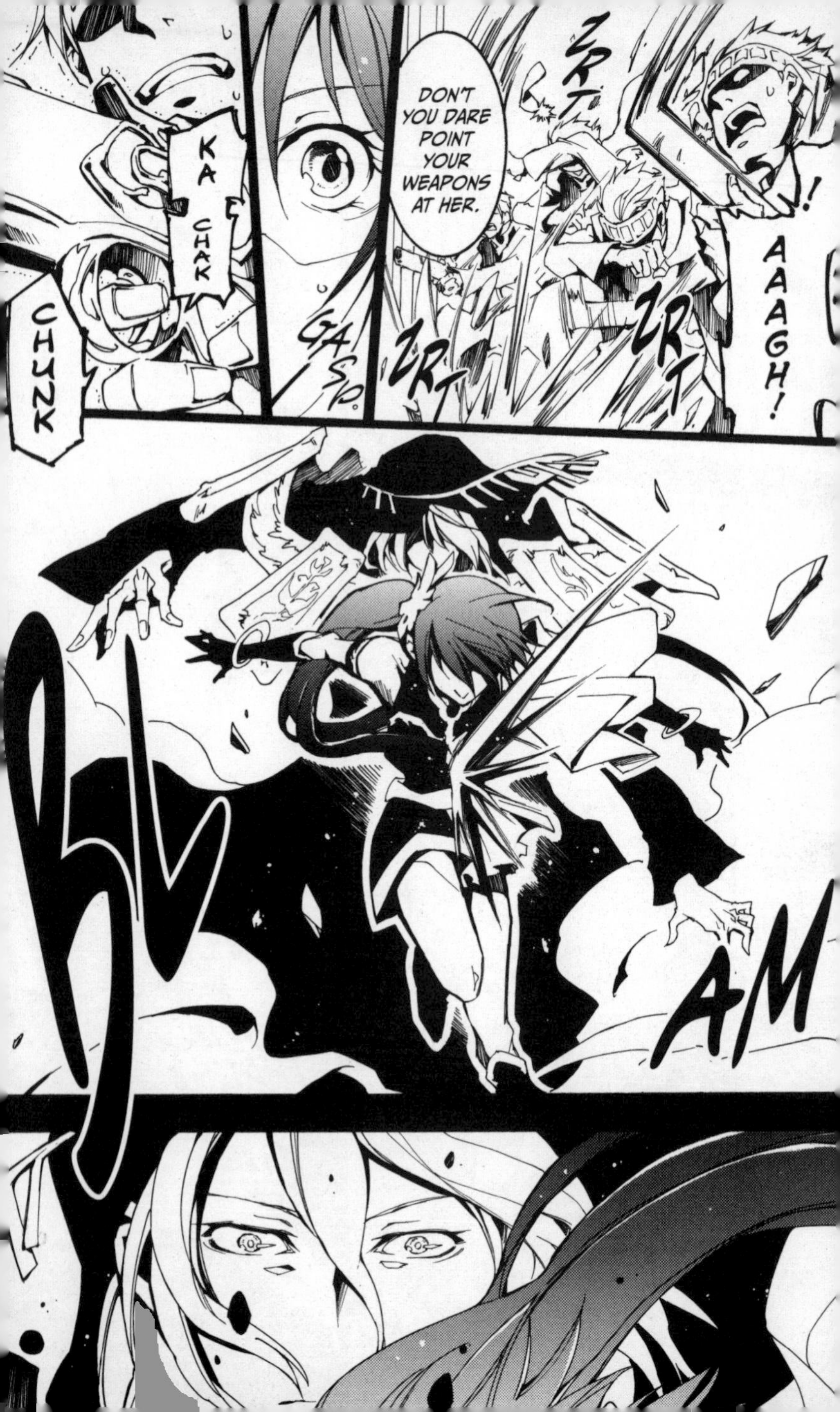
ZRT
AAAAGH!
DON'T YOU DARE POINT YOUR WEAPONS AT HER.
ZRT
ZRT
GASP
KA CHAK
CHUNK
SLAM

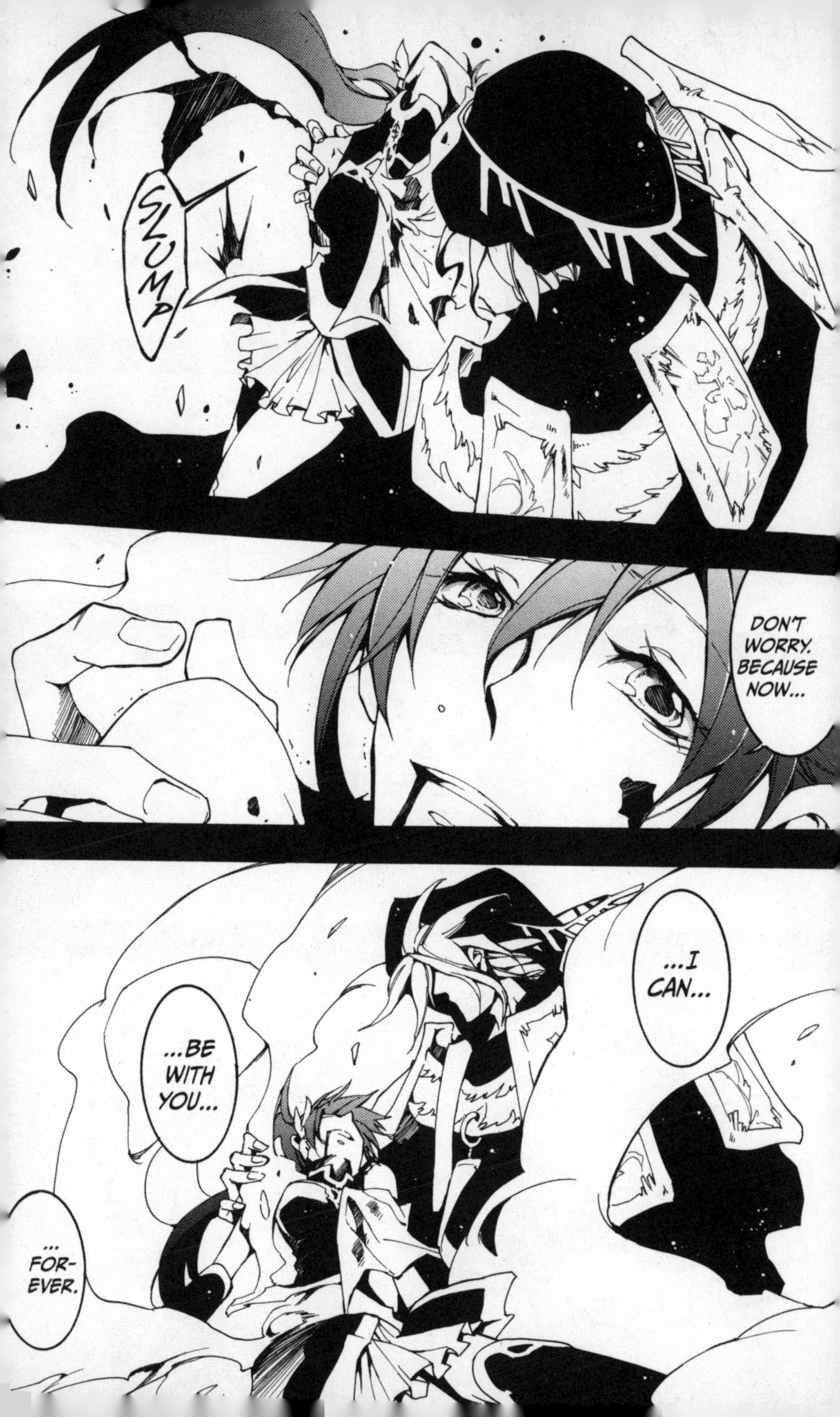
SLUMP
DON'T WORRY. BECAUSE NOW...
...I CAN...
...BE WITH YOU...
...FOR-EVER.

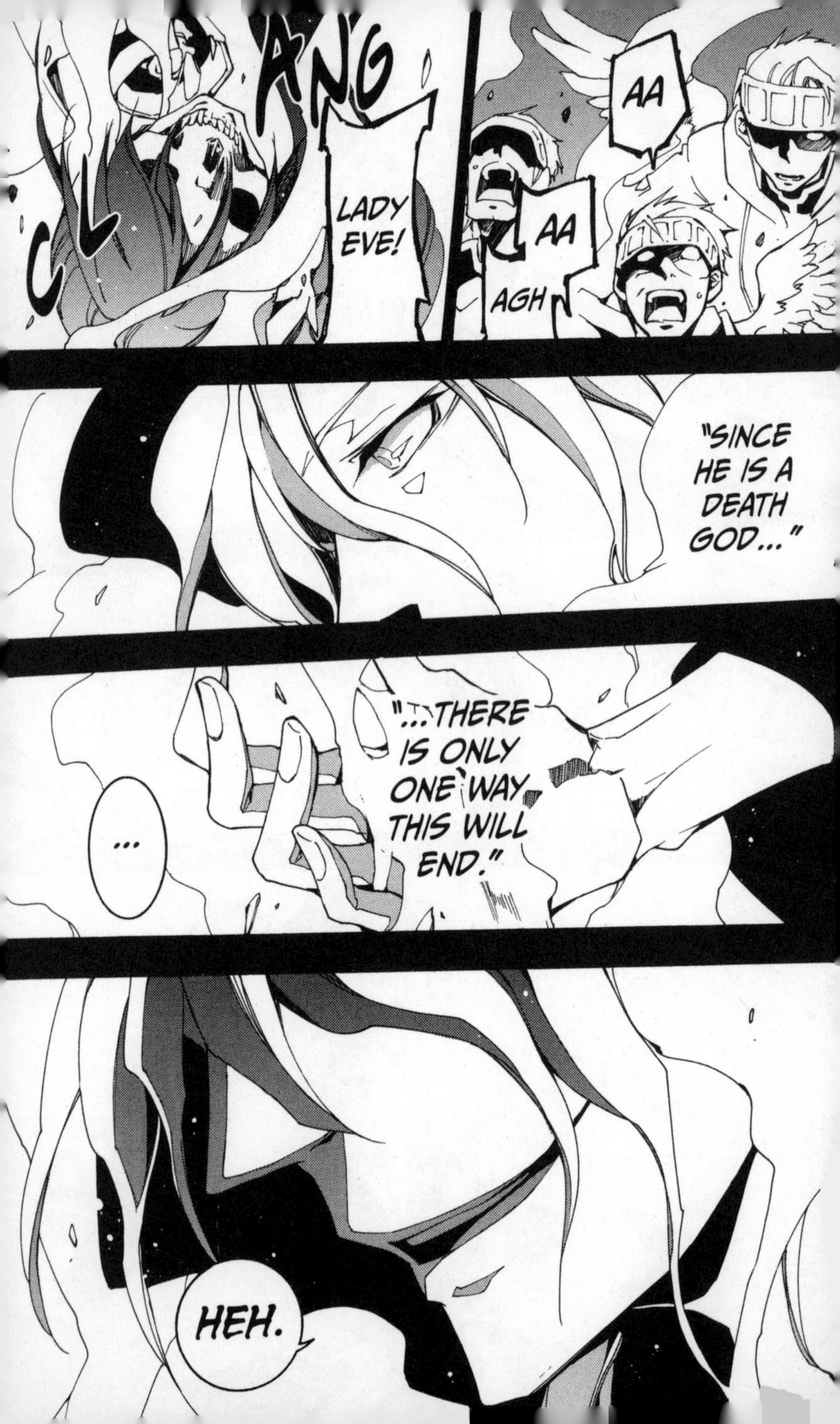
AA
AA
AGH
LADY EVE!
CLANG
"SINCE HE IS A DEATH GOD..."
"...THERE IS ONLY ONE WAY THIS WILL END."
...
HEH.

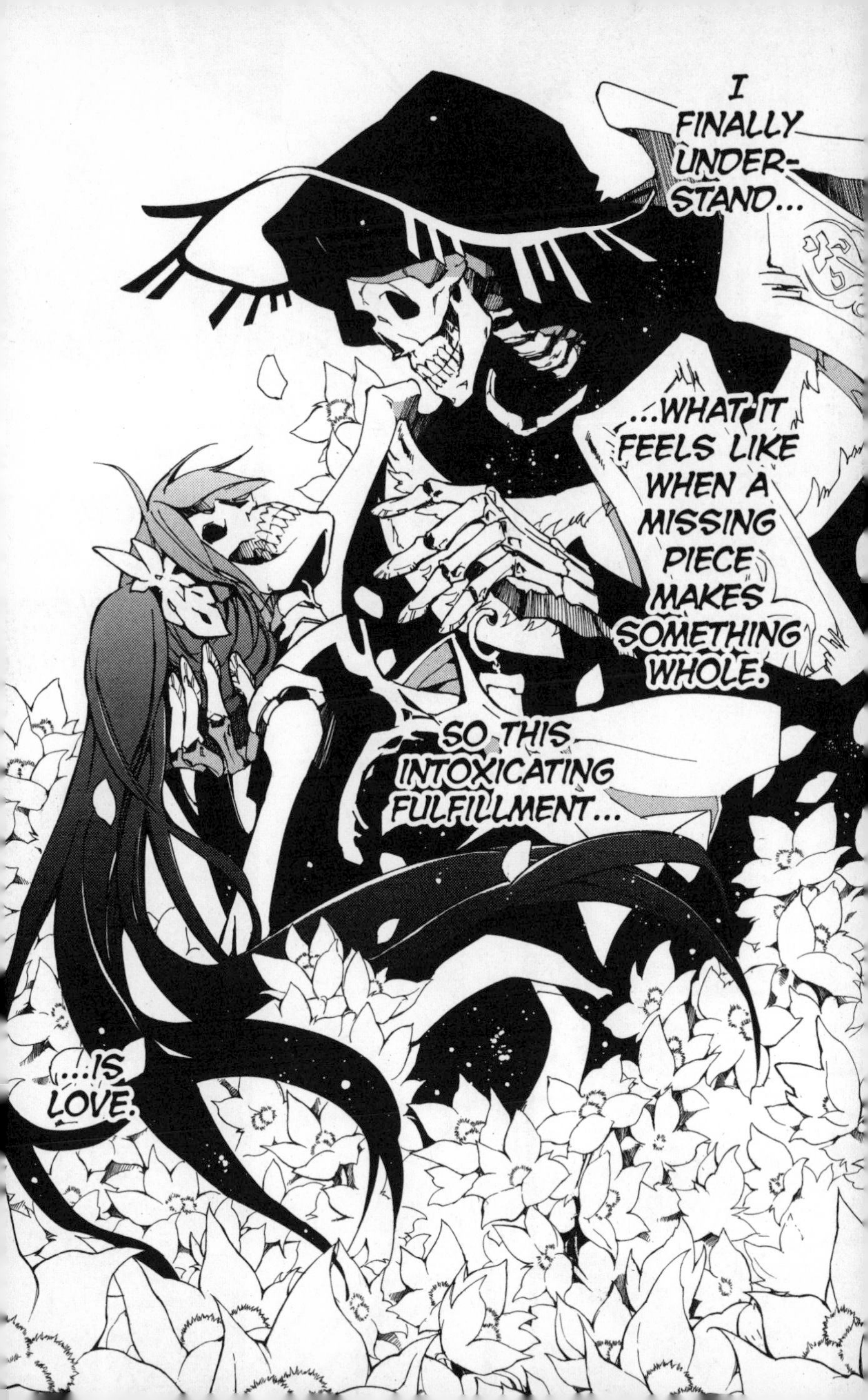
I FINALLY UNDER-STAND...
...WHAT IT FEELS LIKE WHEN A MISSING PIECE MAKES SOMETHING WHOLE.
SO THIS INTOXICATING FULFILLMENT...
...IS LOVE.

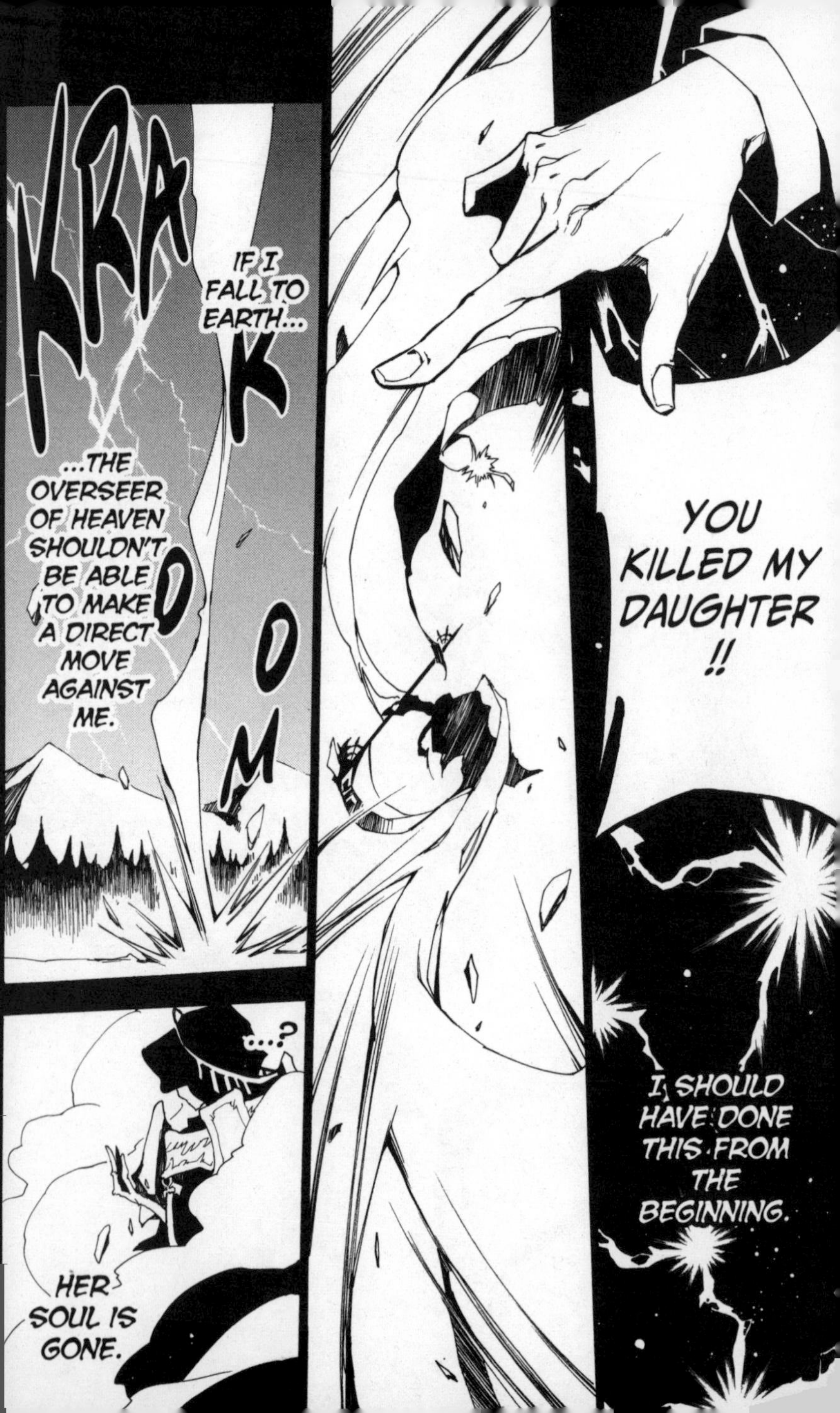
YOU KILLED MY DAUGHTER !!
I SHOULD HAVE DONE THIS FROM THE BEGINNING.
KRAKOOM
IF I FALL TO EARTH...
...THE OVERSEER OF HEAVEN SHOULDN'T BE ABLE TO MAKE A DIRECT MOVE AGAINST ME.
....?
HER SOUL IS GONE.

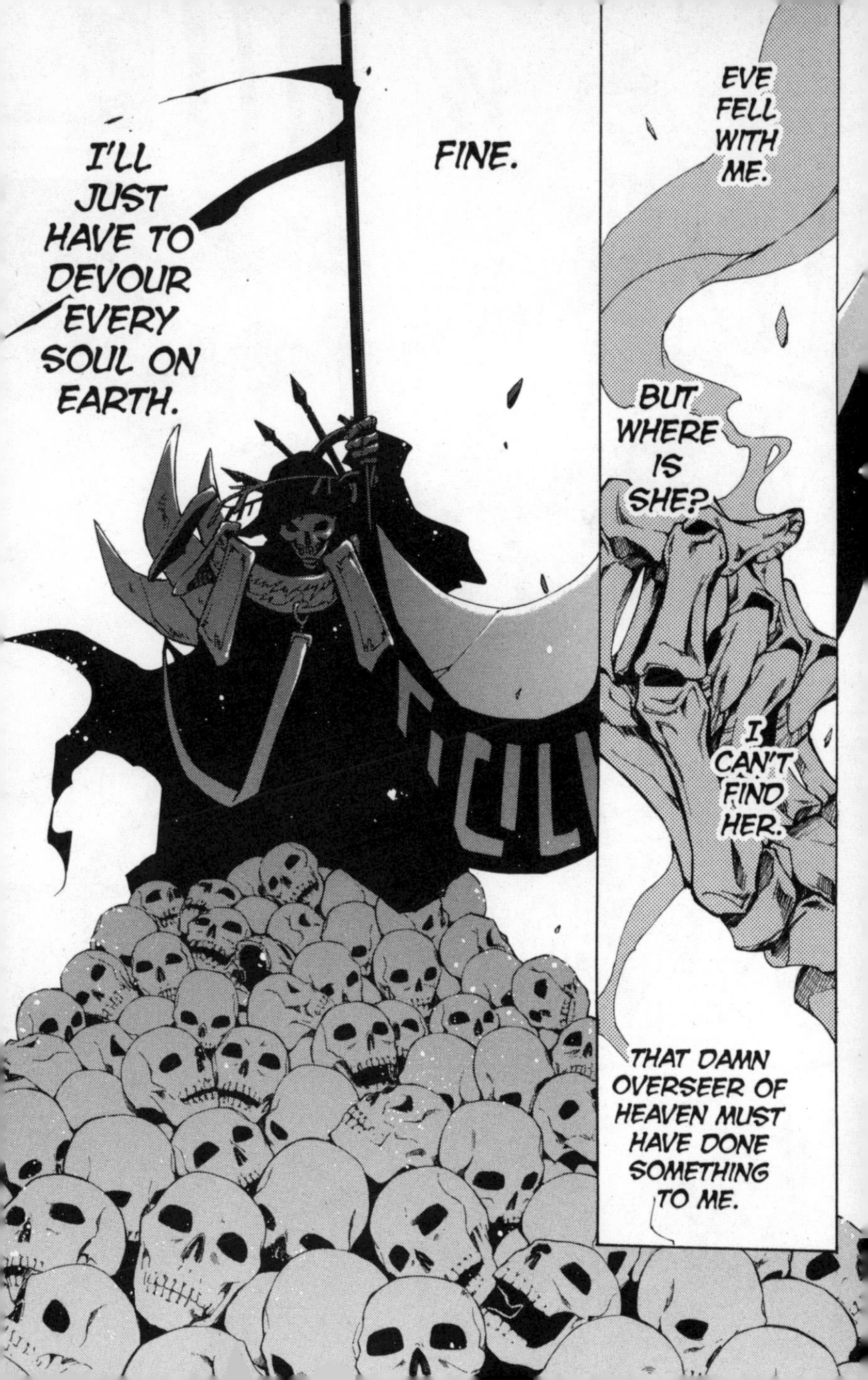
EVE FELL WITH ME.
BUT WHERE IS SHE?
I CAN'T FIND HER.
THAT DAMN OVERSEER OF HEAVEN MUST HAVE DONE SOMETHING TO ME.
FINE.
I'LL JUST HAVE TO DEVOUR EVERY SOUL ON EARTH.

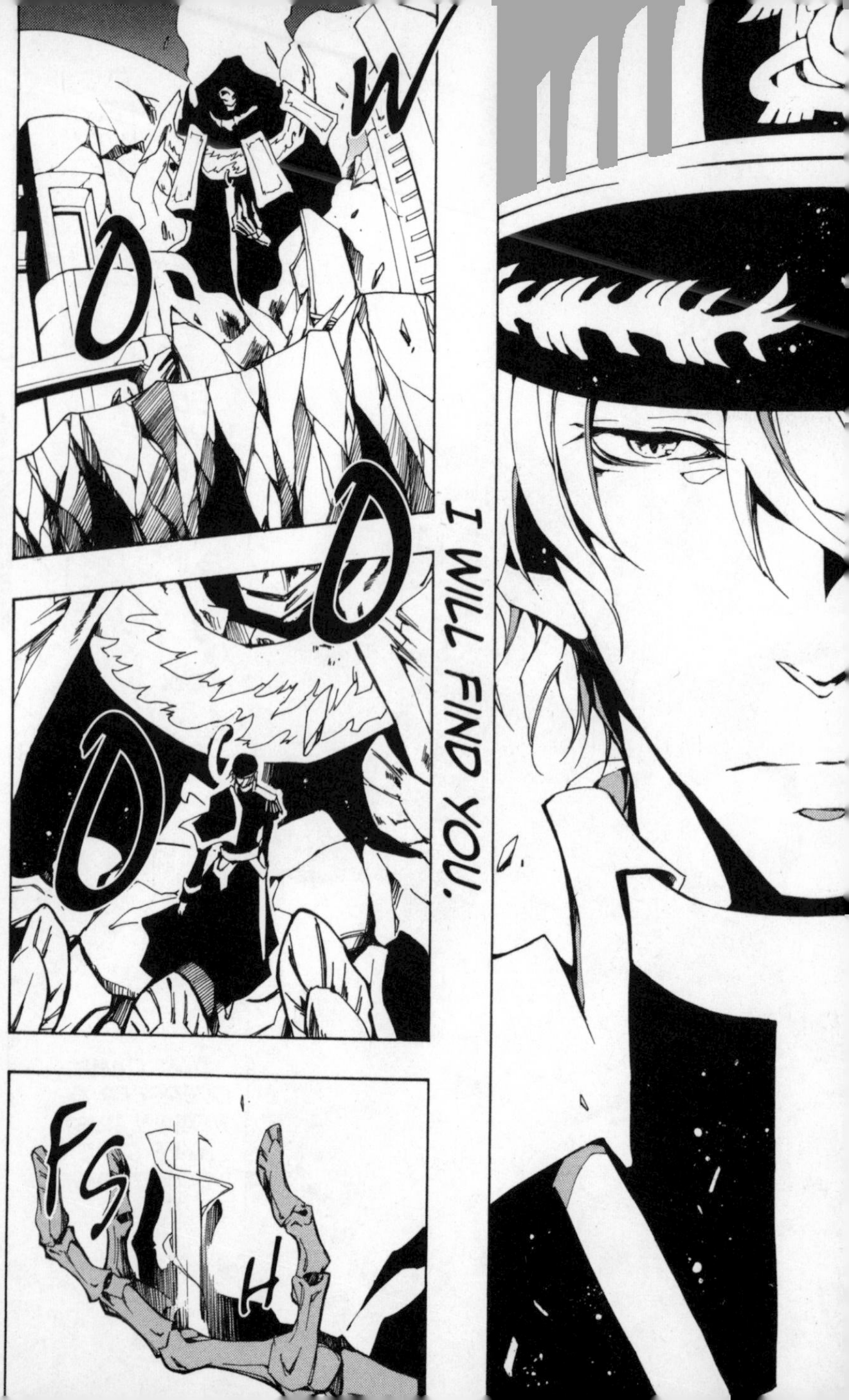
I WILL FIND YOU.
WDDD
FSSH

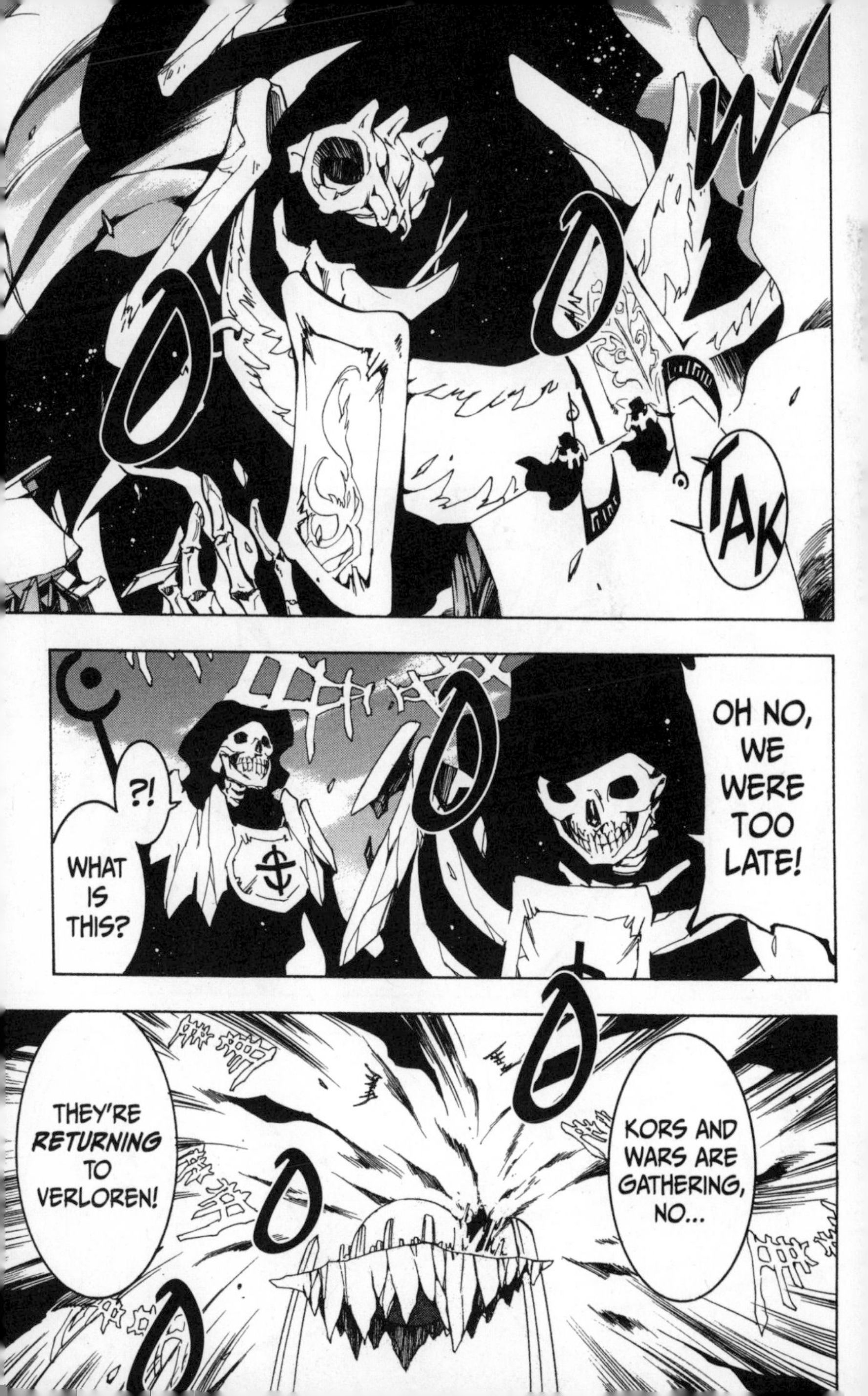
TAK
OH NO, WE WERE TOO LATE!
?!
WHAT IS THIS?
KORS AND WARS ARE GATHERING, NO...
THEY'RE *RETURNING* TO VERLOREN!

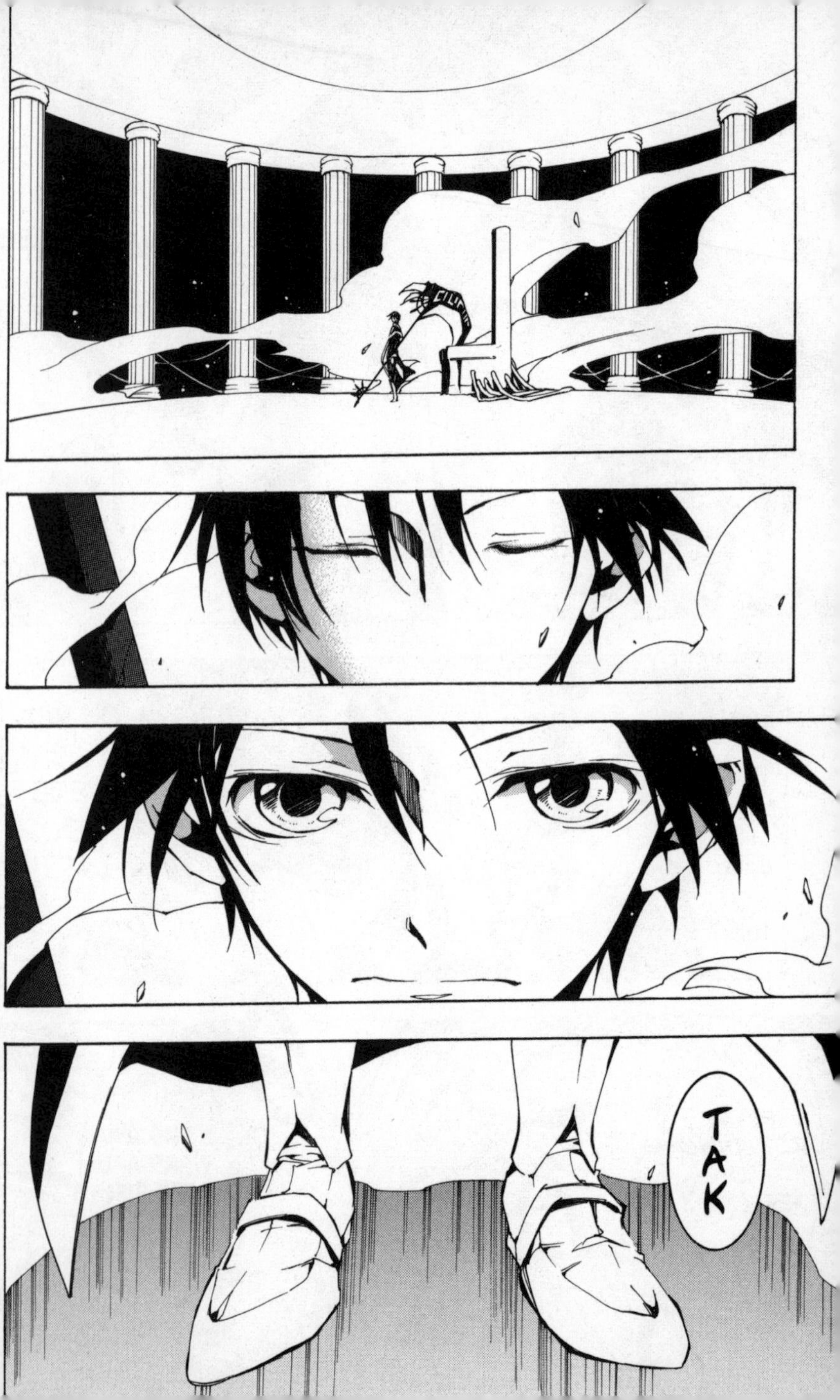
TAK

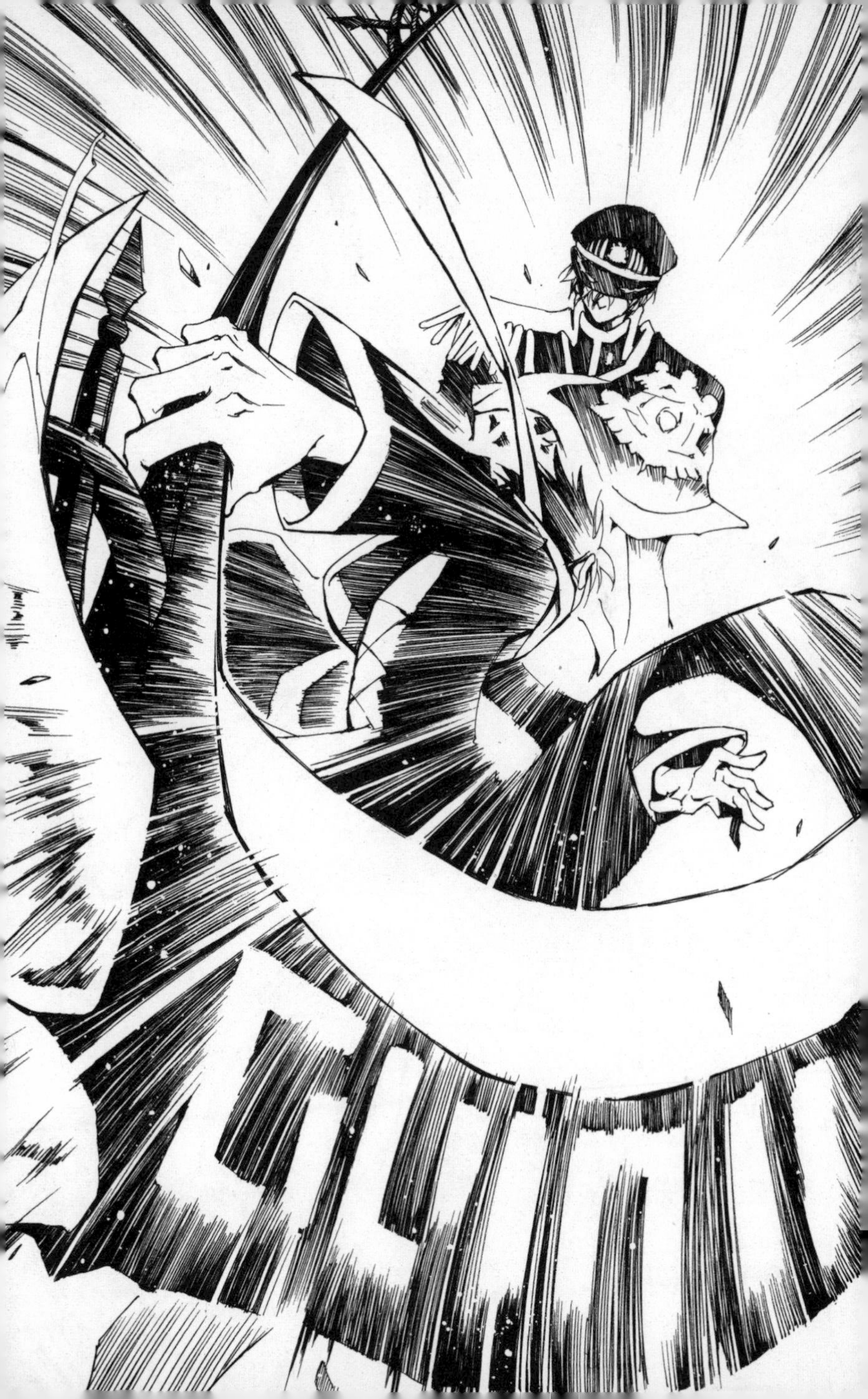

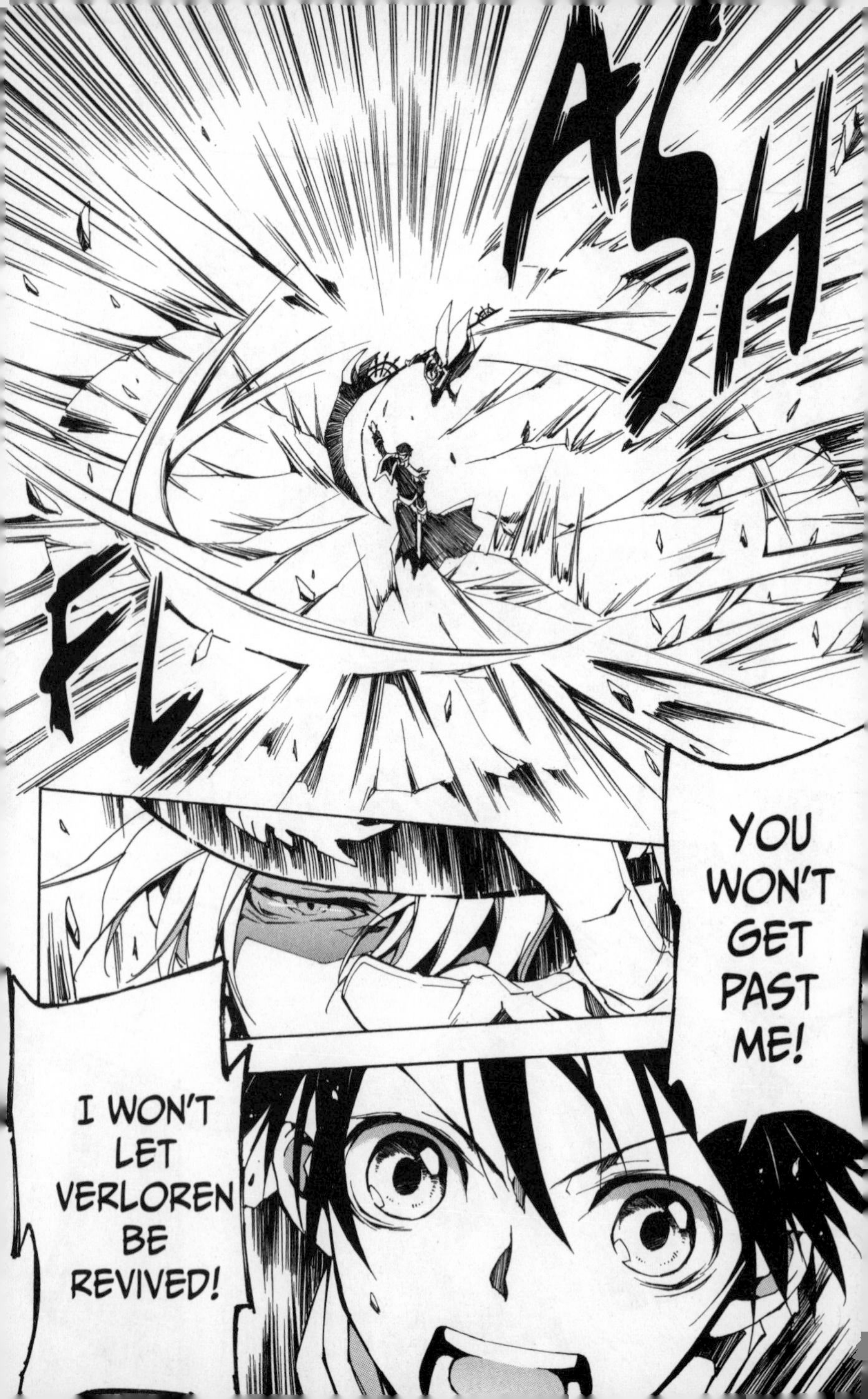
FLASH
YOU WON'T GET PAST ME!
I WON'T LET VERLOREN BE REVIVED!

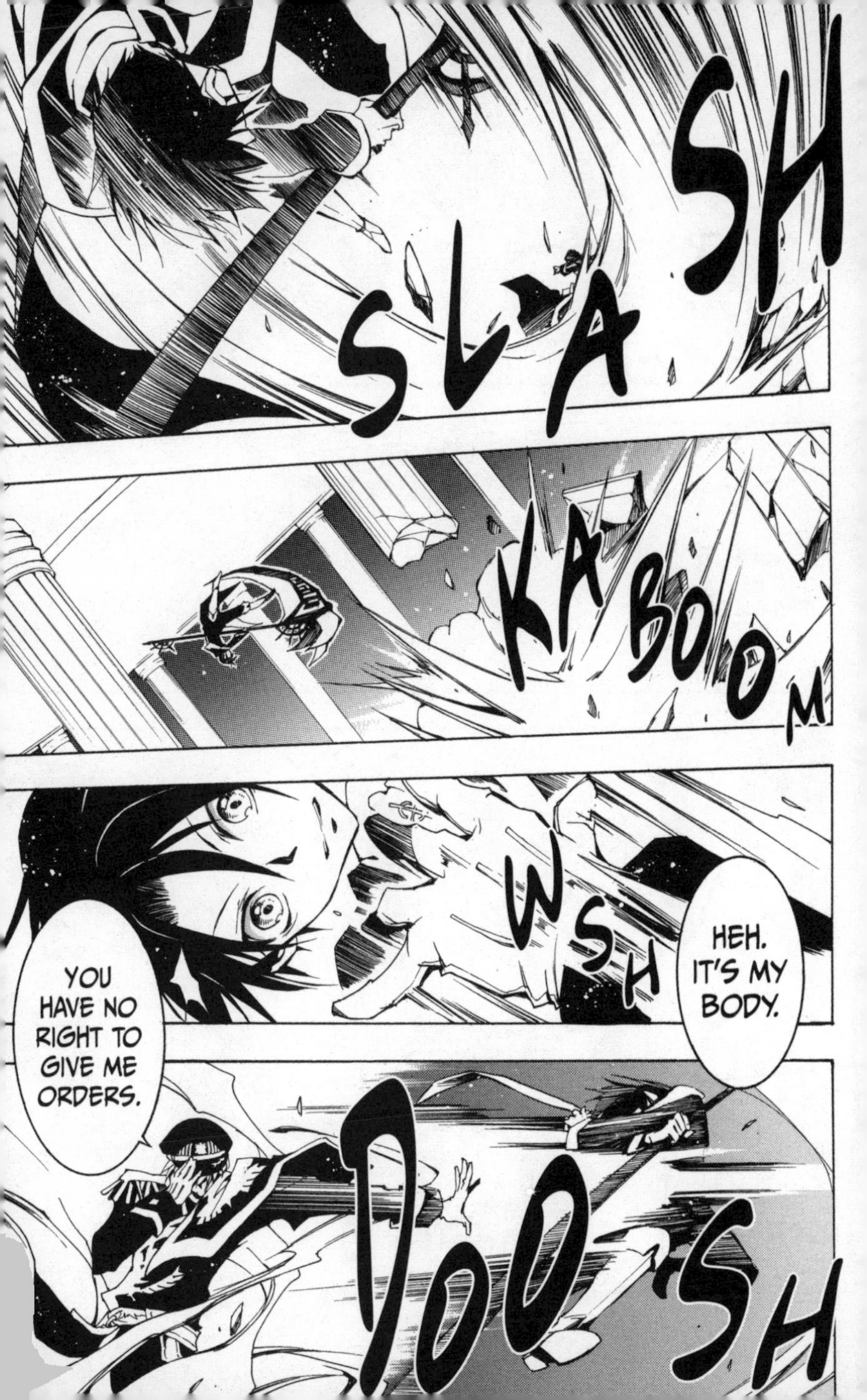
SLASH
KABOOM
WSH
HEH. IT'S MY BODY.
YOU HAVE NO RIGHT TO GIVE ME ORDERS.
FOOSH

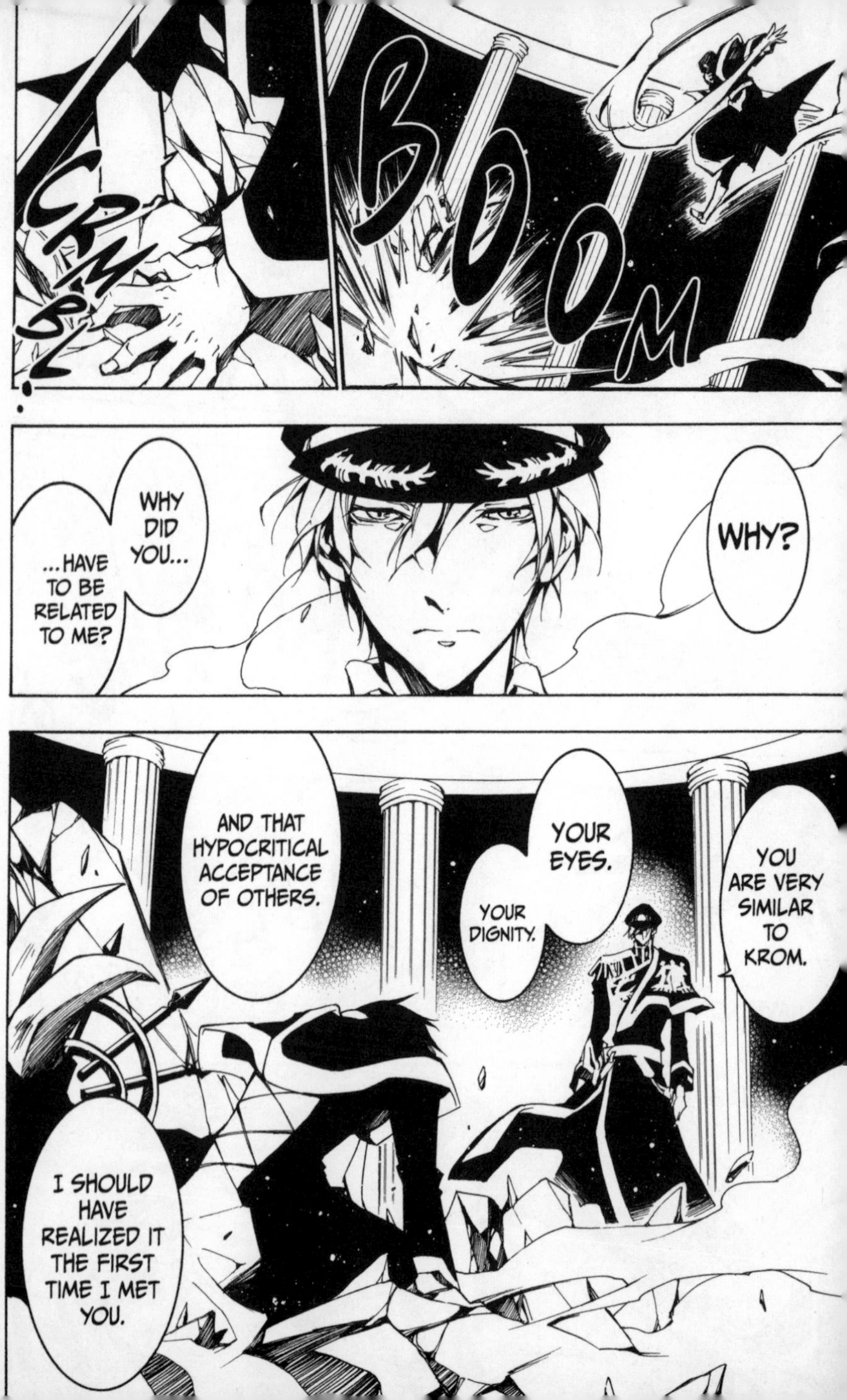
BOOOM
CRMBL
WHY?
WHY DID YOU...
...HAVE TO BE RELATED TO ME?
YOU ARE VERY SIMILAR TO KROM.
YOUR EYES.
YOUR DIGNITY.
AND THAT HYPOCRITICAL ACCEPTANCE OF OTHERS.
I SHOULD HAVE REALIZED IT THE FIRST TIME I MET YOU.

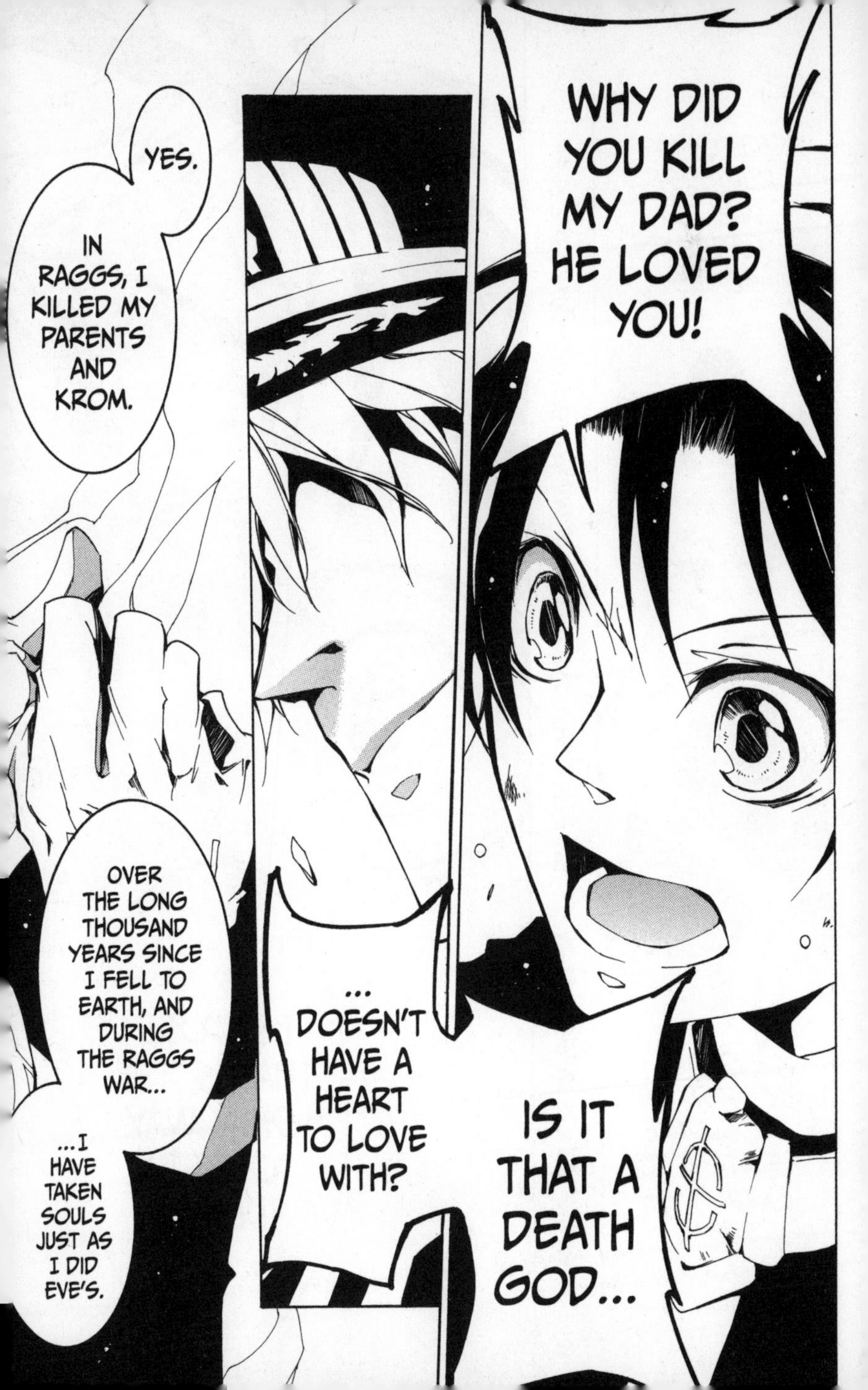
WHY DID YOU KILL MY DAD? HE LOVED YOU!
IS IT THAT A DEATH GOD...
...DOESN'T HAVE A HEART TO LOVE WITH?
YES.
IN RAGGS, I KILLED MY PARENTS AND KROM.
OVER THE LONG THOUSAND YEARS SINCE I FELL TO EARTH, AND DURING THE RAGGS WAR...
...I HAVE TAKEN SOULS JUST AS I DID EVE'S.

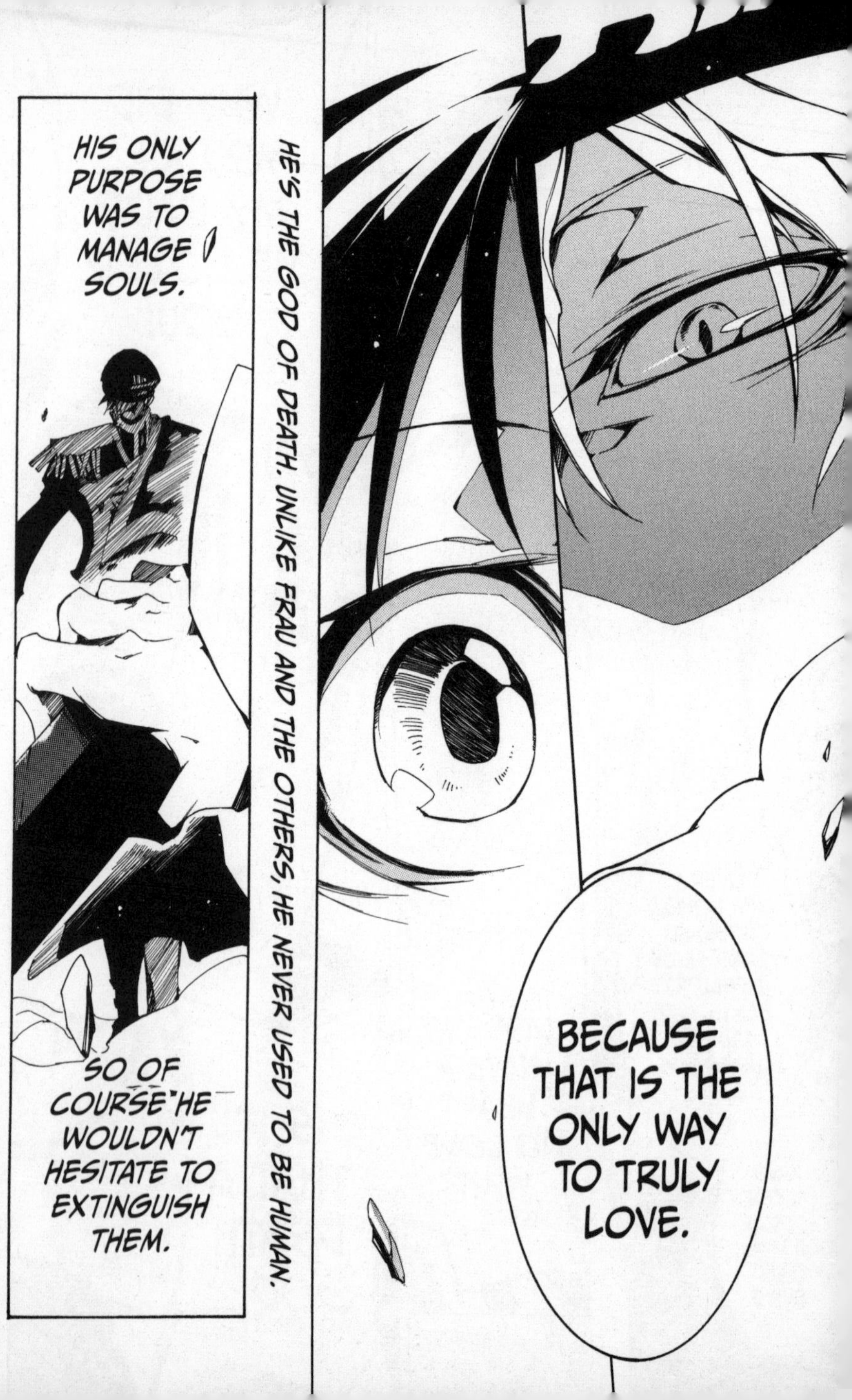
BECAUSE THAT IS THE ONLY WAY TO TRULY LOVE.
HE'S THE GOD OF DEATH. UNLIKE FRAU AND THE OTHERS, HE NEVER USED TO BE HUMAN.
HIS ONLY PURPOSE WAS TO MANAGE SOULS.
SO OF COURSE HE WOULDN'T HESITATE TO EXTINGUISH THEM.

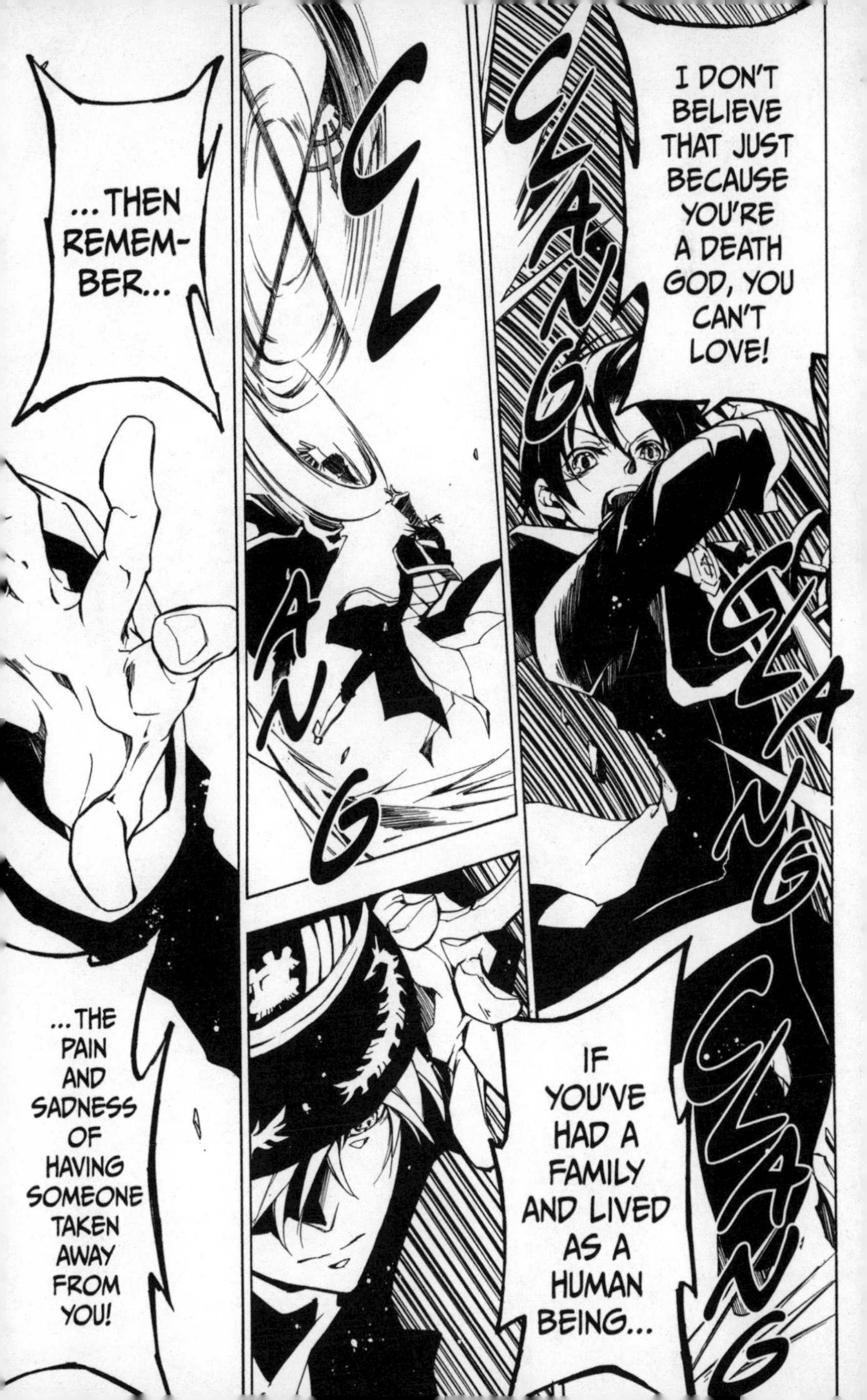
I DON'T BELIEVE THAT JUST BECAUSE YOU'RE A DEATH GOD, YOU CAN'T LOVE!
CLANG
CLANG
CLANG
CLANG
IF YOU'VE HAD A FAMILY AND LIVED AS A HUMAN BEING...
...THEN REMEMBER...
...THE PAIN AND SADNESS OF HAVING SOMEONE TAKEN AWAY FROM YOU!

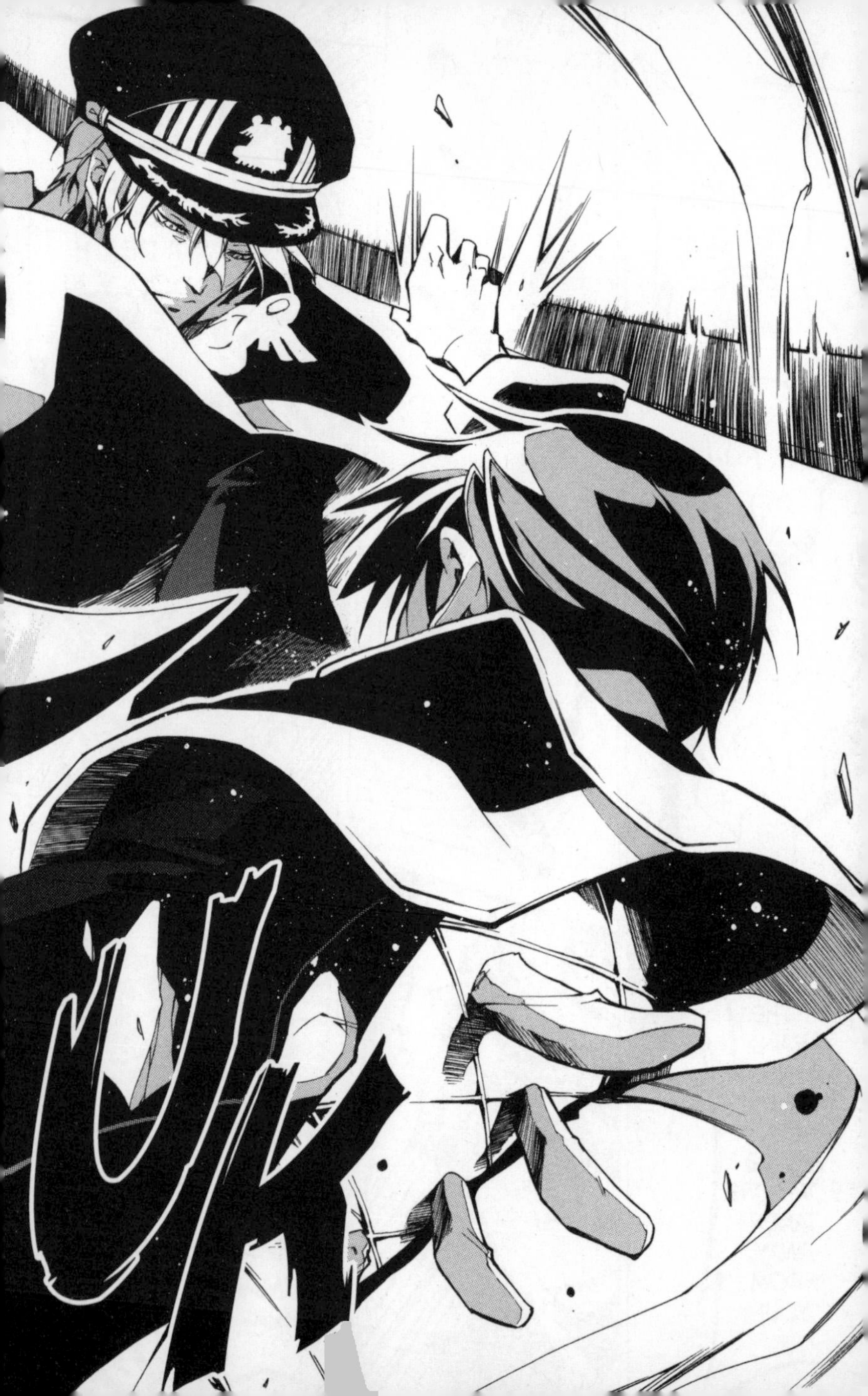

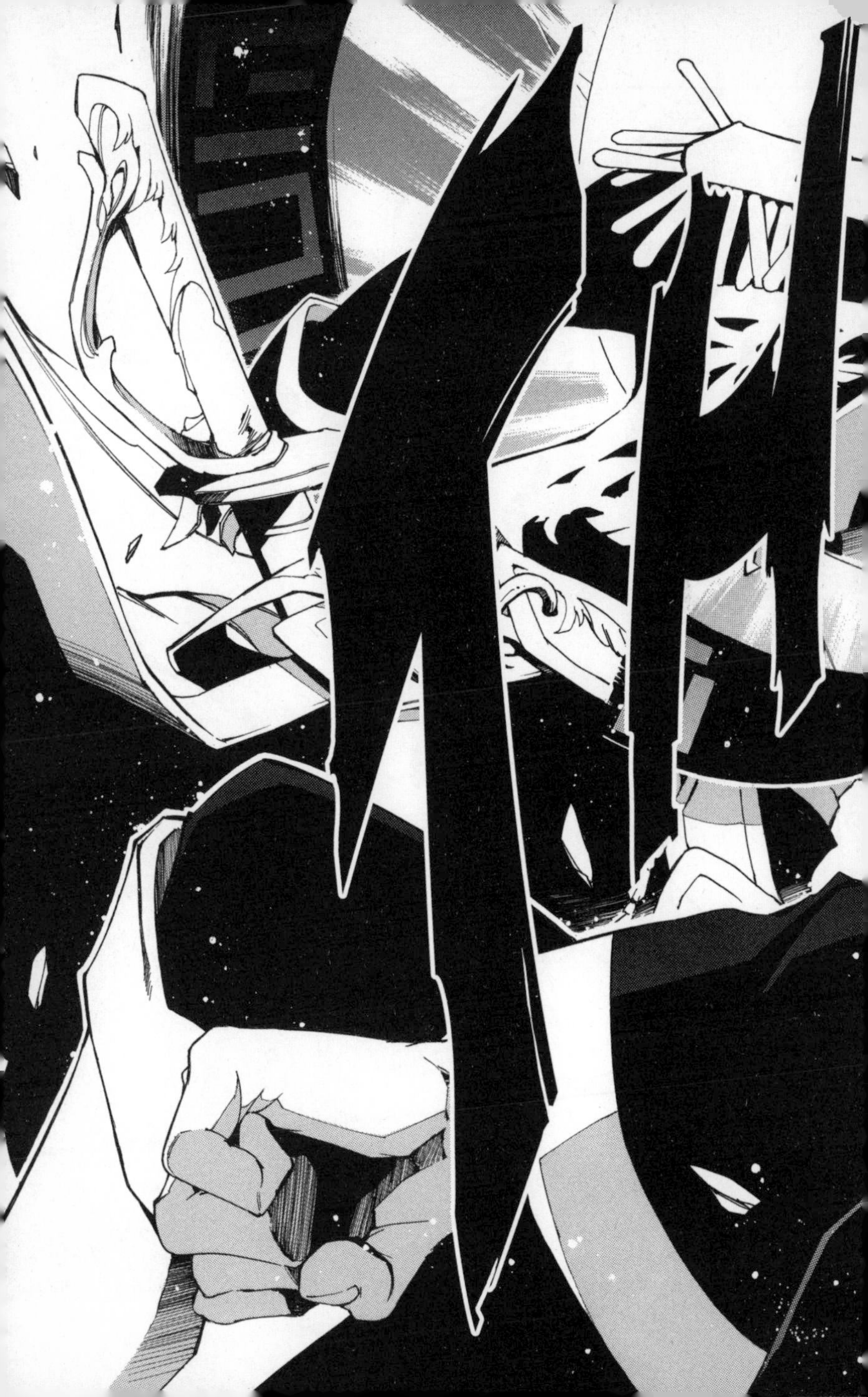

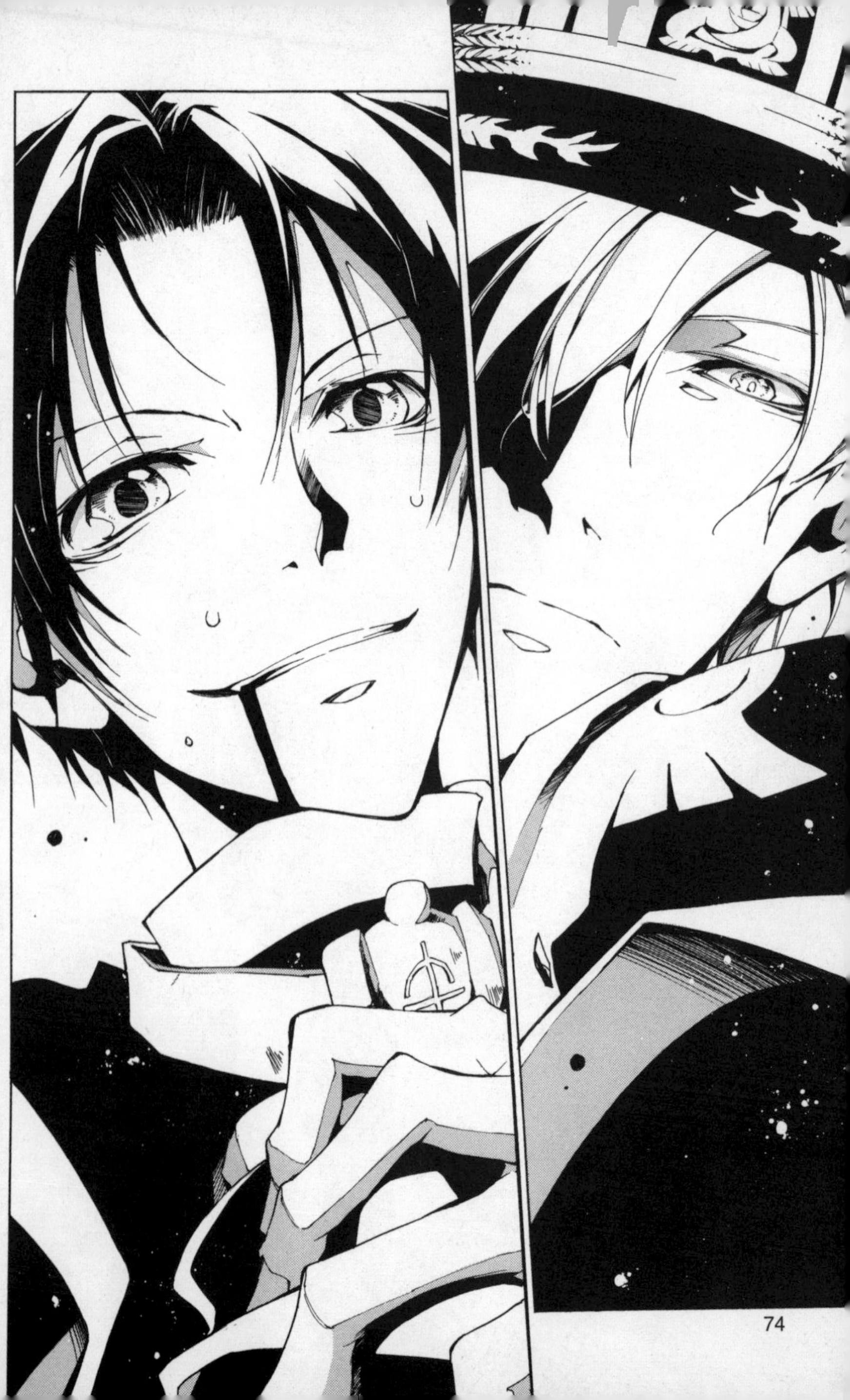

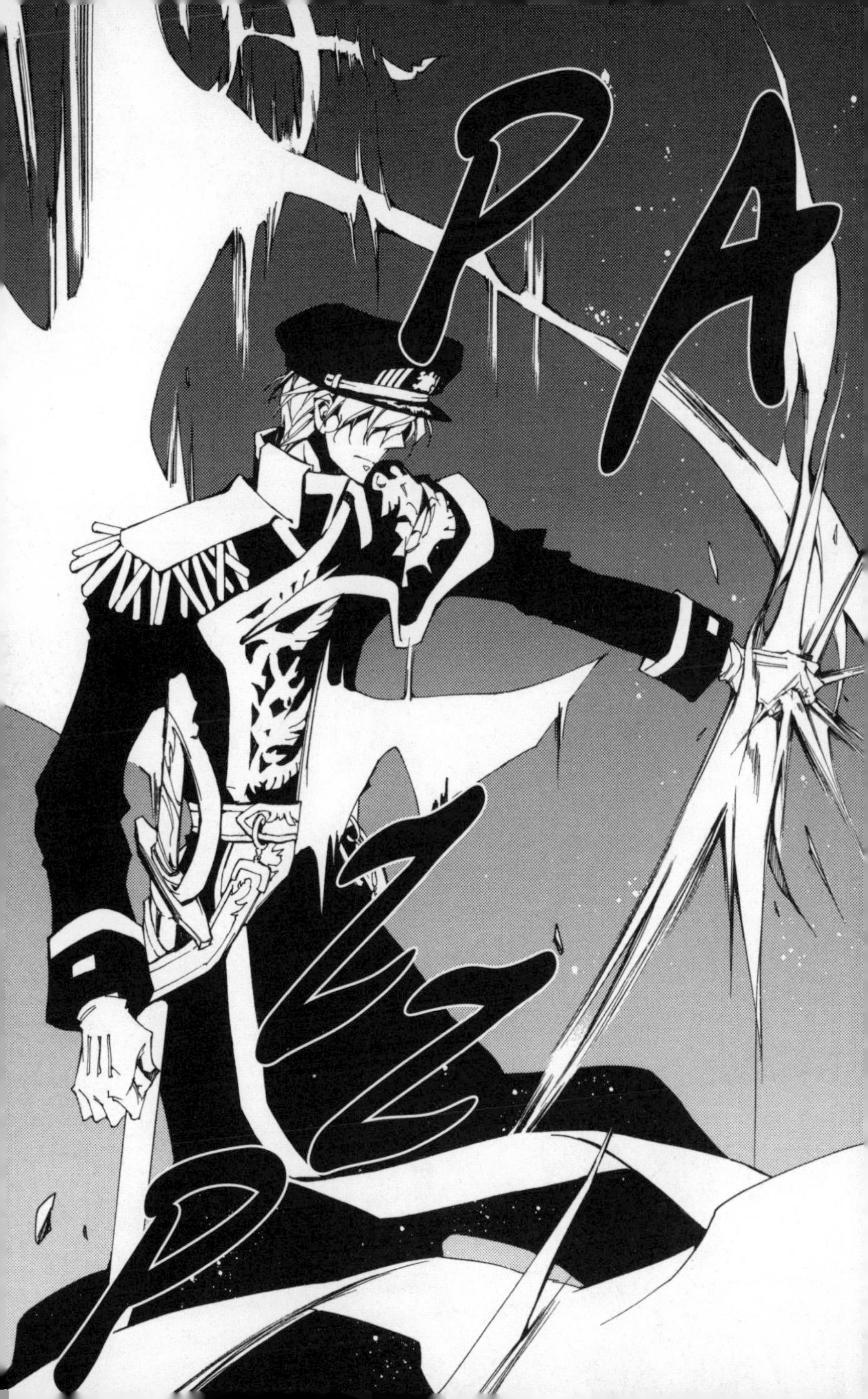

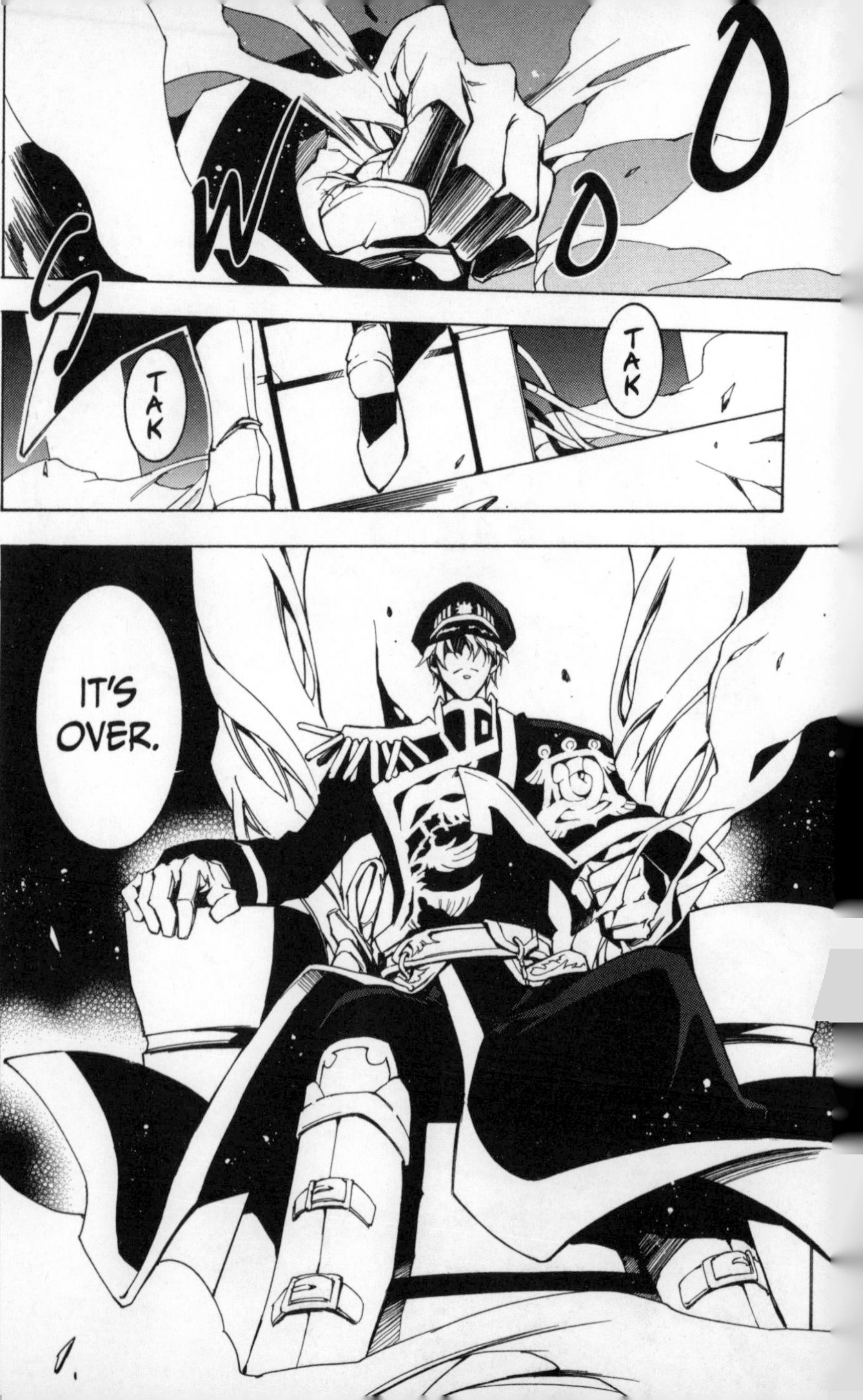
SWOOD
TAK
TAK
IT'S OVER.

It Always Goes Like This

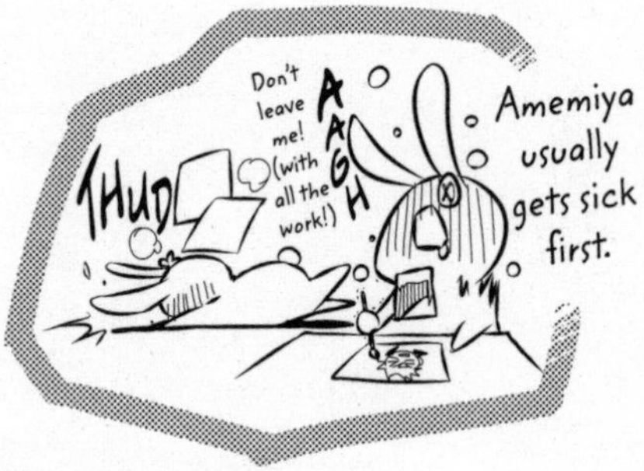

Amemiya usually gets sick first.
AAGH
Don't leave me! (with all the work!)
THUD

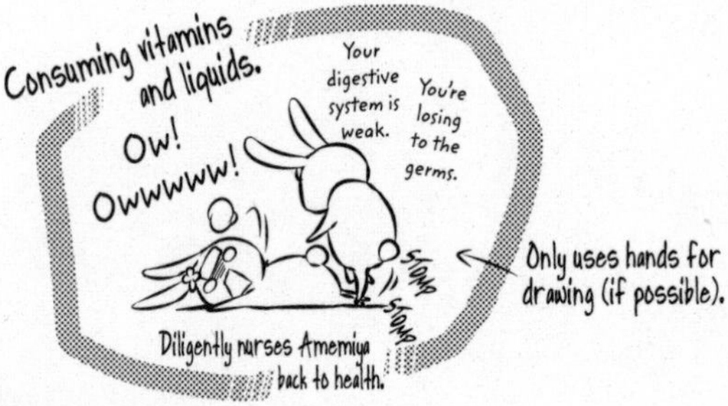

Consuming vitamins and liquids.
You're losing to the germs.
Your digestive system is weak.
Ow! Owwwww!
STOMP STOMP
Only uses hands for drawing (if possible).
Diligently nurses Amemiya back to health.

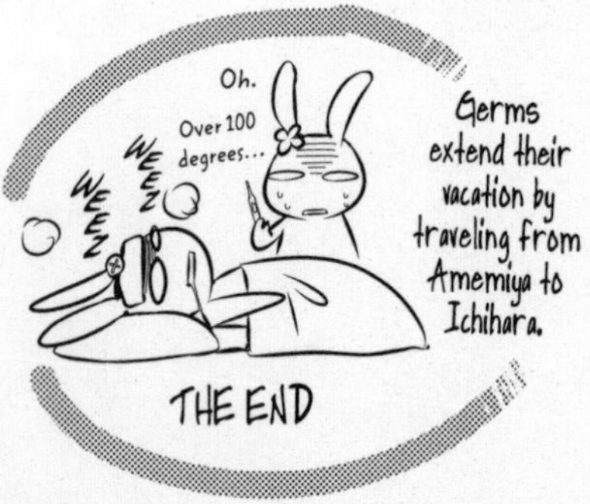

Germs extend their vacation by traveling from Amemiya to Ichihara.
Oh.
Over 100 degrees...
WEEZ WEEZ
THE END

Kapitel.98 “The Shape of Love”

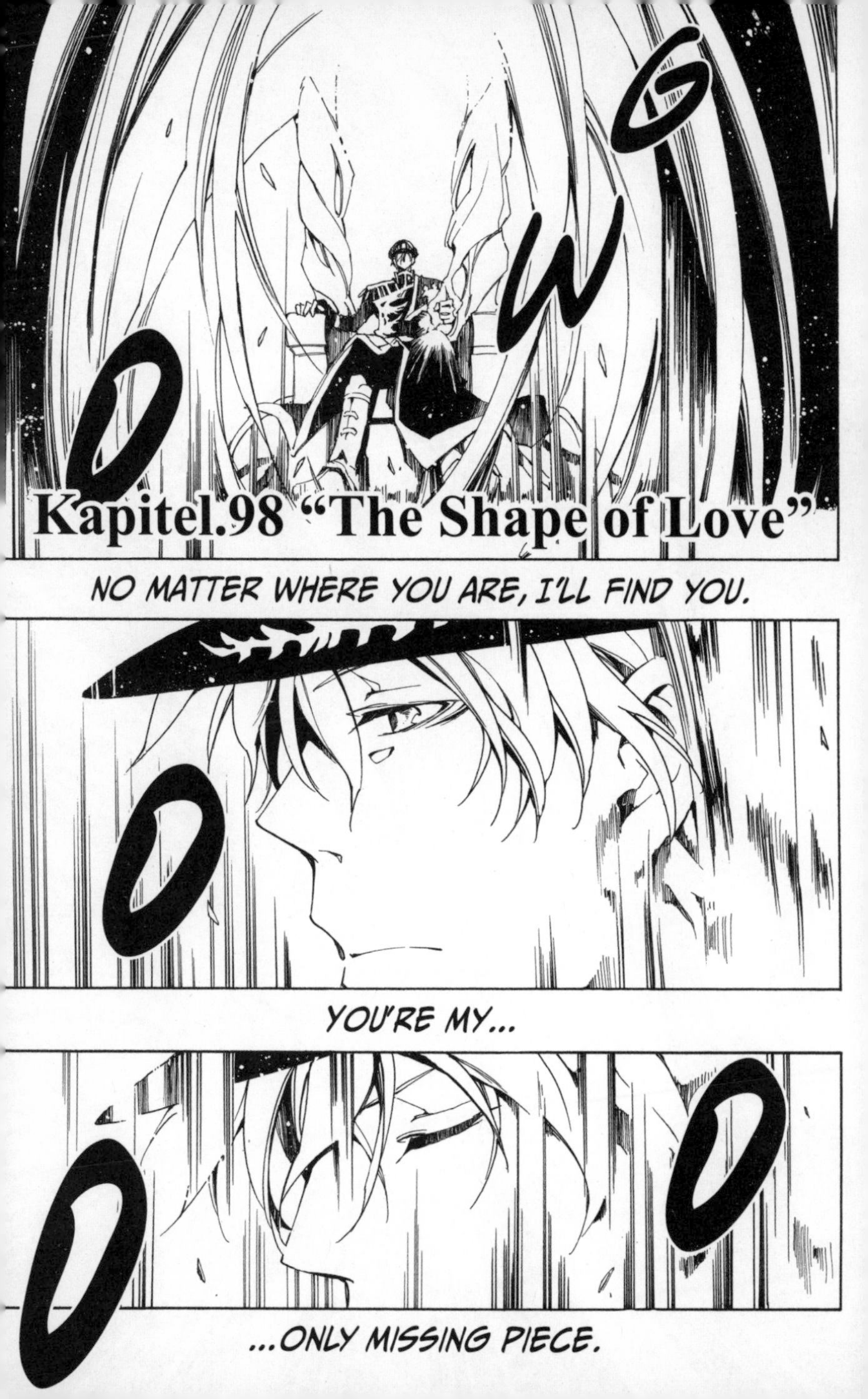
GWOOOO
NO MATTER WHERE YOU ARE, I'LL FIND YOU.
YOU'RE MY...
...ONLY MISSING PIECE.

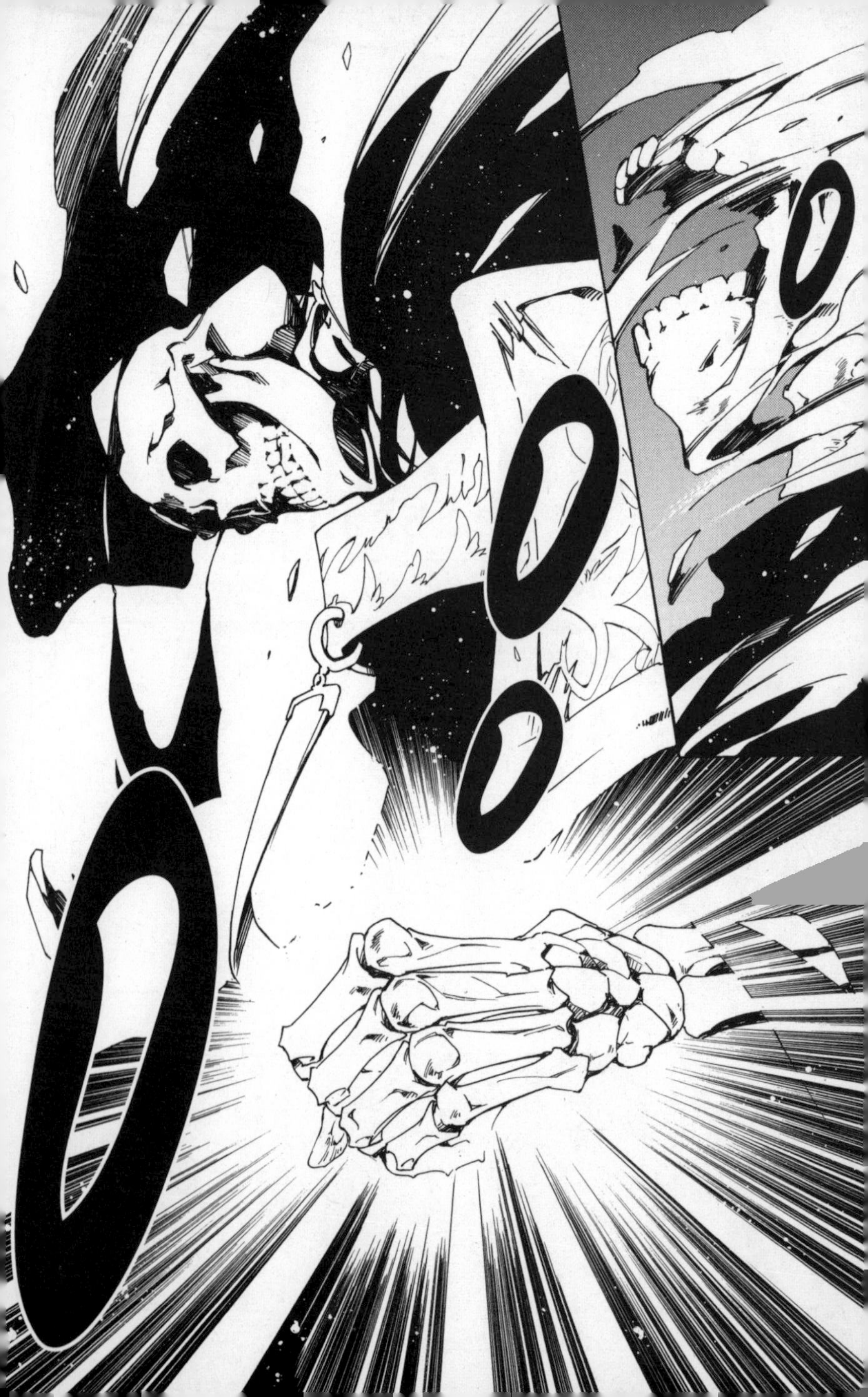

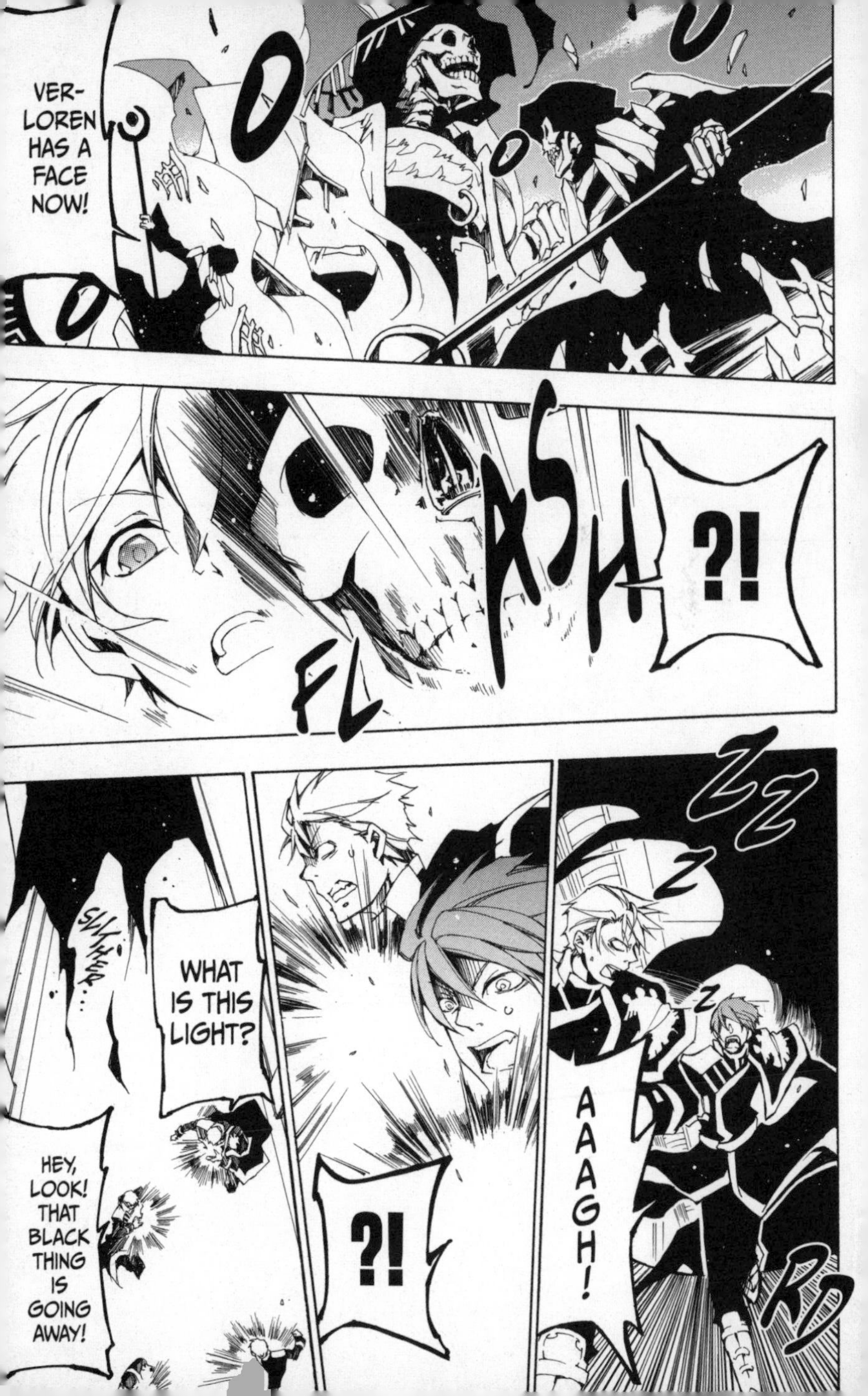
VER-LOREN HAS A FACE NOW!
?!
FLASH
AAAGH!
?!
WHAT IS THIS LIGHT?
HEY, LOOK! THAT BLACK THING IS GOING AWAY!

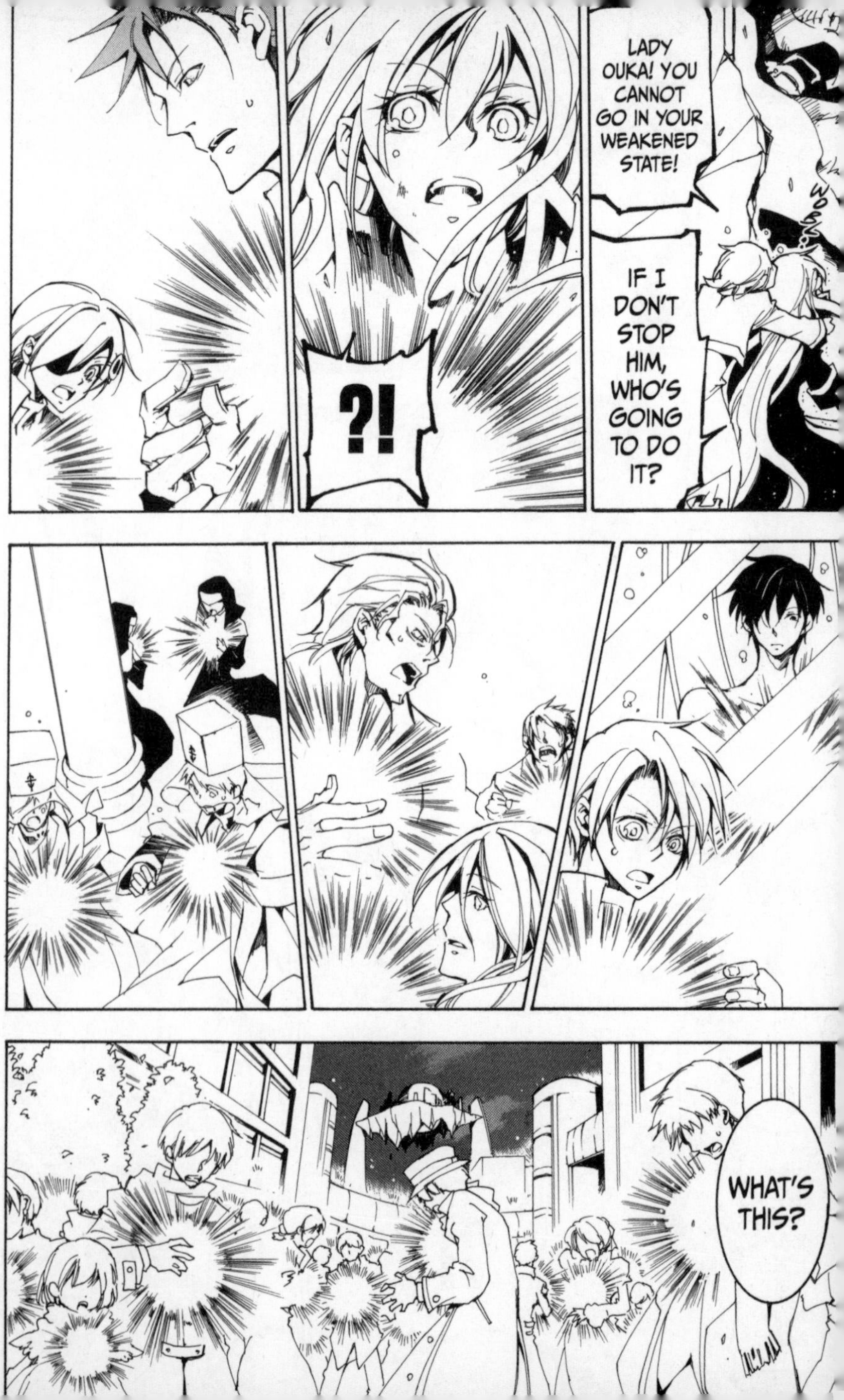
LADY OUKA! YOU CANNOT GO IN YOUR WEAKENED STATE!
IF I DON'T STOP HIM, WHO'S GOING TO DO IT?
?!
WHAT'S THIS?

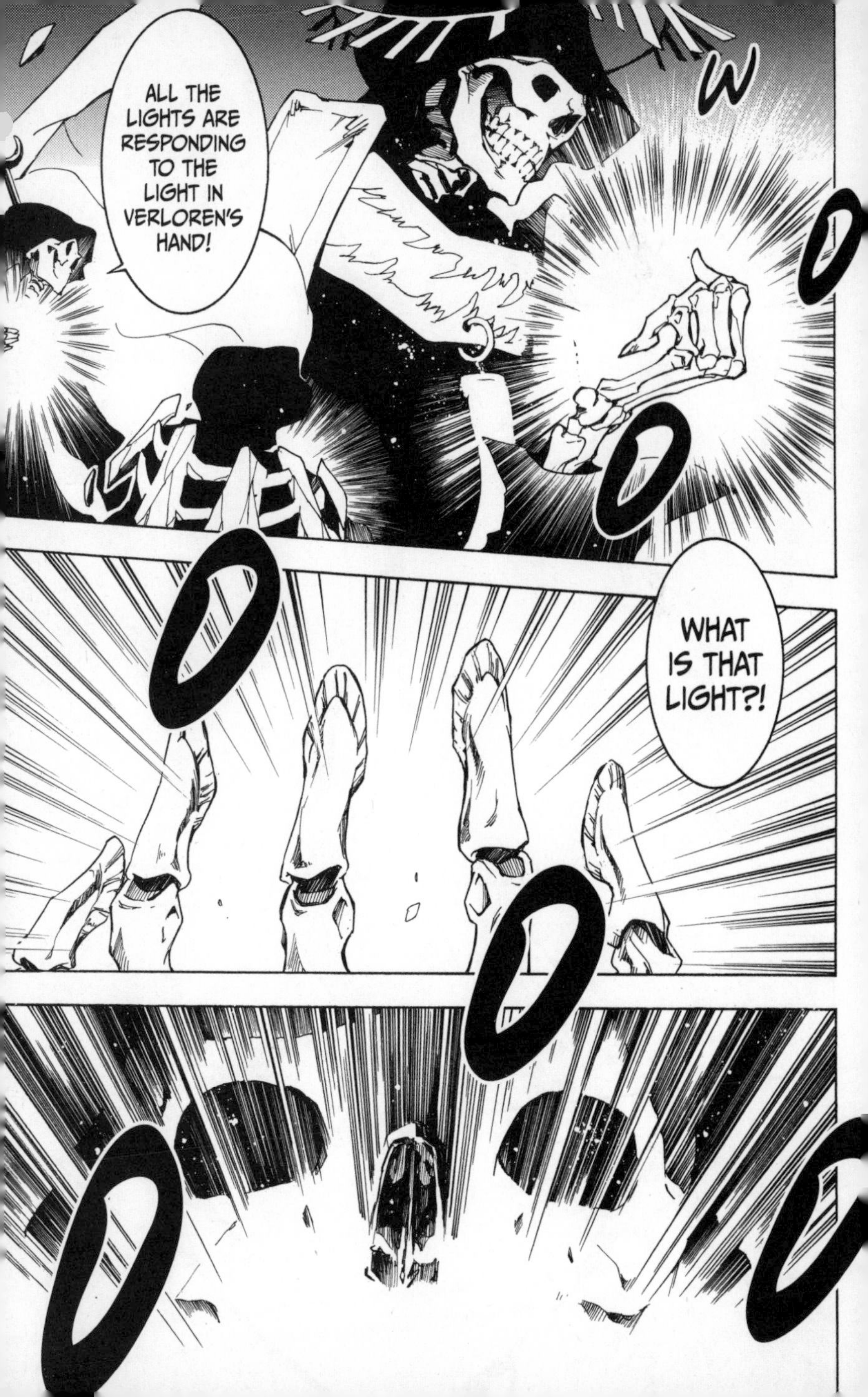
W
ALL THE LIGHTS ARE RESPONDING TO THE LIGHT IN VERLOREN'S HAND!
WHAT IS THAT LIGHT?!

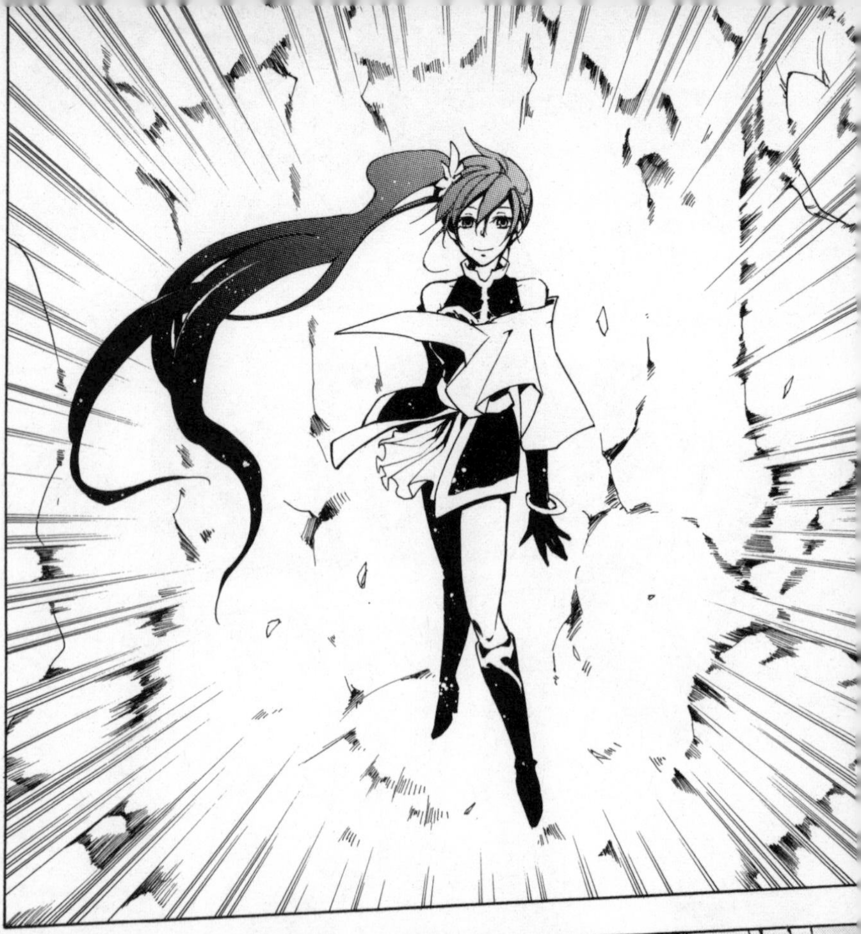
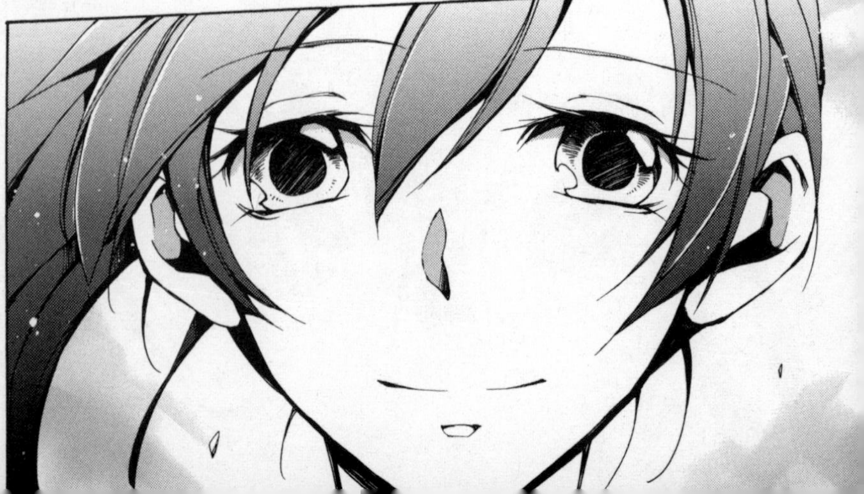

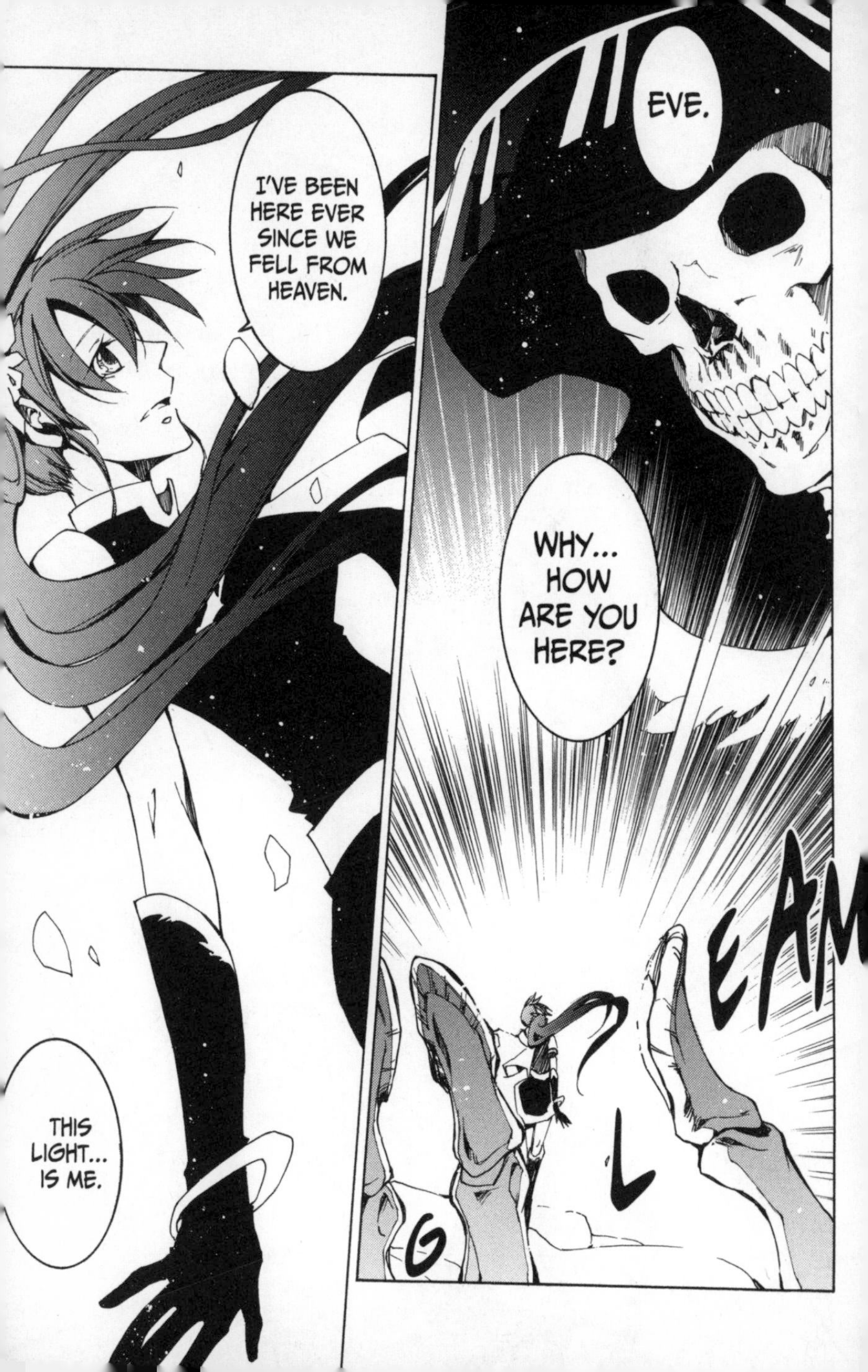
EVE.
WHY... HOW ARE YOU HERE?
GLEAM
I'VE BEEN HERE EVER SINCE WE FELL FROM HEAVEN.
THIS LIGHT... IS ME.

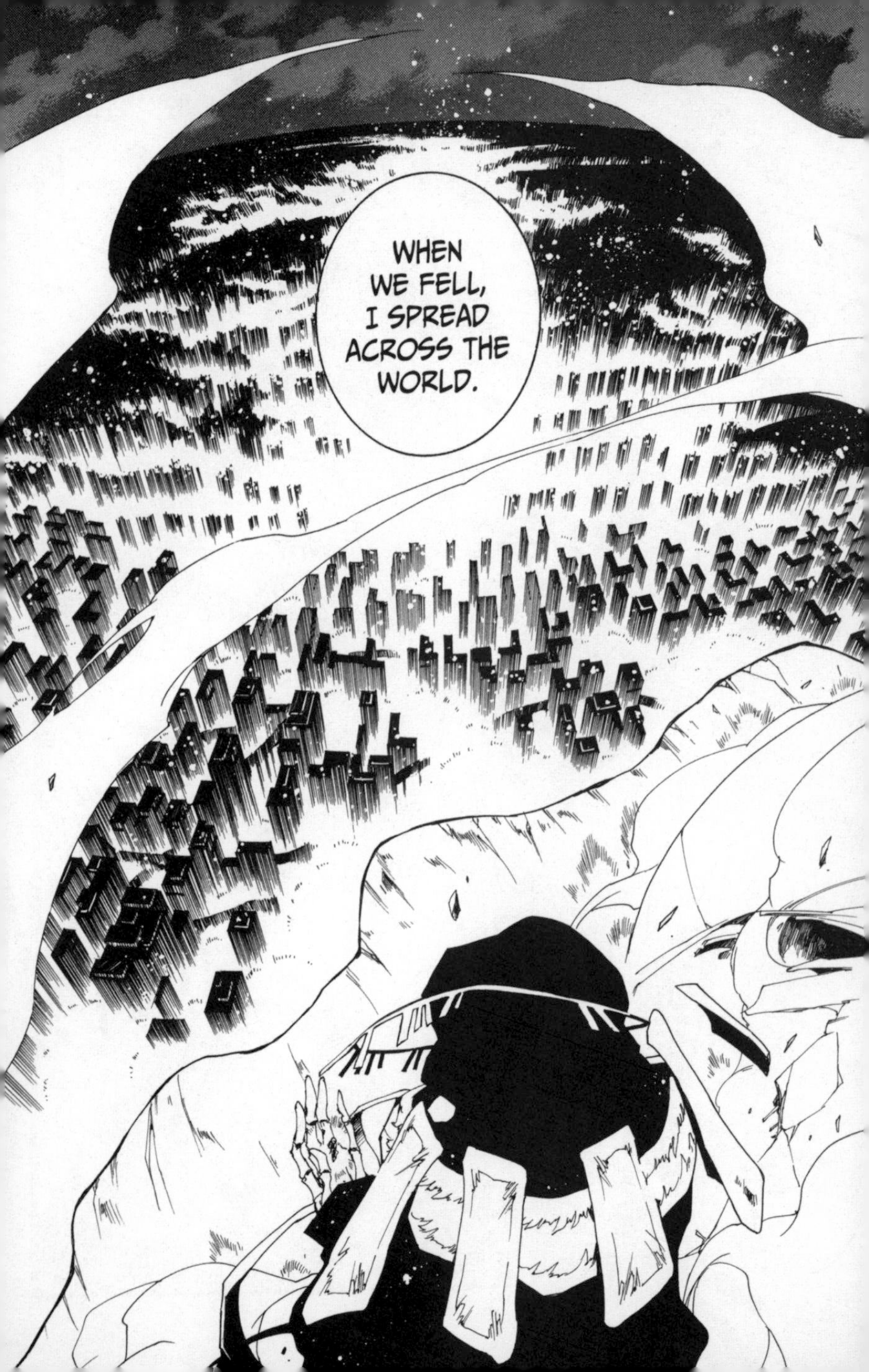
WHEN WE FELL, I SPREAD ACROSS THE WORLD.

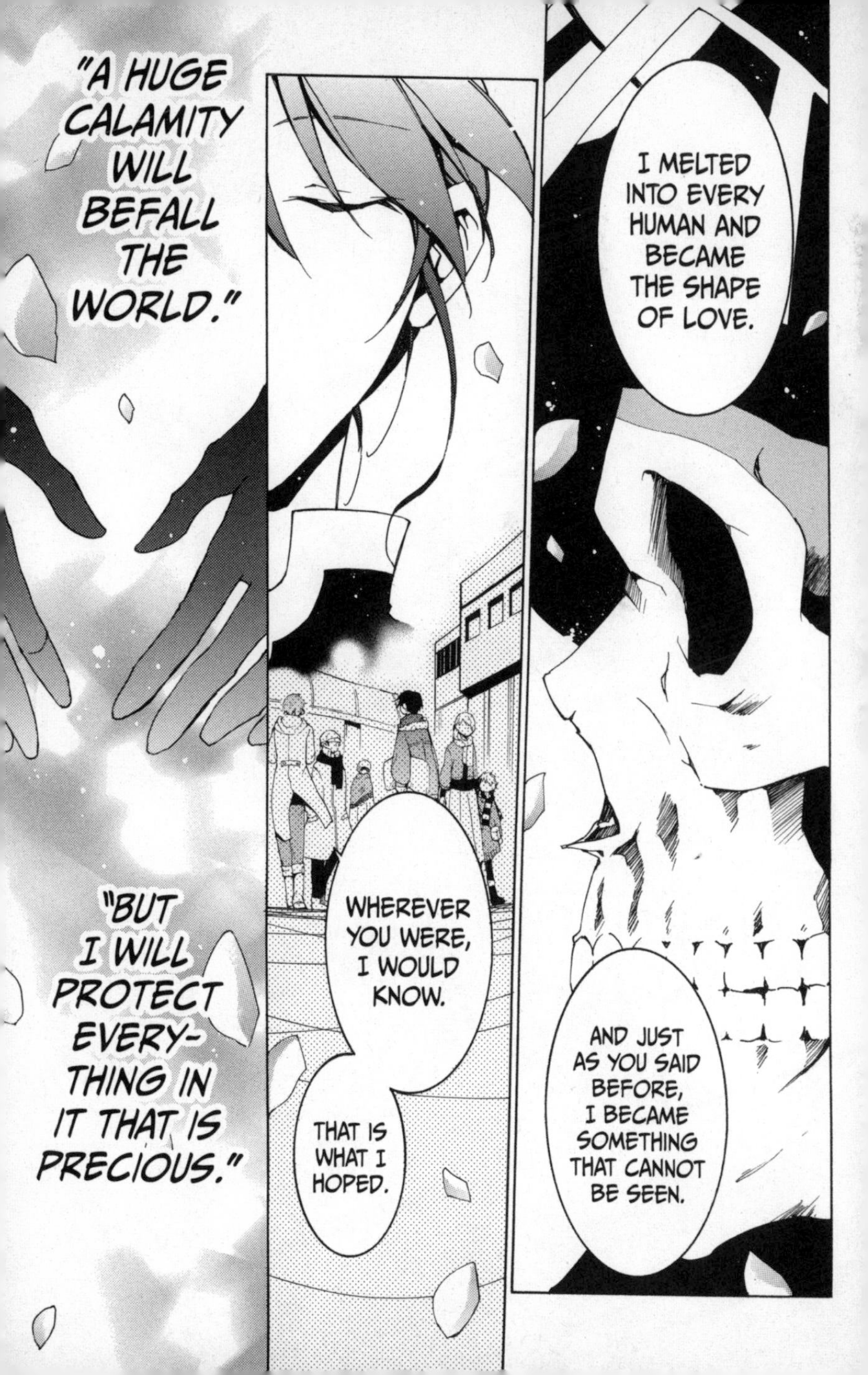
I MELTED INTO EVERY HUMAN AND BECAME THE SHAPE OF LOVE.
AND JUST AS YOU SAID BEFORE, I BECAME SOMETHING THAT CANNOT BE SEEN.
WHEREVER YOU WERE, I WOULD KNOW.
THAT IS WHAT I HOPED.
"A HUGE CALAMITY WILL BEFALL THE WORLD."
"BUT I WILL PROTECT EVERY-THING IN IT THAT IS PRECIOUS."

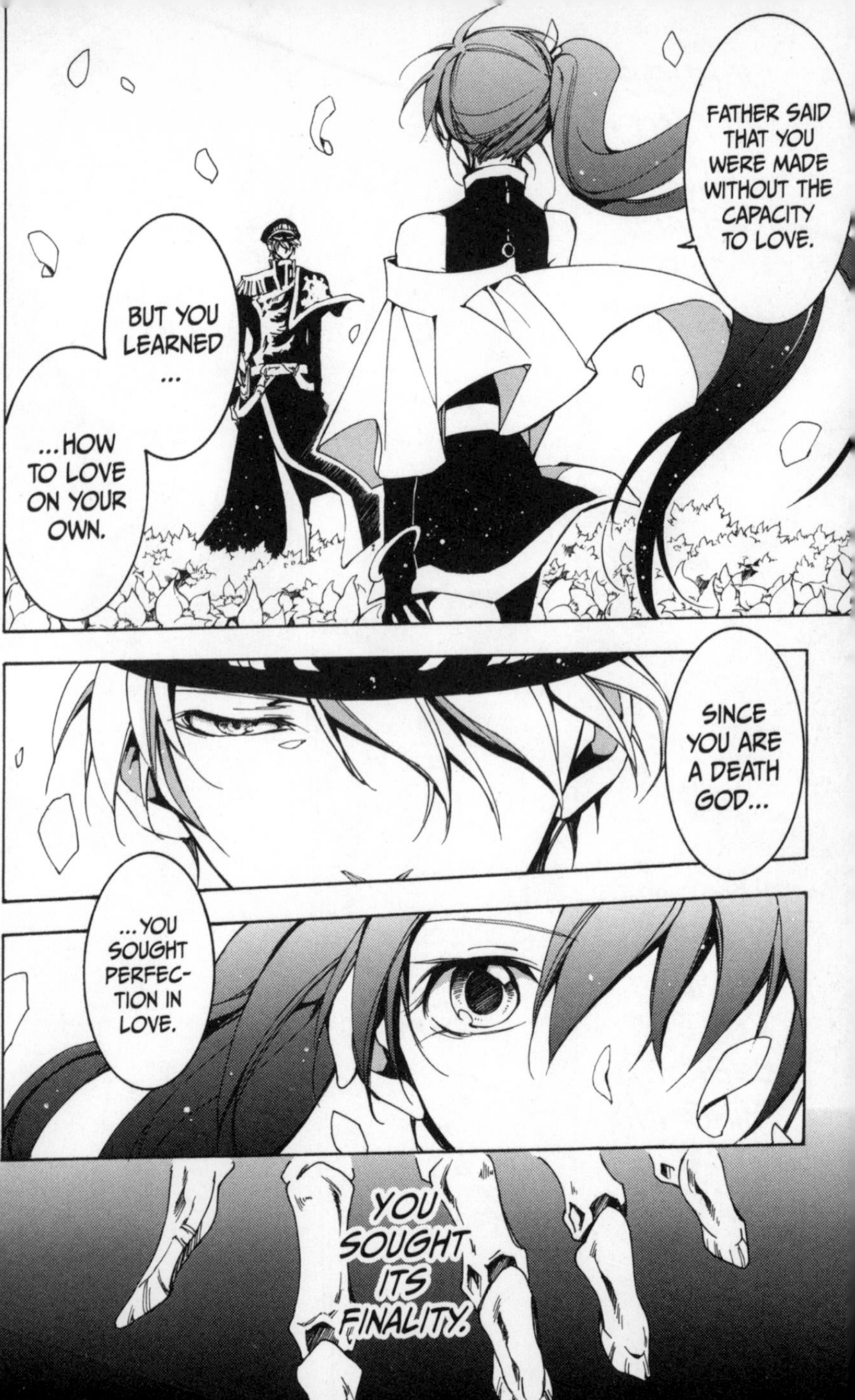
FATHER SAID THAT YOU WERE MADE WITHOUT THE CAPACITY TO LOVE.
BUT YOU LEARNED ...
...HOW TO LOVE ON YOUR OWN.
SINCE YOU ARE A DEATH GOD...
...YOU SOUGHT PERFEC-TION IN LOVE.
YOU SOUGHT ITS FINALITY.

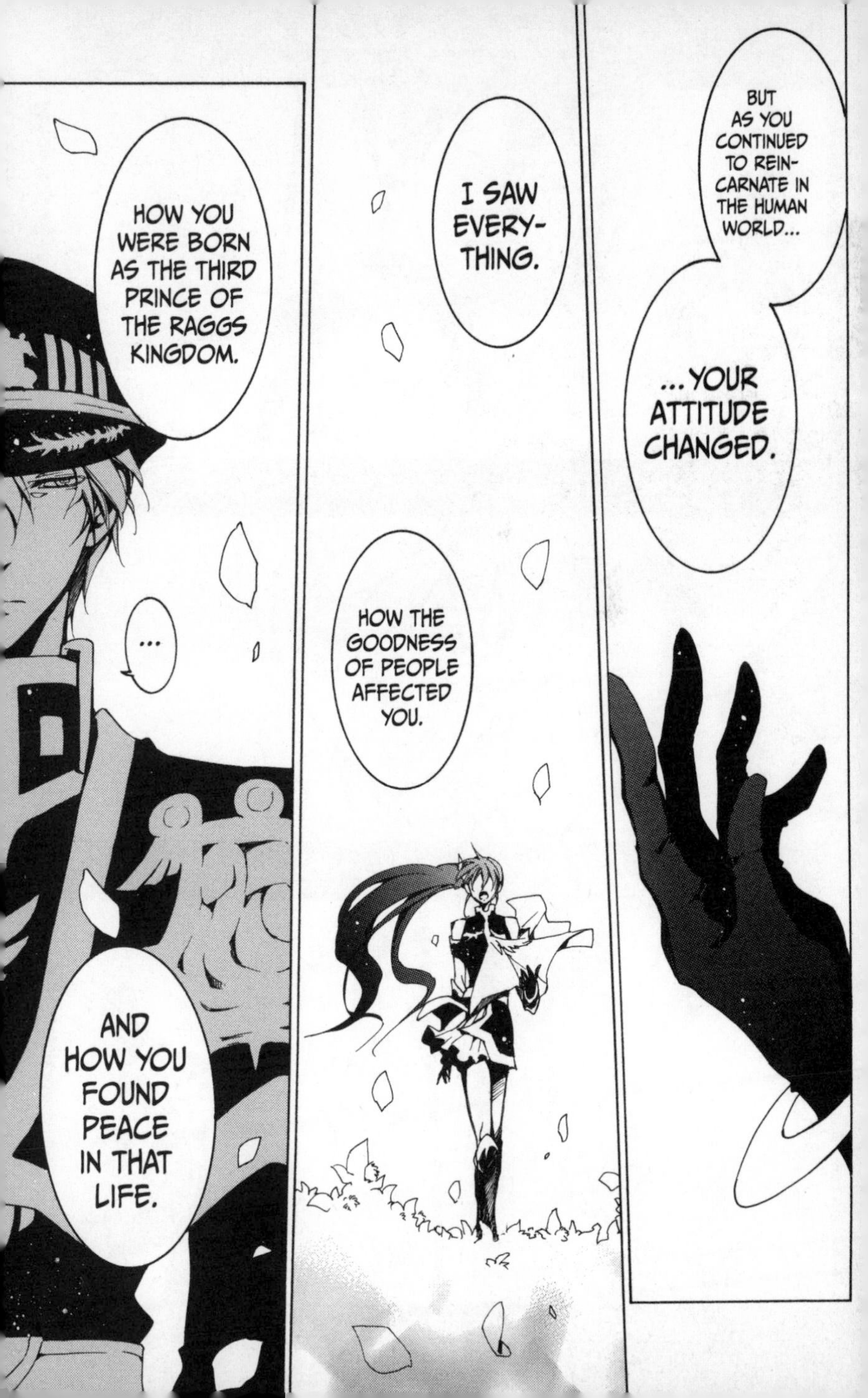
BUT AS YOU CONTINUED TO REIN-CARNATE IN THE HUMAN WORLD...
...YOUR ATTITUDE CHANGED.
I SAW EVERY-THING.
HOW THE GOODNESS OF PEOPLE AFFECTED YOU.
HOW YOU WERE BORN AS THE THIRD PRINCE OF THE RAGGS KINGDOM.
...
AND HOW YOU FOUND PEACE IN THAT LIFE.

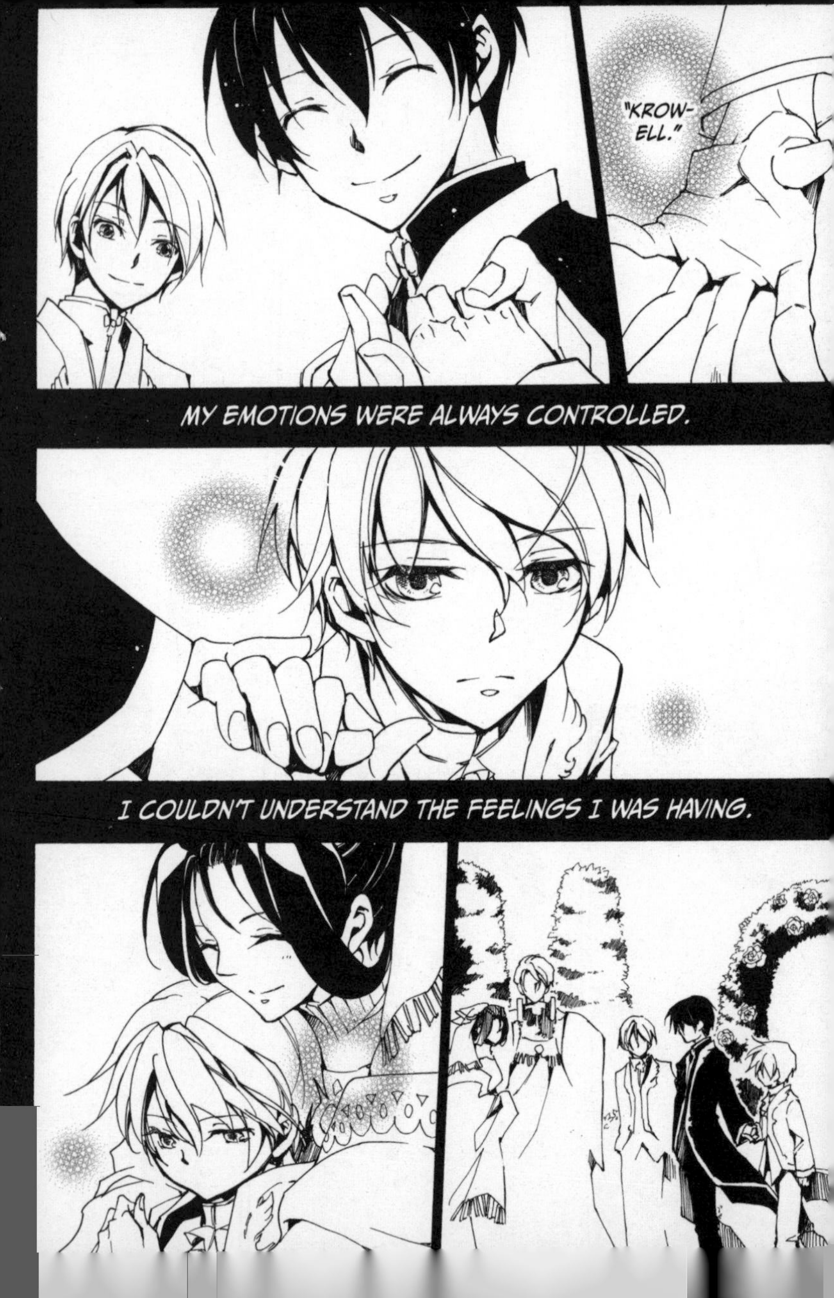
"KROW-ELL."
MY EMOTIONS WERE ALWAYS CONTROLLED.
I COULDN'T UNDERSTAND THE FEELINGS I WAS HAVING.

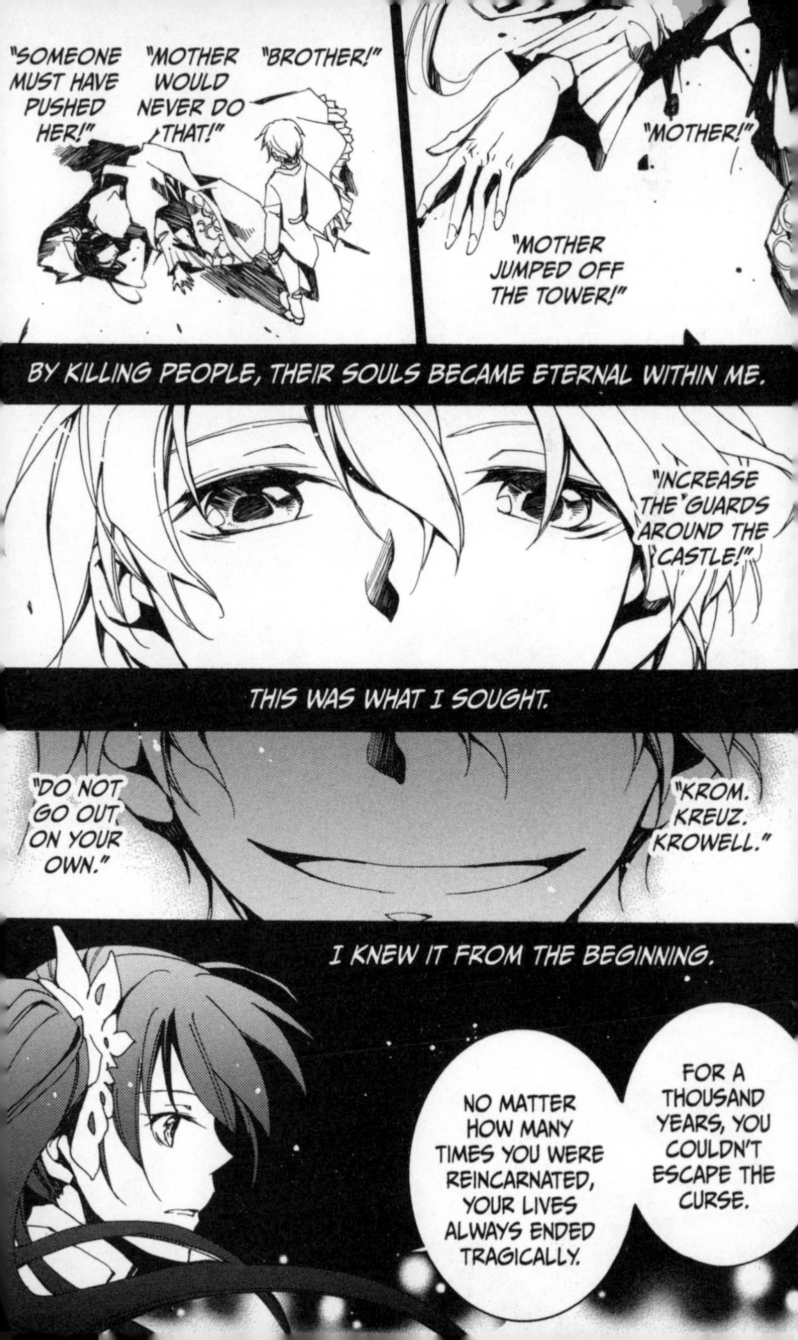
"MOTHER!"
"MOTHER JUMPED OFF THE TOWER!"
"BROTHER!"
"MOTHER WOULD NEVER DO THAT!"
"SOMEONE MUST HAVE PUSHED HER!"
BY KILLING PEOPLE, THEIR SOULS BECAME ETERNAL WITHIN ME.
"INCREASE THE GUARDS AROUND THE CASTLE!"
THIS WAS WHAT I SOUGHT.
"KROM. KREUZ. KROWELL."
"DO NOT GO OUT ON YOUR OWN."
I KNEW IT FROM THE BEGINNING.
FOR A THOUSAND YEARS, YOU COULDN'T ESCAPE THE CURSE.
NO MATTER HOW MANY TIMES YOU WERE REINCARNATED, YOUR LIVES ALWAYS ENDED TRAGICALLY.

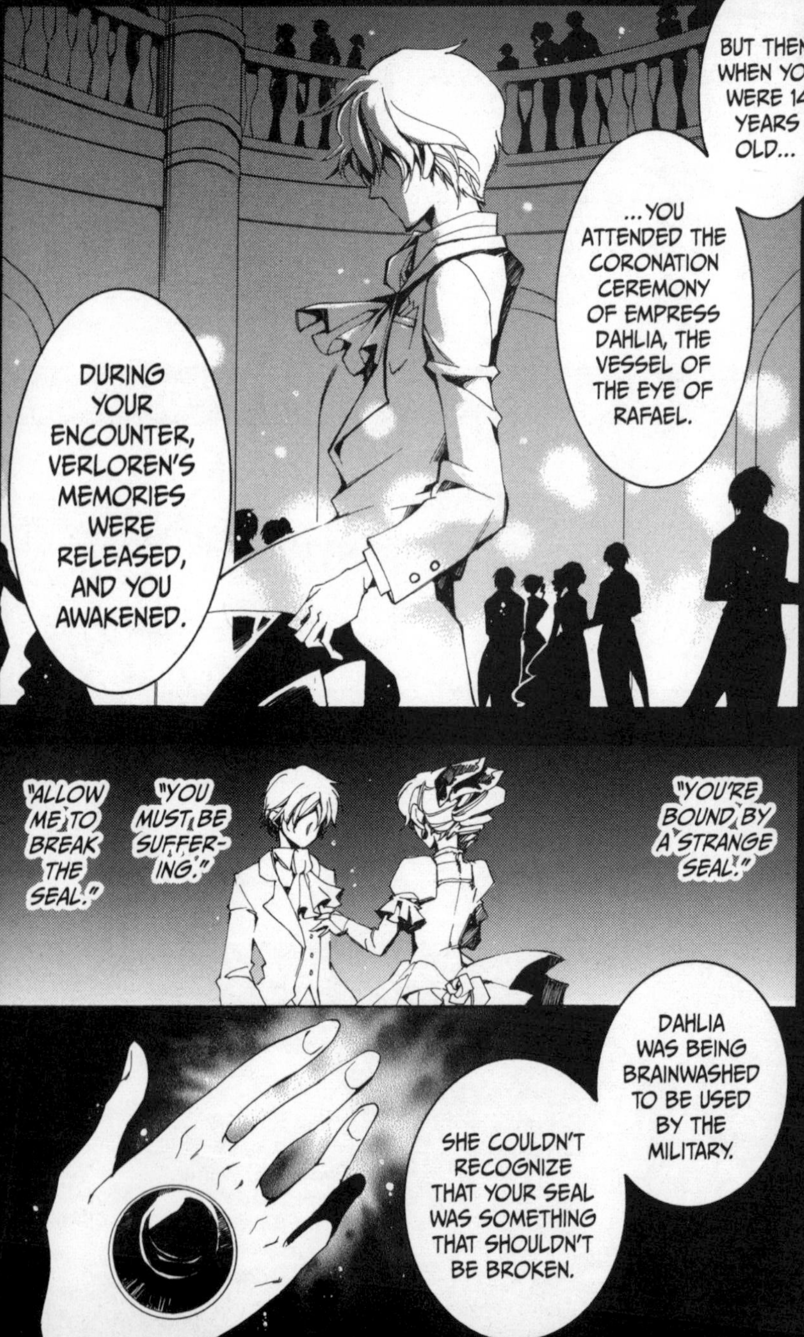
BUT THEN, WHEN YOU WERE 14 YEARS OLD...
...YOU ATTENDED THE CORONATION CEREMONY OF EMPRESS DAHLIA, THE VESSEL OF THE EYE OF RAFAEL.
DURING YOUR ENCOUNTER, VERLOREN'S MEMORIES WERE RELEASED, AND YOU AWAKENED.
"YOU'RE BOUND BY A STRANGE SEAL."
"YOU MUST BE SUFFER-ING."
"ALLOW ME TO BREAK THE SEAL."
DAHLIA WAS BEING BRAINWASHED TO BE USED BY THE MILITARY.
SHE COULDN'T RECOGNIZE THAT YOUR SEAL WAS SOMETHING THAT SHOULDN'T BE BROKEN.

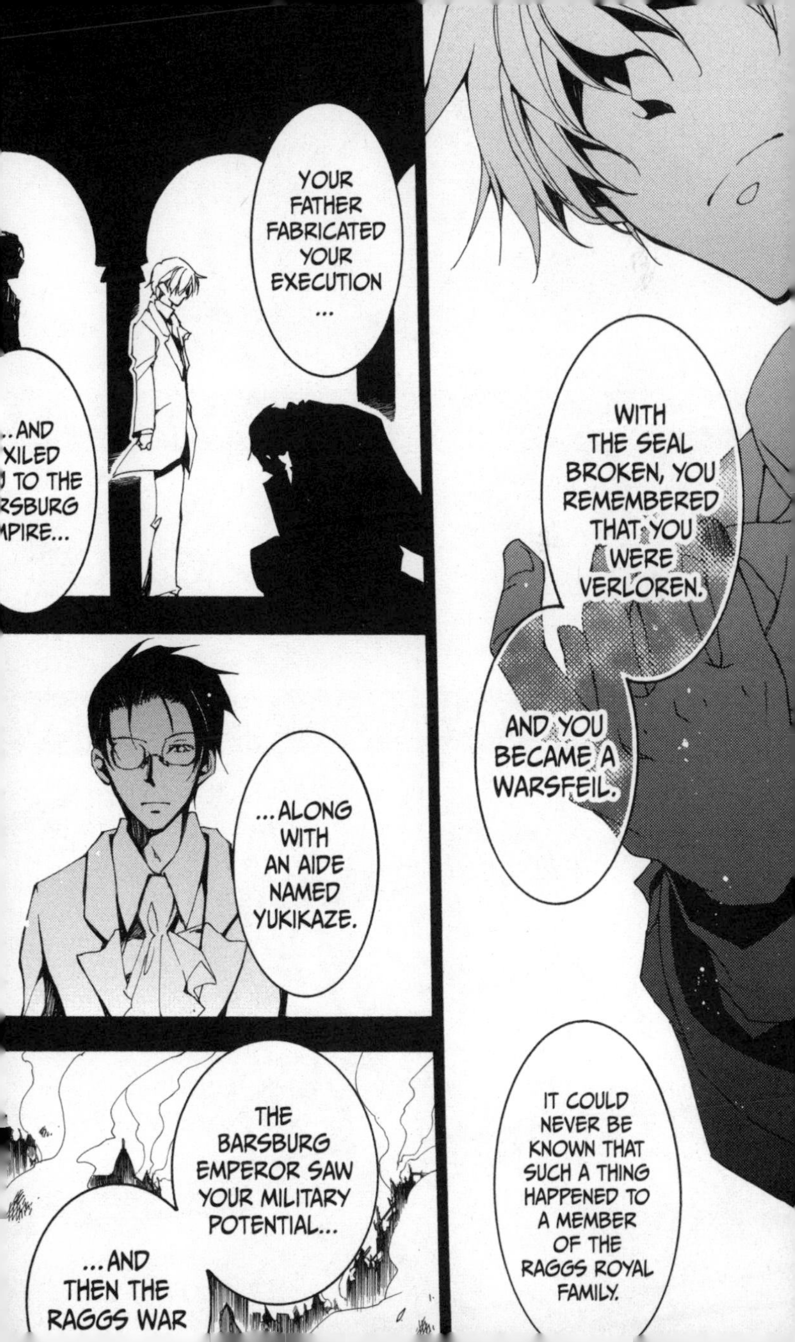
WITH THE SEAL BROKEN, YOU REMEMBERED THAT YOU WERE VERLOREN.
AND YOU BECAME A WARSFEIL.
IT COULD NEVER BE KNOWN THAT SUCH A THING HAPPENED TO A MEMBER OF THE RAGGS ROYAL FAMILY.
YOUR FATHER FABRICATED YOUR EXECUTION ...
...AND XILED TO THE RSBURG MPIRE...
...ALONG WITH AN AIDE NAMED YUKIKAZE.
THE BARSBURG EMPEROR SAW YOUR MILITARY POTENTIAL...
...AND THEN THE RAGGS WAR

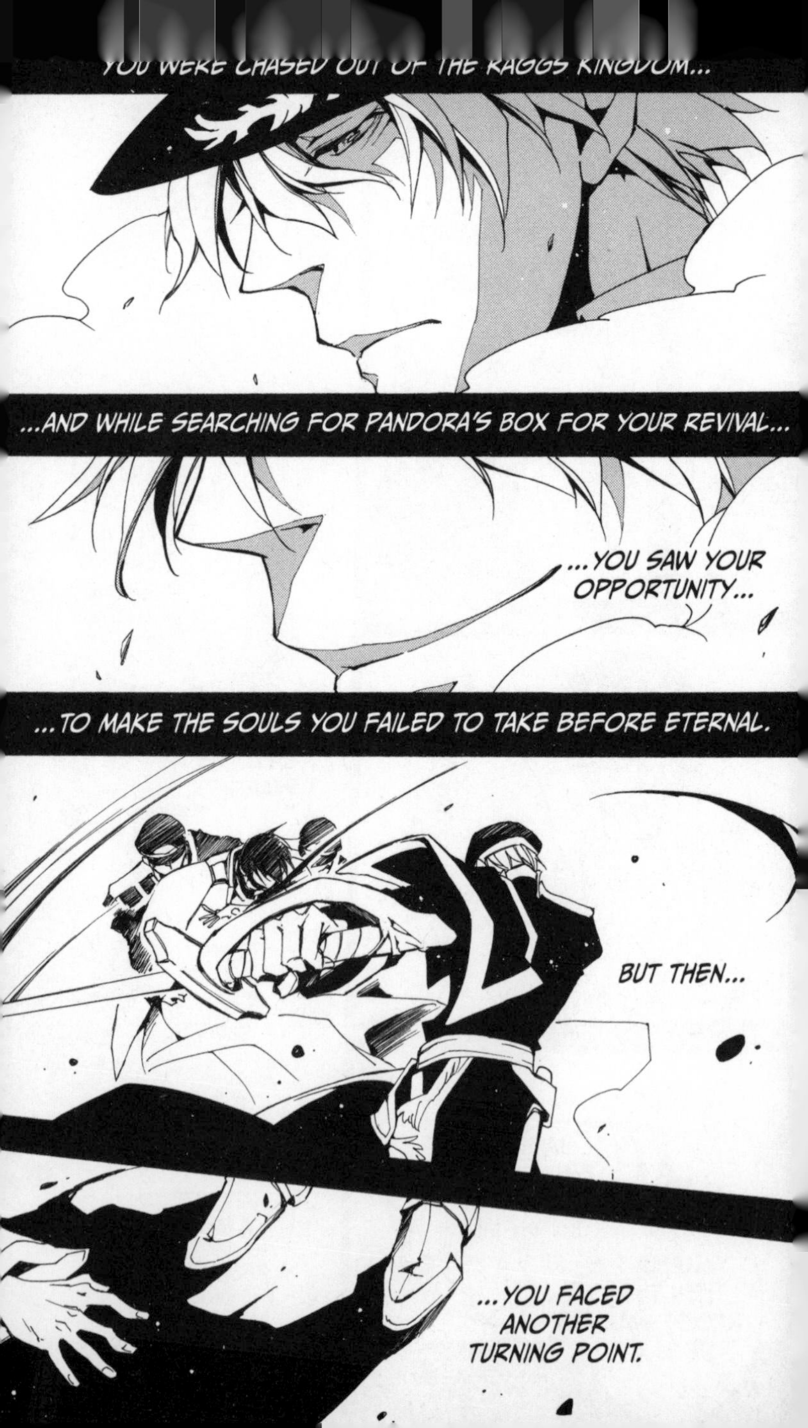
YOU WERE CHASED OUT OF THE RAGGS KINGDOM...
...AND WHILE SEARCHING FOR PANDORA'S BOX FOR YOUR REVIVAL...
...YOU SAW YOUR OPPORTUNITY...
...TO MAKE THE SOULS YOU FAILED TO TAKE BEFORE ETERNAL.
BUT THEN...
...YOU FACED ANOTHER TURNING POINT.

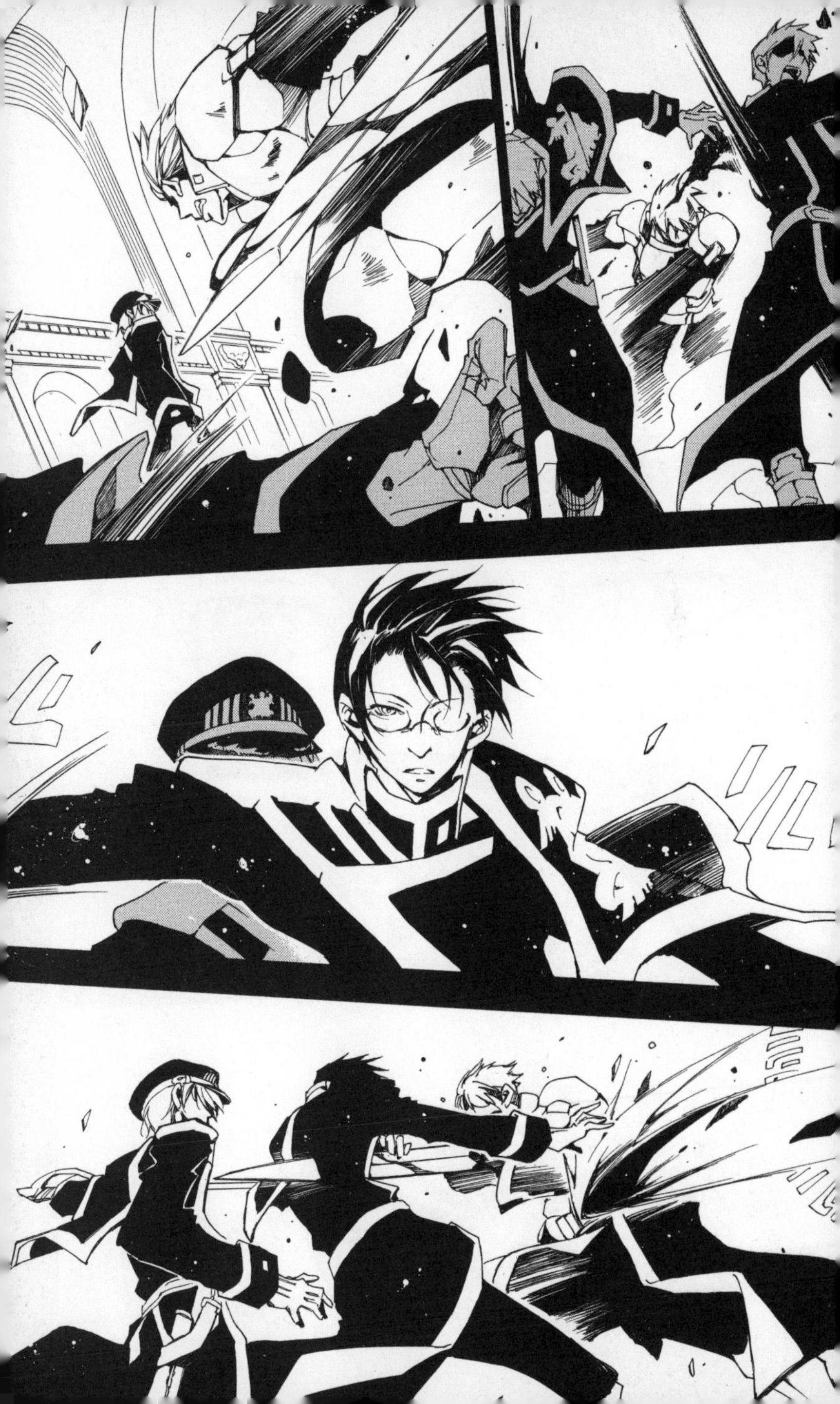

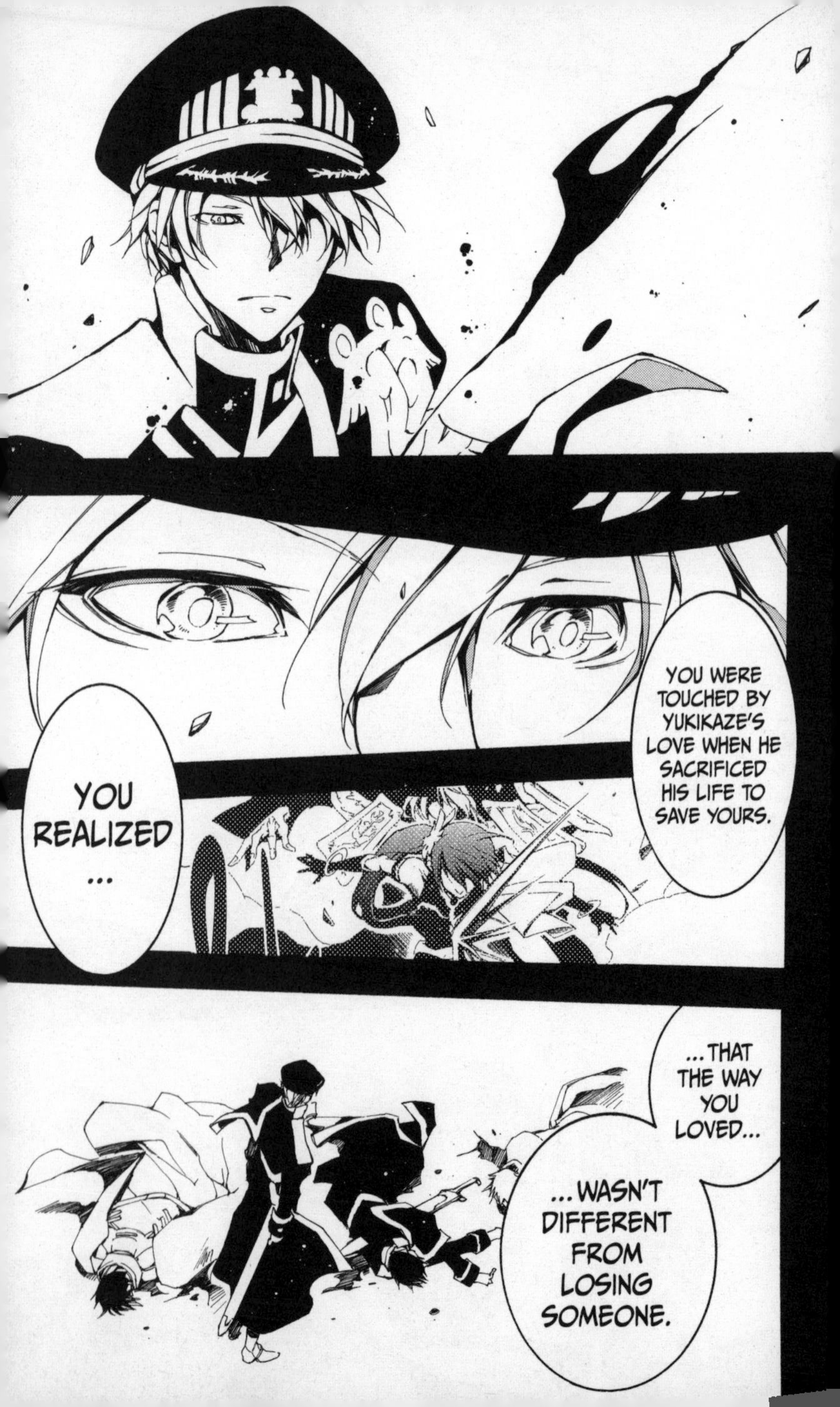
YOU WERE TOUCHED BY YUKIKAZE'S LOVE WHEN HE SACRIFICED HIS LIFE TO SAVE YOURS.
YOU REALIZED ...
...THAT THE WAY YOU LOVED...
...WASN'T DIFFERENT FROM LOSING SOMEONE.

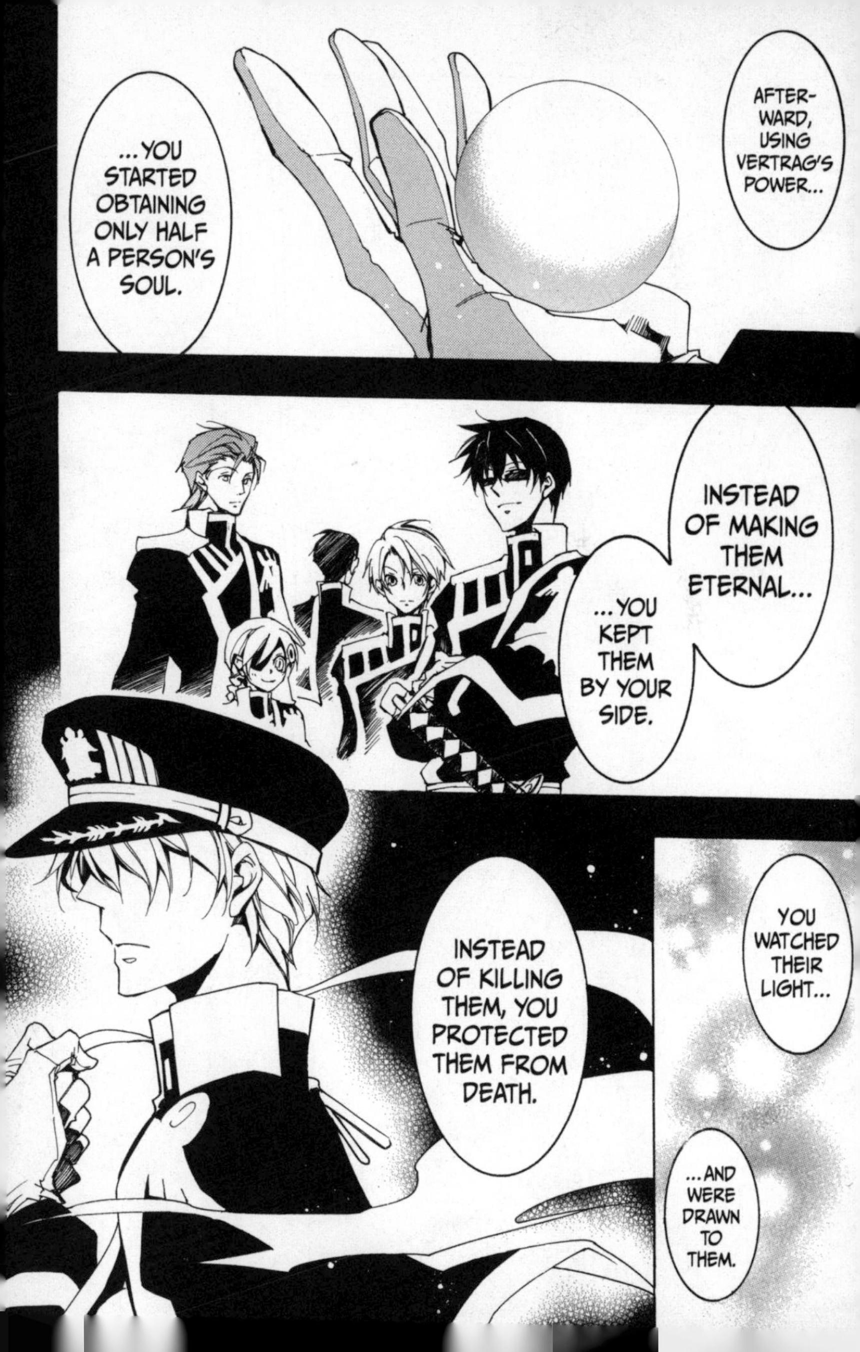
AFTER-WARD, USING VERTRAG'S POWER...
...YOU STARTED OBTAINING ONLY HALF A PERSON'S SOUL.
INSTEAD OF MAKING THEM ETERNAL...
...YOU KEPT THEM BY YOUR SIDE.
YOU WATCHED THEIR LIGHT...
...AND WERE DRAWN TO THEM.
INSTEAD OF KILLING THEM, YOU PROTECTED THEM FROM DEATH.

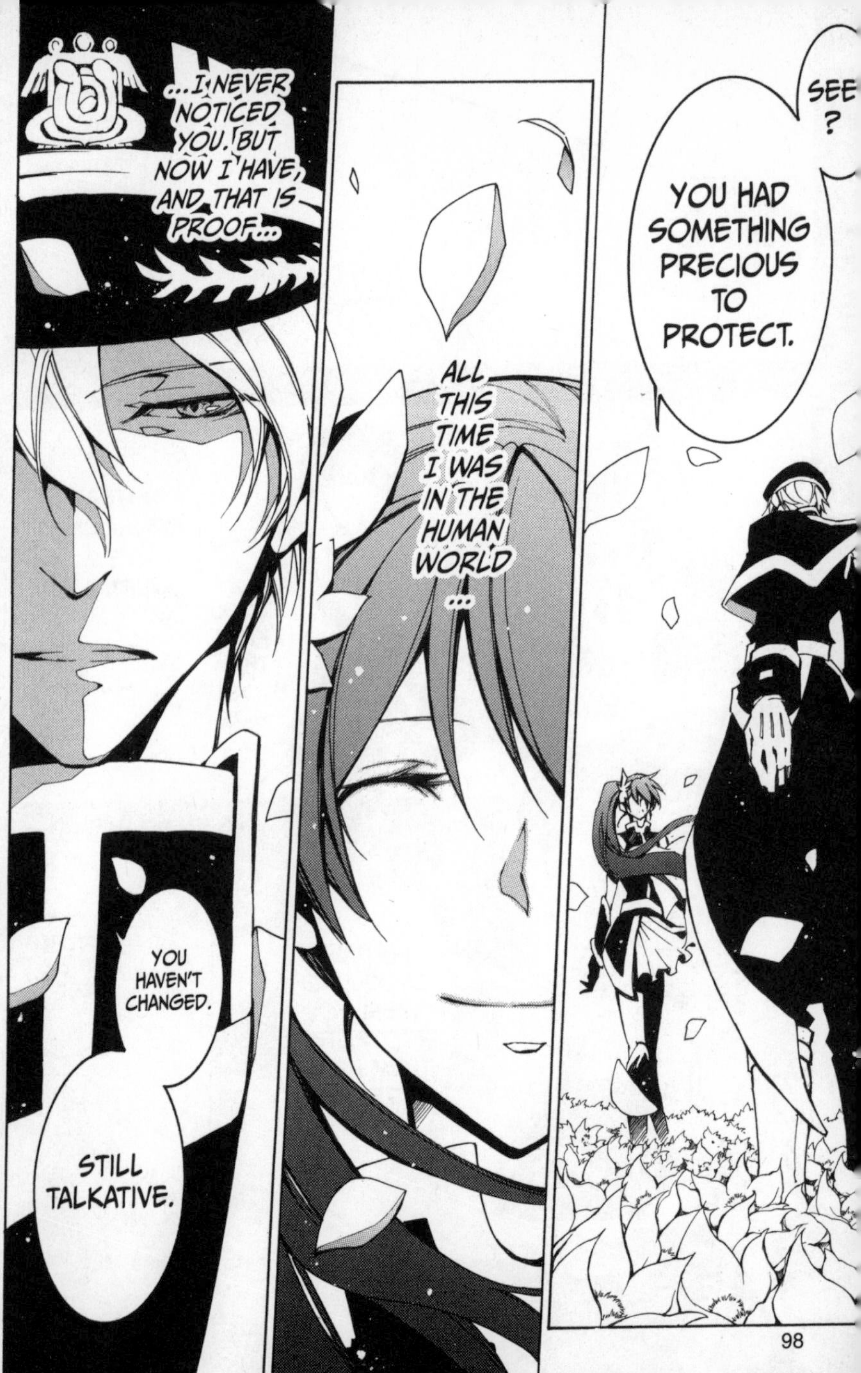
SEE?
YOU HAD SOMETHING PRECIOUS TO PROTECT.
ALL THIS TIME I WAS IN THE HUMAN WORLD...
...I NEVER NOTICED YOU. BUT NOW I HAVE, AND THAT IS PROOF...
YOU HAVEN'T CHANGED.
STILL TALKATIVE.

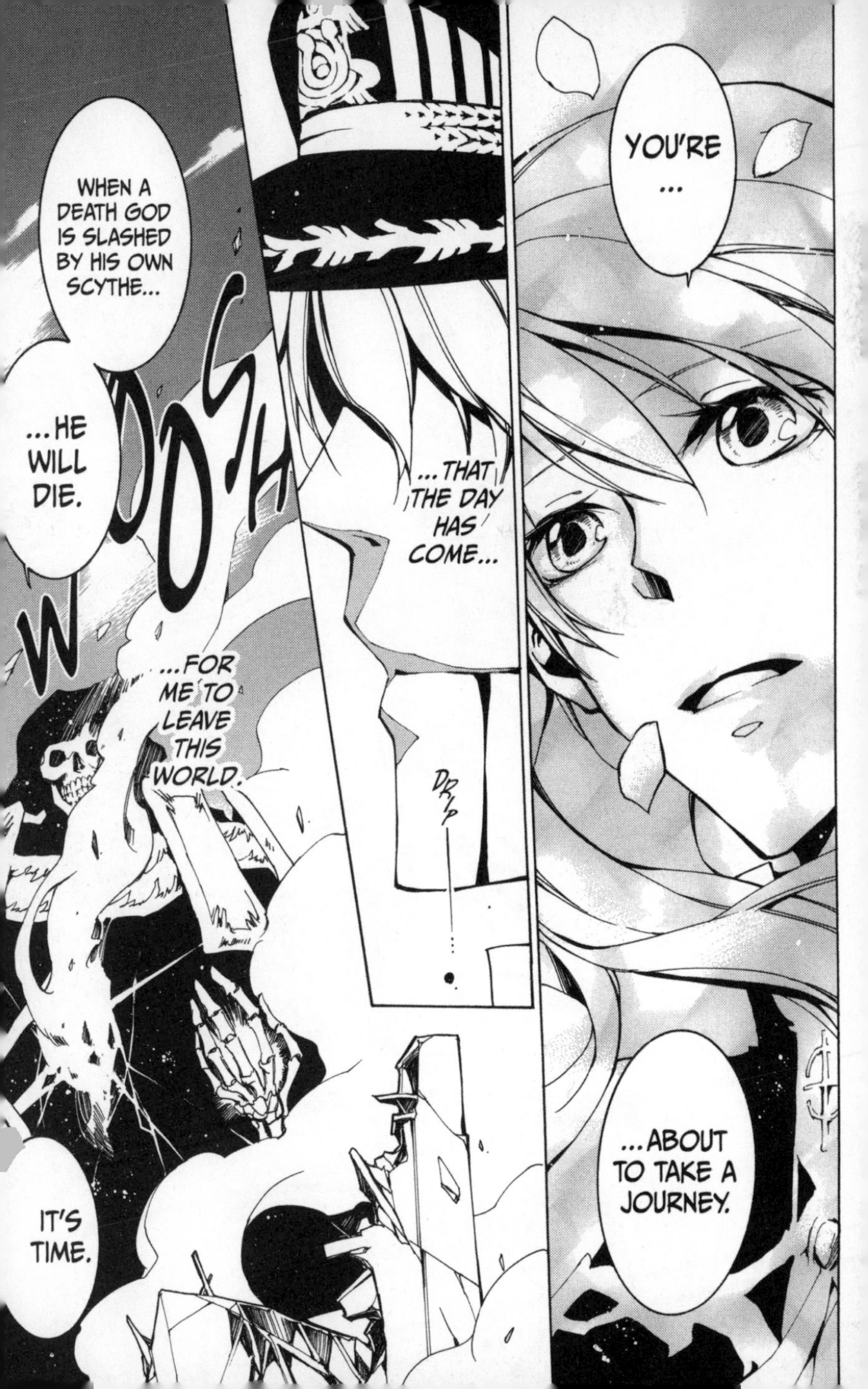
YOU'RE ...
...ABOUT TO TAKE A JOURNEY.
...THAT THE DAY HAS COME...
DRIP
WHEN A DEATH GOD IS SLASHED BY HIS OWN SCYTHE...
...HE WILL DIE.
WHOOSH
...FOR ME TO LEAVE THIS WORLD.
IT'S TIME.

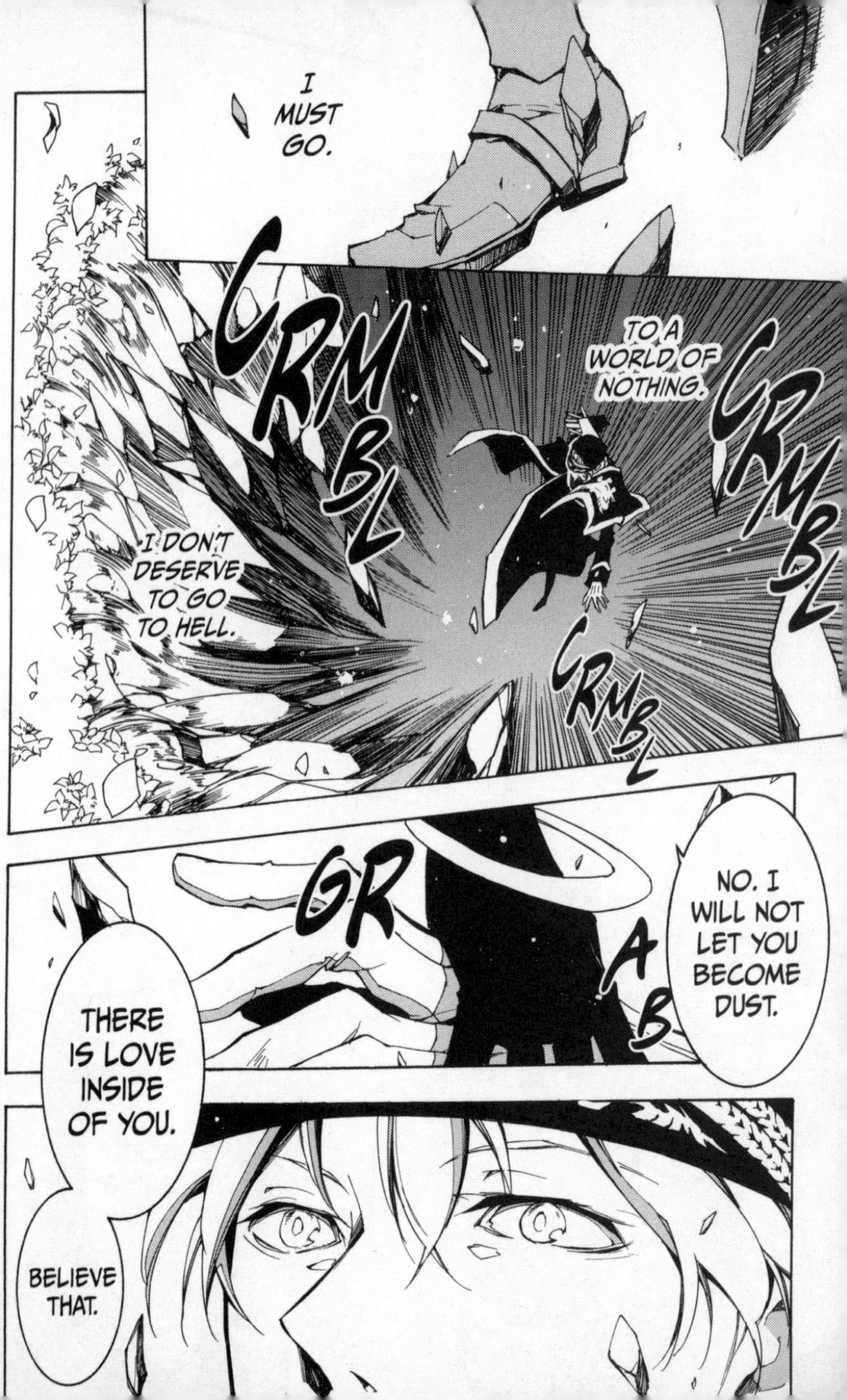

I MUST GO.
TO A WORLD OF NOTHING.
CRMBL
CRMBL
I DON'T DESERVE TO GO TO HELL.
CRMBL
NO. I WILL NOT LET YOU BECOME DUST.
GRAB
THERE IS LOVE INSIDE OF YOU.
BELIEVE THAT.

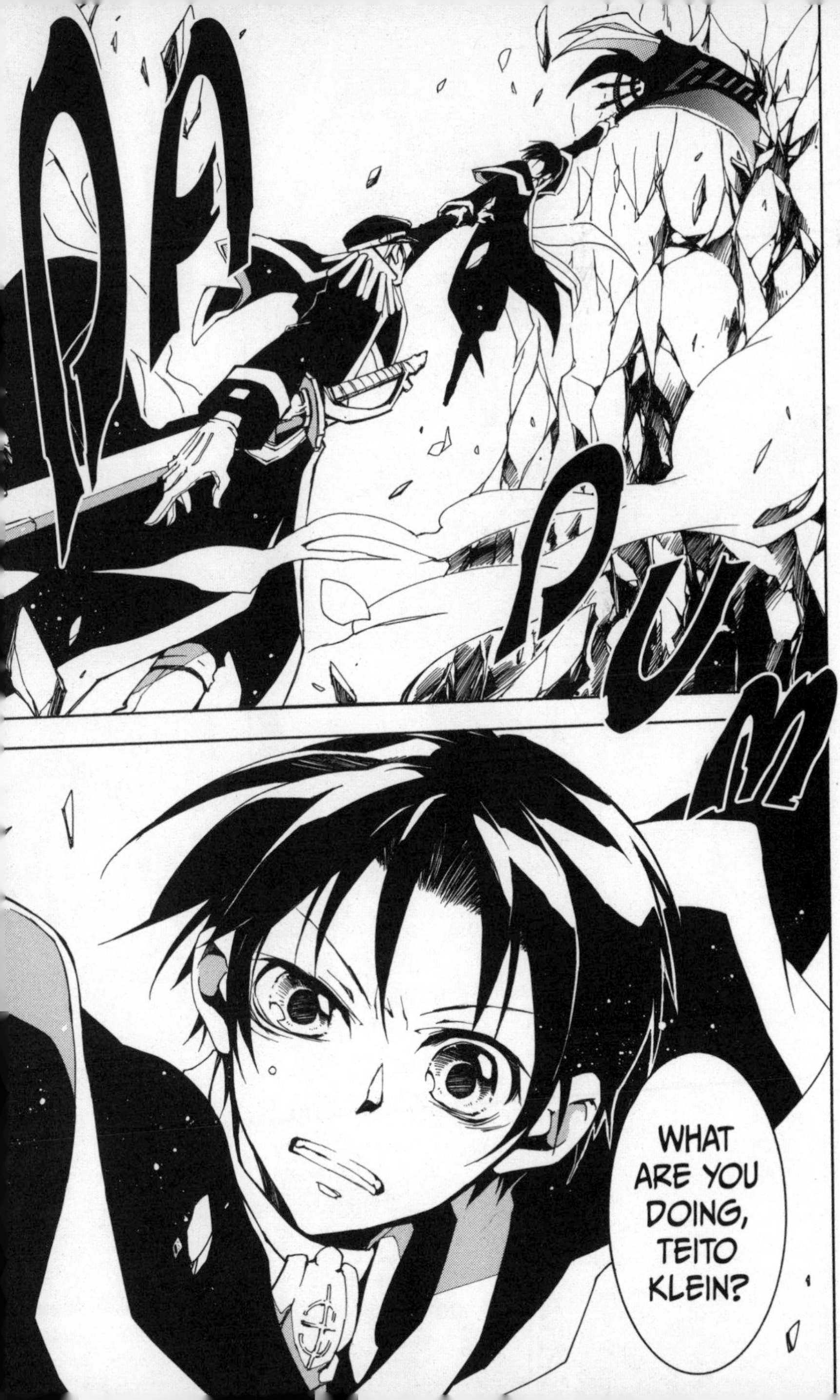
WHAT ARE YOU DOING, TEITO KLEIN?

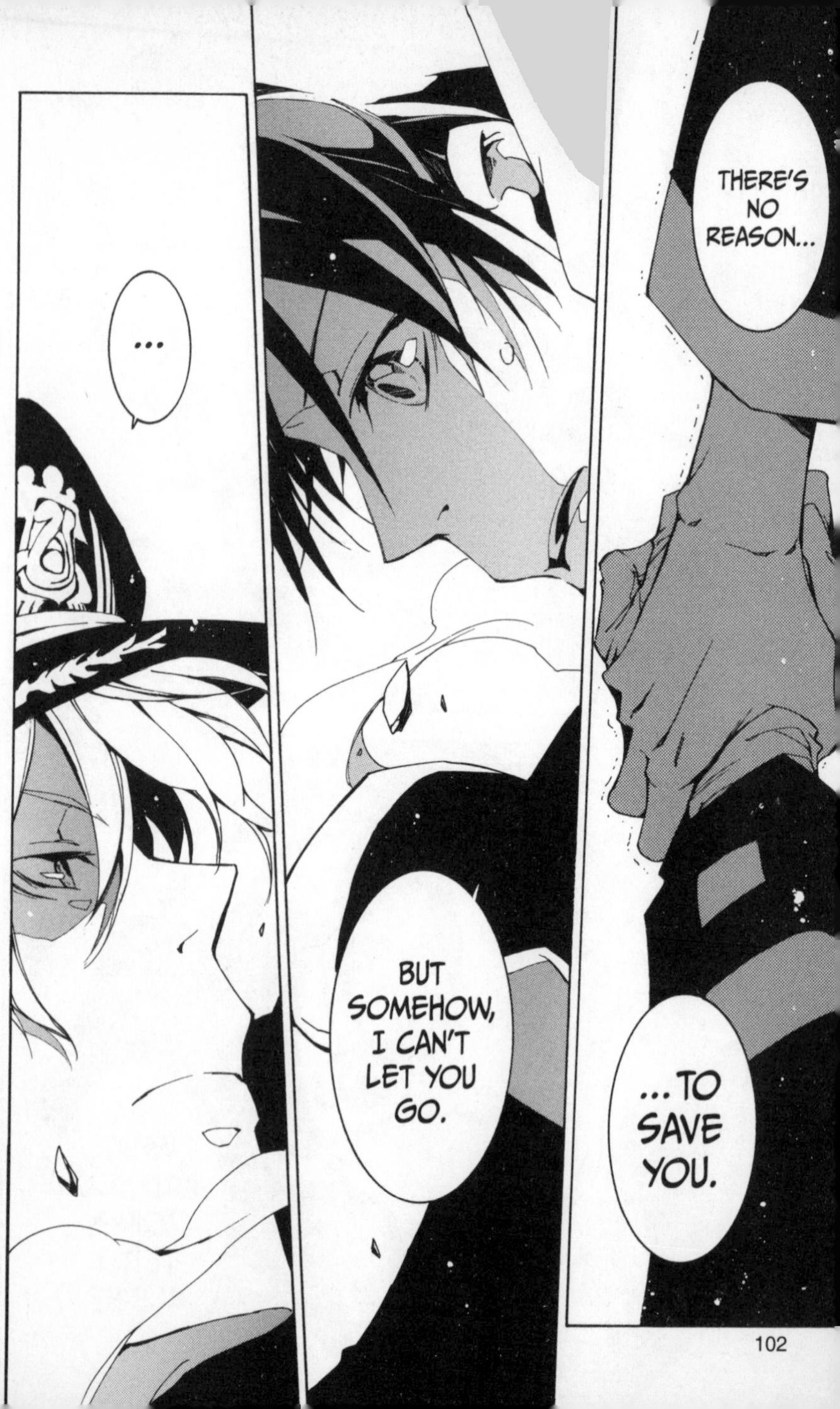
THERE'S NO REASON...
...TO SAVE YOU.
BUT SOMEHOW, I CAN'T LET YOU GO.
...

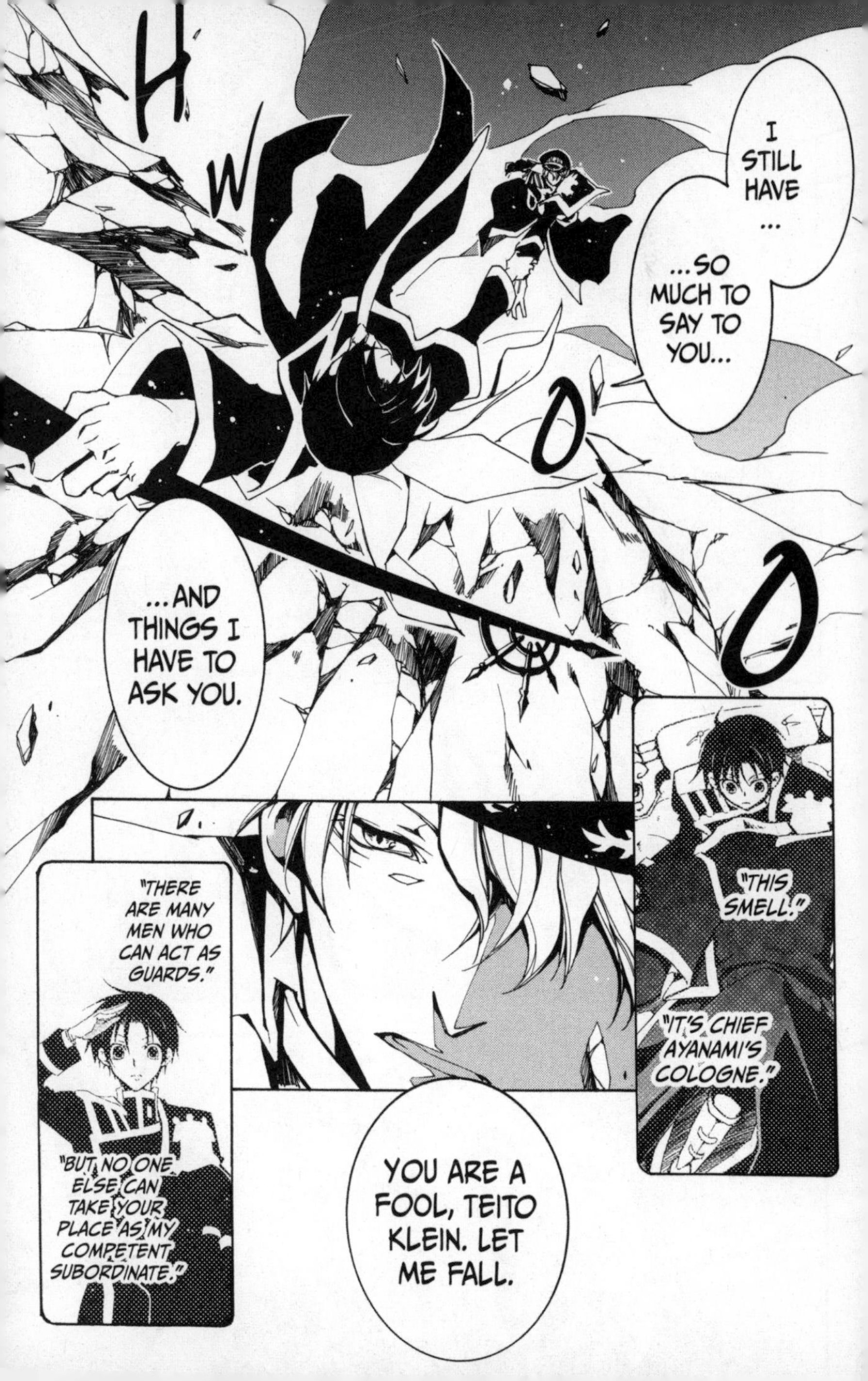
I STILL HAVE ...
...SO MUCH TO SAY TO YOU...
...AND THINGS I HAVE TO ASK YOU.
"THIS SMELL."
"IT'S CHIEF AYANAMI'S COLOGNE."
YOU ARE A FOOL, TEITO KLEIN. LET ME FALL.
"THERE ARE MANY MEN WHO CAN ACT AS GUARDS."
"BUT NO ONE ELSE CAN TAKE YOUR PLACE AS MY COMPETENT SUBORDINATE."

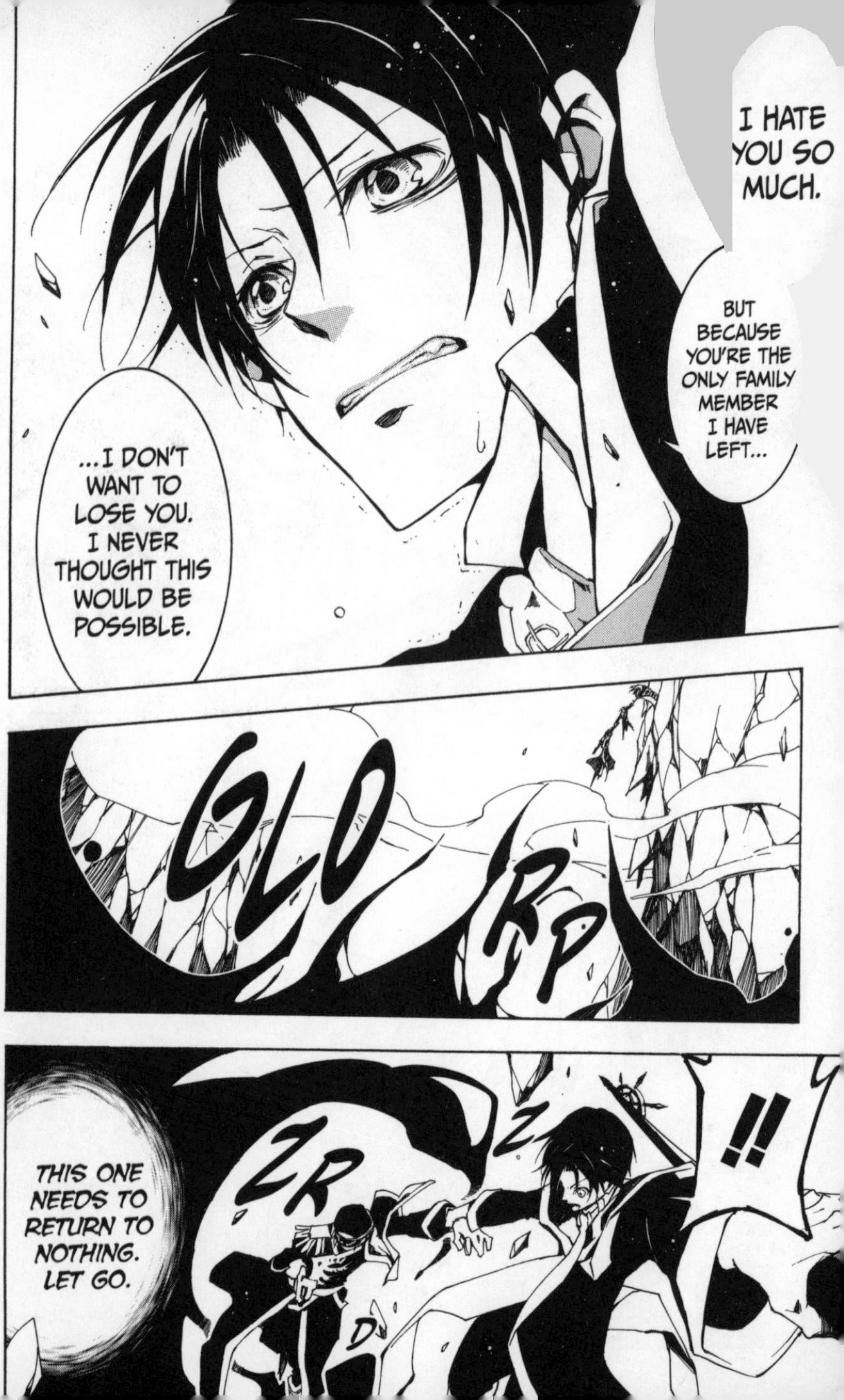
I HATE YOU SO MUCH.
BUT BECAUSE YOU'RE THE ONLY FAMILY MEMBER I HAVE LEFT...
...I DON'T WANT TO LOSE YOU. I NEVER THOUGHT THIS WOULD BE POSSIBLE.
GLORP
!!
THIS ONE NEEDS TO RETURN TO NOTHING. LET GO.

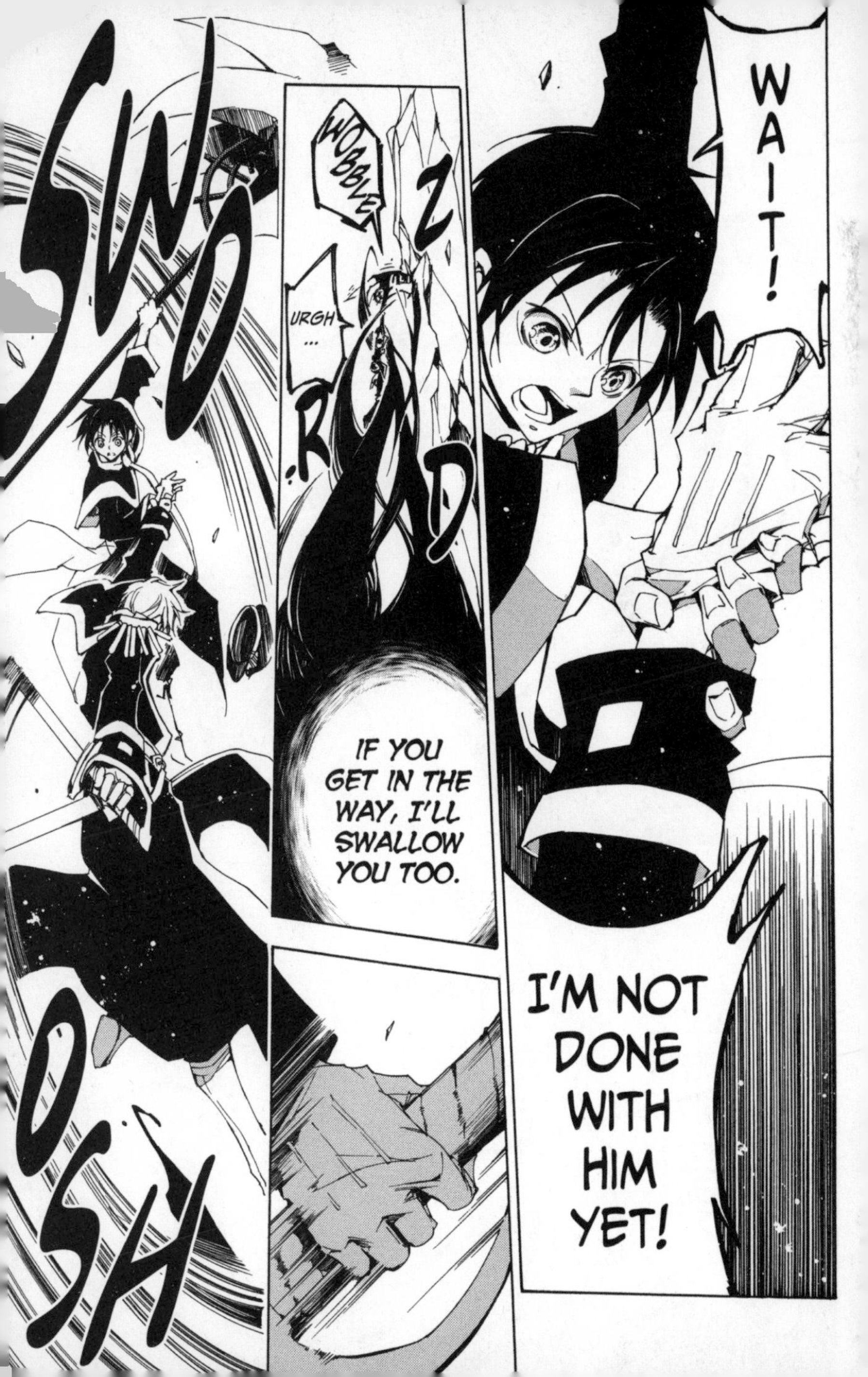
WAIT!
I'M NOT DONE WITH HIM YET!
WOBBLE
URGH...
IF YOU GET IN THE WAY, I'LL SWALLOW YOU TOO.
SWOOSH

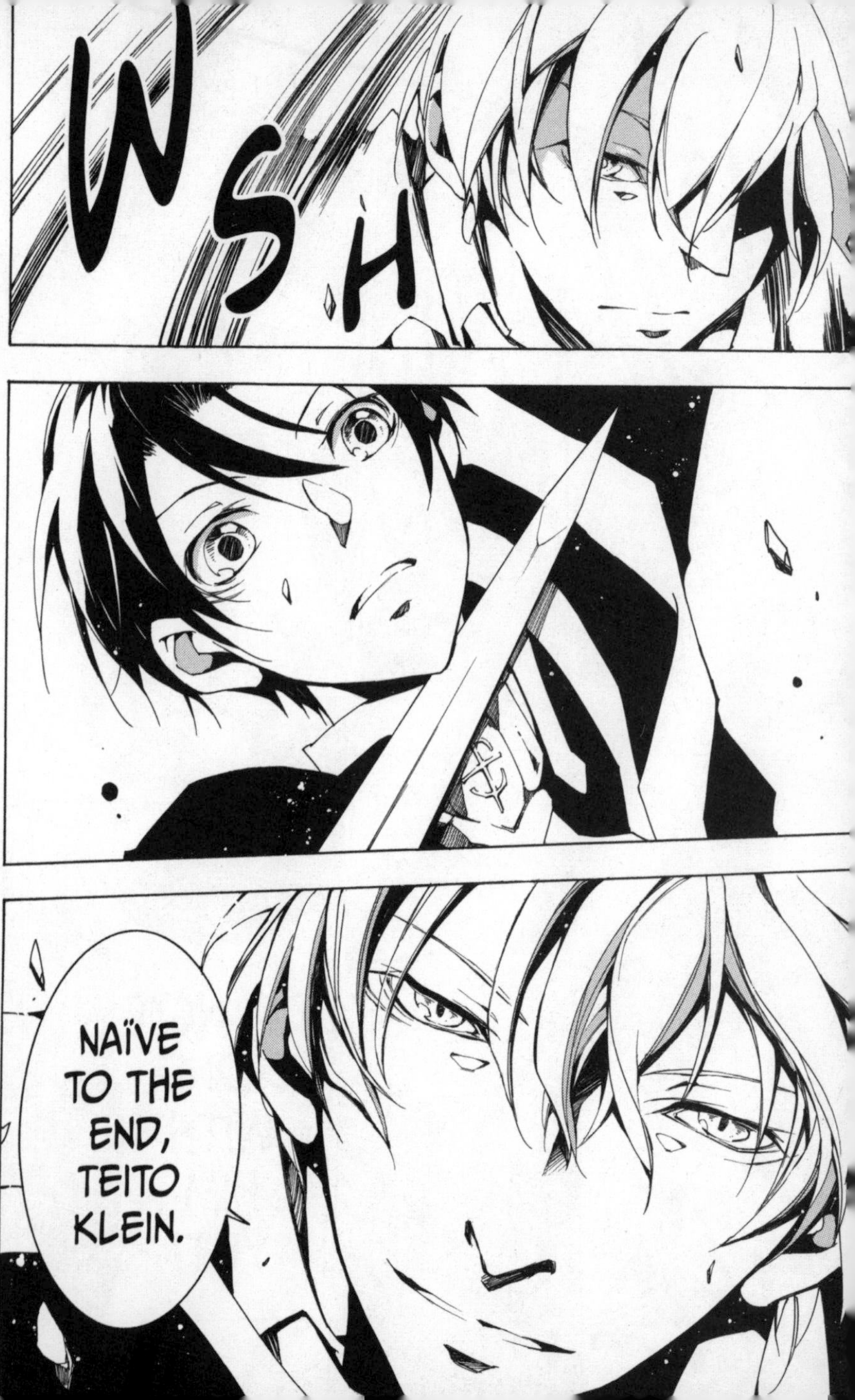
WSH
NAÏVE TO THE END, TEITO KLEIN.

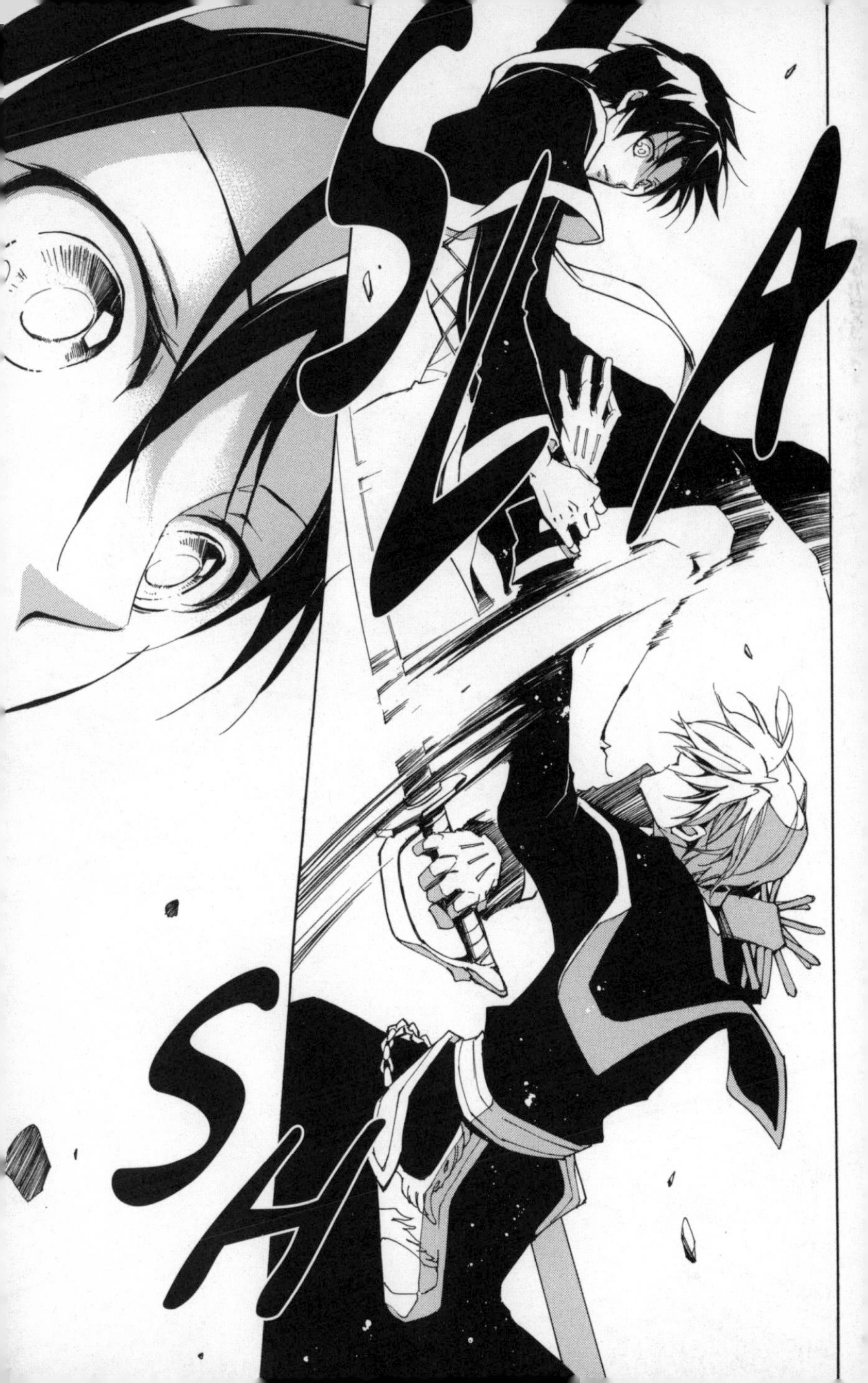
SHA
SH

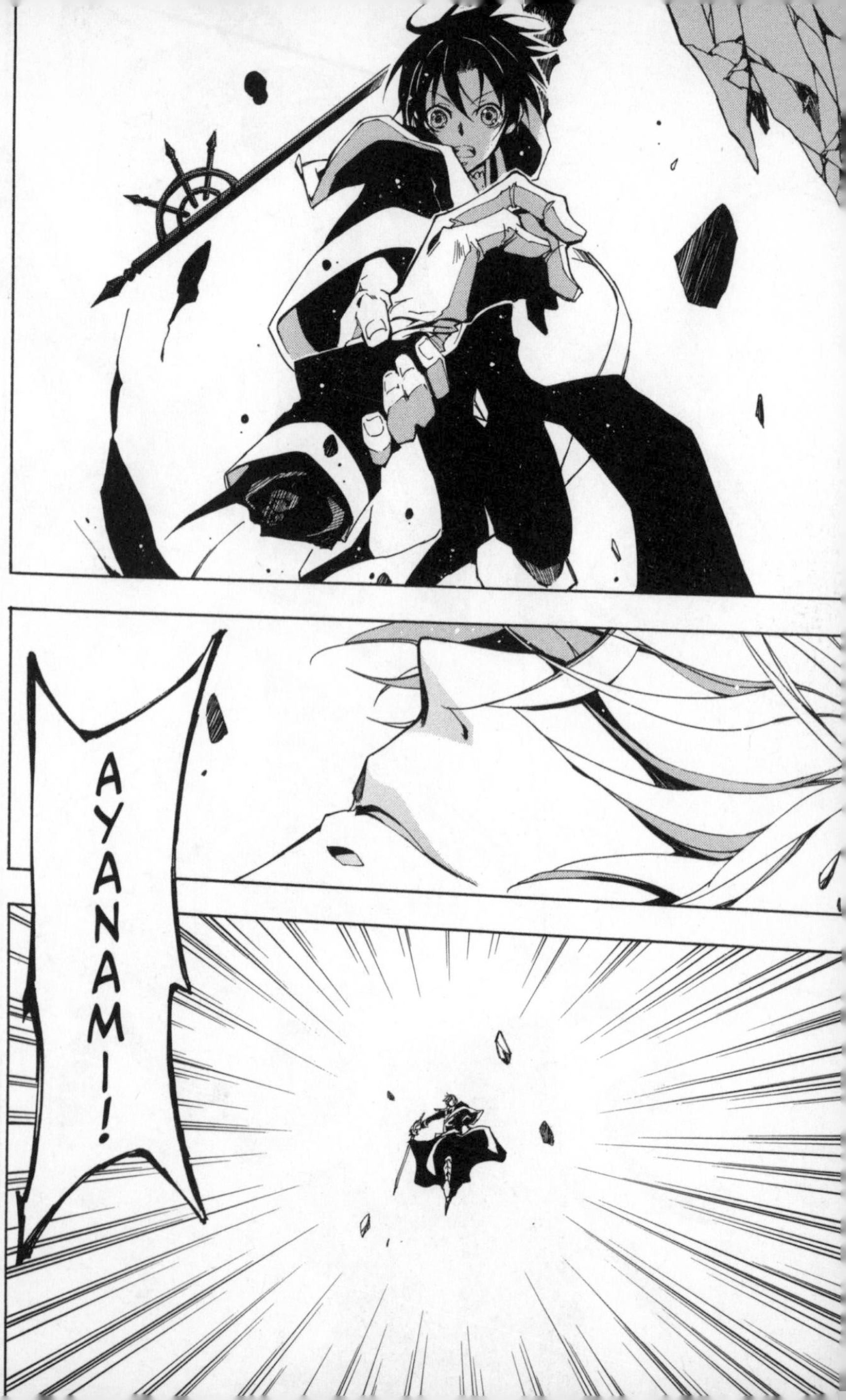
AYANAMI!

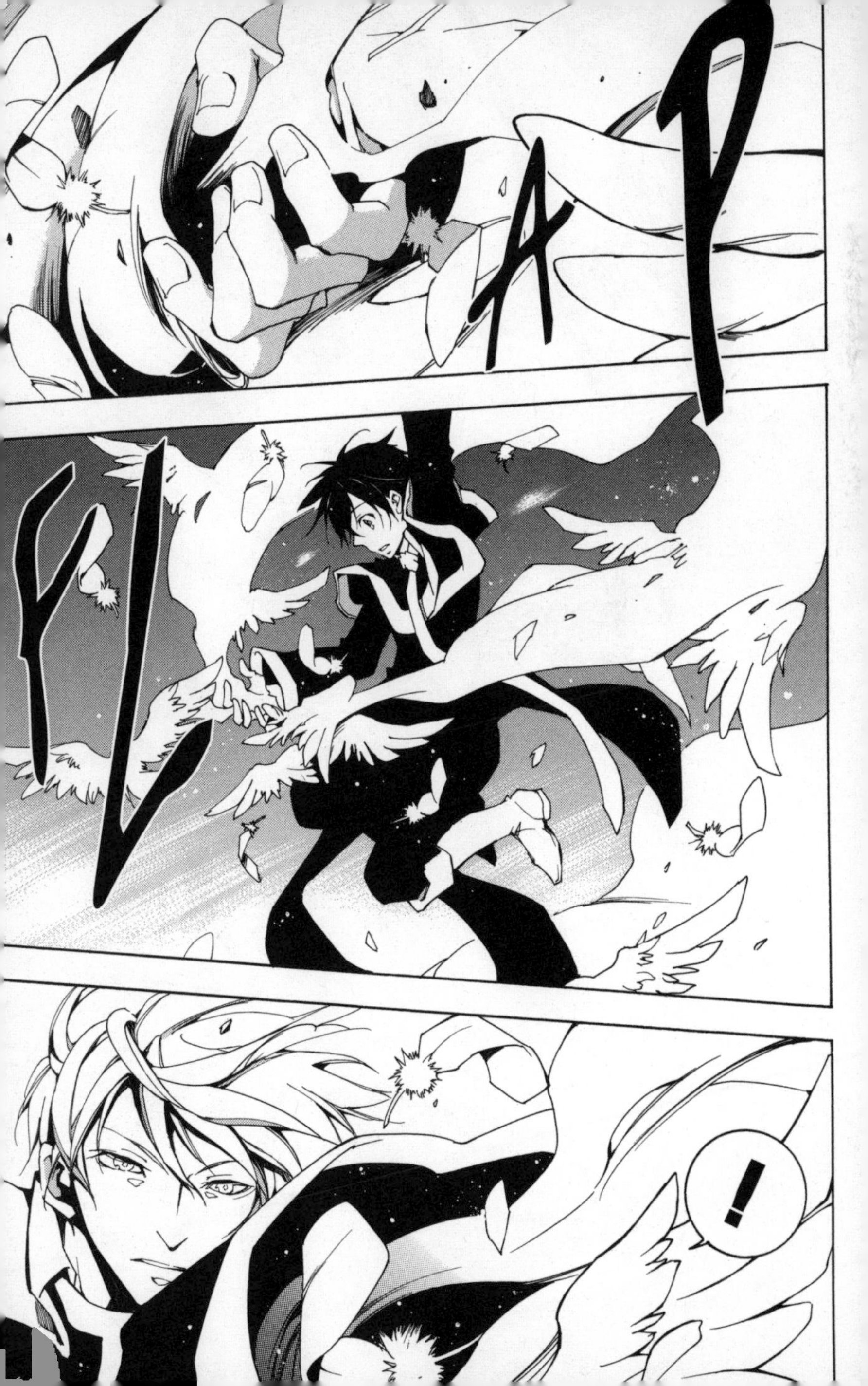
!

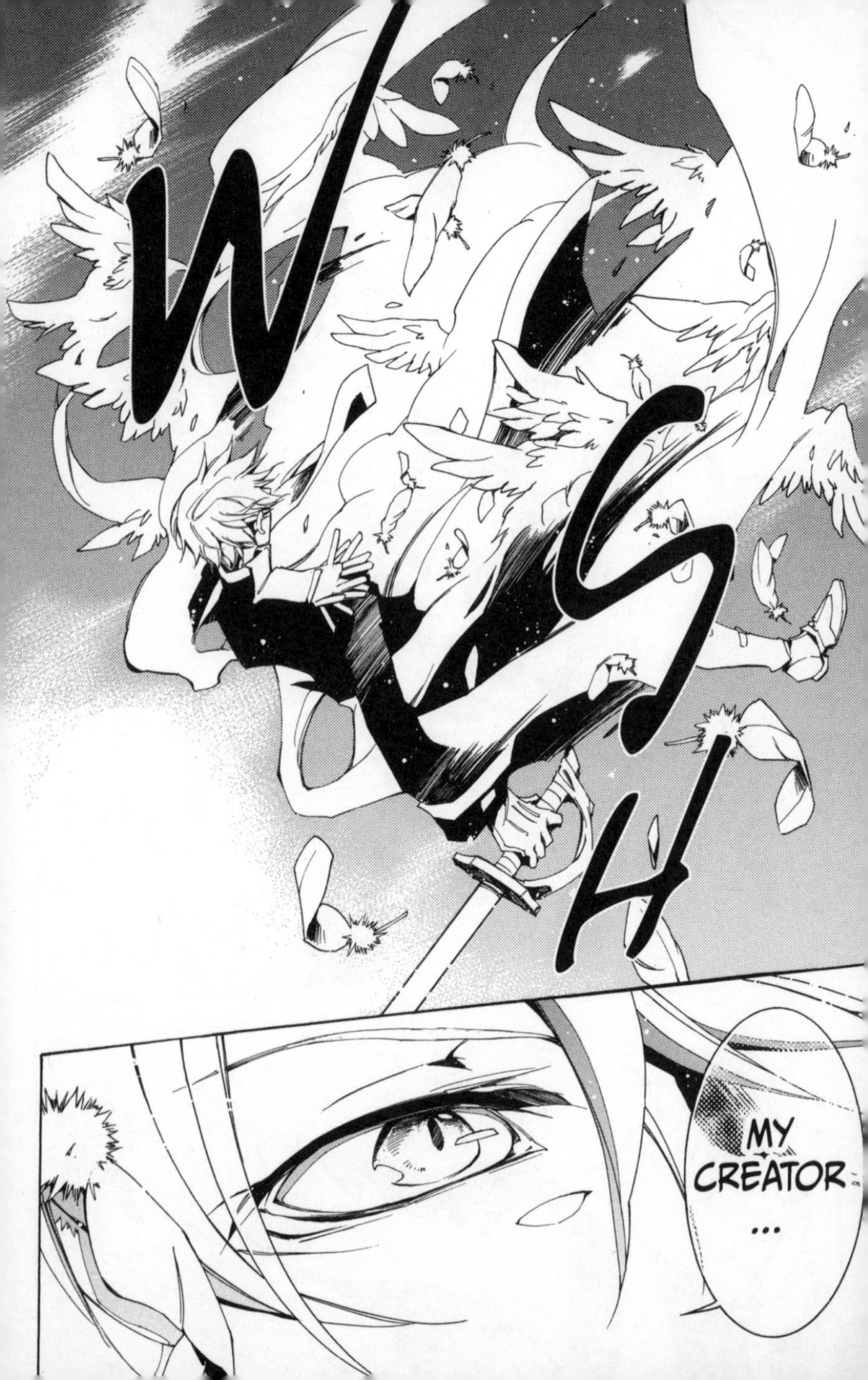
MY CREATOR...

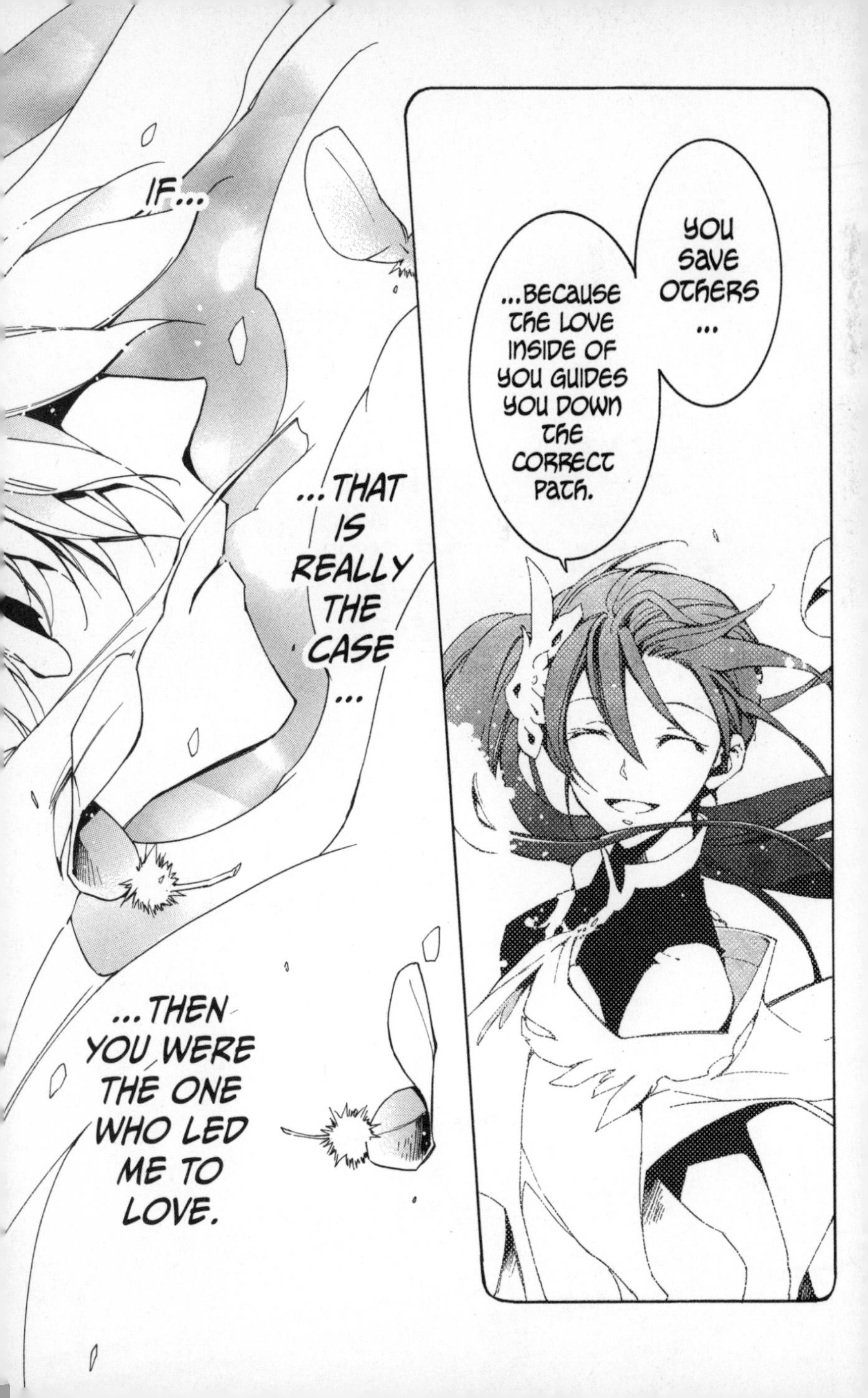
YOU SAVE OTHERS...
...BECAUSE THE LOVE INSIDE OF YOU GUIDES YOU DOWN THE CORRECT PATH.
IF...
...THAT IS REALLY THE CASE...
...THEN YOU WERE THE ONE WHO LED ME TO LOVE.

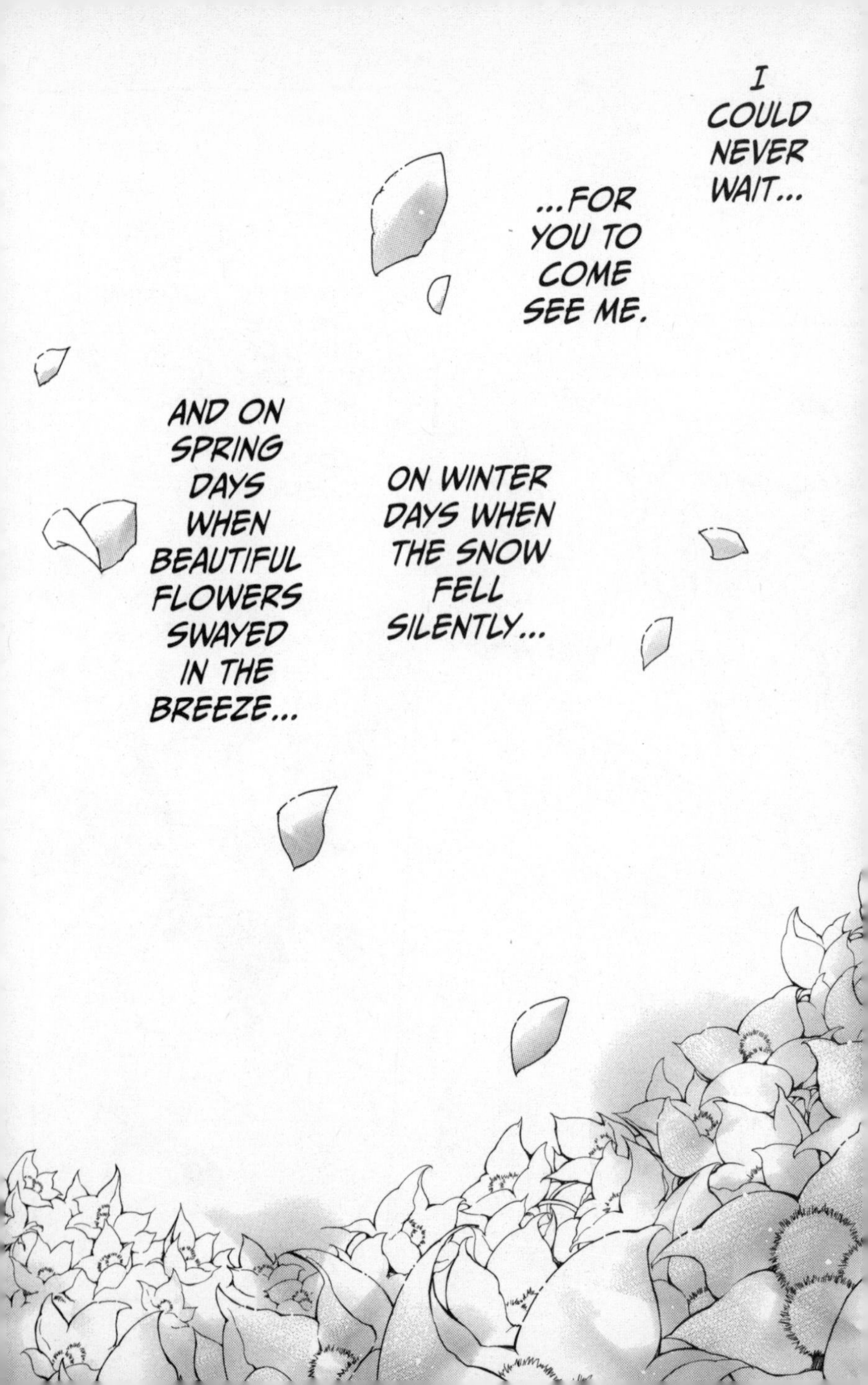
I COULD NEVER WAIT...
...FOR YOU TO COME SEE ME.
ON WINTER DAYS WHEN THE SNOW FELL SILENTLY...
AND ON SPRING DAYS WHEN BEAUTIFUL FLOWERS SWAYED IN THE BREEZE...

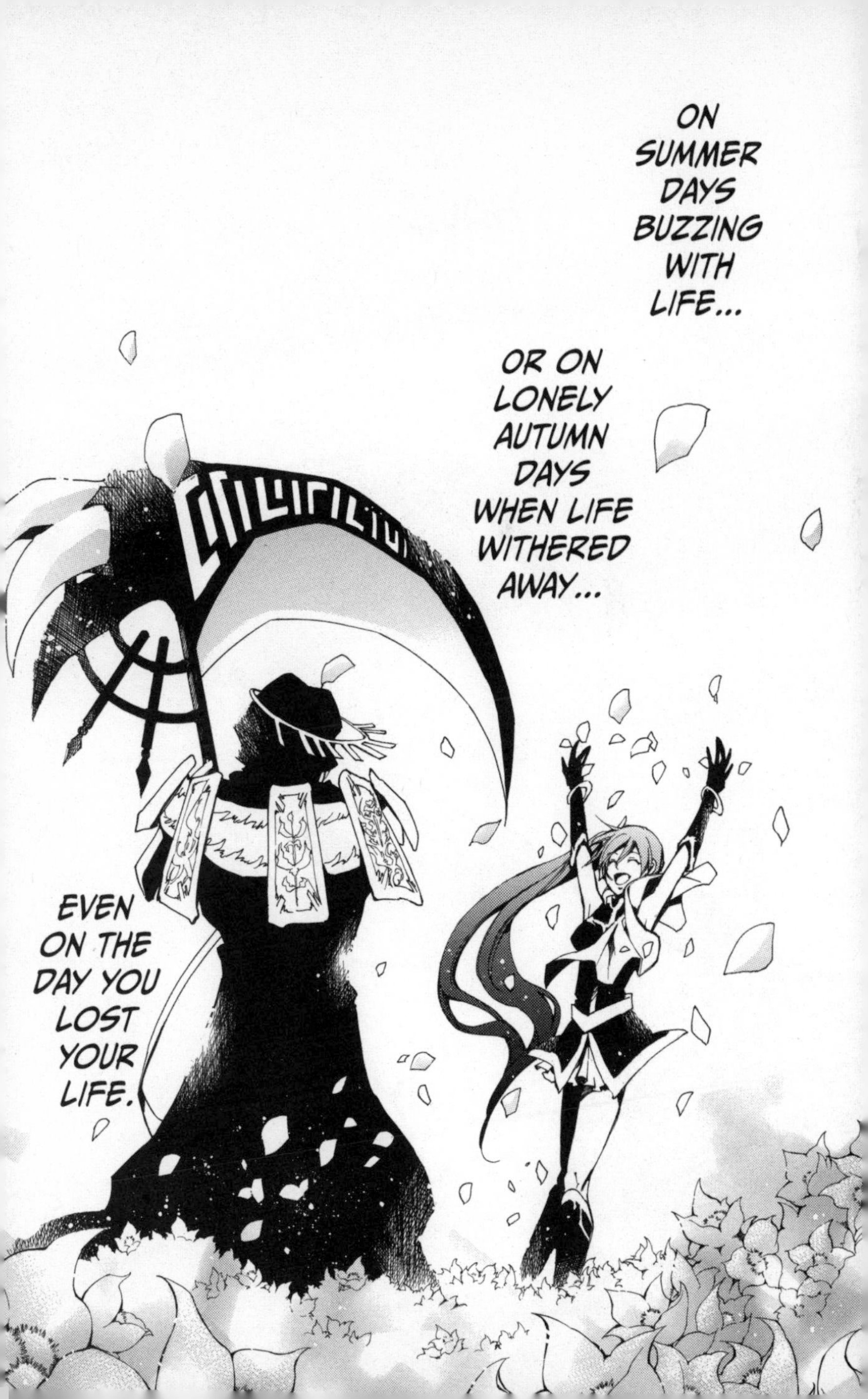
ON SUMMER DAYS BUZZING WITH LIFE...
OR ON LONELY AUTUMN DAYS WHEN LIFE WITHERED AWAY...
EVEN ON THE DAY YOU LOST YOUR LIFE.

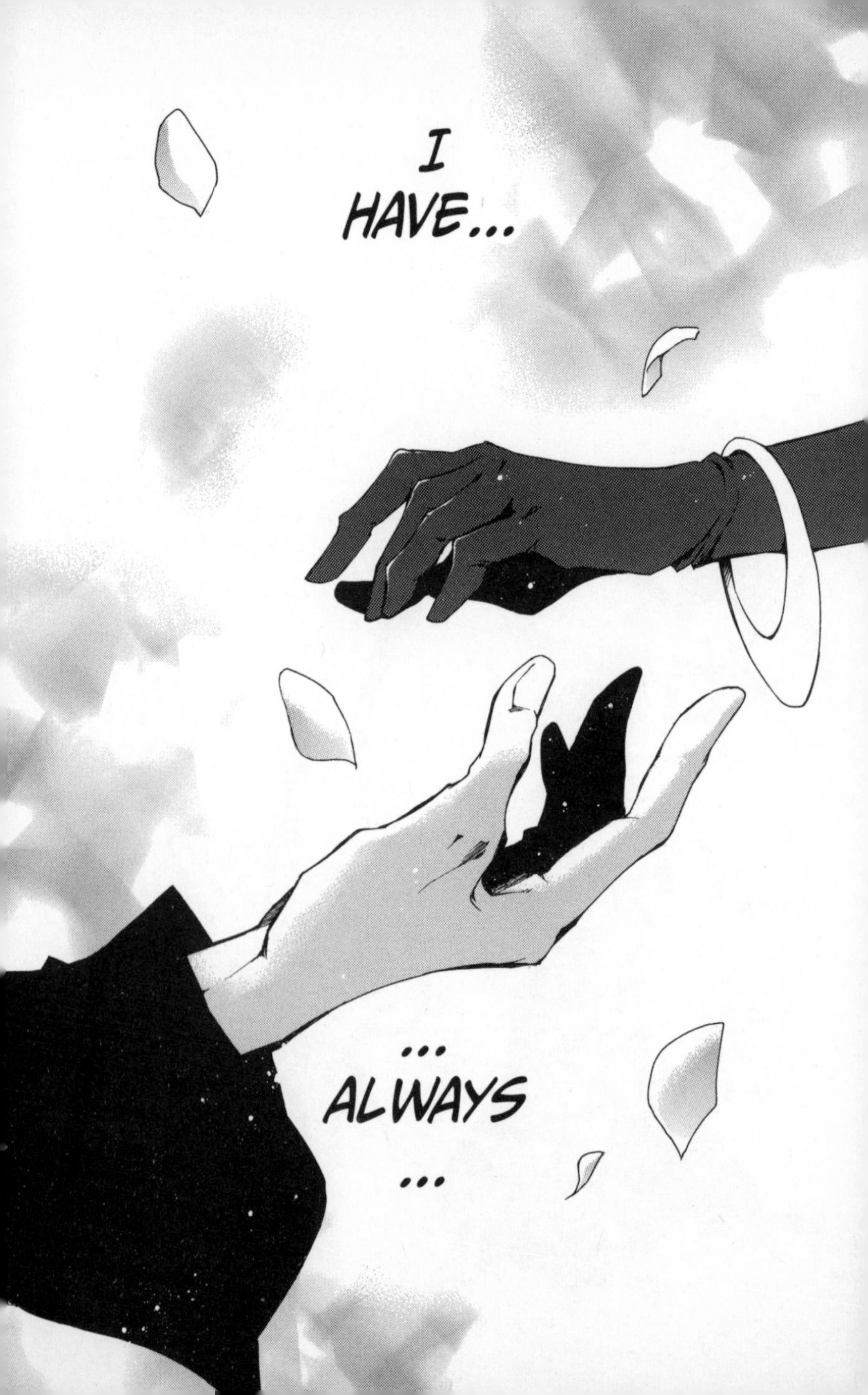
I HAVE...
...ALWAYS...

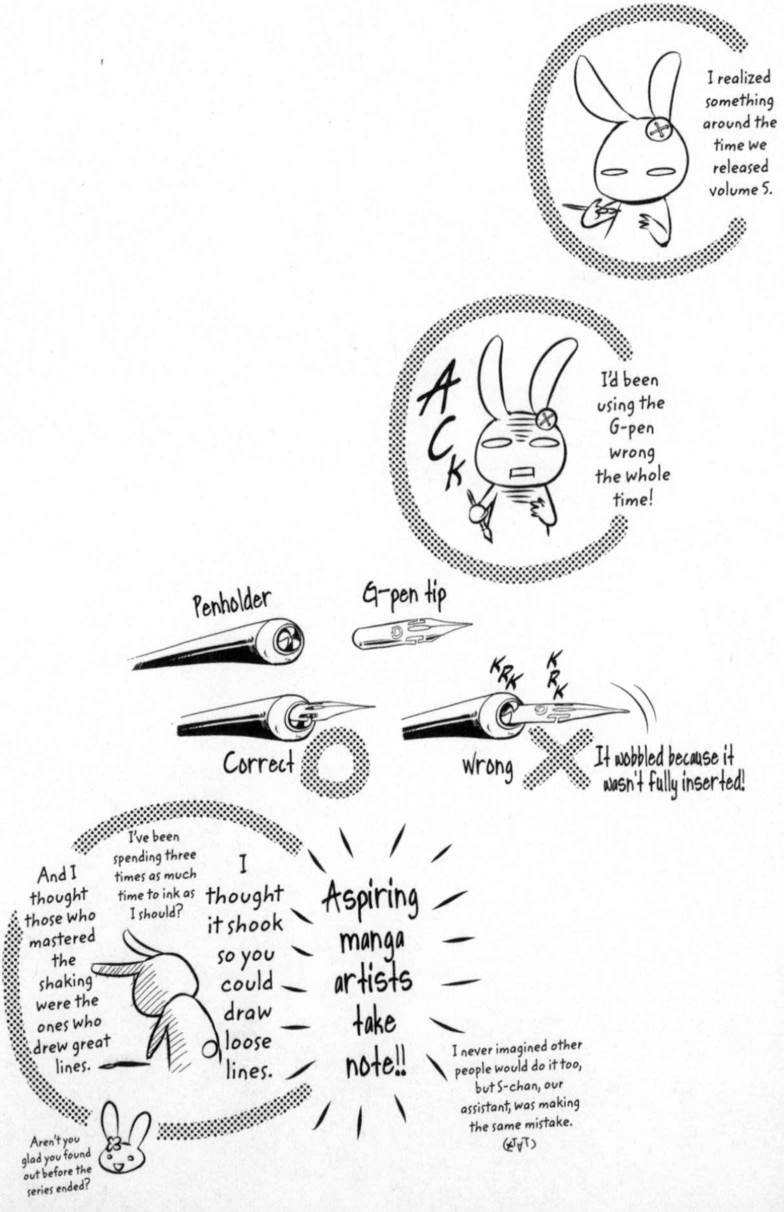
I realized something around the time we released volume 5.
I'd been using the G-pen wrong the whole time!
ACK
G-pen tip
Penholder
KRK
KRK
Wrong
It wobbled because it wasn't fully inserted!
Correct
Aspiring manga artists take note!!
I never imagined other people would do it too, but S-chan, our assistant, was making the same mistake.
I thought it shook so you could draw loose lines.
I've been spending three times as much time to ink as I should?
And I thought those who mastered the shaking were the ones who drew great lines.
Aren't you glad you found out before the series ended?

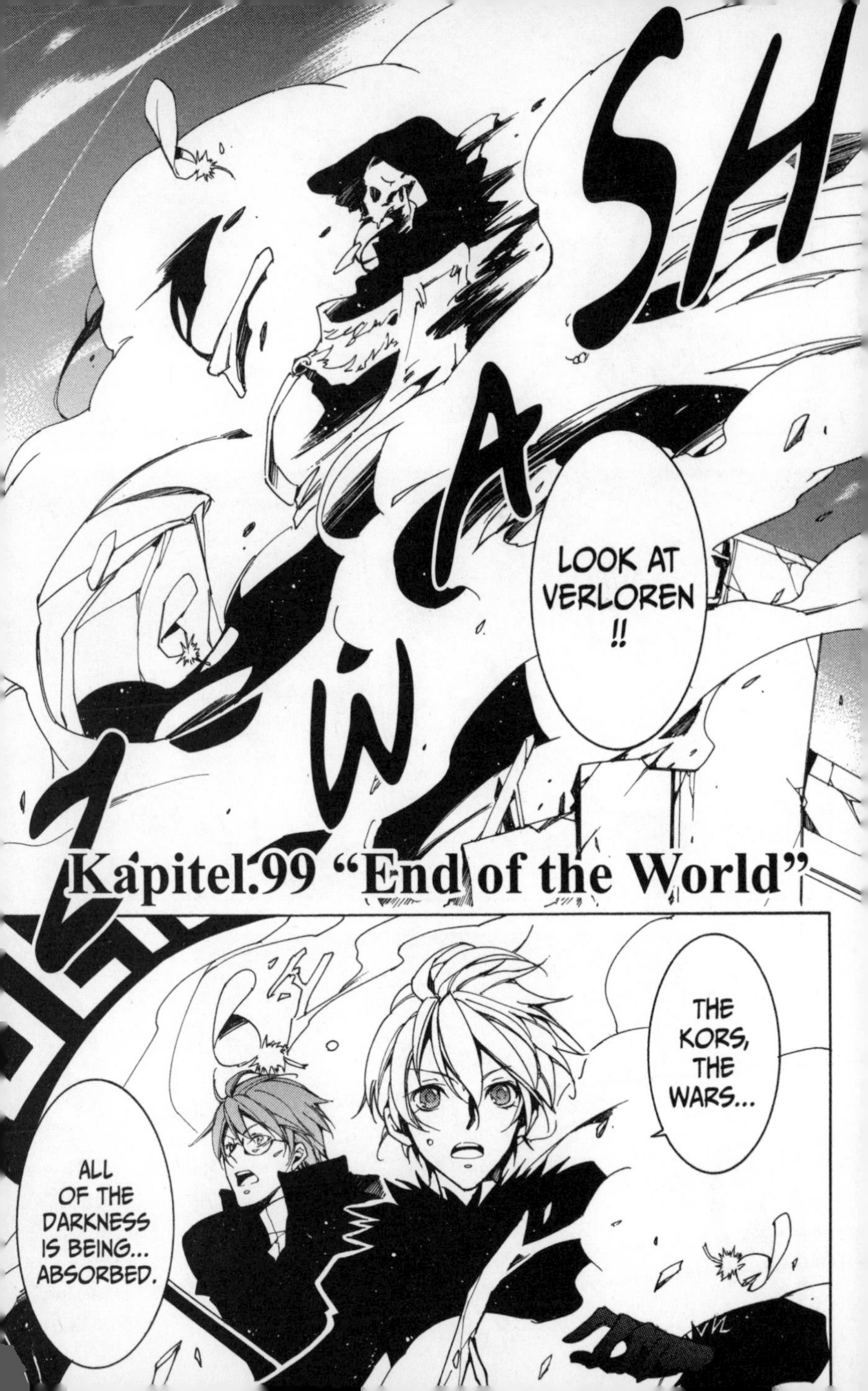
SWASH
LOOK AT VERLOREN !!
Kapitel.99 "End of the World"
THE KORS, THE WARS...
ALL OF THE DARKNESS IS BEING... ABSORBED.

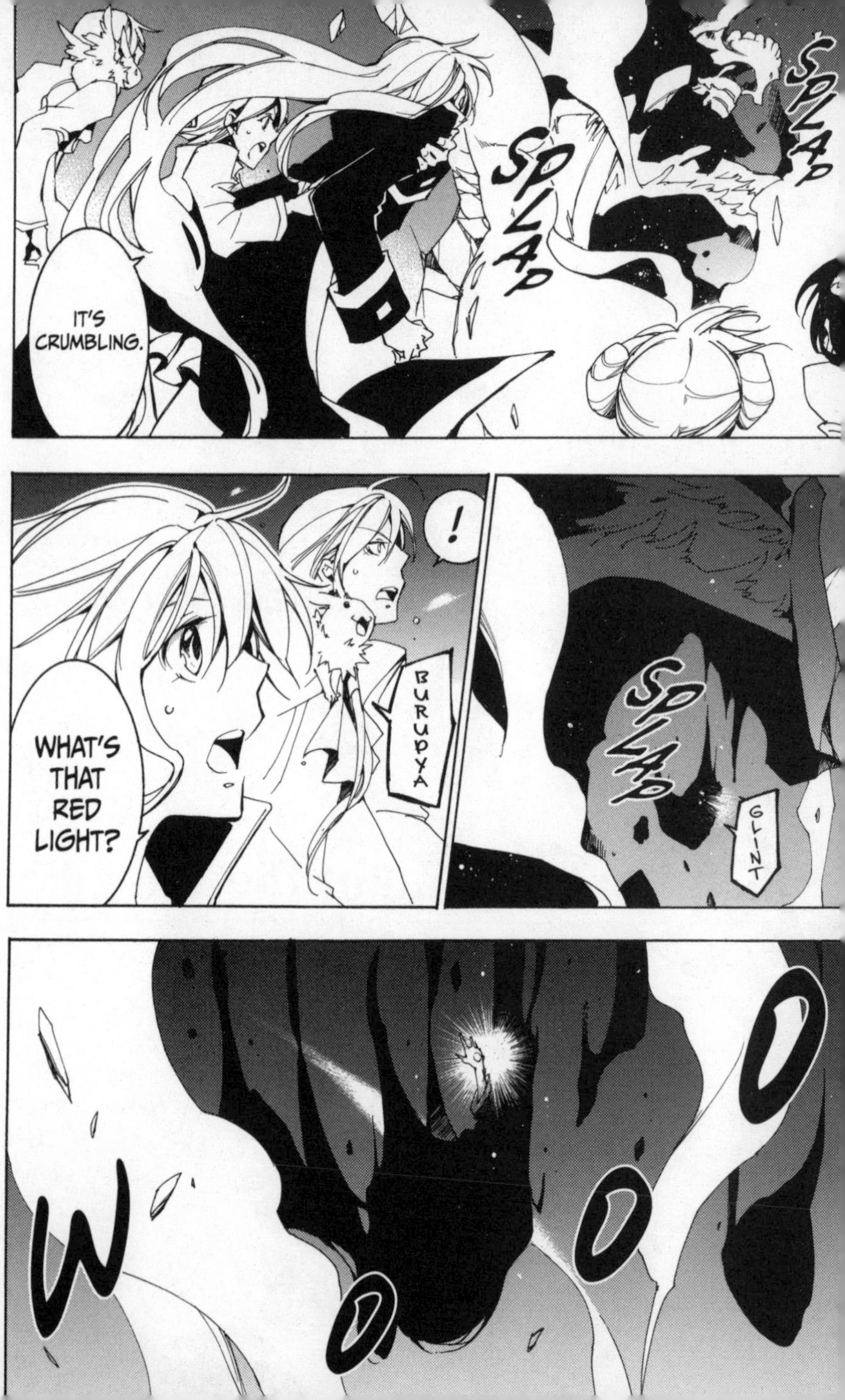
SPLAP
SPLAP
IT'S CRUMBLING.
SPLAP
GLINT
!
BURUDYA
WHAT'S THAT RED LIGHT?
WOOOOO

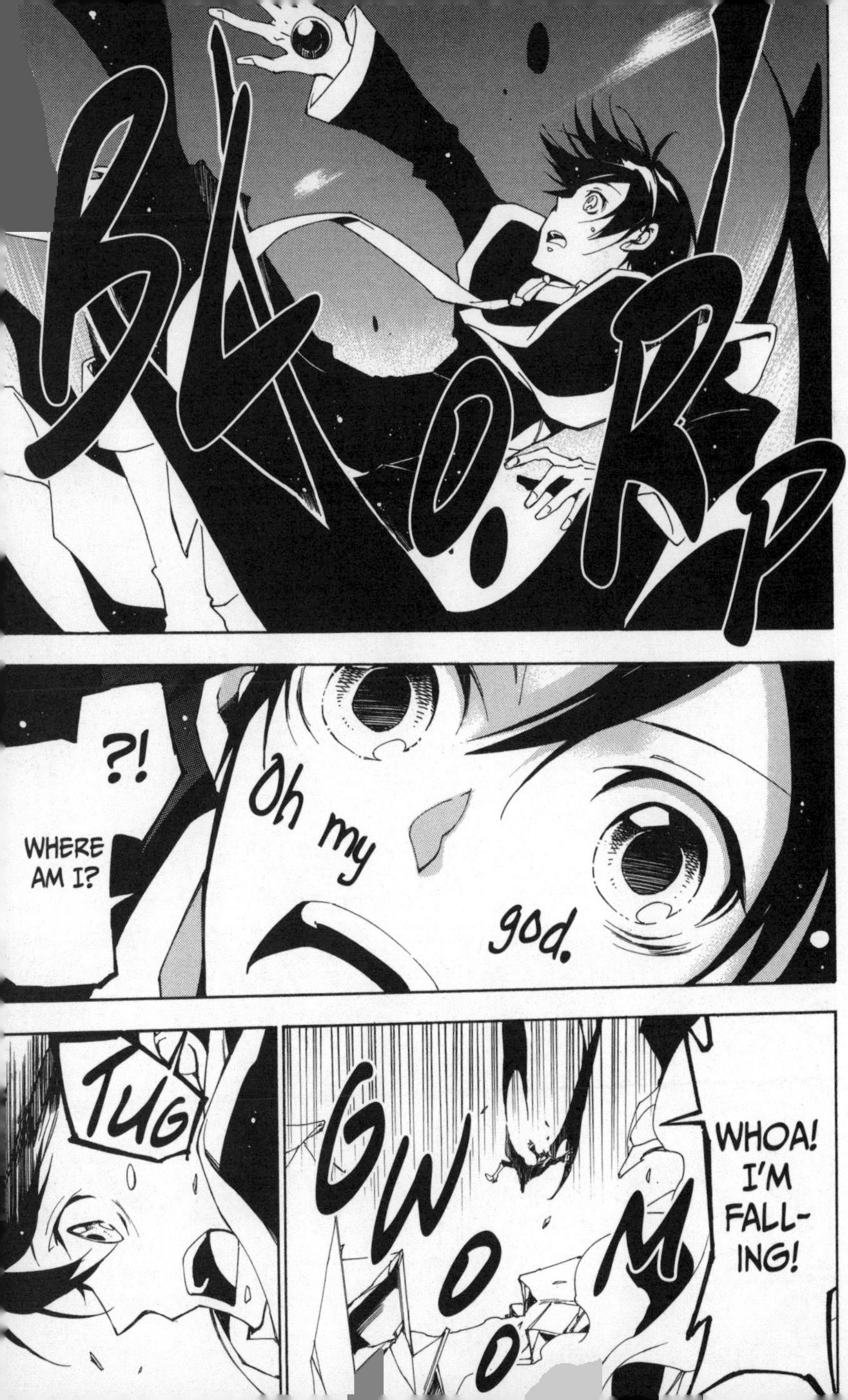
BLORP
Oh my god.
?!
WHERE AM I?
GWOOM
WHOA! I'M FALL-ING!
TUG

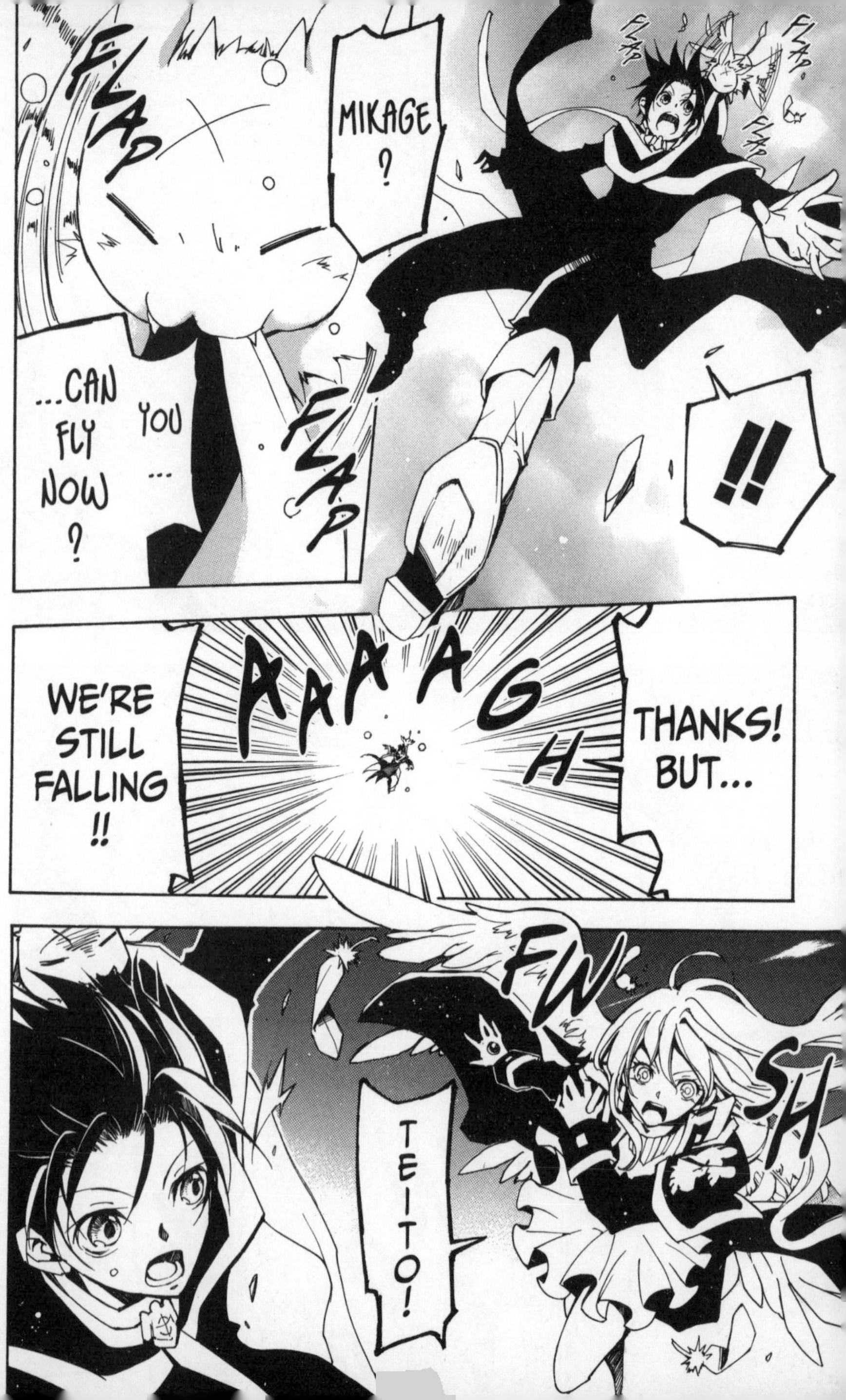
FLAP
FLAP
FLAP
!!
FLAP
MIKAGE?
FLAP
YOU...
...CAN FLY NOW?
THANKS! BUT...
AAAAGH
WE'RE STILL FALLING!!
FWSH
TEITO!

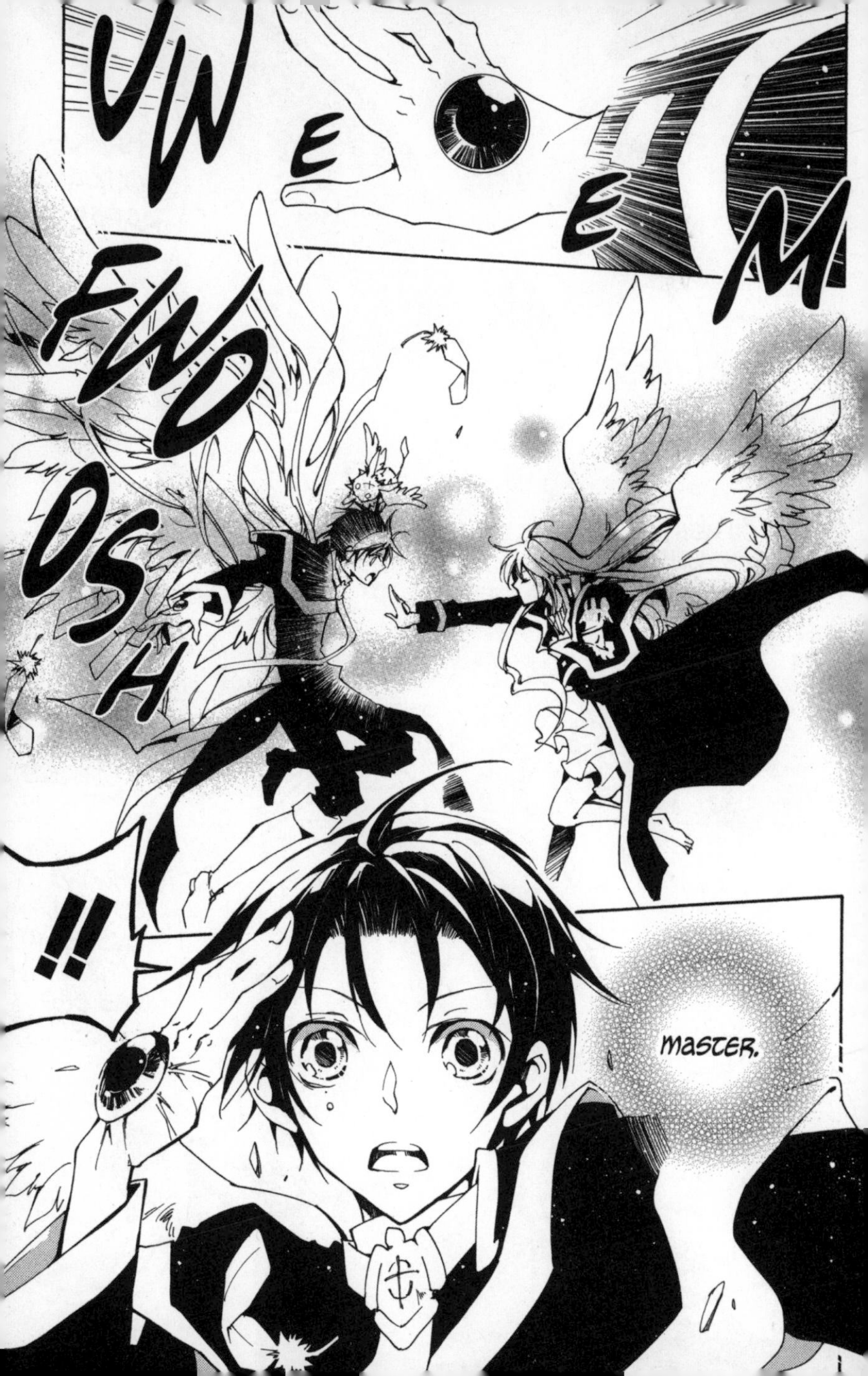
VWEEM
FWOOSH
MASTER.
!!

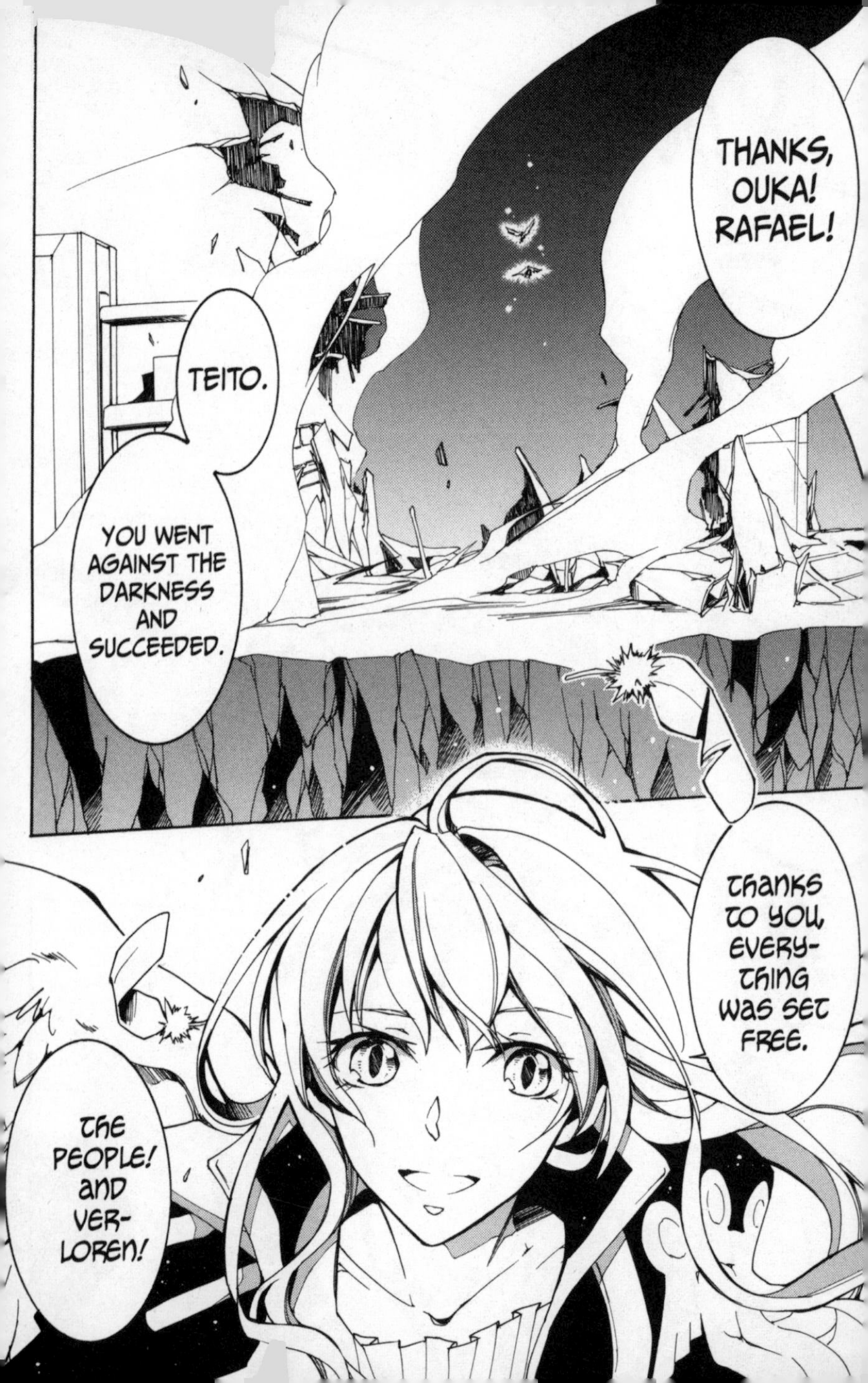
THANKS, OUKA! RAFAEL!
TEITO.
YOU WENT AGAINST THE DARKNESS AND SUCCEEDED.
THANKS TO YOU, EVERY-THING WAS SET FREE.
THE PEOPLE! AND VER-LOREN!

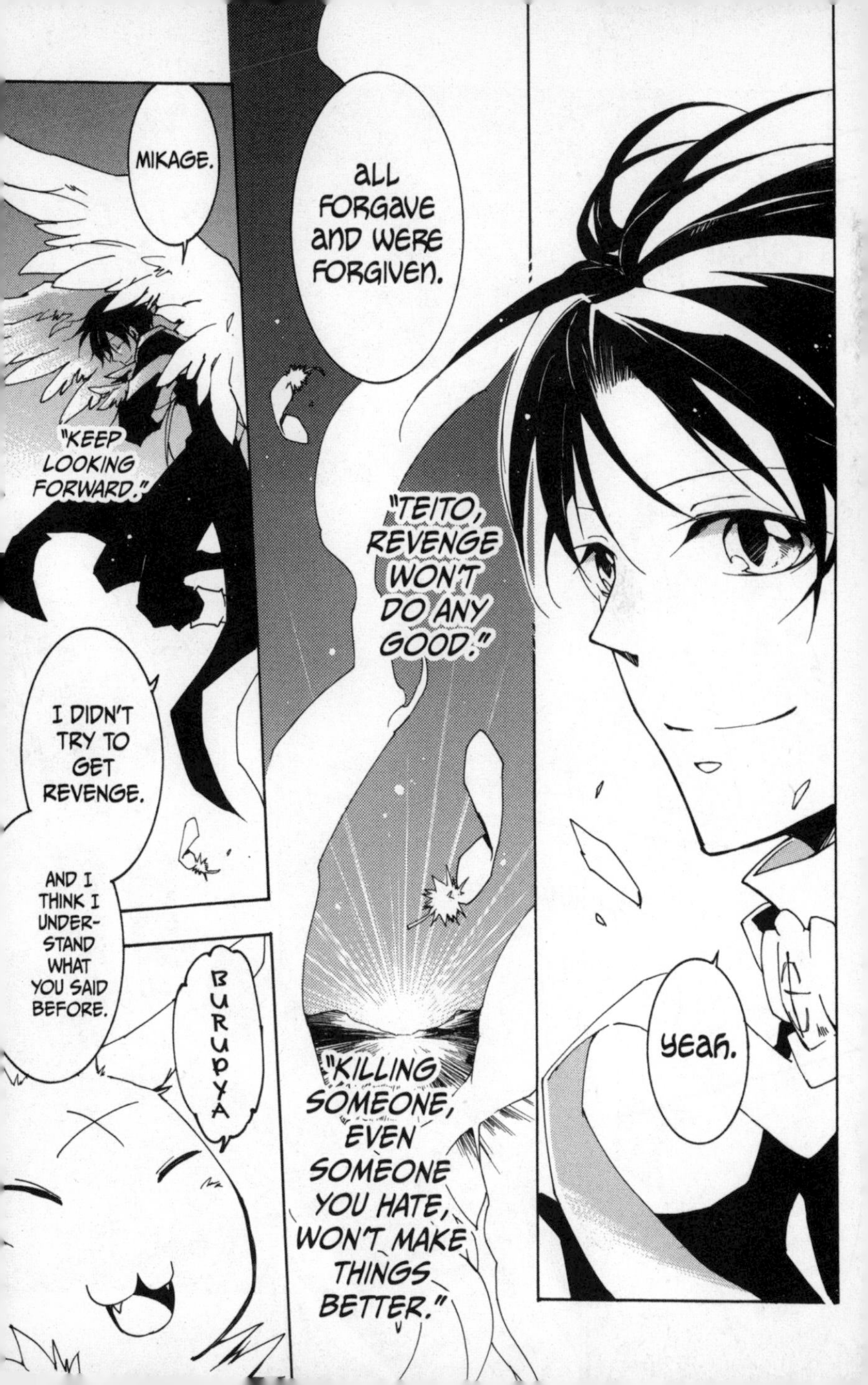
Yeah.
All forgave and were forgiven.
"Teito, revenge won't do any good."
"Killing someone, even someone you hate, won't make things better."
Mikage.
"Keep looking forward."
I didn't try to get revenge.
And I think I understand what you said before.
Burupya

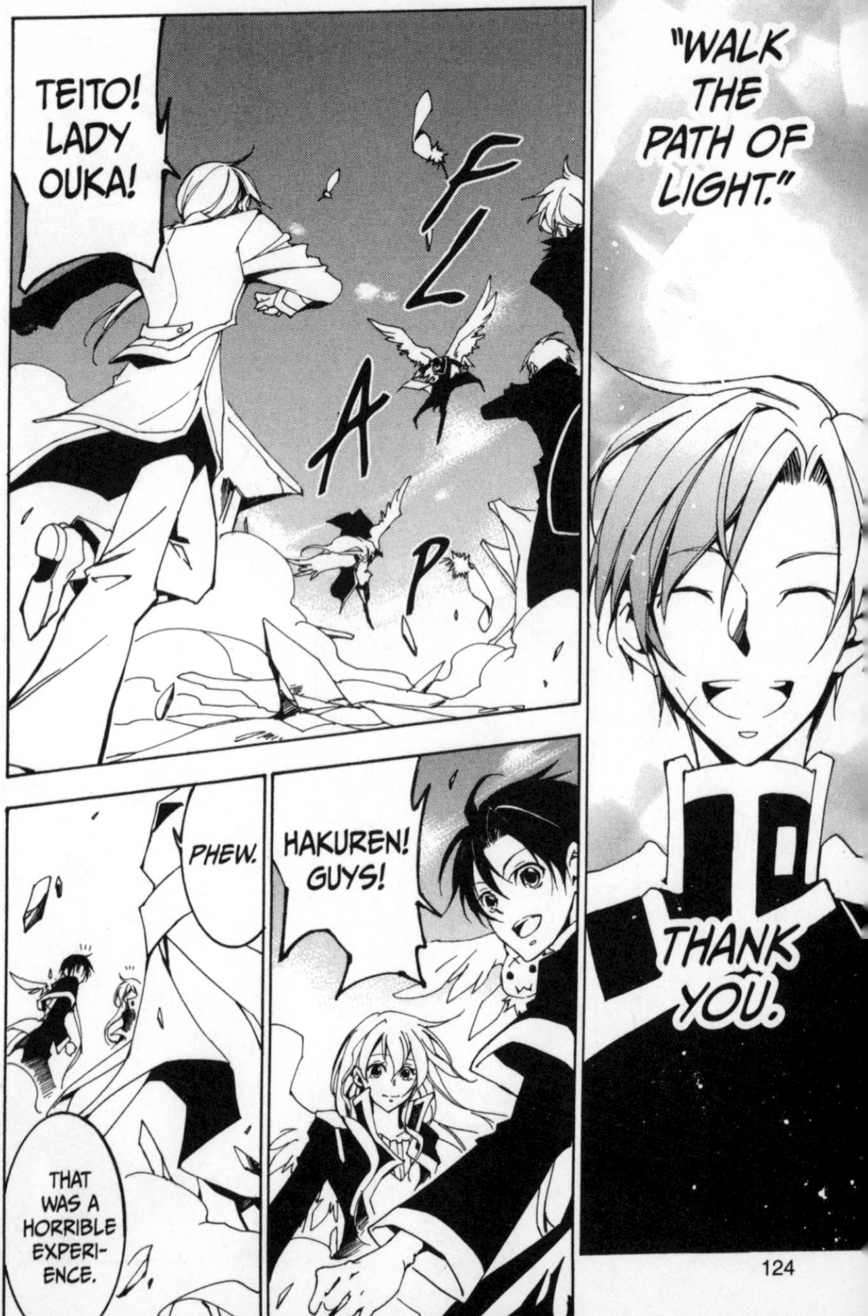
"WALK THE PATH OF LIGHT."
THANK YOU.
TEITO! LADY OUKA!
FLAP
HAKUREN! GUYS!
PHEW.
THAT WAS A HORRIBLE EXPERI-ENCE.

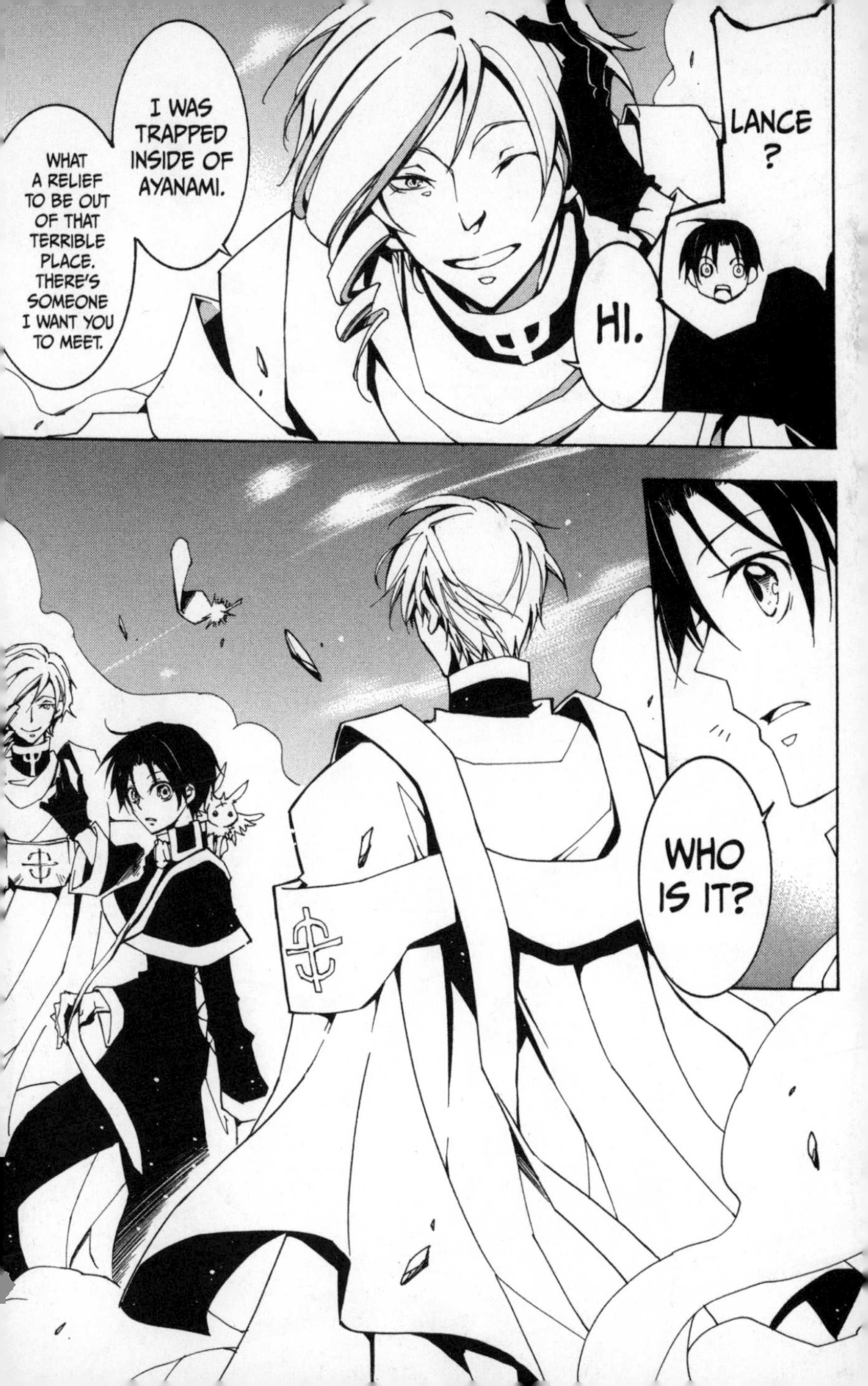
LANCE ?
HI.
I WAS TRAPPED INSIDE OF AYANAMI.
WHAT A RELIEF TO BE OUT OF THAT TERRIBLE PLACE. THERE'S SOMEONE I WANT YOU TO MEET.
WHO IS IT?

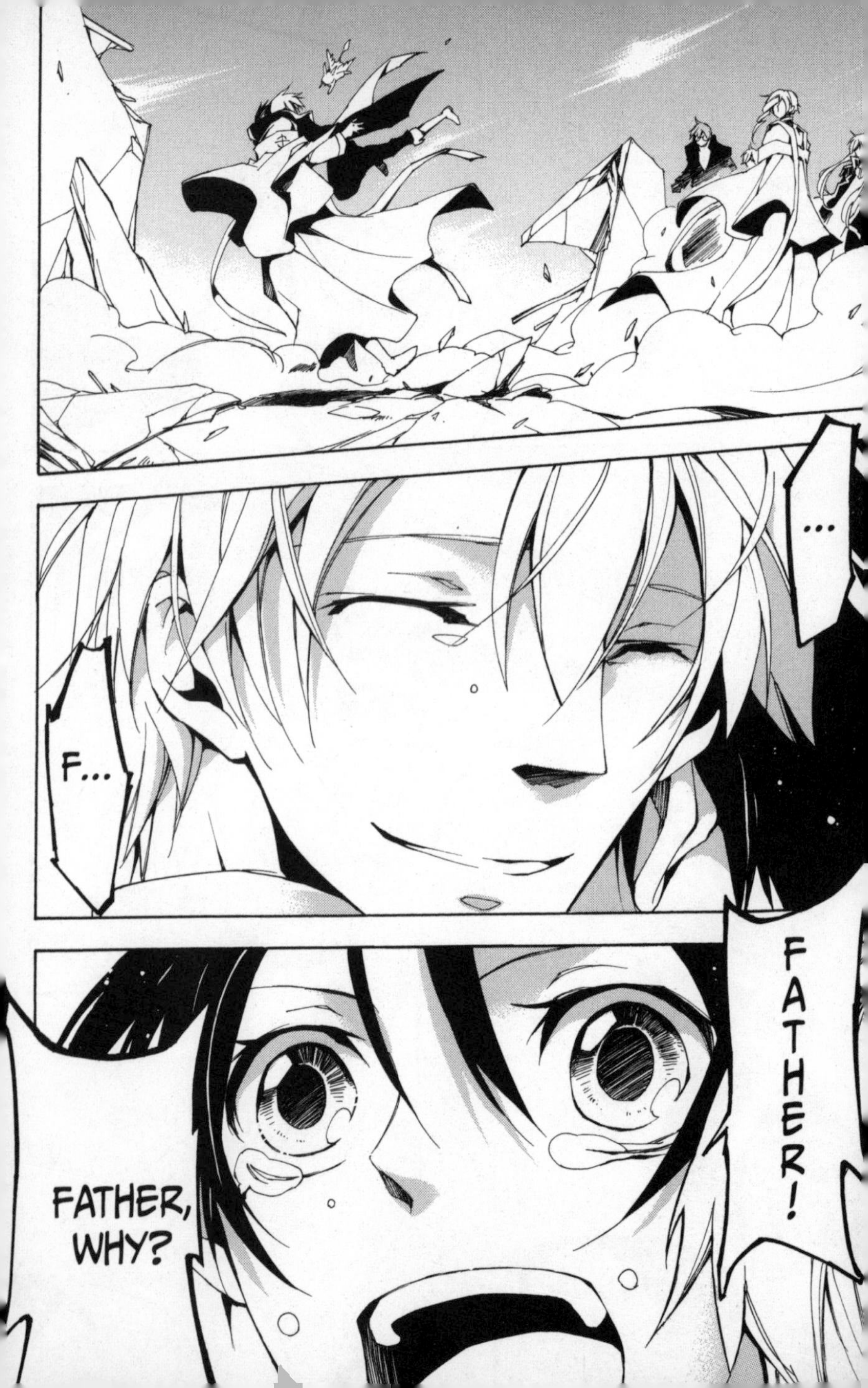
...
F...
FATHER!
FATHER, WHY?

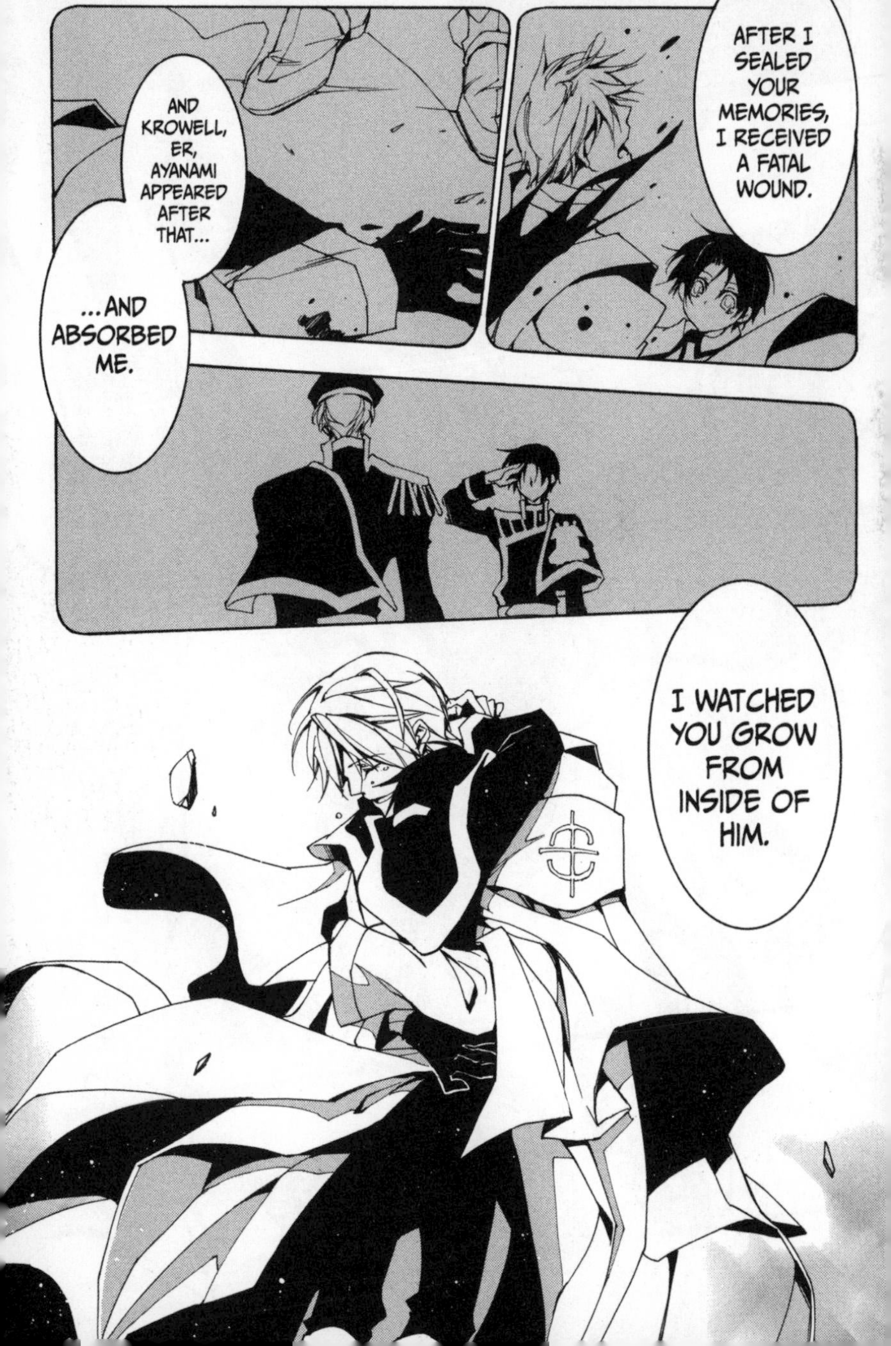
AFTER I SEALED YOUR MEMORIES, I RECEIVED A FATAL WOUND.
AND KROWELL, ER, AYANAMI APPEARED AFTER THAT...
...AND ABSORBED ME.
I WATCHED YOU GROW FROM INSIDE OF HIM.

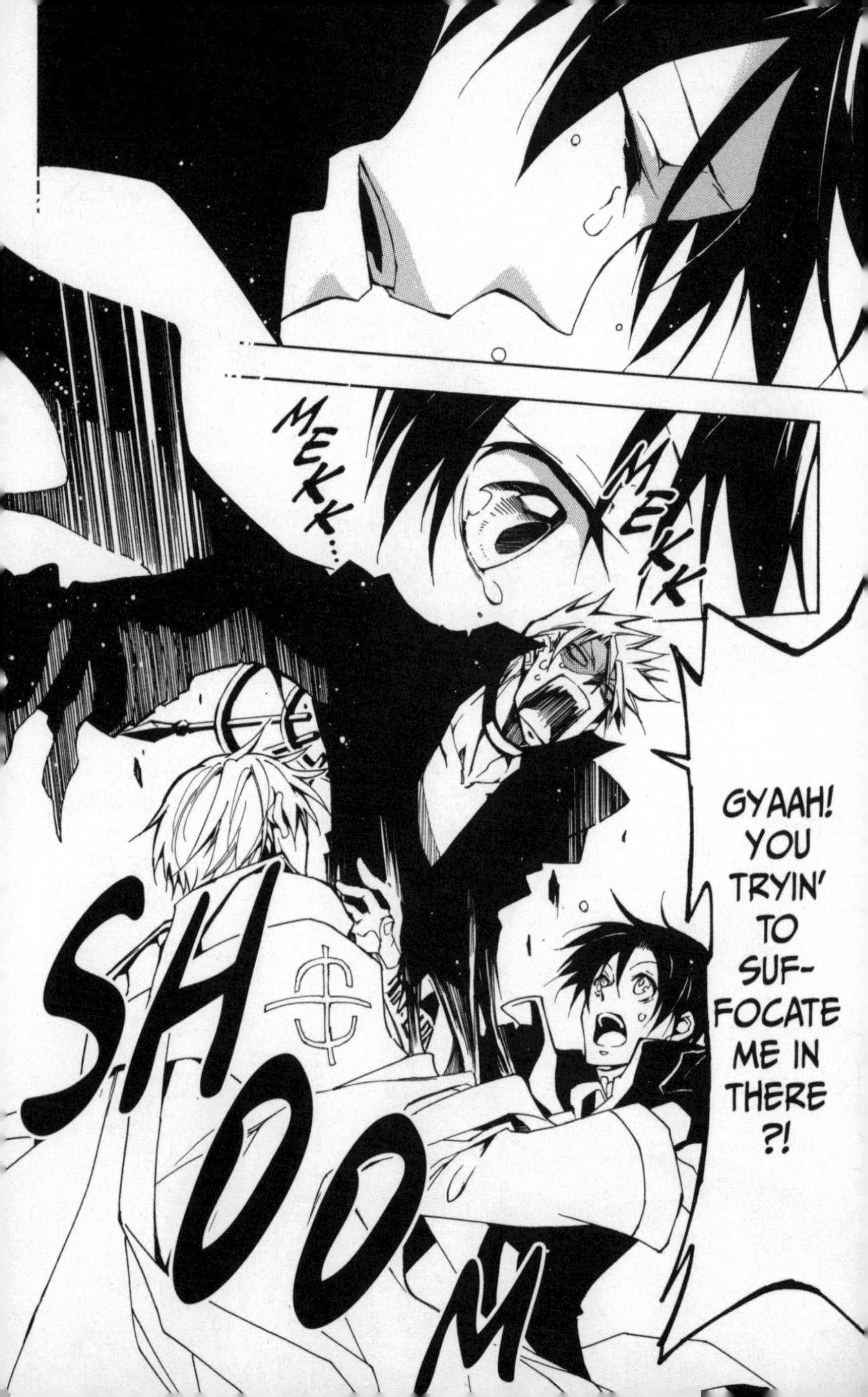
MEKK
MEKK...
SHOOM
GYAAH! YOU TRYIN' TO SUF-FOCATE ME IN THERE?!

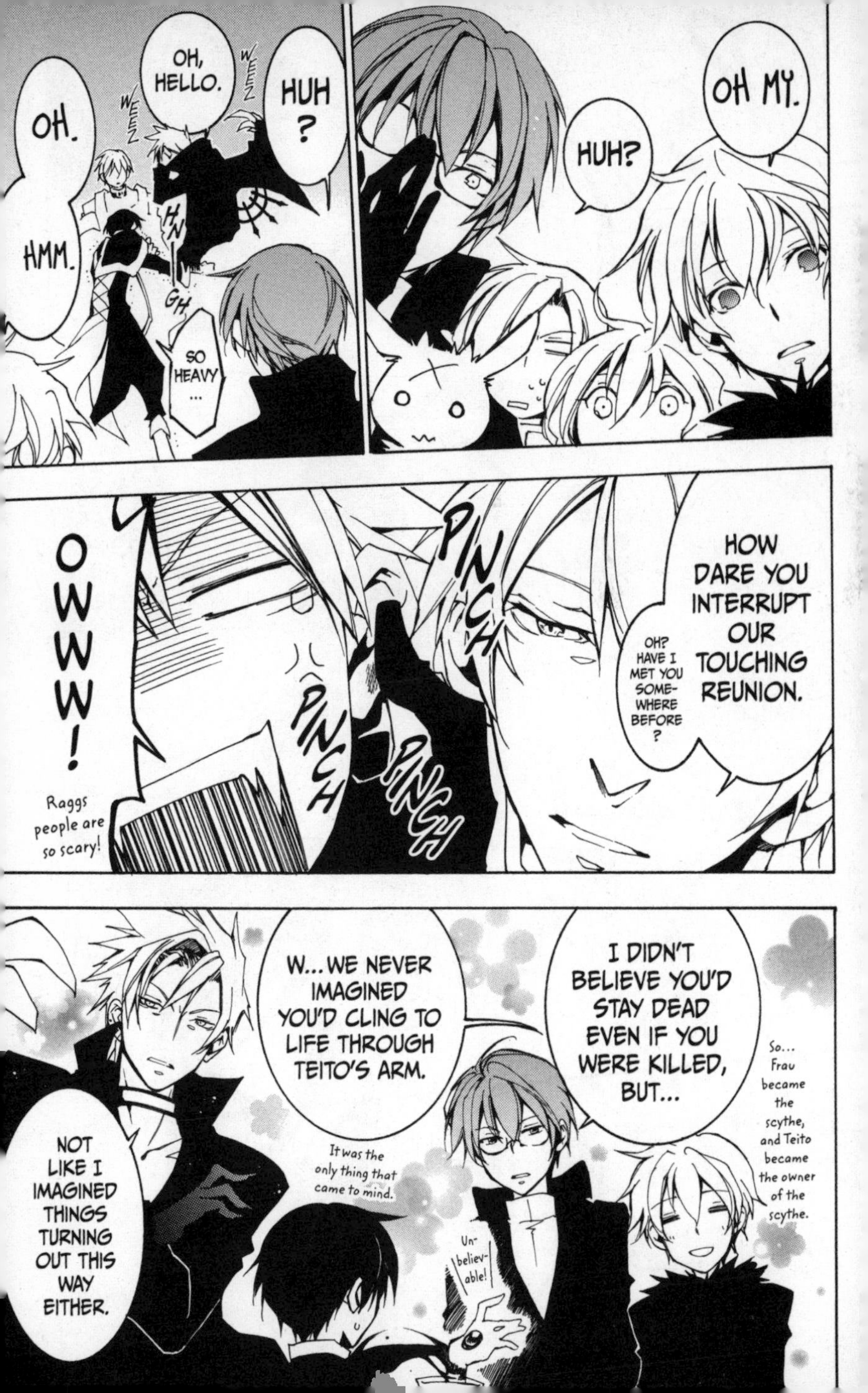
OH MY.
HUH?
HUH ?
OH, HELLO.
WEEZ
WEEZ
OH.
HMM.
HN
GH
SO HEAVY ...
HOW DARE YOU INTERRUPT OUR TOUCHING REUNION.
OH? HAVE I MET YOU SOME-WHERE BEFORE ?
PINCH
PINCH
PINCH
OWWWW!
Raggs people are so scary!
I DIDN'T BELIEVE YOU'D STAY DEAD EVEN IF YOU WERE KILLED, BUT...
So... Frau became the scythe, and Teito became the owner of the scythe.
W...WE NEVER IMAGINED YOU'D CLING TO LIFE THROUGH TEITO'S ARM.
It was the only thing that came to mind.
Unbeliev-able!
NOT LIKE I IMAGINED THINGS TURNING OUT THIS WAY EITHER.

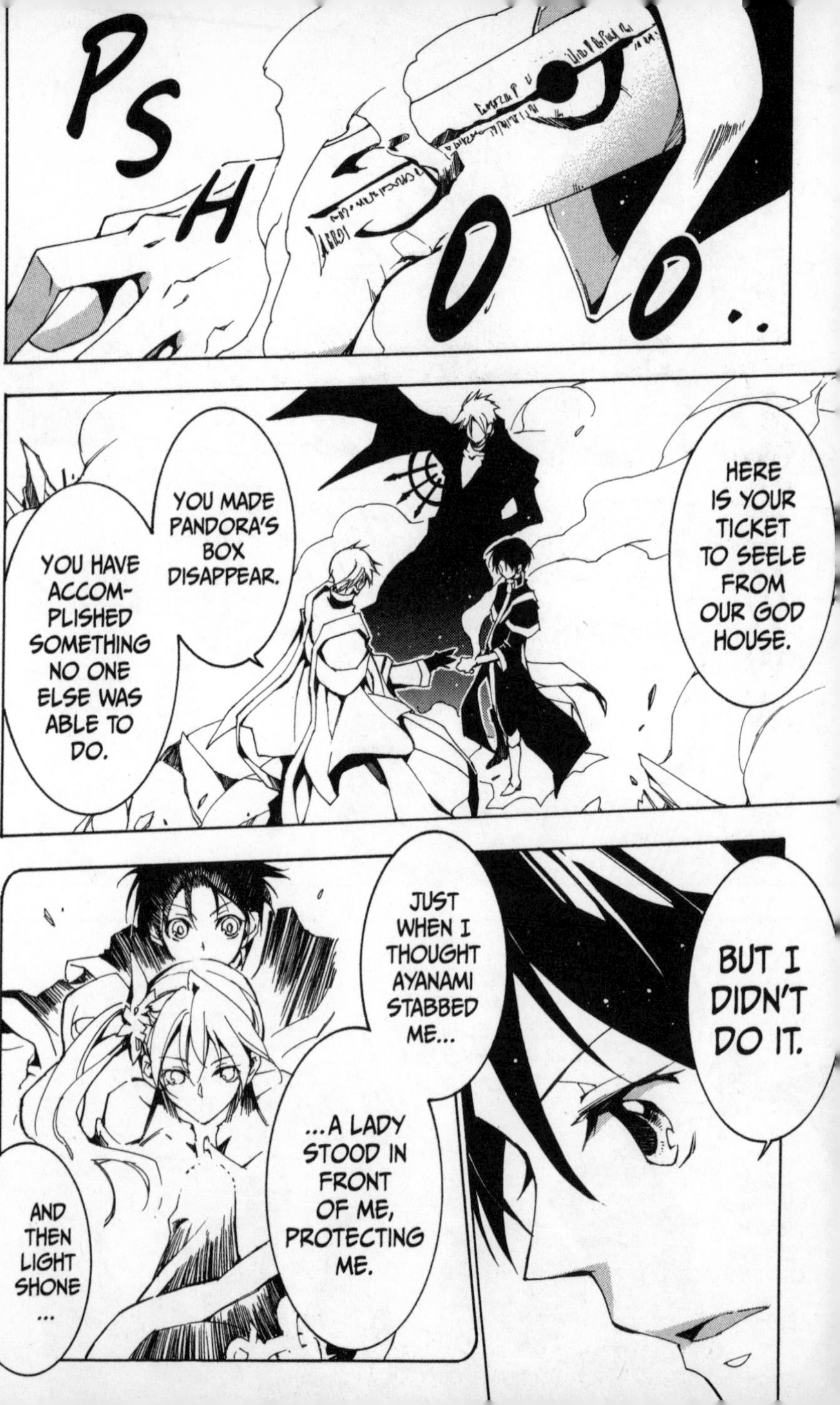
PSHOOO..
HERE IS YOUR TICKET TO SEELE FROM OUR GOD HOUSE.
YOU MADE PANDORA'S BOX DISAPPEAR.
YOU HAVE ACCOMPLISHED SOMETHING NO ONE ELSE WAS ABLE TO DO.
BUT I DIDN'T DO IT.
JUST WHEN I THOUGHT AYANAMI STABBED ME...
...A LADY STOOD IN FRONT OF ME, PROTECTING ME.
AND THEN LIGHT SHONE...

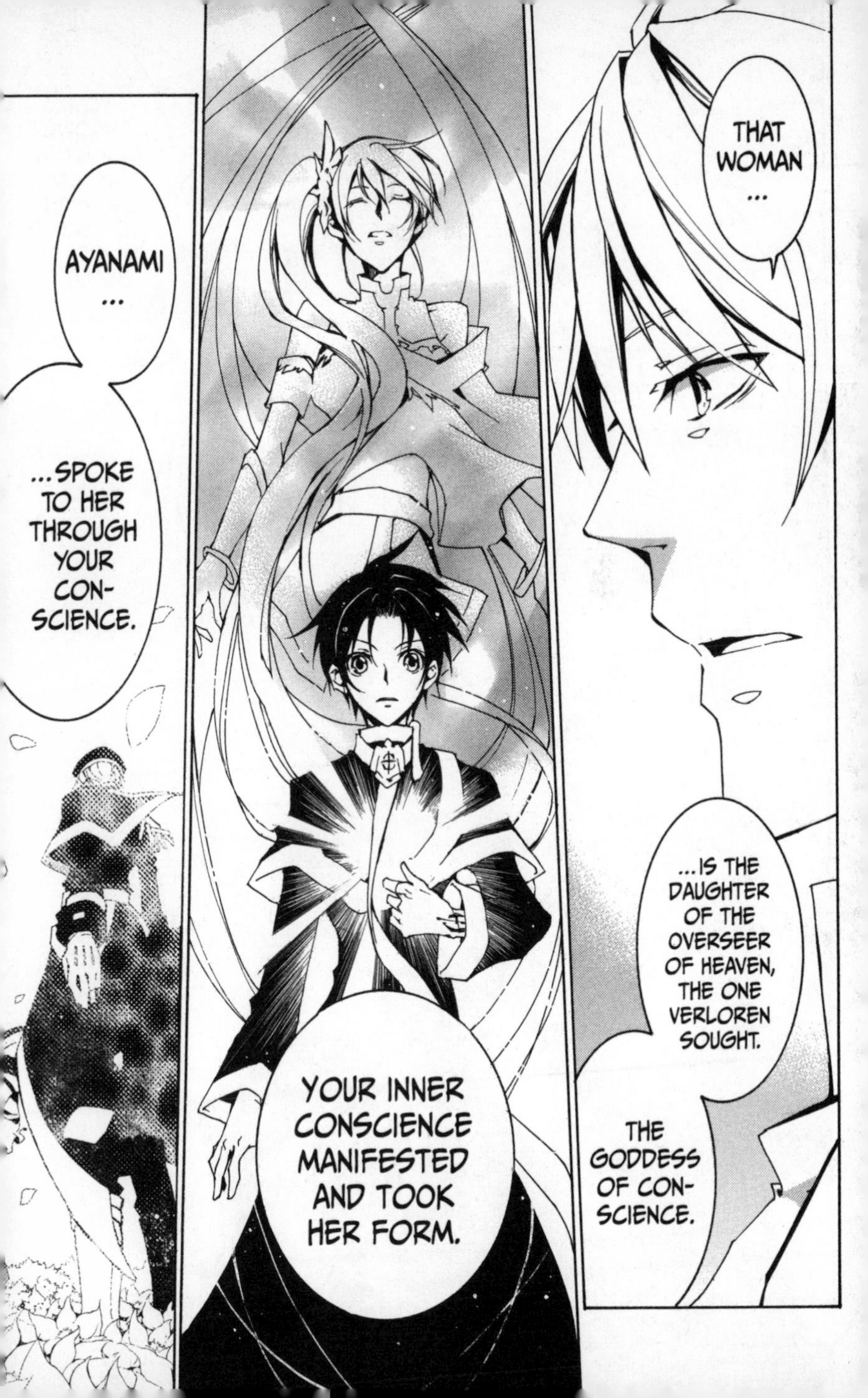
THAT WOMAN ...
...IS THE DAUGHTER OF THE OVERSEER OF HEAVEN, THE ONE VERLOREN SOUGHT.
THE GODDESS OF CON- SCIENCE.
YOUR INNER CONSCIENCE MANIFESTED AND TOOK HER FORM.
AYANAMI ...
...SPOKE TO HER THROUGH YOUR CON- SCIENCE.

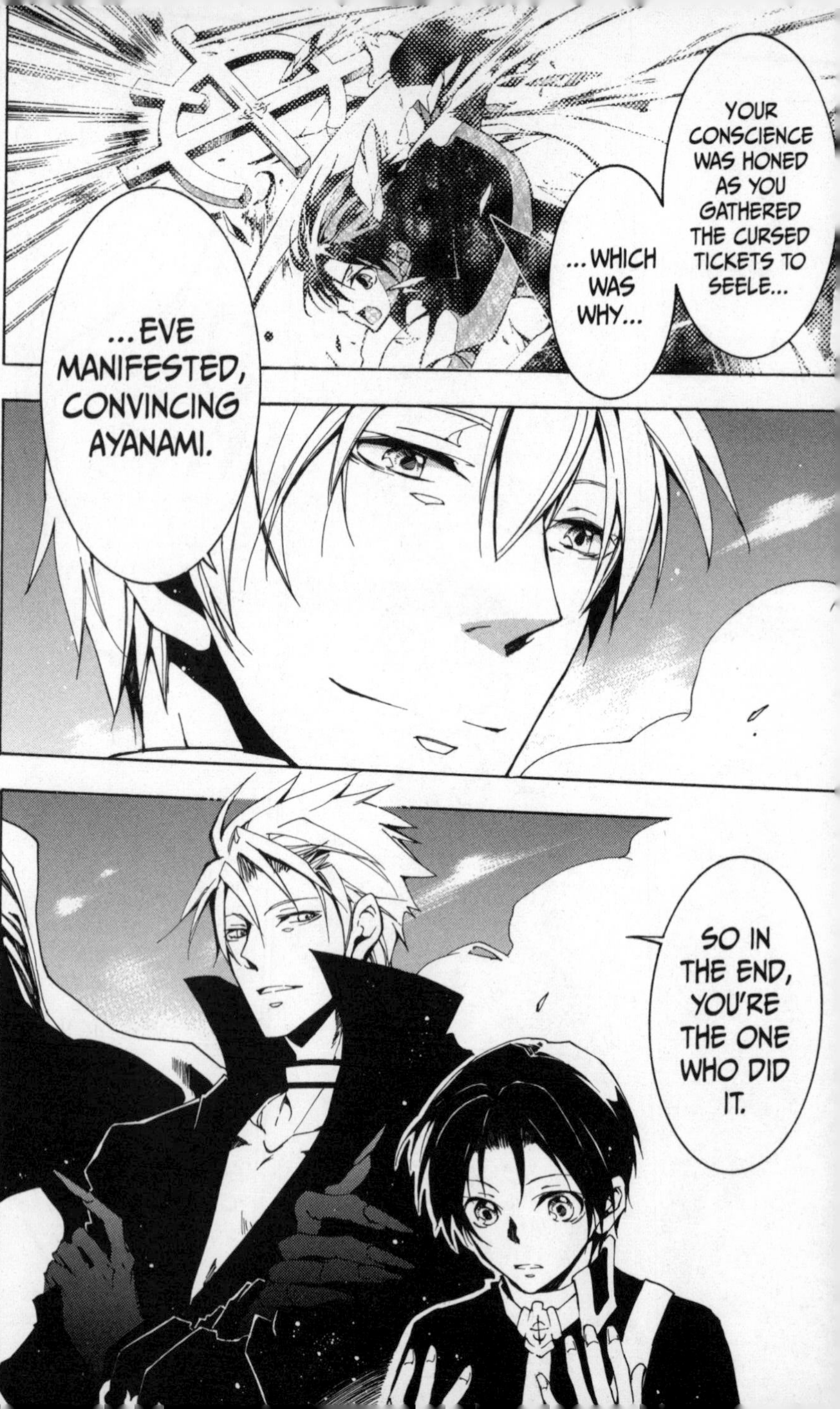
YOUR CONSCIENCE WAS HONED AS YOU GATHERED THE CURSED TICKETS TO SEELE...
...WHICH WAS WHY...
...EVE MANIFESTED, CONVINCING AYANAMI.
SO IN THE END, YOU'RE THE ONE WHO DID IT.

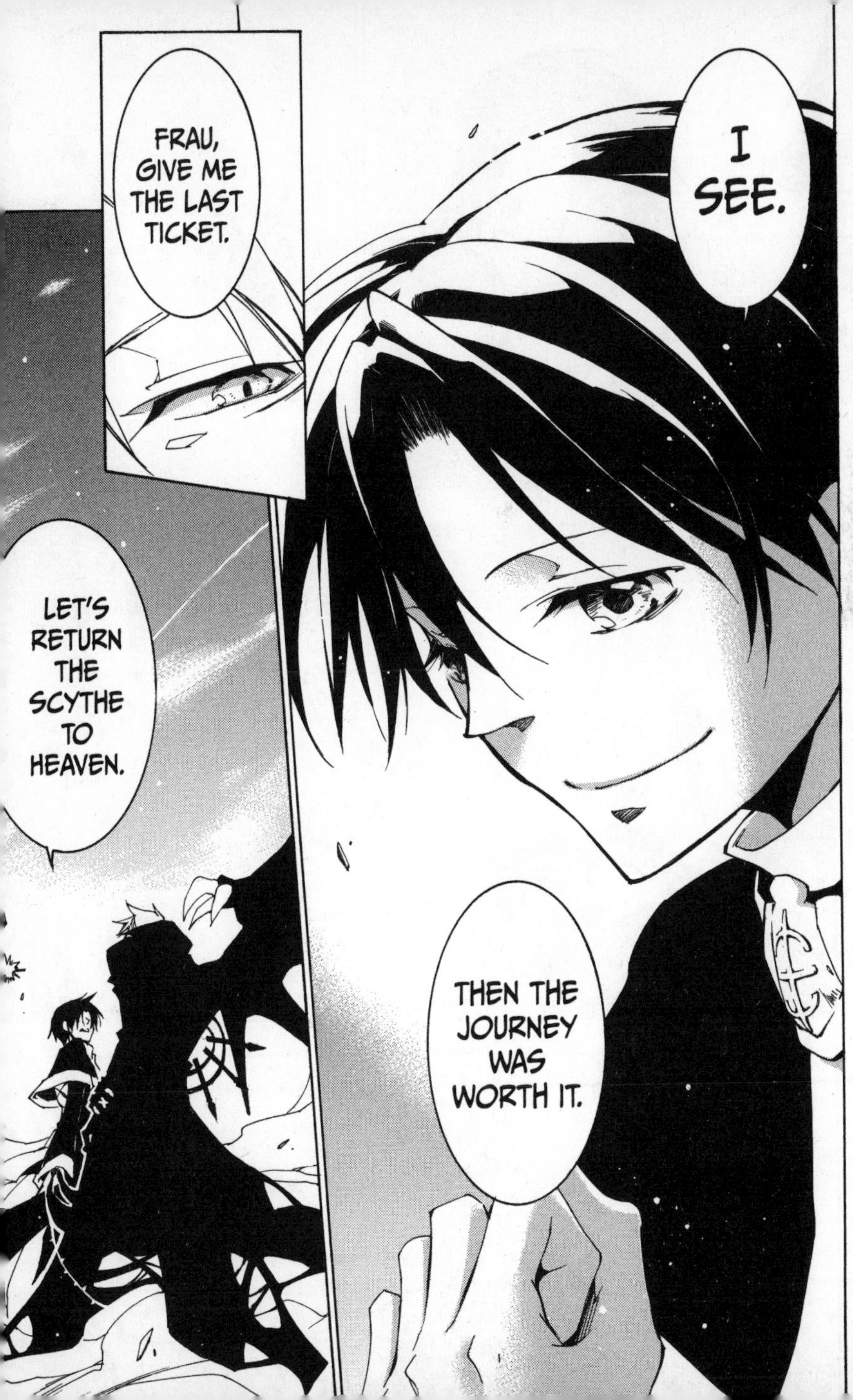
I SEE.
THEN THE JOURNEY WAS WORTH IT.
FRAU, GIVE ME THE LAST TICKET.
LET'S RETURN THE SCYTHE TO HEAVEN.

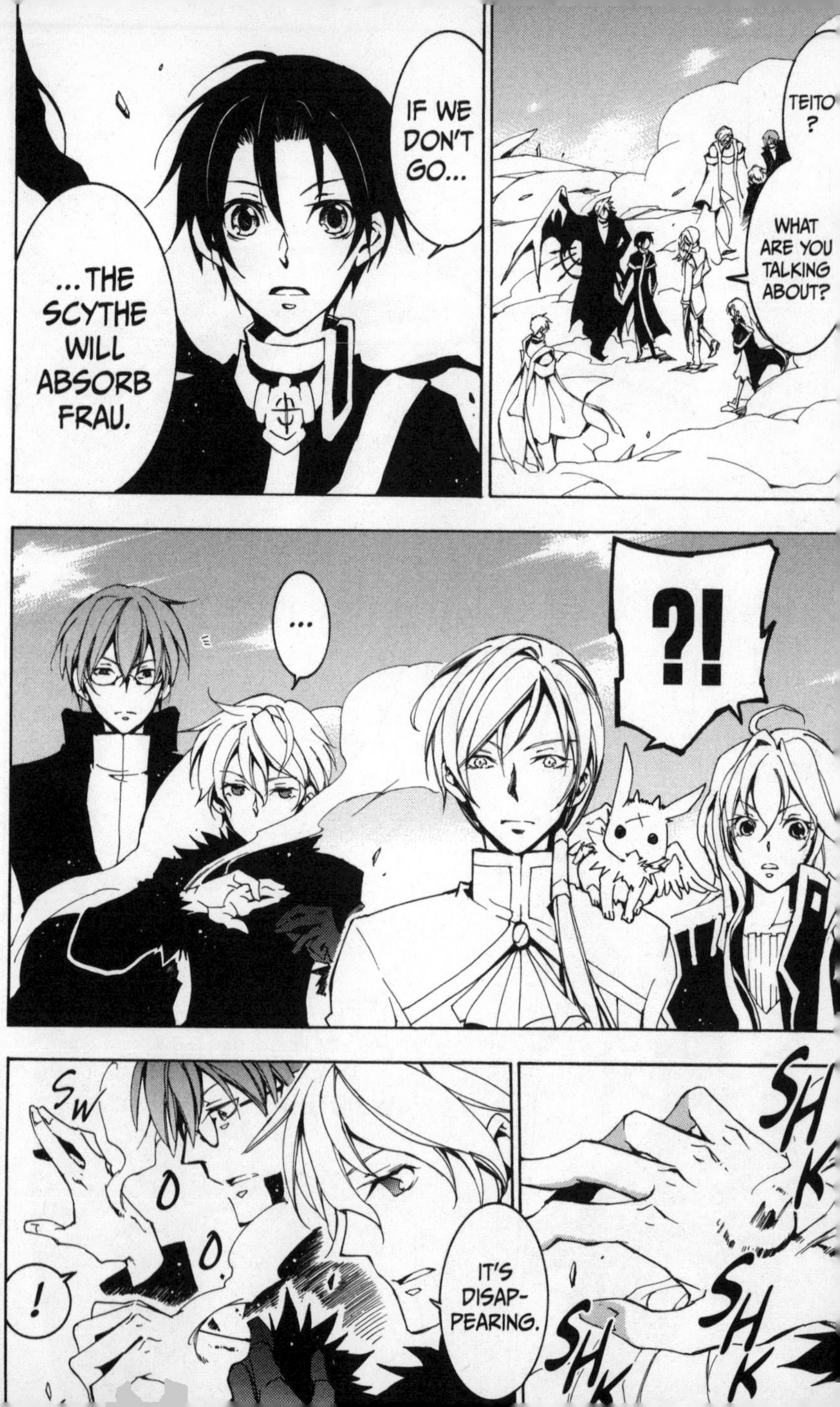
TEITO?
WHAT ARE YOU TALKING ABOUT?
IF WE DON'T GO...
...THE SCYTHE WILL ABSORB FRAU.
?!
...
SHK
SHK
SHK
IT'S DISAP-PEARING.
SWOOO
!

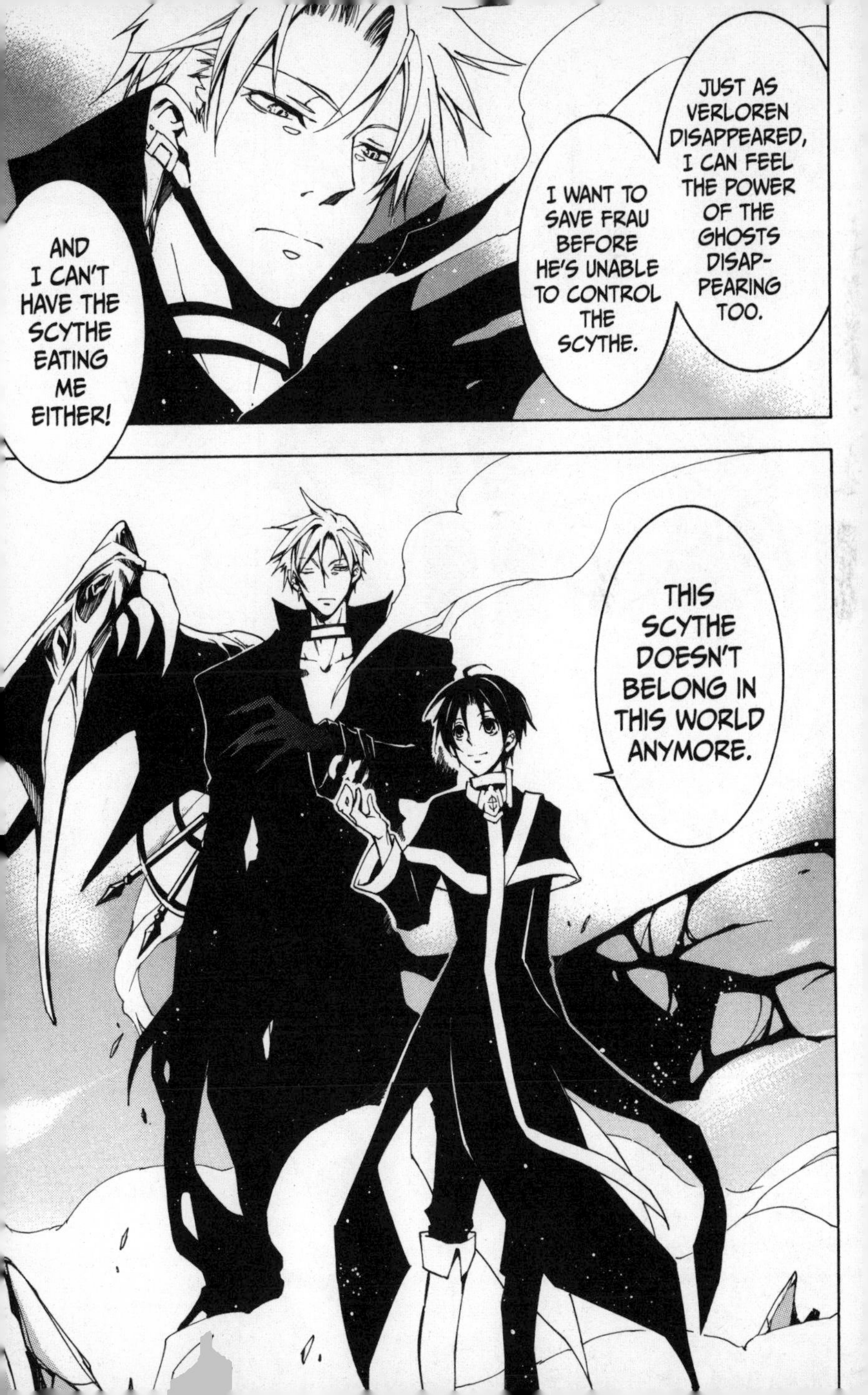
JUST AS VERLOREN DISAPPEARED, I CAN FEEL THE POWER OF THE GHOSTS DISAP-PEARING TOO.
I WANT TO SAVE FRAU BEFORE HE'S UNABLE TO CONTROL THE SCYTHE.
AND I CAN'T HAVE THE SCYTHE EATING ME EITHER!
THIS SCYTHE DOESN'T BELONG IN THIS WORLD ANYMORE.

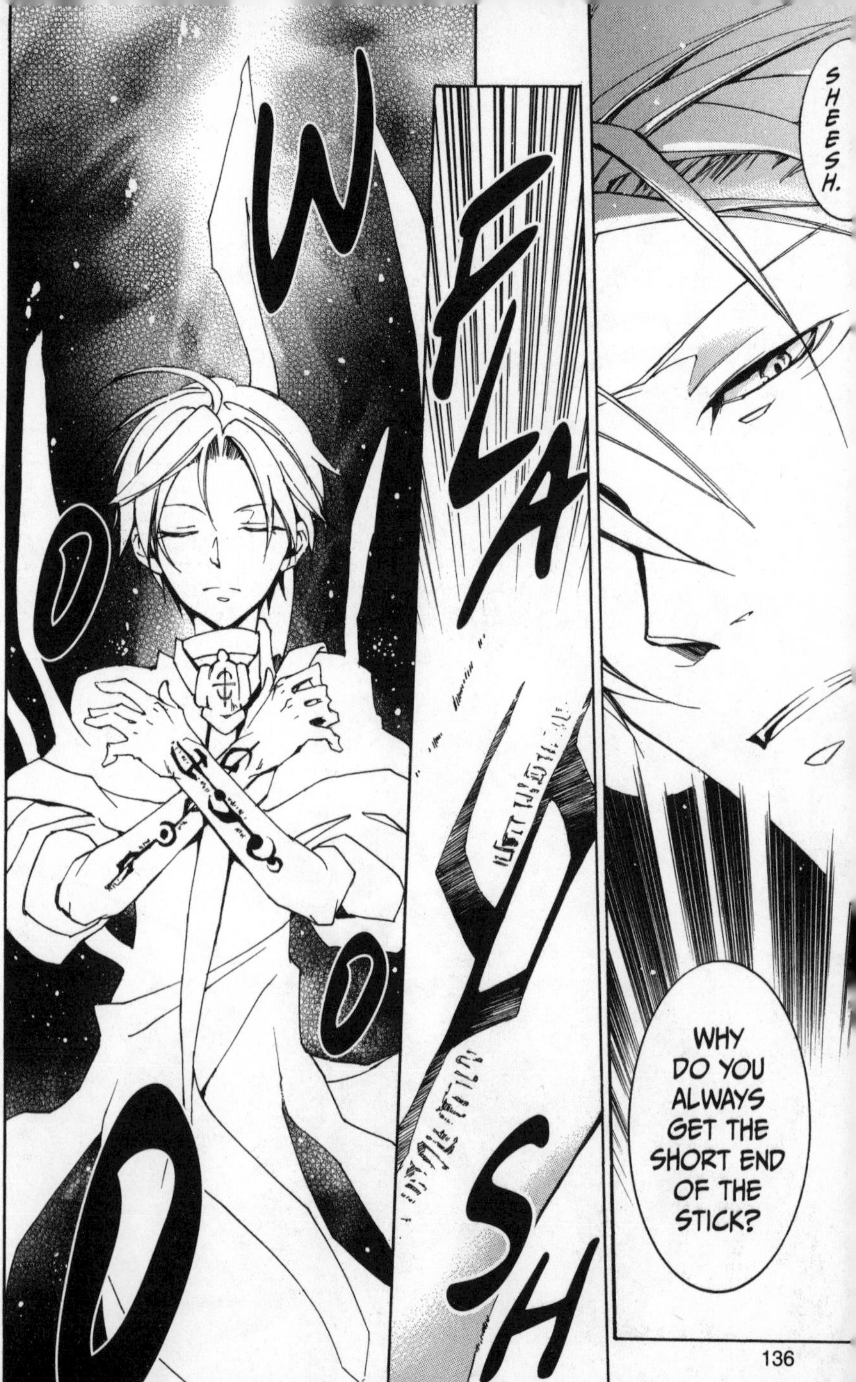
SHEESH.
WHY DO YOU ALWAYS GET THE SHORT END OF THE STICK?
WHOOSH
WHOOO

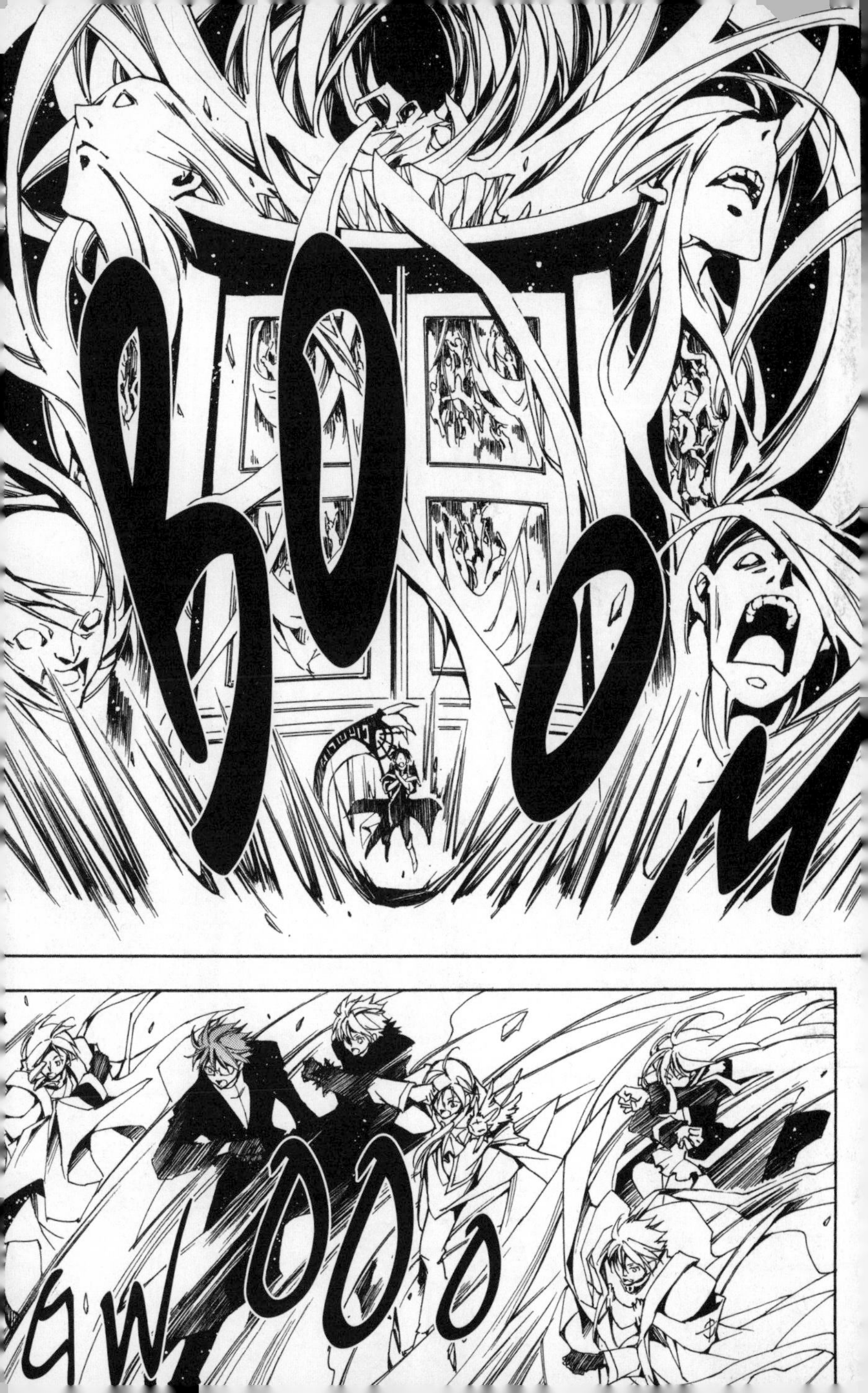
BOOOM
GWOOOO

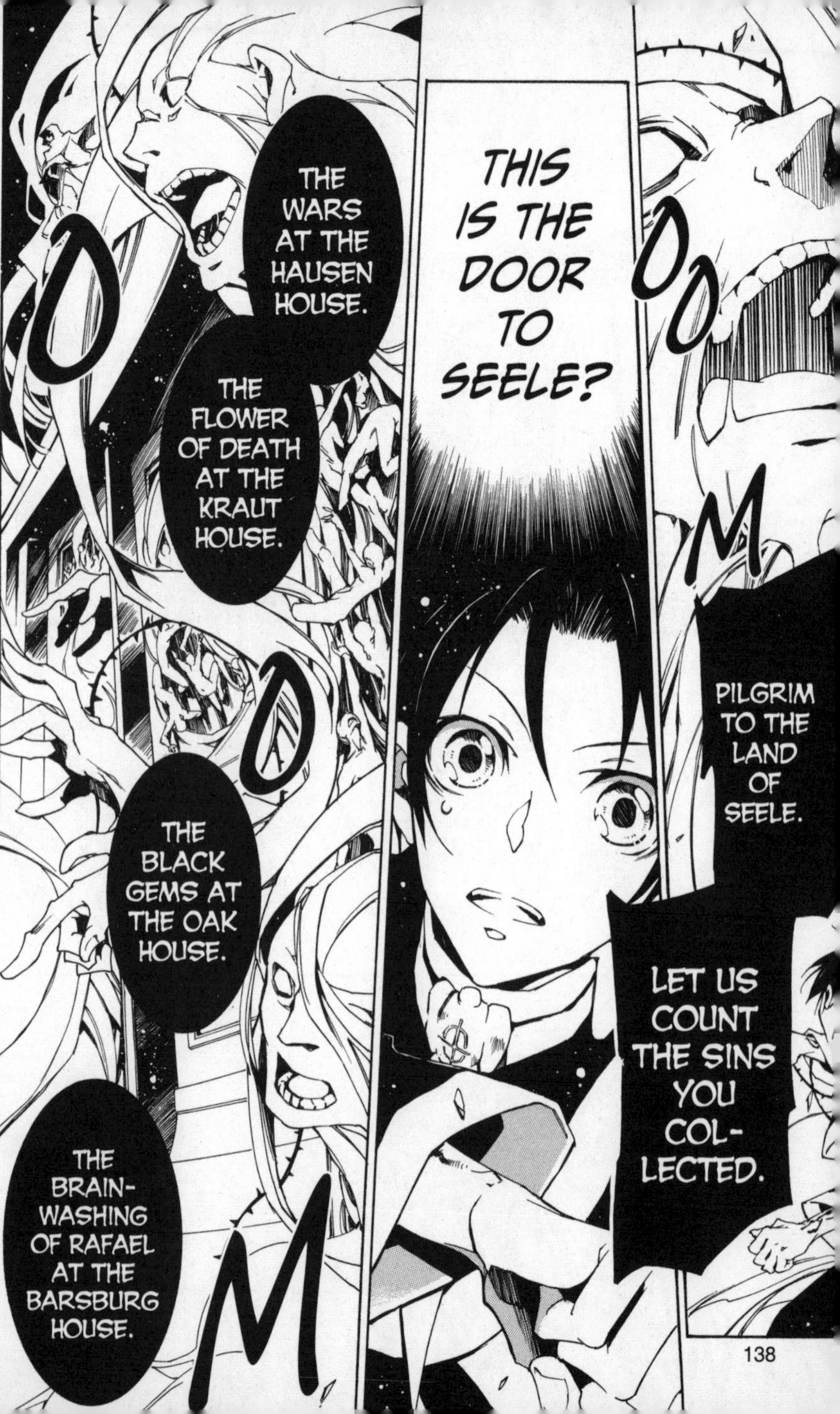
DOOM
PILGRIM TO THE LAND OF SEELE.
LET US COUNT THE SINS YOU COL-LECTED.
THIS IS THE DOOR TO SEELE?
THE WARS AT THE HAUSEN HOUSE.
THE FLOWER OF DEATH AT THE KRAUT HOUSE.
THE BLACK GEMS AT THE OAK HOUSE.
THE BRAIN-WASHING OF RAFAEL AT THE BARSBURG HOUSE.
DOOM

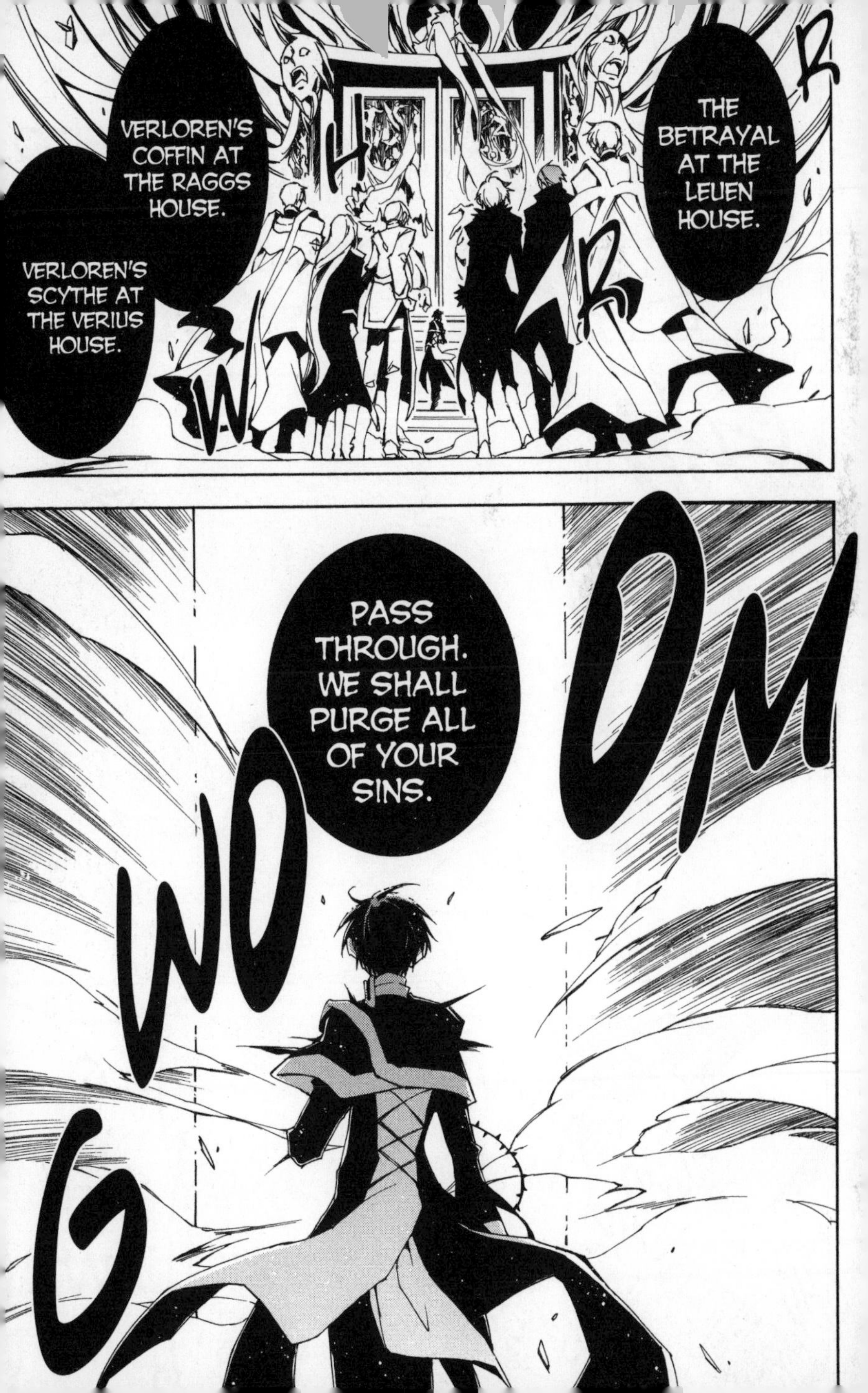
THE BETRAYAL AT THE LEUEN HOUSE.
VERLOREN'S COFFIN AT THE RAGGS HOUSE.
VERLOREN'S SCYTHE AT THE VERIUS HOUSE.
PASS THROUGH. WE SHALL PURGE ALL OF YOUR SINS.
GWOOM

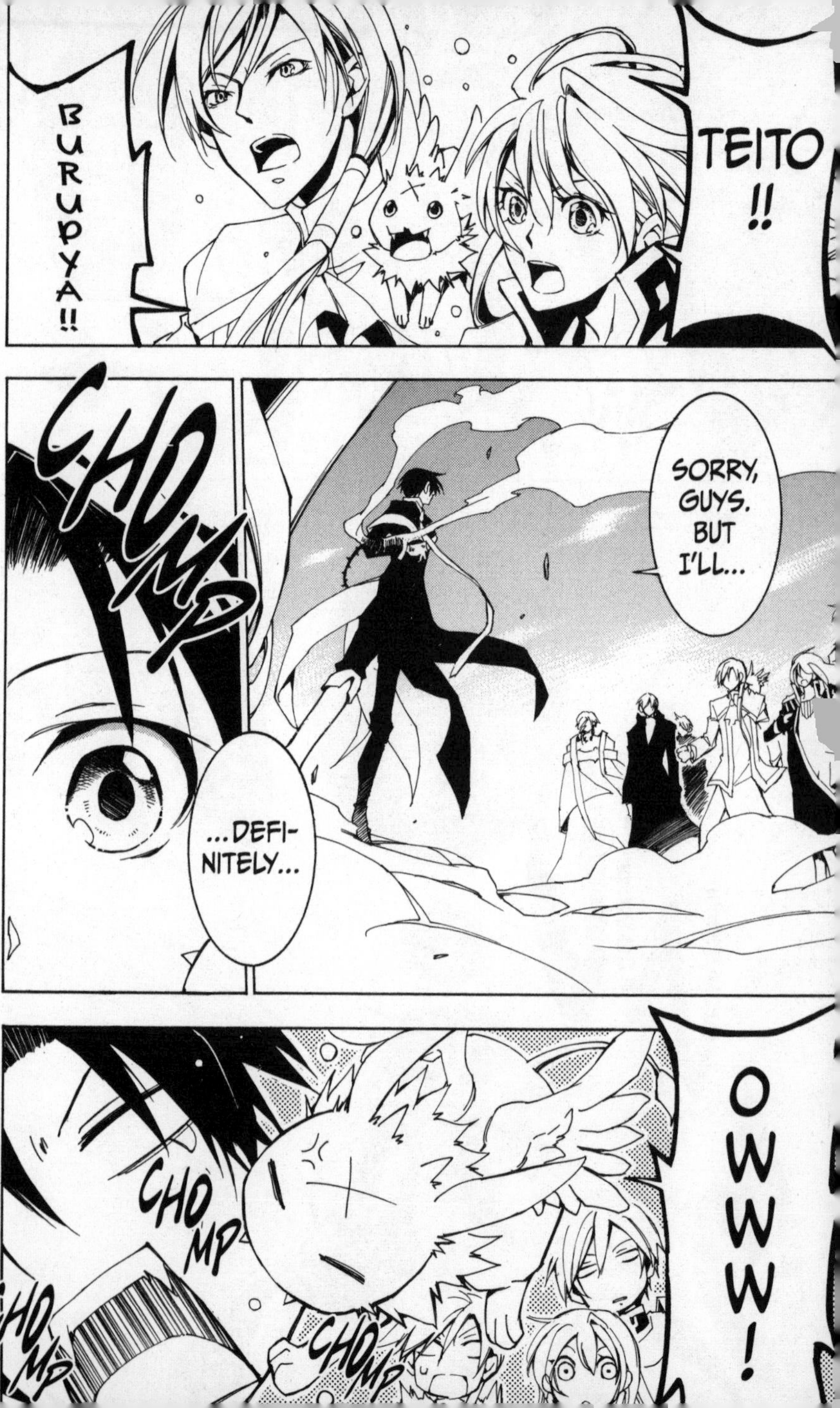
TEITO!!
BURUPYA!!
SORRY, GUYS. BUT I'LL...
...DEFI-NITELY...
CHOMP
OWWW!
CHOMP
CHOMP
CHOMP
CHOMP

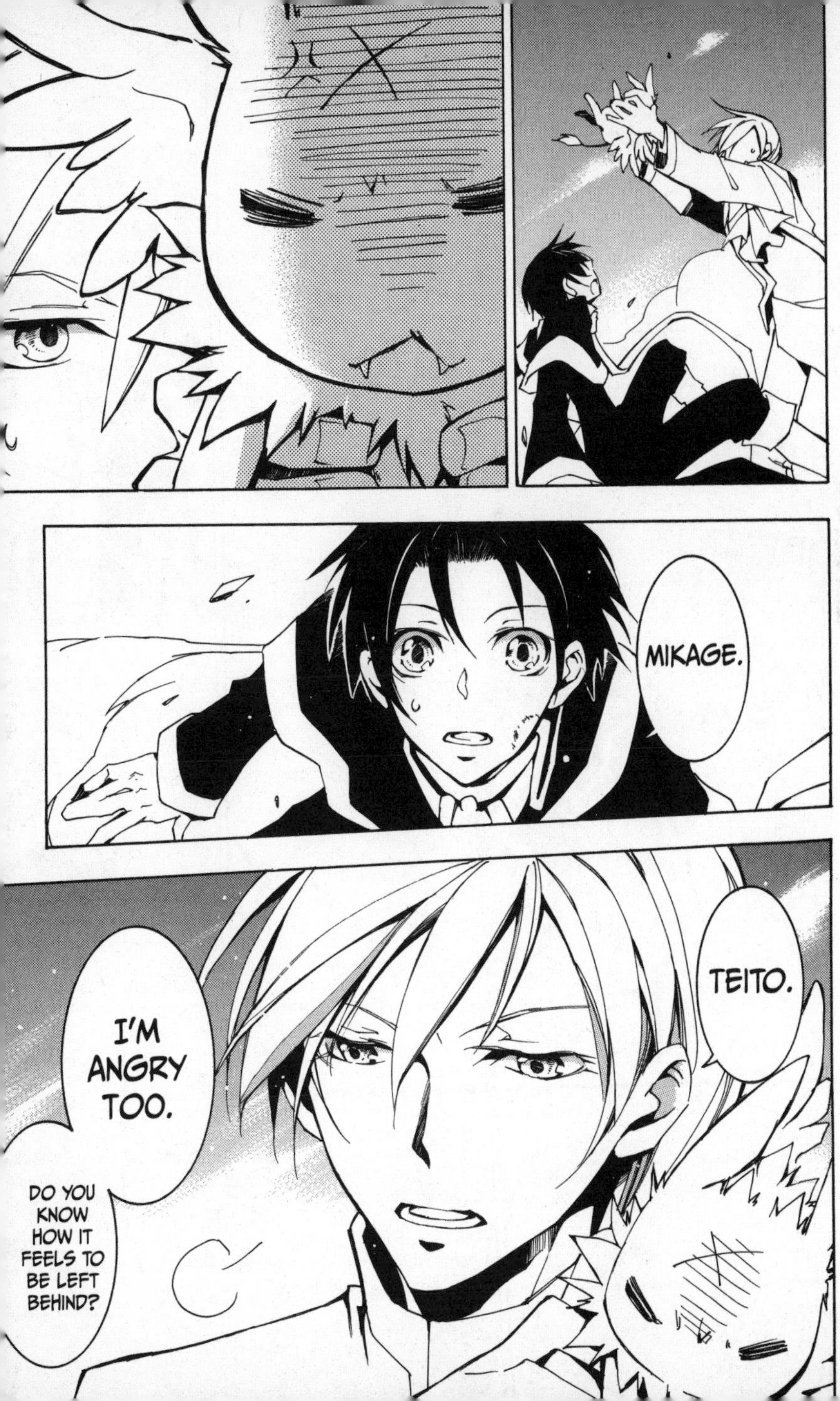
MIKAGE.
TEITO.
I'M ANGRY TOO.
DO YOU KNOW HOW IT FEELS TO BE LEFT BEHIND?

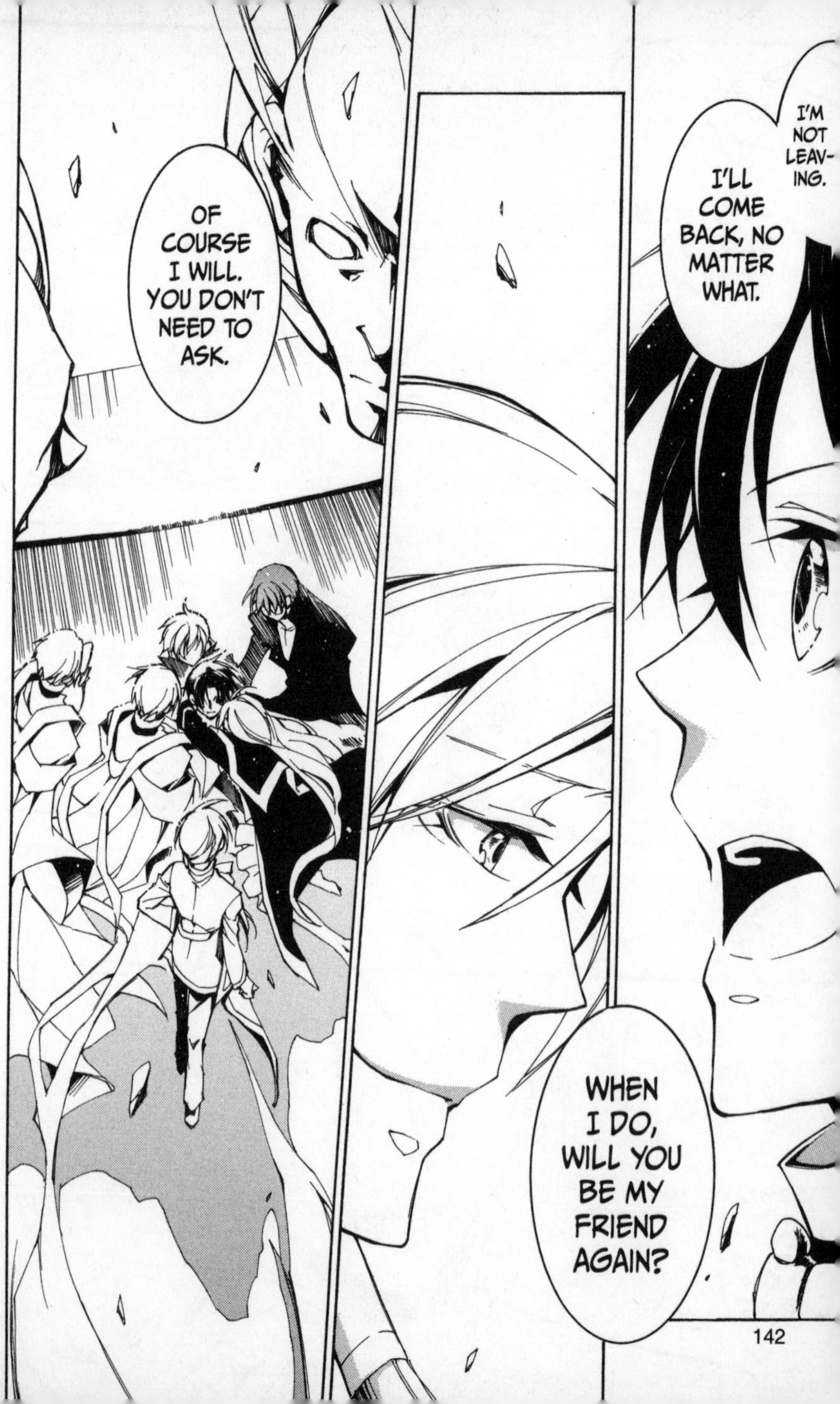
I'M NOT LEAVING.
I'LL COME BACK, NO MATTER WHAT.
WHEN I DO, WILL YOU BE MY FRIEND AGAIN?
OF COURSE I WILL. YOU DON'T NEED TO ASK.

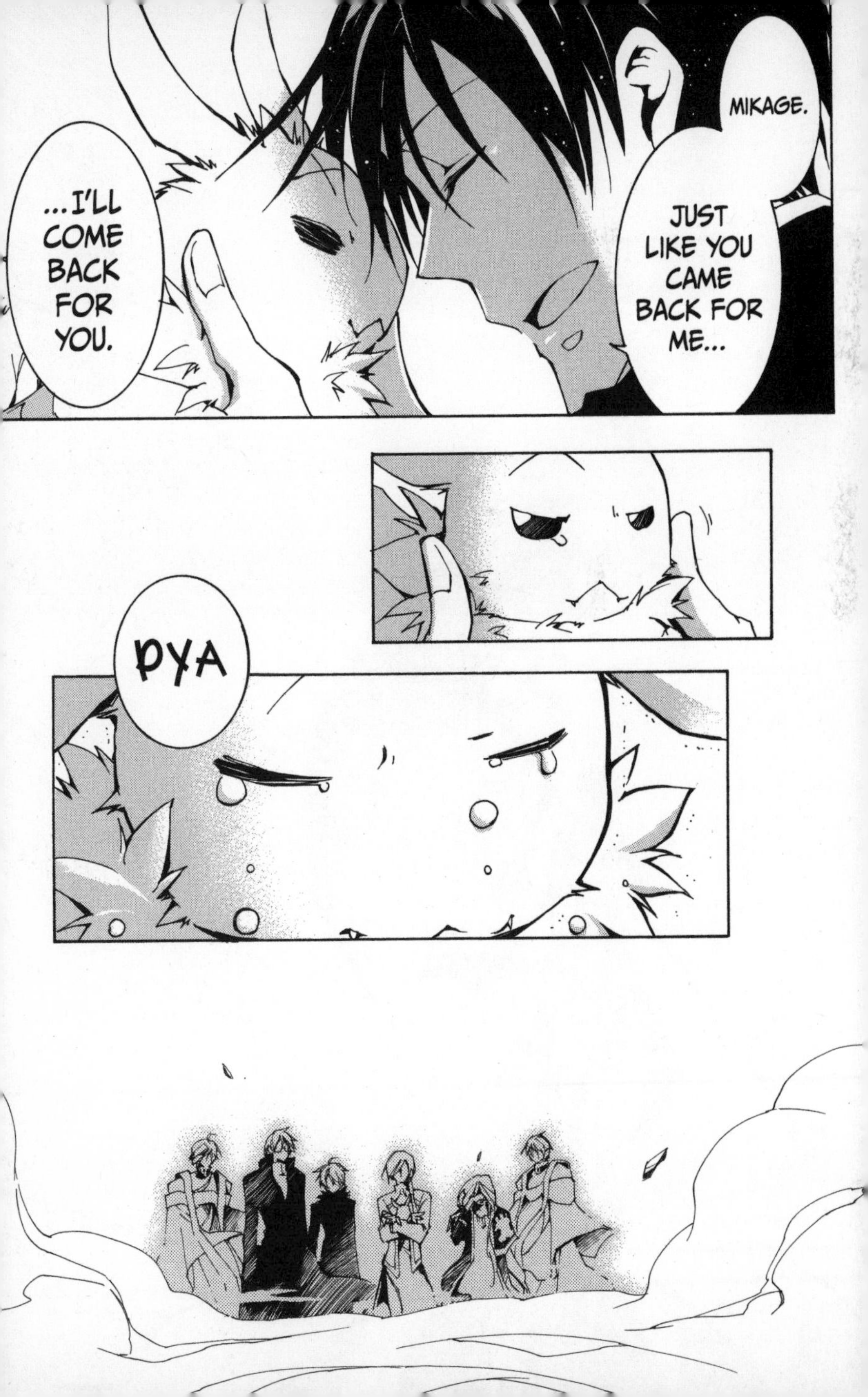
MIKAGE.
JUST LIKE YOU CAME BACK FOR ME...
...I'LL COME BACK FOR YOU.
PYA

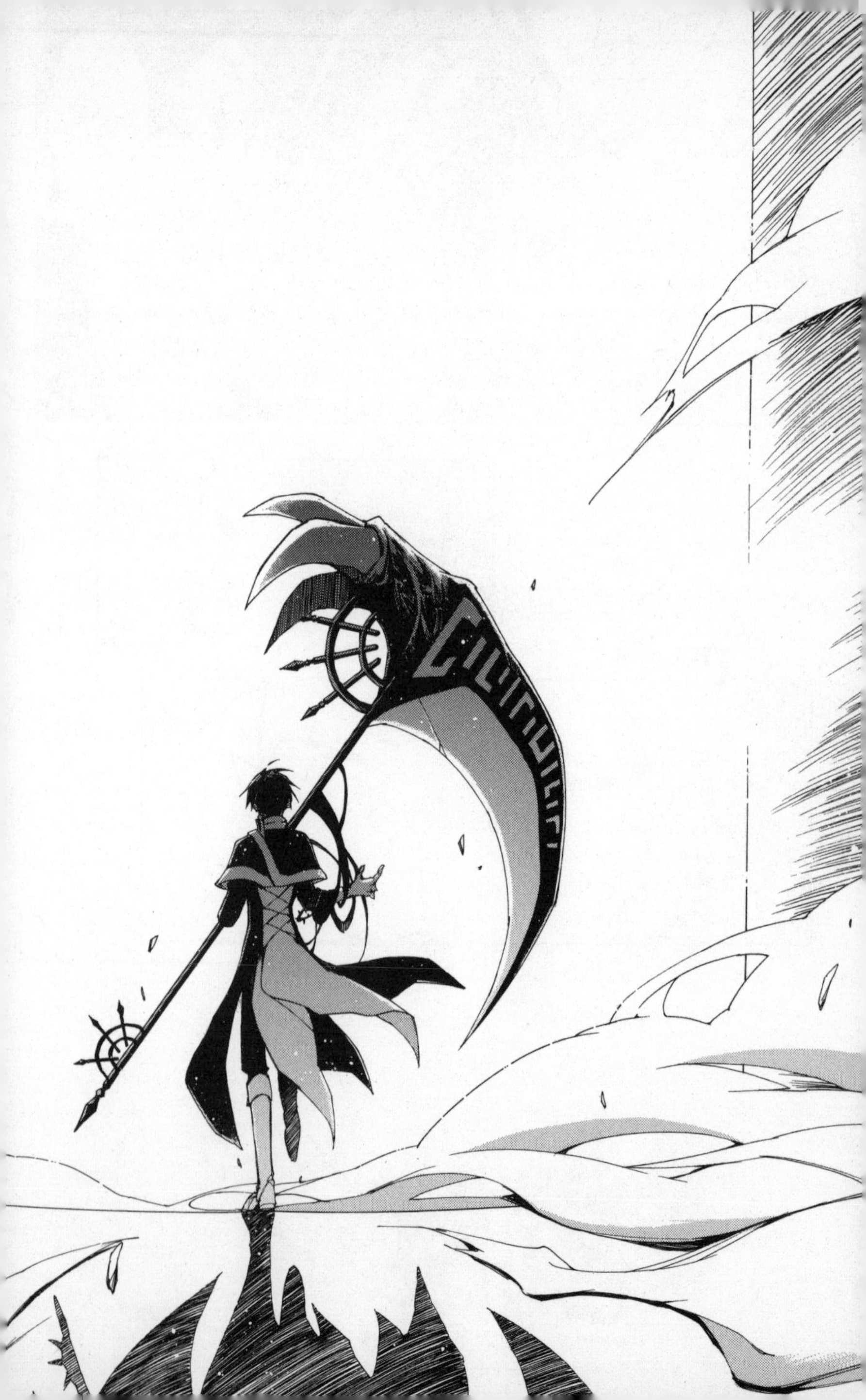

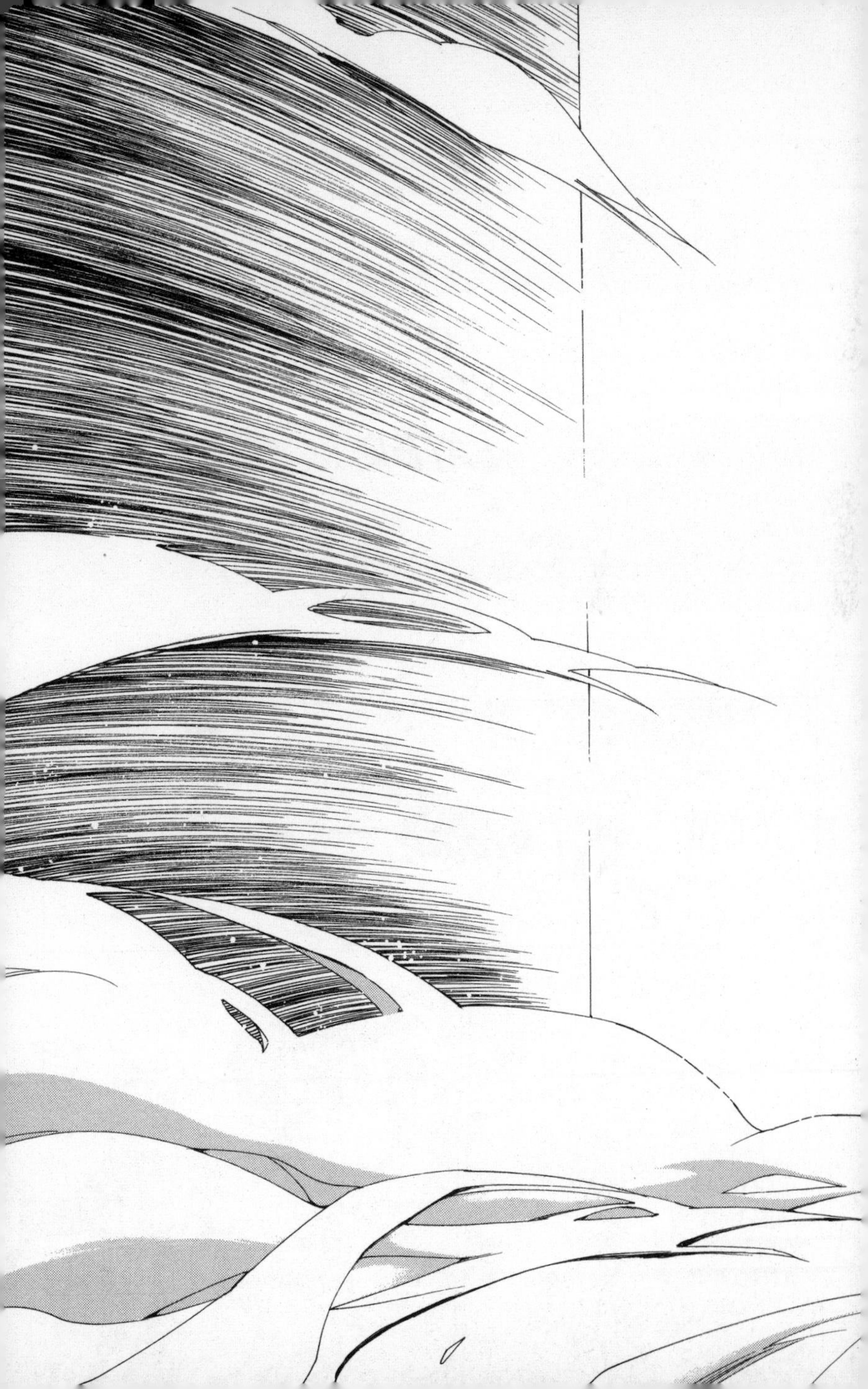

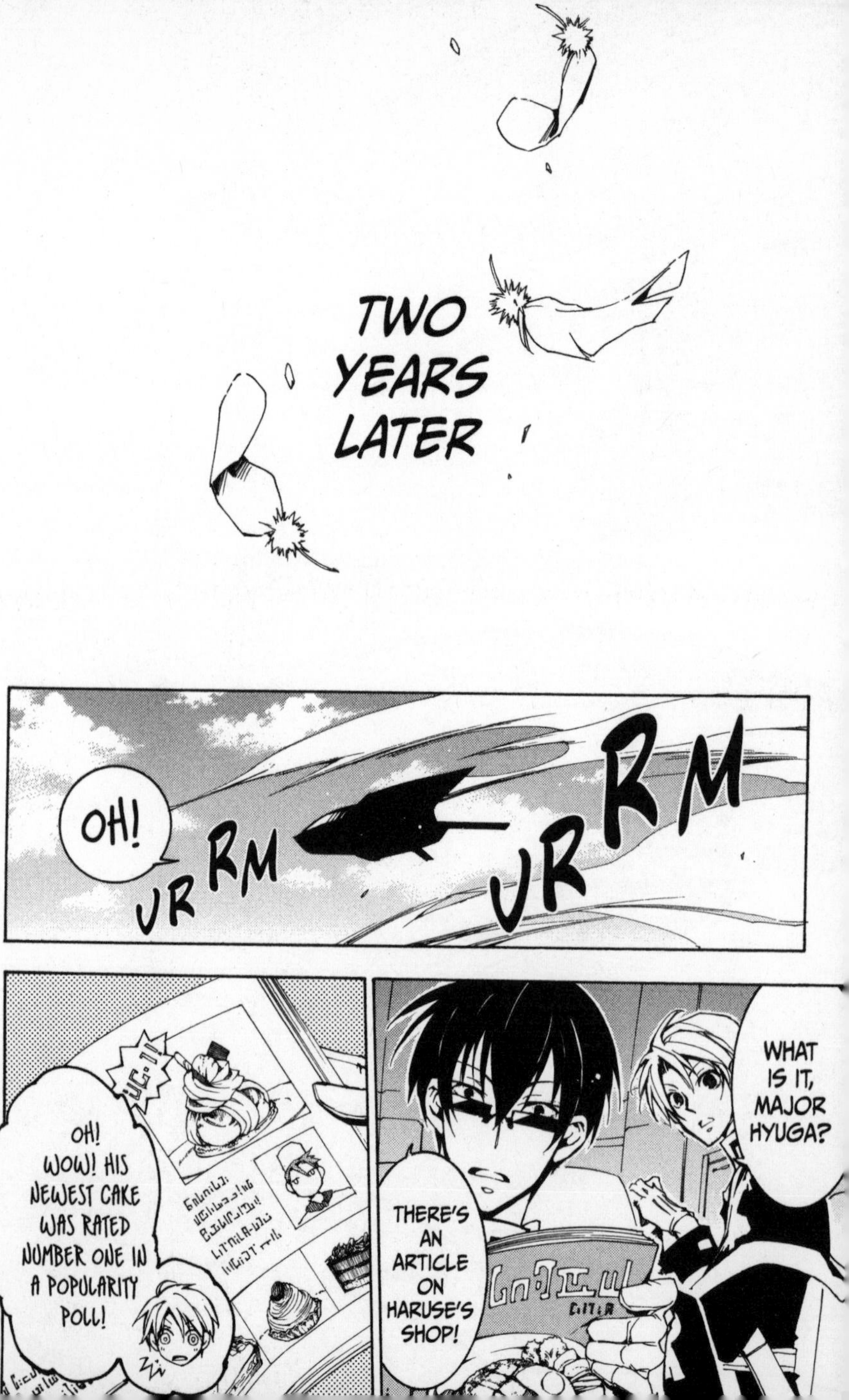
TWO YEARS LATER
OH!
VRRM
VRRM
WHAT IS IT, MAJOR HYUGA?
THERE'S AN ARTICLE ON HARUSE'S SHOP!
OH! WOW! HIS NEWEST CAKE WAS RATED NUMBER ONE IN A POPULARITY POLL!

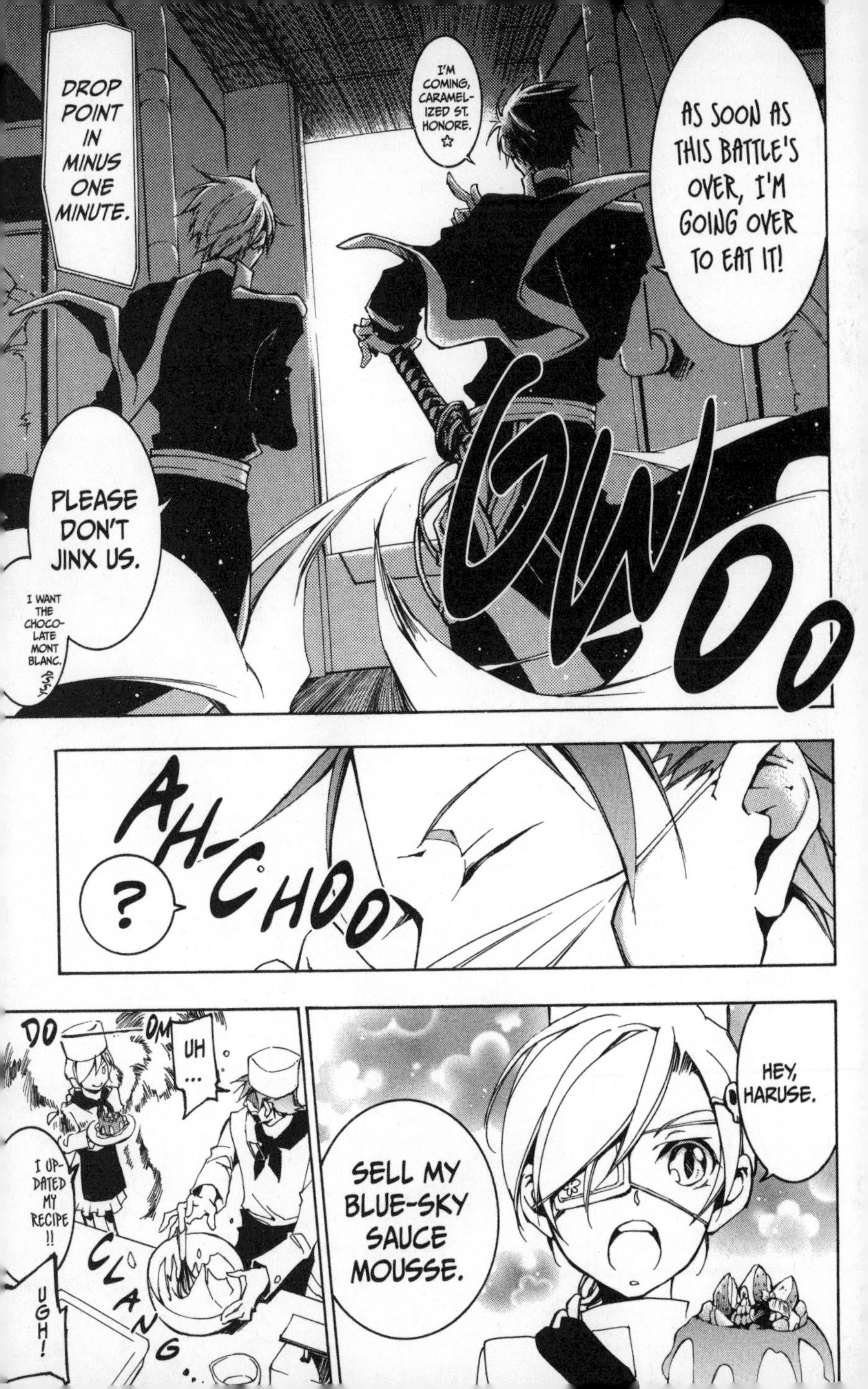
AS SOON AS THIS BATTLE'S OVER, I'M GOING OVER TO EAT IT!
I'M COMING, CARAMEL-IZED ST. HONORE. ☆
DROP POINT IN MINUS ONE MINUTE.
GWOOO
PLEASE DON'T JINX US.
I WANT THE CHOCO-LATE MONT BLANC.
AH-CHOO
?
HEY, HARUSE.
SELL MY BLUE-SKY SAUCE MOUSSE.
DOOM
UH ...
I UP-DATED MY RECIPE !!
CLANG...
UGH!

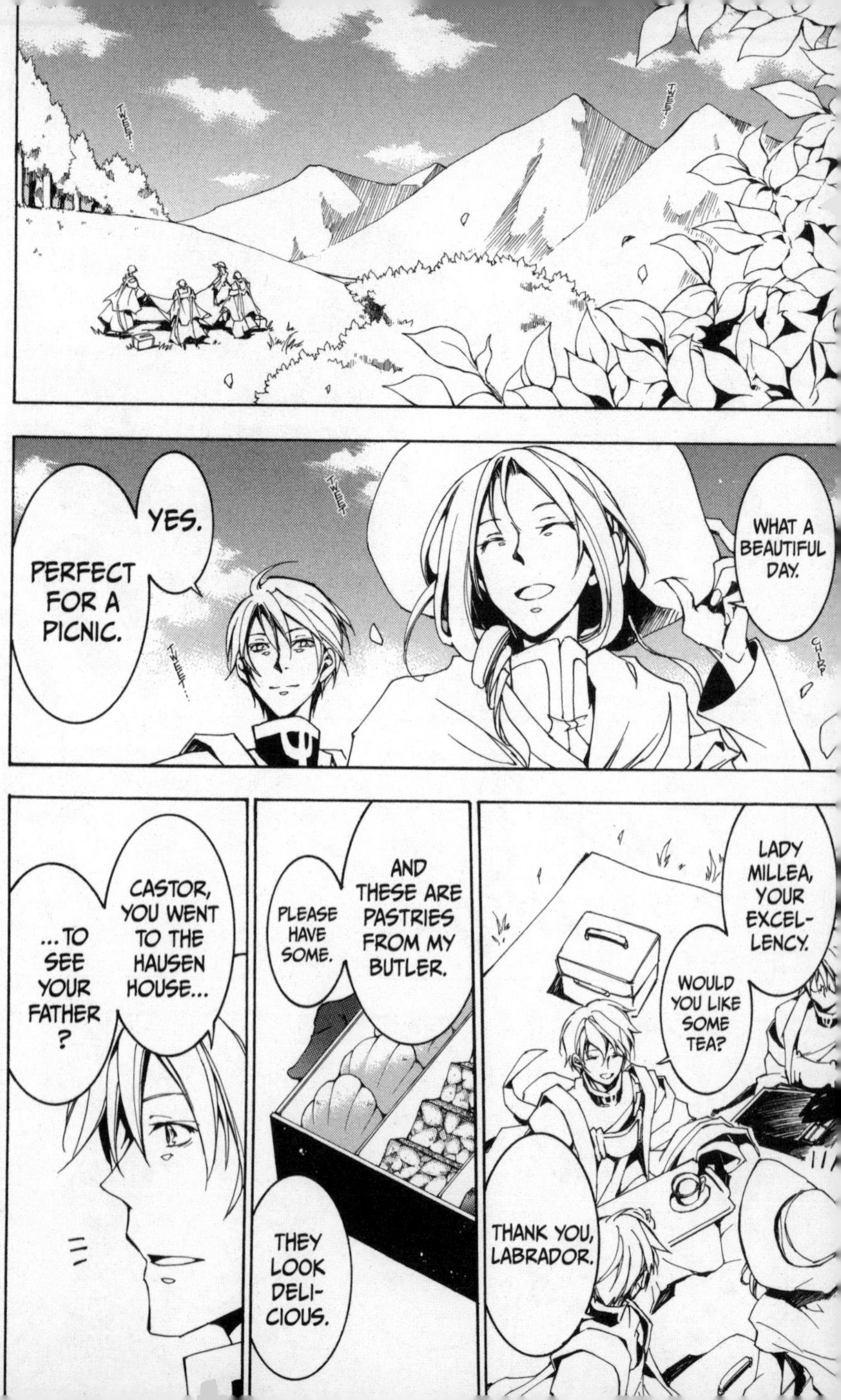
TWEET...
TWEET...
WHAT A BEAUTIFUL DAY.
CHIRP
TWEET
YES.
PERFECT FOR A PICNIC.
TWEET...
LADY MILLEA, YOUR EXCELLENCY.
WOULD YOU LIKE SOME TEA?
THANK YOU, LABRADOR.
AND THESE ARE PASTRIES FROM MY BUTLER.
PLEASE HAVE SOME.
THEY LOOK DELICIOUS.
CASTOR, YOU WENT TO THE HAUSEN HOUSE...
...TO SEE YOUR FATHER?

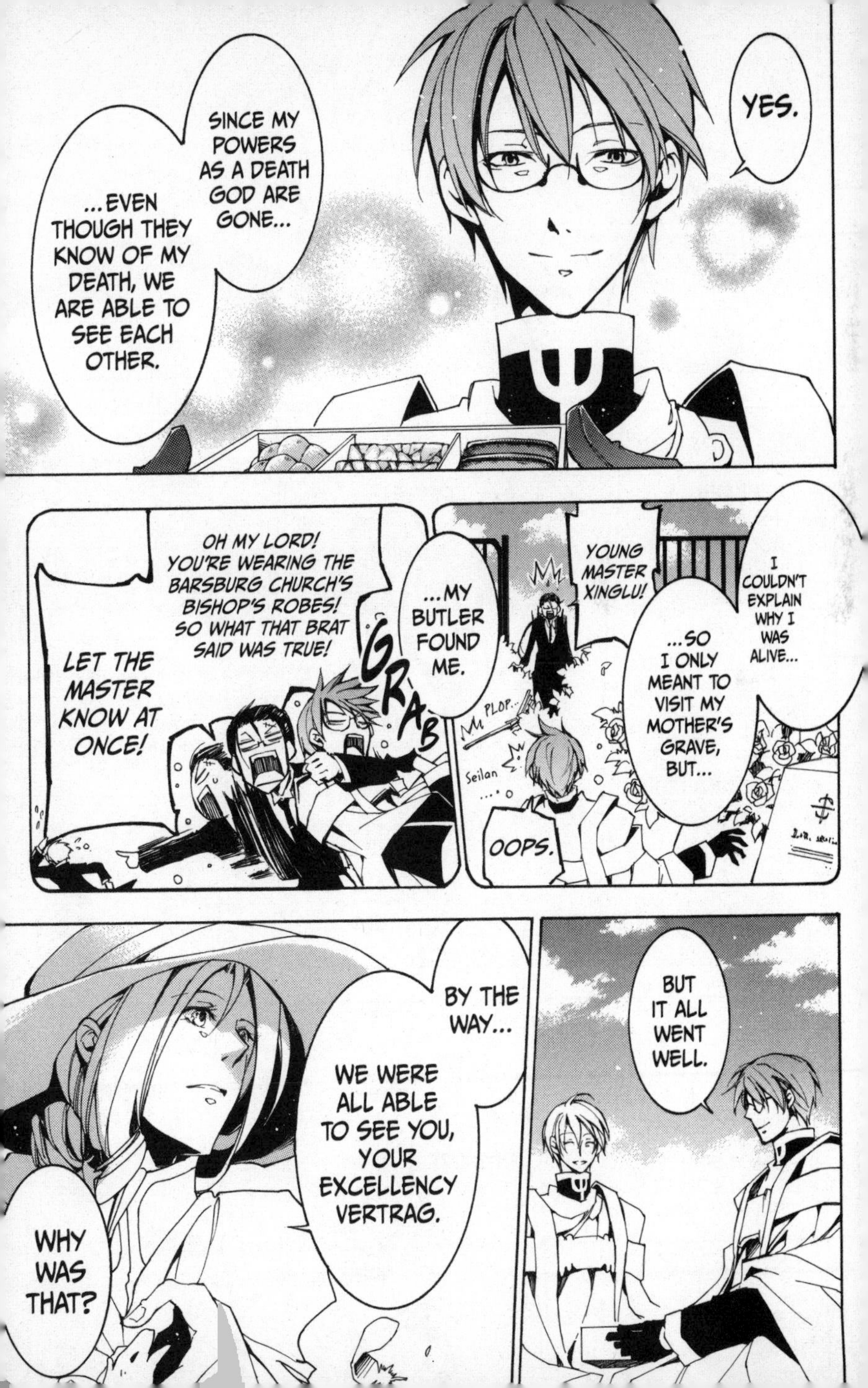
YES.
SINCE MY POWERS AS A DEATH GOD ARE GONE...
...EVEN THOUGH THEY KNOW OF MY DEATH, WE ARE ABLE TO SEE EACH OTHER.
I COULDN'T EXPLAIN WHY I WAS ALIVE...
...SO I ONLY MEANT TO VISIT MY MOTHER'S GRAVE, BUT...
YOUNG MASTER XINGLU!
...MY BUTLER FOUND ME.
PLOP...
Seilan ...
OOPS.
OH MY LORD! YOU'RE WEARING THE BARSBURG CHURCH'S BISHOP'S ROBES! SO WHAT THAT BRAT SAID WAS TRUE!
GRAB
LET THE MASTER KNOW AT ONCE!
BUT IT ALL WENT WELL.
BY THE WAY...
WE WERE ALL ABLE TO SEE YOU, YOUR EXCELLENCY VERTRAG.
WHY WAS THAT?

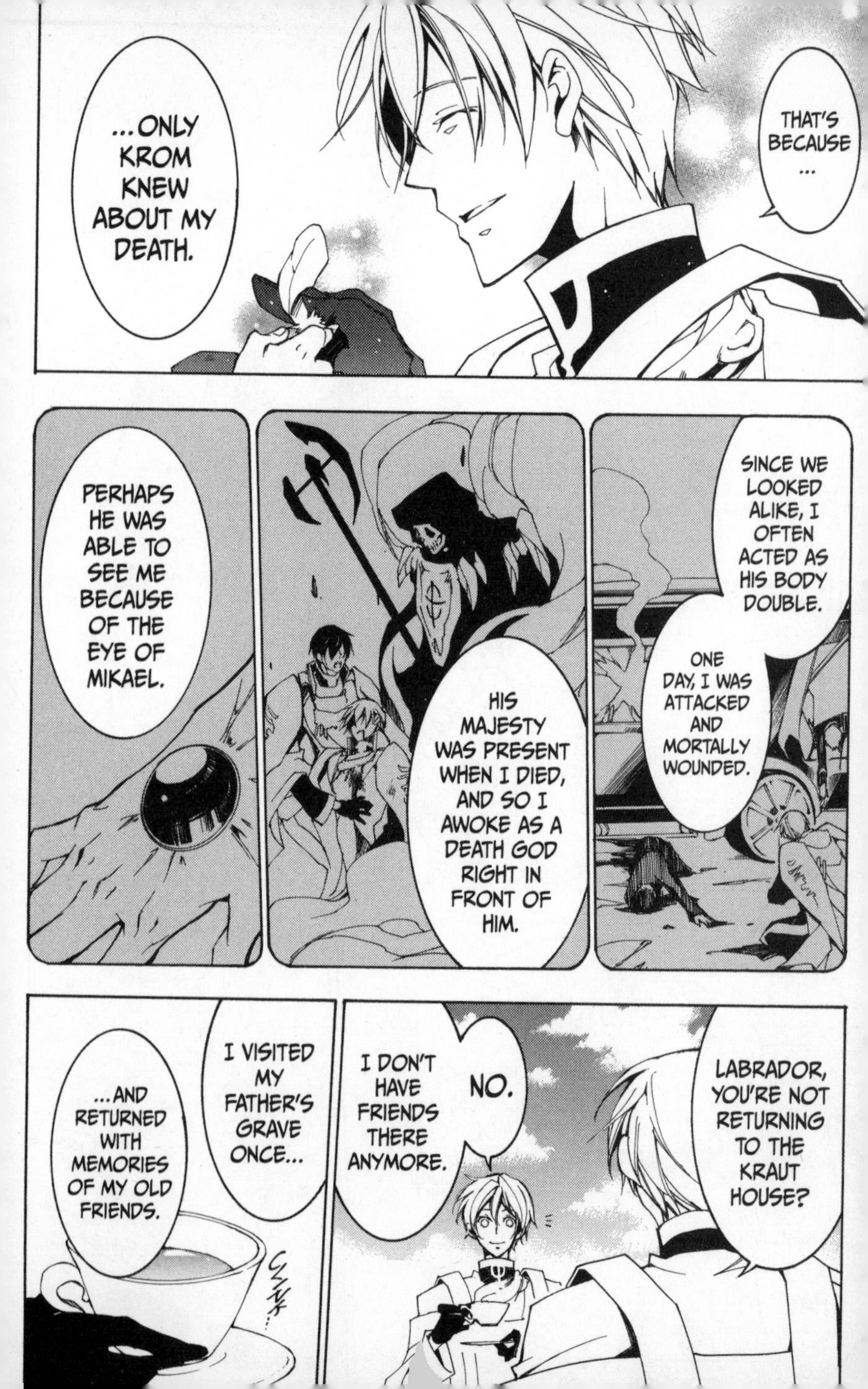
THAT'S BECAUSE ...
...ONLY KROM KNEW ABOUT MY DEATH.
SINCE WE LOOKED ALIKE, I OFTEN ACTED AS HIS BODY DOUBLE.
ONE DAY, I WAS ATTACKED AND MORTALLY WOUNDED.
HIS MAJESTY WAS PRESENT WHEN I DIED, AND SO I AWOKE AS A DEATH GOD RIGHT IN FRONT OF HIM.
PERHAPS HE WAS ABLE TO SEE ME BECAUSE OF THE EYE OF MIKAEL.
LABRADOR, YOU'RE NOT RETURNING TO THE KRAUT HOUSE?
NO.
I DON'T HAVE FRIENDS THERE ANYMORE.
I VISITED MY FATHER'S GRAVE ONCE...
...AND RETURNED WITH MEMORIES OF MY OLD FRIENDS.
CLINK...

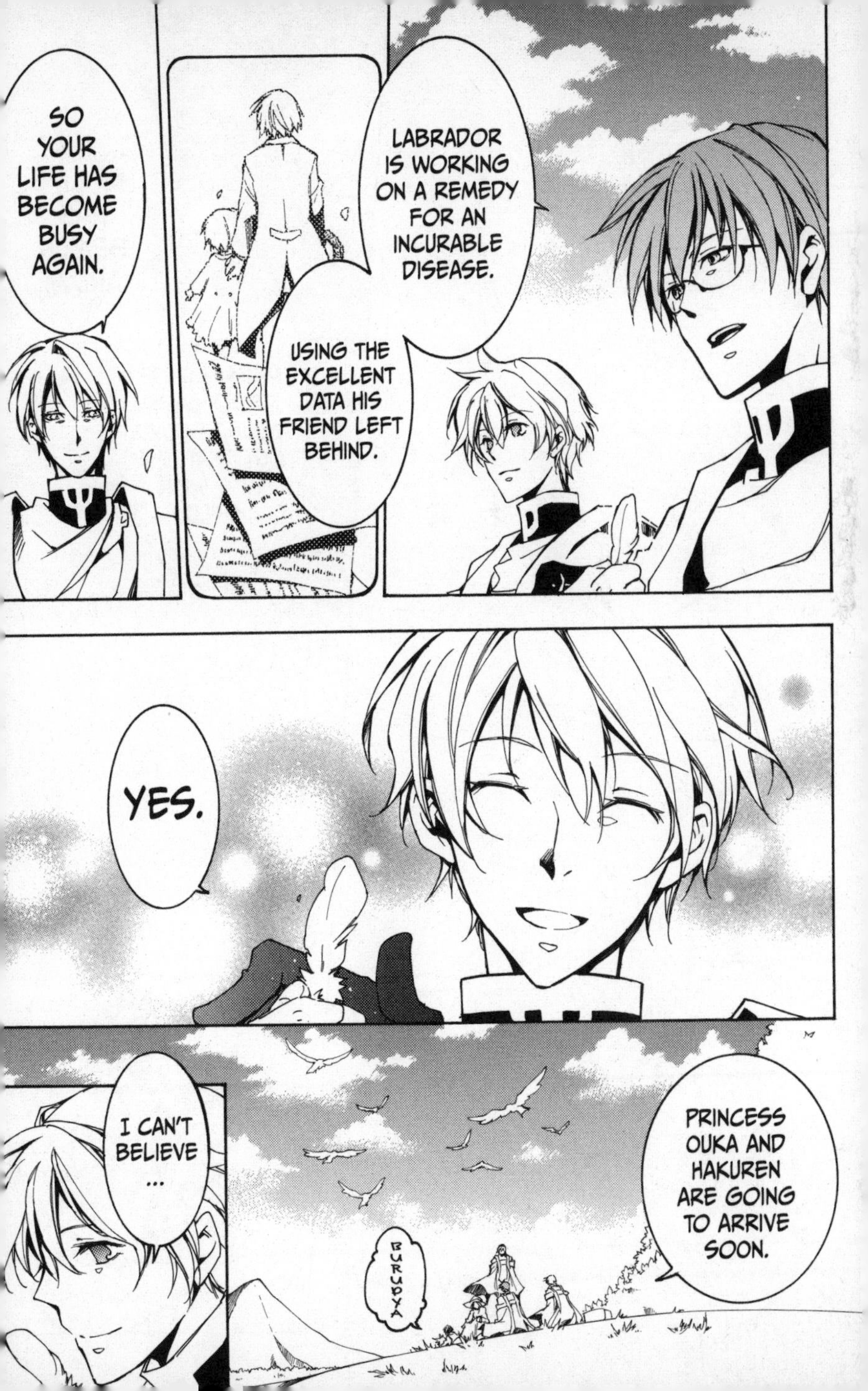
LABRADOR IS WORKING ON A REMEDY FOR AN INCURABLE DISEASE.
USING THE EXCELLENT DATA HIS FRIEND LEFT BEHIND.
SO YOUR LIFE HAS BECOME BUSY AGAIN.
YES.
PRINCESS OUKA AND HAKUREN ARE GOING TO ARRIVE SOON.
BURUDYA
I CAN'T BELIEVE ...

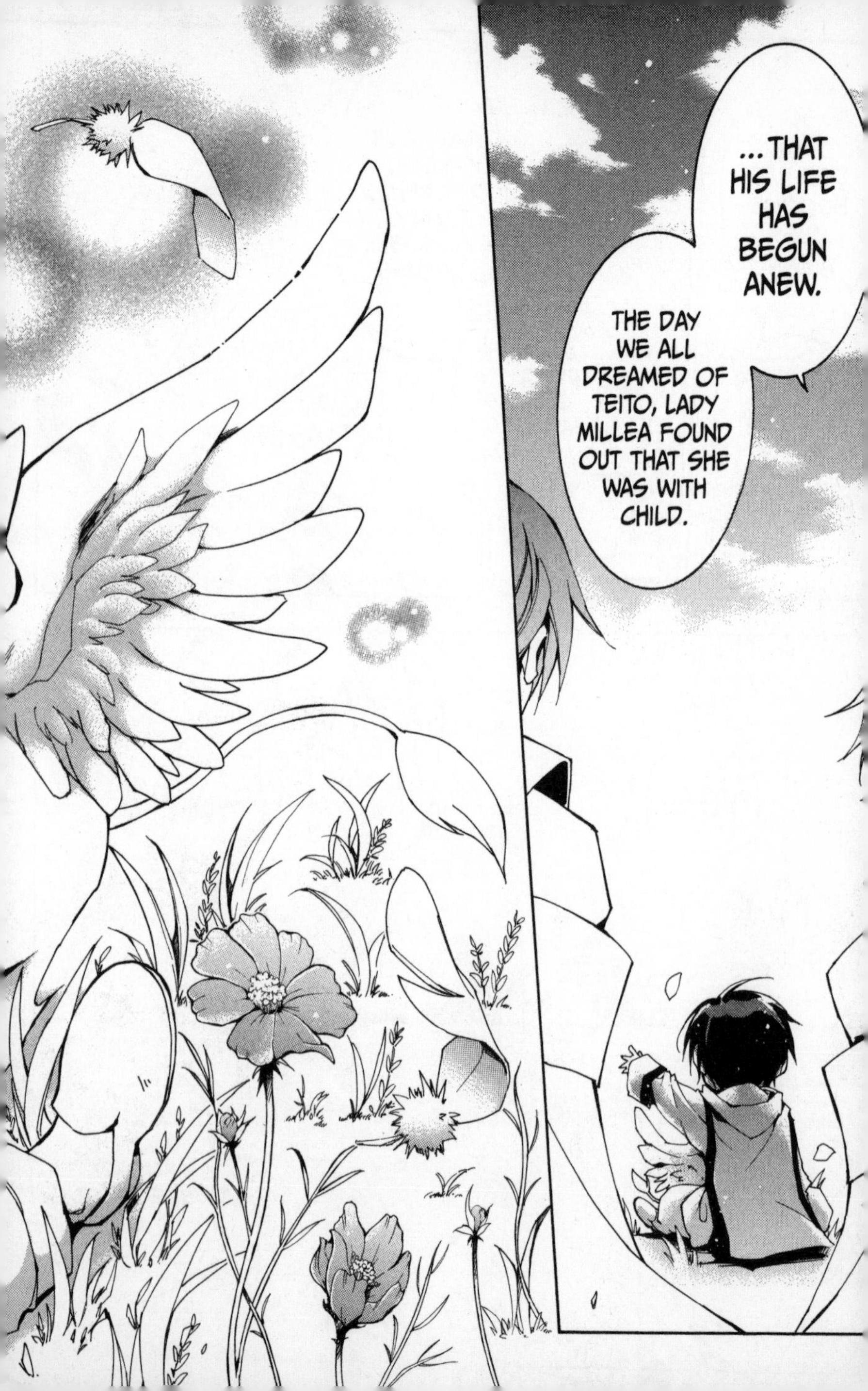
...THAT HIS LIFE HAS BEGUN ANEW.
THE DAY WE ALL DREAMED OF TEITO, LADY MILLEA FOUND OUT THAT SHE WAS WITH CHILD.

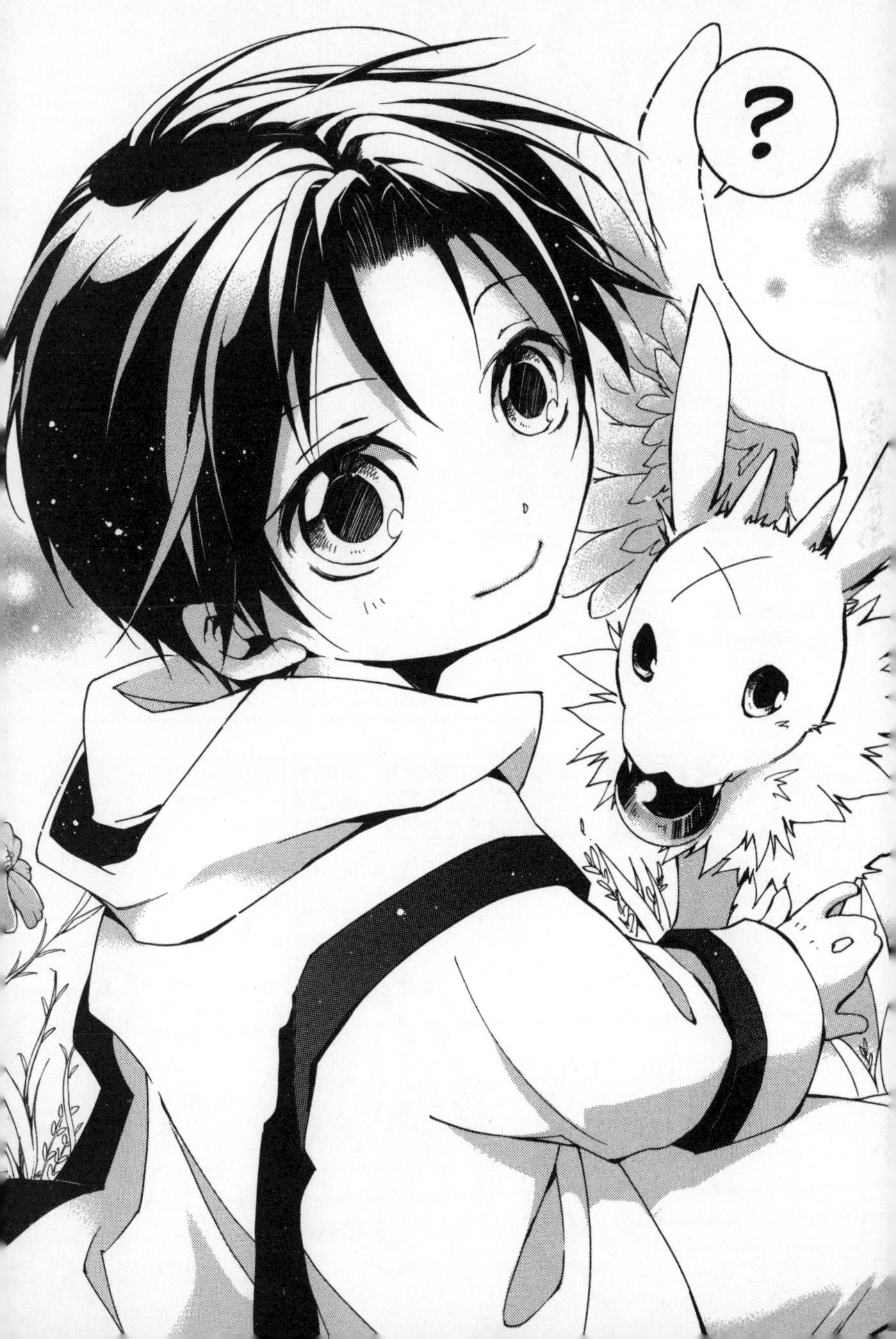
?

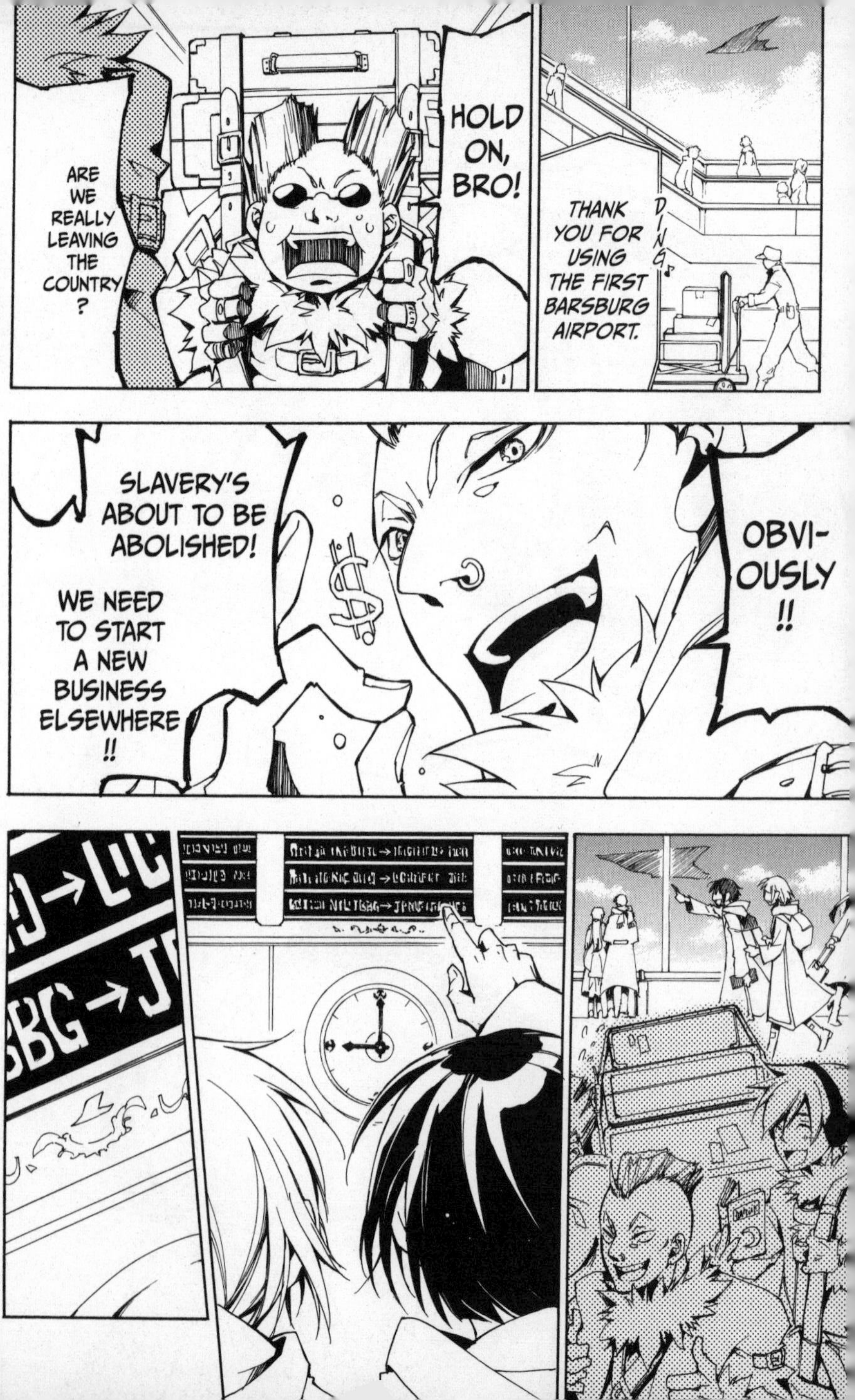
THANK YOU FOR USING THE FIRST BARSBURG AIRPORT.
DING♪
HOLD ON, BRO!
ARE WE REALLY LEAVING THE COUNTRY?
OBVIOUSLY!!
SLAVERY'S ABOUT TO BE ABOLISHED!
WE NEED TO START A NEW BUSINESS ELSEWHERE!!

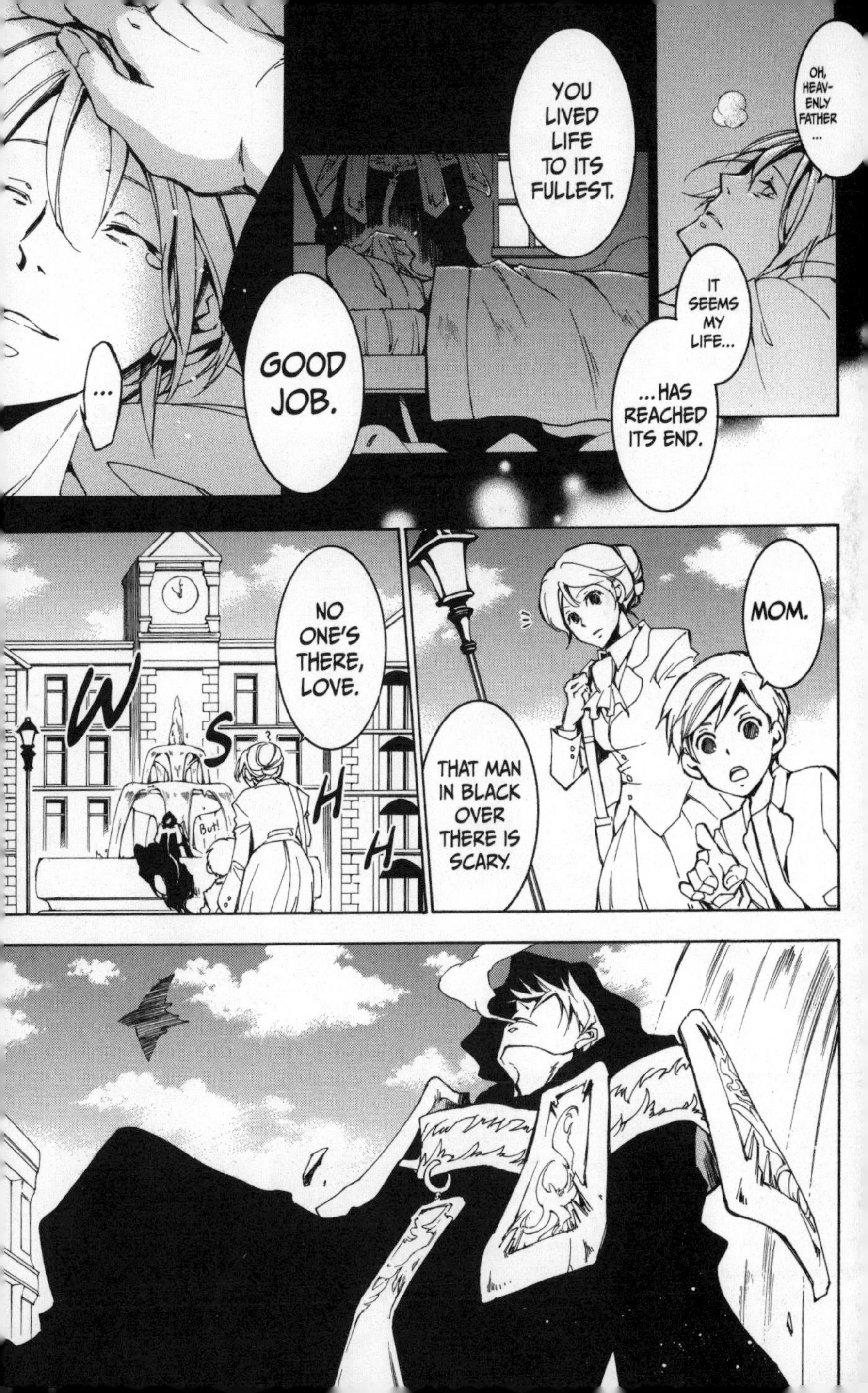
OH, HEAV-ENLY FATHER ...
IT SEEMS MY LIFE...
...HAS REACHED ITS END.
YOU LIVED LIFE TO ITS FULLEST.
GOOD JOB.
...
MOM.
THAT MAN IN BLACK OVER THERE IS SCARY.
NO ONE'S THERE, LOVE.
But!
WSHH

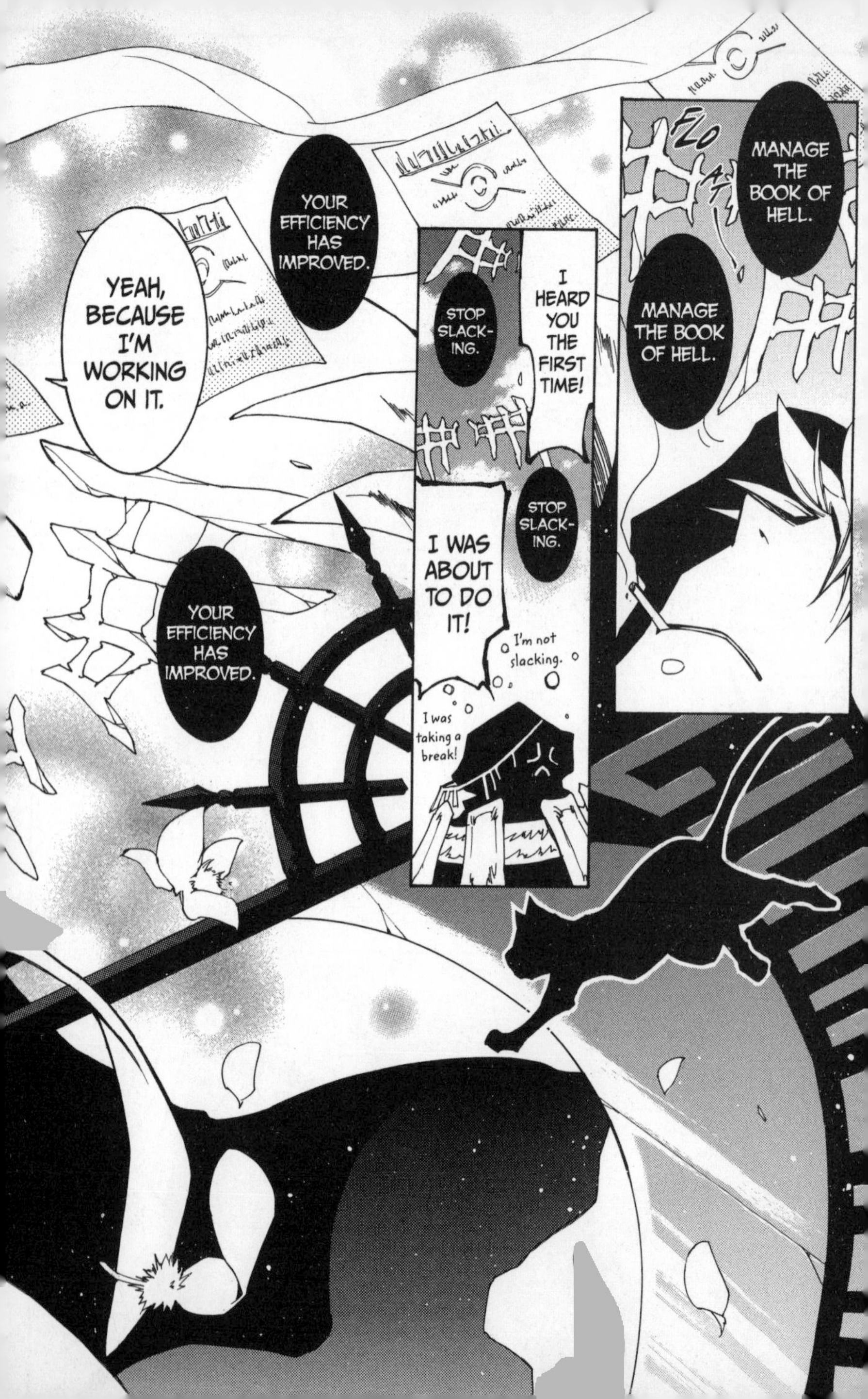
MANAGE THE BOOK OF HELL.
MANAGE THE BOOK OF HELL.
I HEARD YOU THE FIRST TIME!
STOP SLACKING.
STOP SLACKING.
I WAS ABOUT TO DO IT!
I'm not slacking.
I was taking a break!
YOUR EFFICIENCY HAS IMPROVED.
YEAH, BECAUSE I'M WORKING ON IT.
YOUR EFFICIENCY HAS IMPROVED.

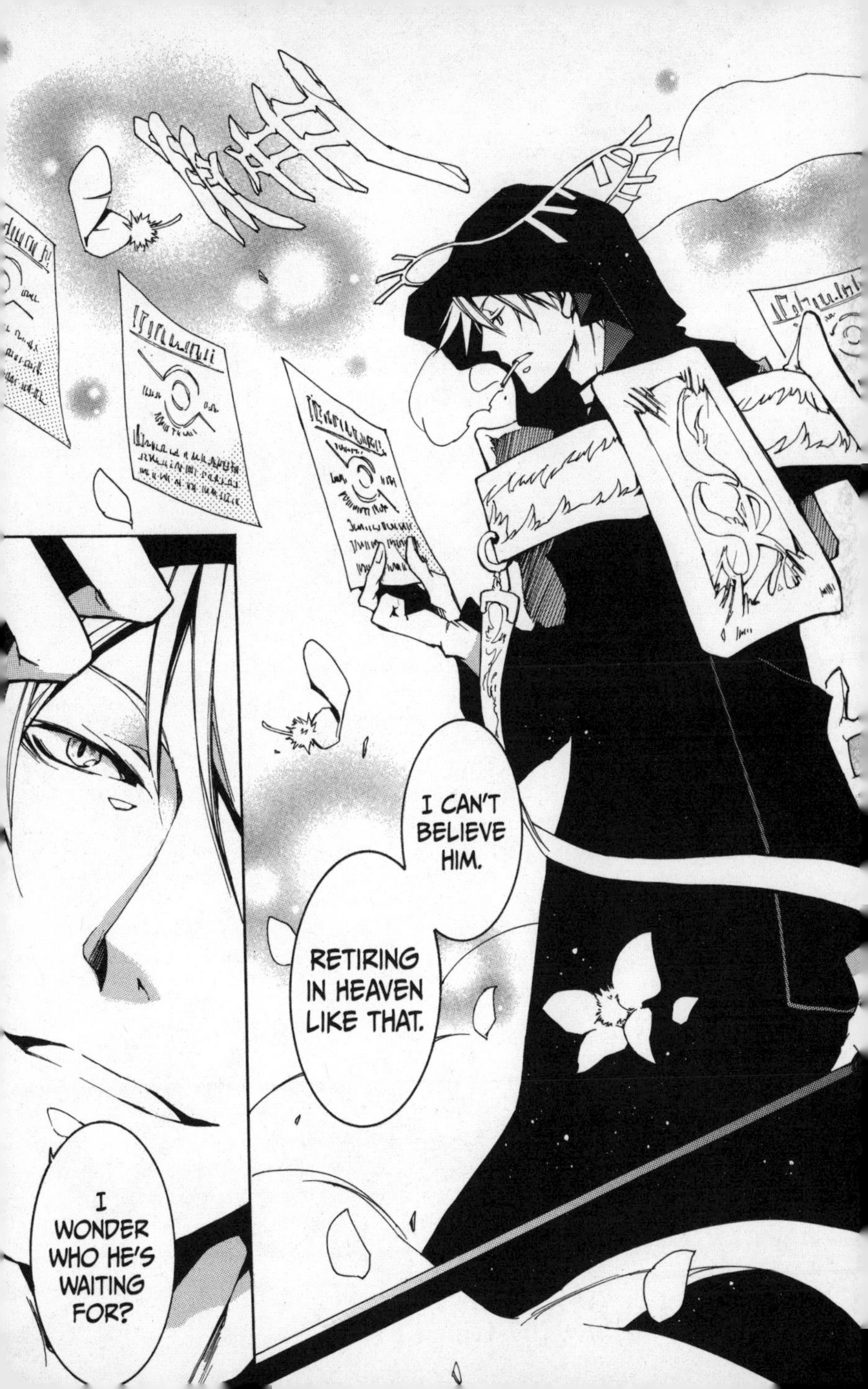
I CAN'T BELIEVE HIM.
RETIRING IN HEAVEN LIKE THAT.
I WONDER WHO HE'S WAITING FOR?

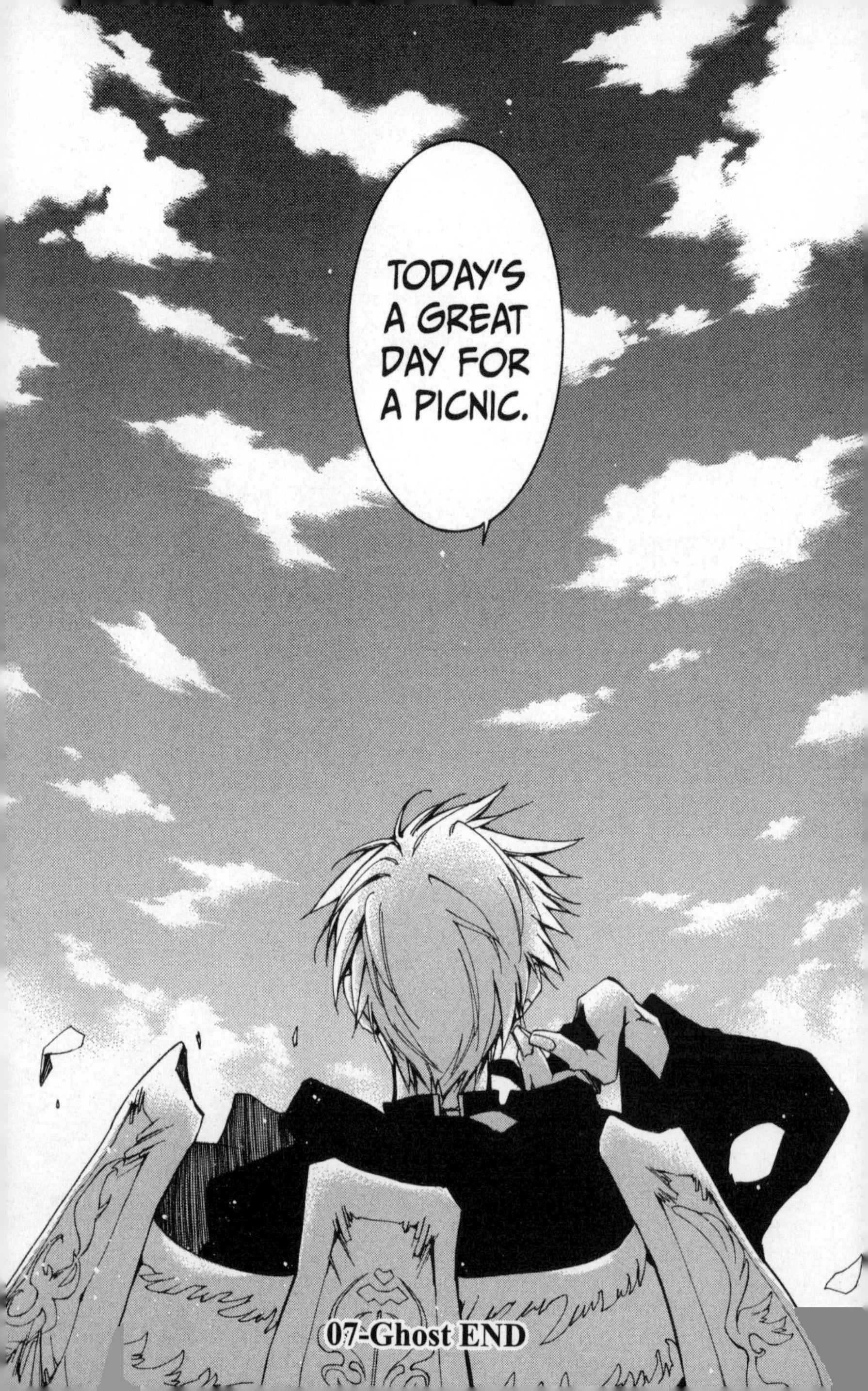
TODAY'S A GREAT DAY FOR A PICNIC.
07-Ghost END

FORTY YEARS LATER, WAHRHEIT TEITO KLEIN WAS ELECTED THE GRAND POPE OF BARSBURG. HE HELD MANY DIALOGUES WITH THE CITIZENS OF THE BARSBURG EMPIRE...

...AND WITHOUT SHEDDING BLOOD, HE GREATLY CONTRIBUTED TO THE REESTABLISHMENT OF THE RAGGS KINGDOM.

BUT THAT IS ANOTHER STORY.

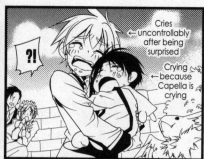

Young Master Xinglu, we're coming too!
Fulfilling a promise from long ago, looking for Lazette's home-town.
STAY HOME !!
Take us with you!
Cries ← uncontrollably after being surprised
Crying ← because Capella is crying
?!
CRUMBLE
CRUMBLE
CRUMBLE
URGH
AYA ...
JUST DO IT.
YOU'RE A DEMON! NO, A DEATH GOD!
...WHAT IS THE PURPOSE OF THIS?
A job crumbling Styrofoam.
URGH
URGH
This sticks to my clothes. You're so mean.

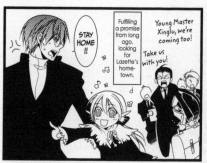

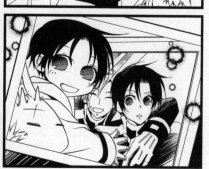

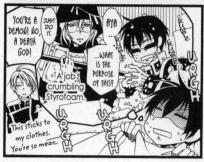

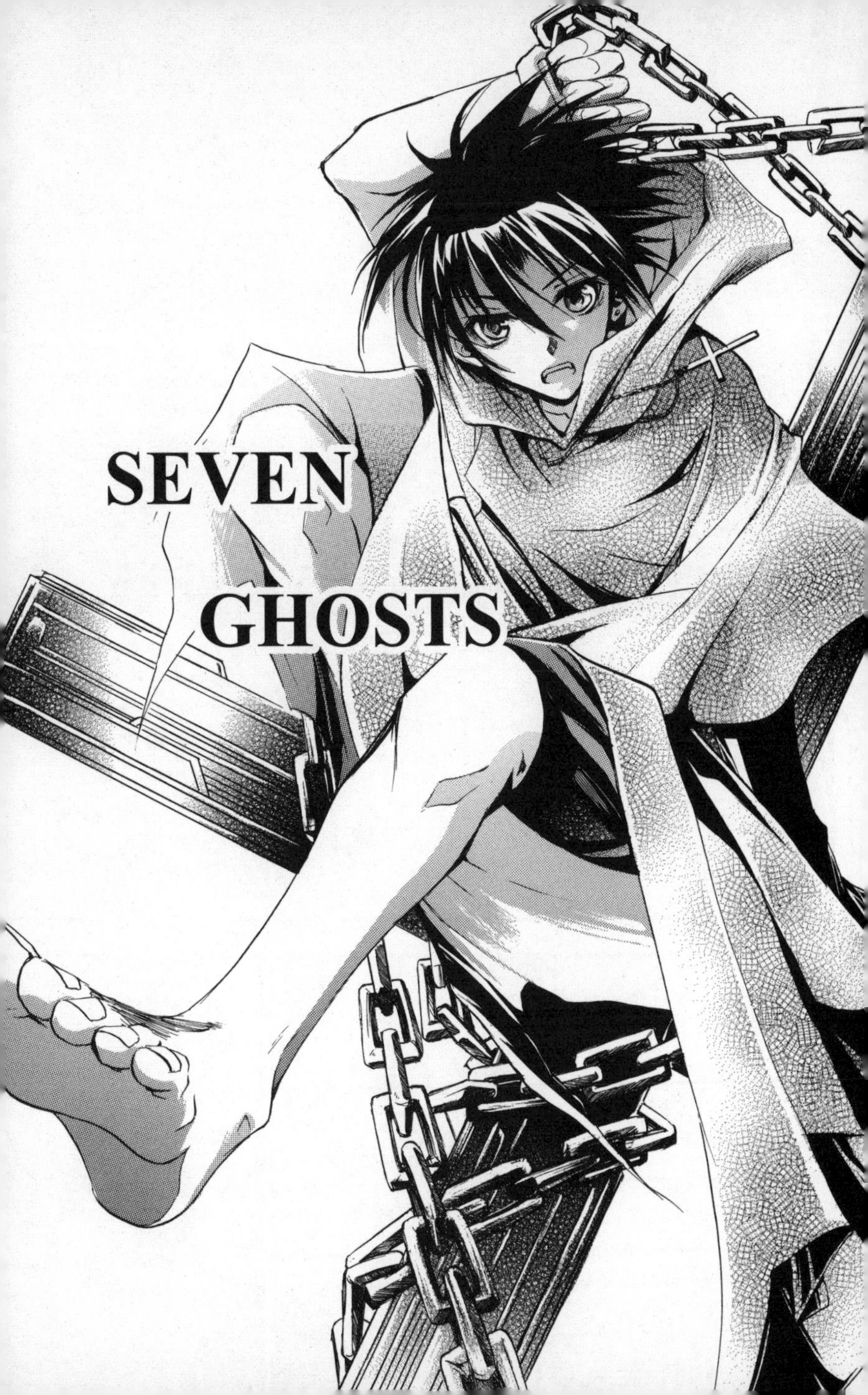
SEVEN
GHOSTS

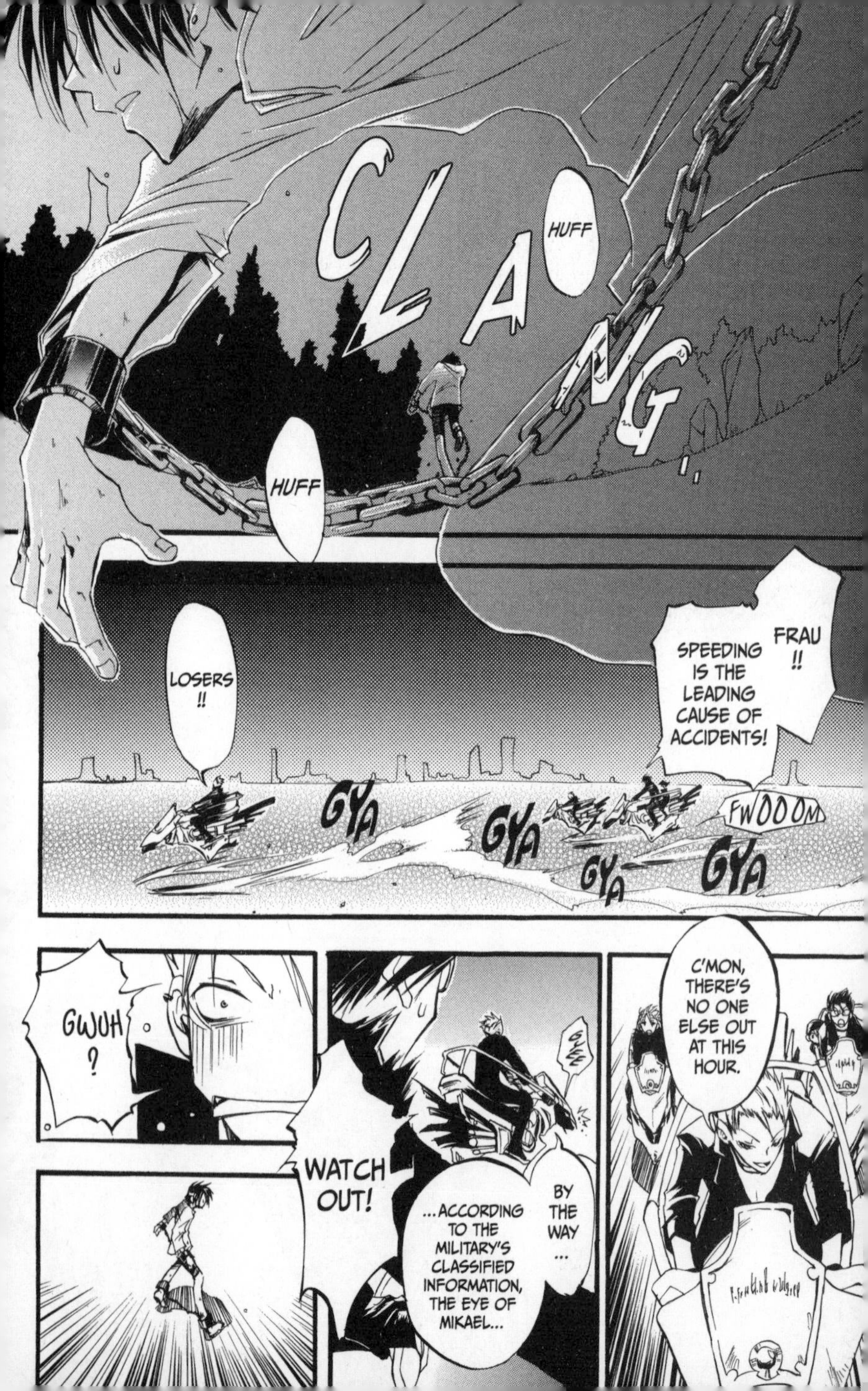
CLANG
HUFF
HUFF
FRAU!!
SPEEDING IS THE LEADING CAUSE OF ACCIDENTS!
FWOOOM
GYA
GYA
GYA
GYA
LOSERS!!
C'MON, THERE'S NO ONE ELSE OUT AT THIS HOUR.
BY THE WAY...
...ACCORDING TO THE MILITARY'S CLASSIFIED INFORMATION, THE EYE OF MIKAEL...
WATCH OUT!
GWUH?

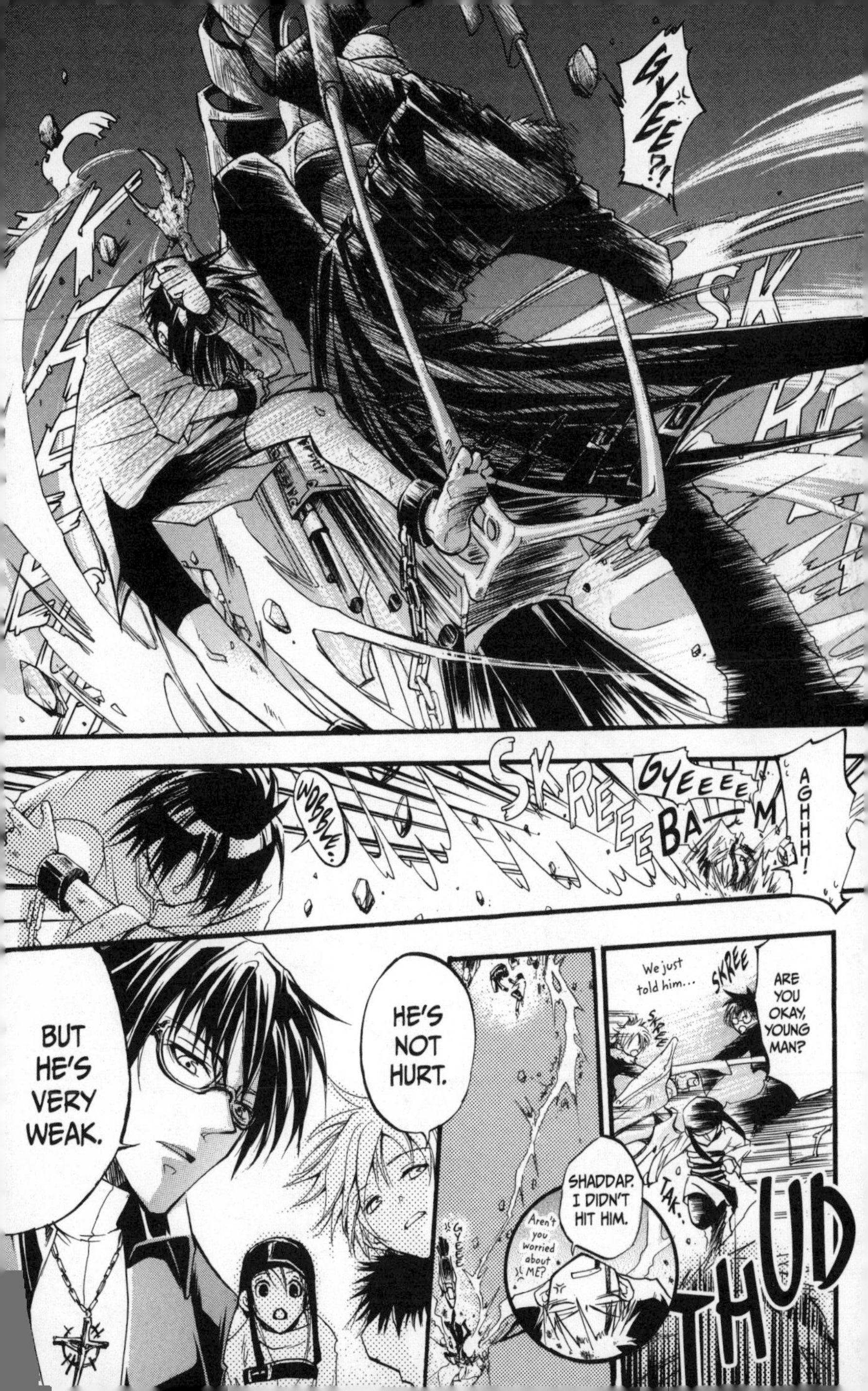

GYEEE?!!
SK
AGHHH!
SKREEEEBAM
GYEEEEM
WOBBLE
ARE YOU OKAY, YOUNG MAN?
SKREE
We just told him...
SHADDAP. I DIDN'T HIT HIM.
Aren't you worried about ME?
TAK...
THUD
GYEEE
HE'S NOT HURT.
BUT HE'S VERY WEAK.

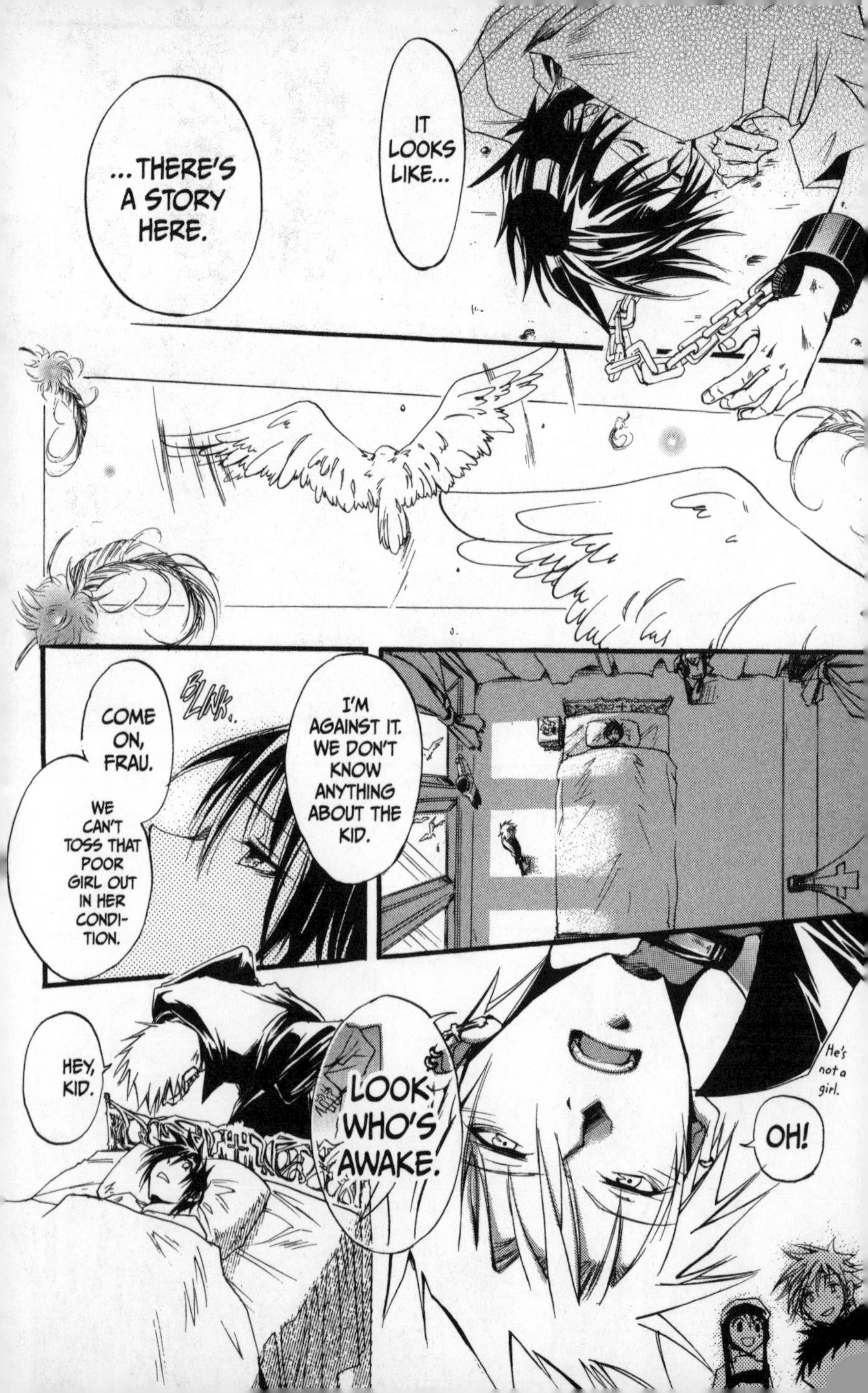
IT LOOKS LIKE...
...THERE'S A STORY HERE.
I'M AGAINST IT. WE DON'T KNOW ANYTHING ABOUT THE KID.
BLINK..
COME ON, FRAU.
WE CAN'T TOSS THAT POOR GIRL OUT IN HER CONDI-TION.
He's not a girl.
OH!
LOOK WHO'S AWAKE.
HEY, KID.

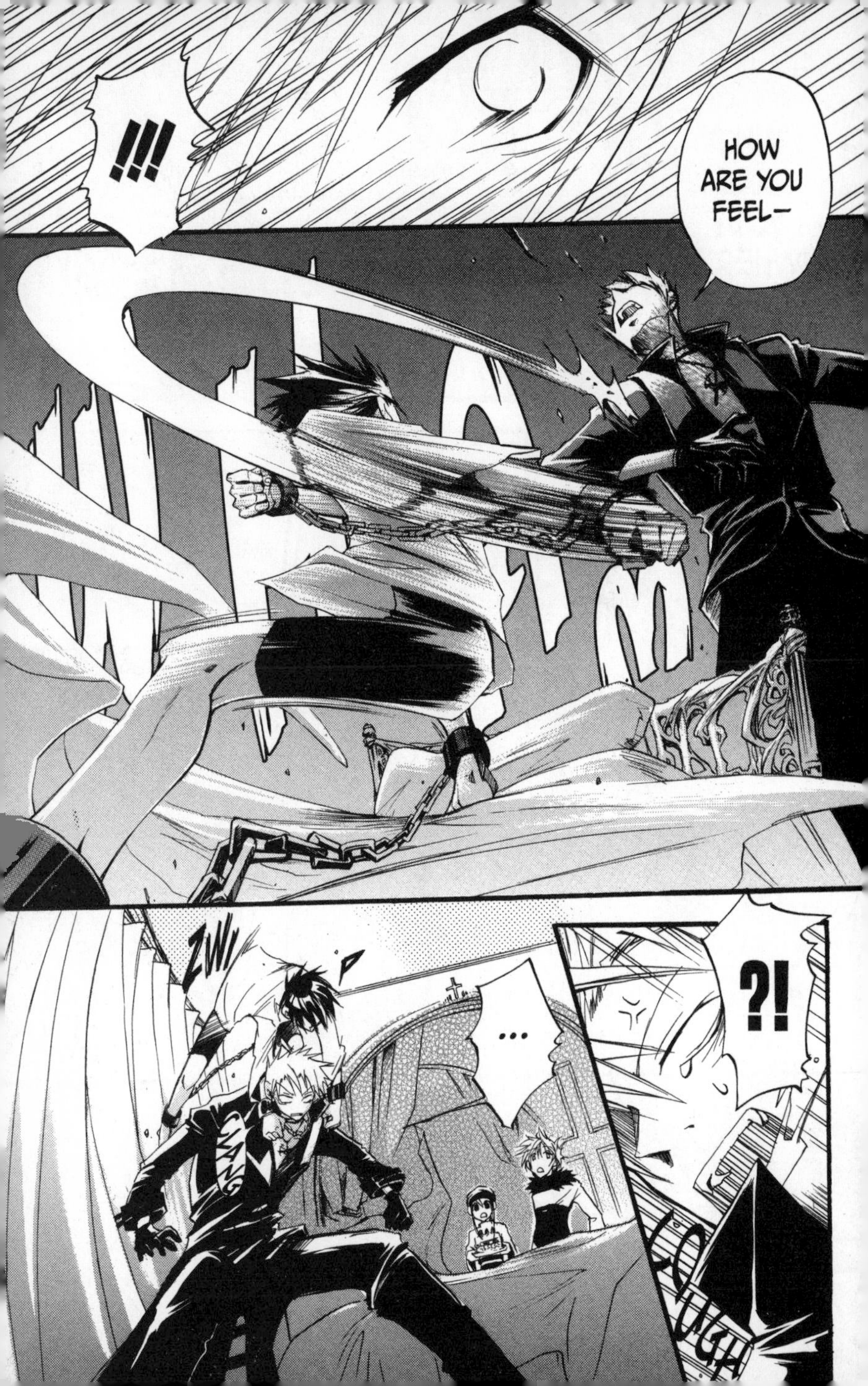
HOW ARE YOU FEEL-
!!!
?!
COUGH
ZWIP
...
CLANG

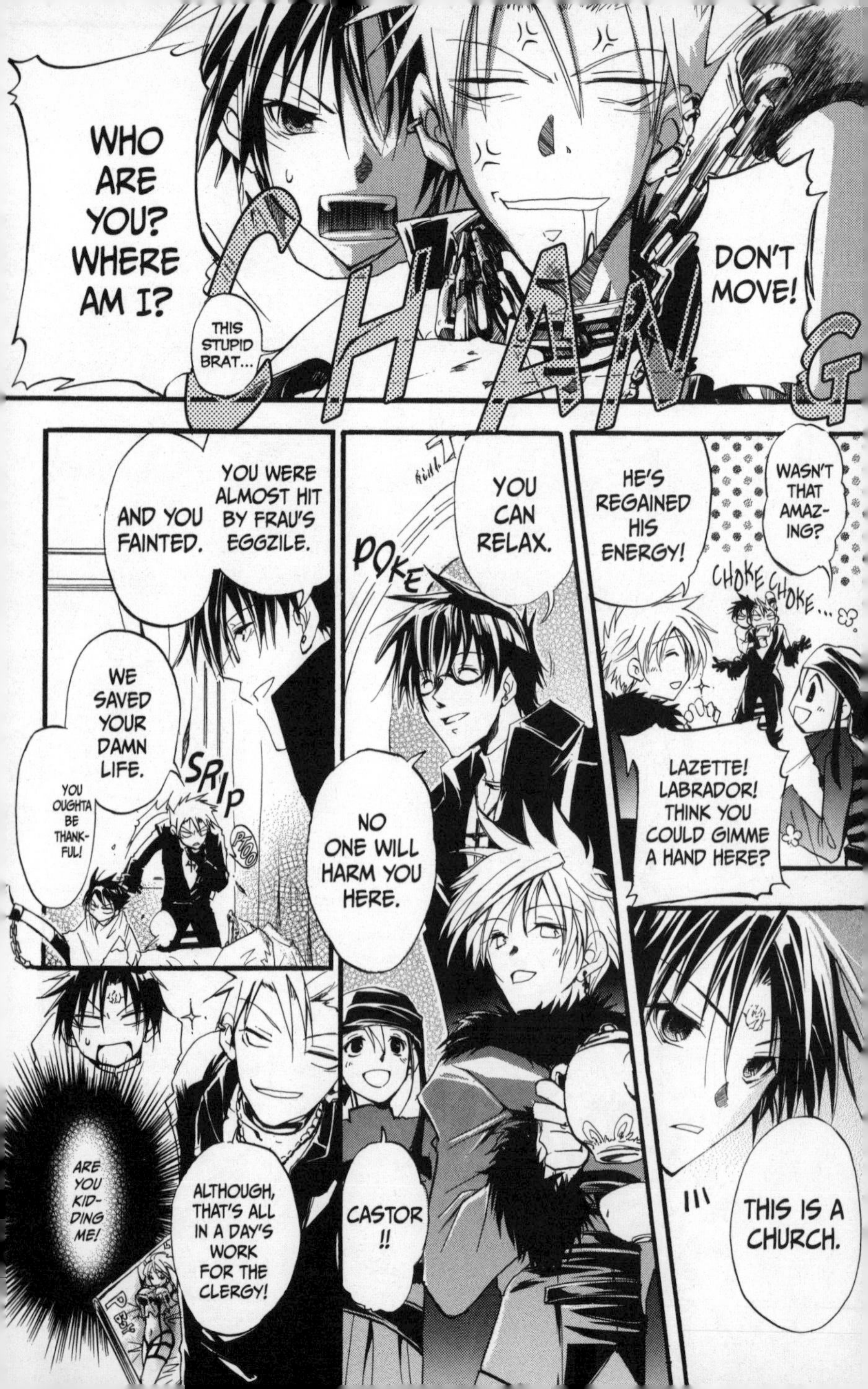
DON'T MOVE!
CHANG
WHO ARE YOU? WHERE AM I?
THIS STUPID BRAT...
WASN'T THAT AMAZ-ING?
HE'S REGAINED HIS ENERGY!
CHOKE CHOKE...
LAZETTE! LABRADOR! THINK YOU COULD GIMME A HAND HERE?
THIS IS A CHURCH.
YOU CAN RELAX.
POKE
NO ONE WILL HARM YOU HERE.
YOU WERE ALMOST HIT BY FRAU'S EGGZILE.
AND YOU FAINTED.
WE SAVED YOUR DAMN LIFE.
SRIP
YOU OUGHTA BE THANK-FUL!
CASTOR !!
ALTHOUGH, THAT'S ALL IN A DAY'S WORK FOR THE CLERGY!
ARE YOU KID-DING ME!

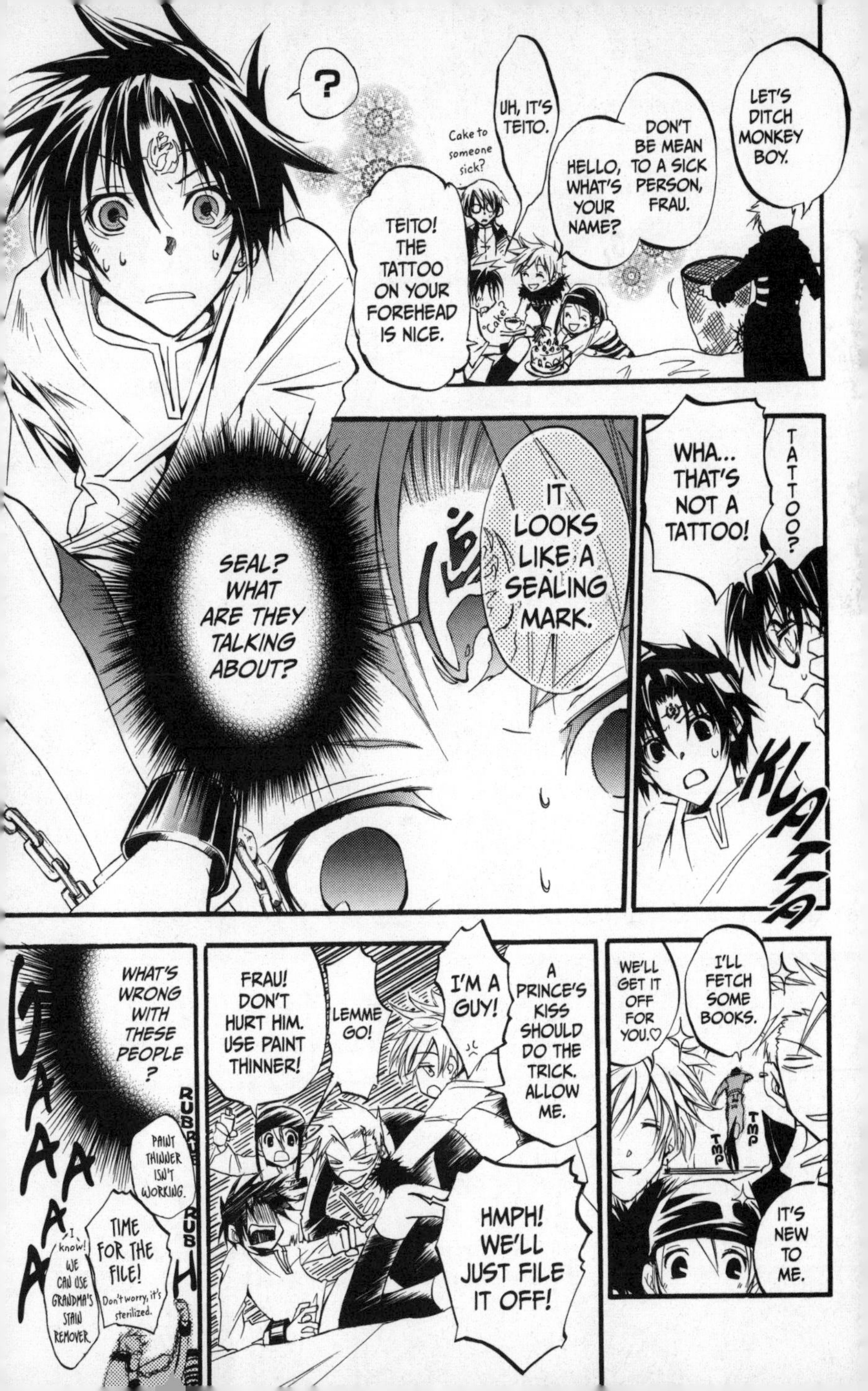
LET'S DITCH MONKEY BOY.
DON'T BE MEAN TO A SICK PERSON, FRAU.
HELLO, WHAT'S YOUR NAME?
UH, IT'S TEITO.
Cake to someone sick?
Cake?
TEITO! THE TATTOO ON YOUR FOREHEAD IS NICE.
?
TATTOO?
WHA... THAT'S NOT A TATTOO!
KLATTA
IT LOOKS LIKE A SEALING MARK.
SEAL? WHAT ARE THEY TALKING ABOUT?
I'LL FETCH SOME BOOKS.
WE'LL GET IT OFF FOR YOU.♡
TMP TMP
IT'S NEW TO ME.
A PRINCE'S KISS SHOULD DO THE TRICK. ALLOW ME.
I'M A GUY!
LEMME GO!
FRAU! DON'T HURT HIM. USE PAINT THINNER!
HMPH! WE'LL JUST FILE IT OFF!
WHAT'S WRONG WITH THESE PEOPLE?
RUB RUB
PAINT THINNER ISN'T WORKING.
RUB RUB
TIME FOR THE FILE! Don't worry, it's sterilized.
I know! WE CAN USE GRANDMA'S STAIN REMOVER
GAAAAAH

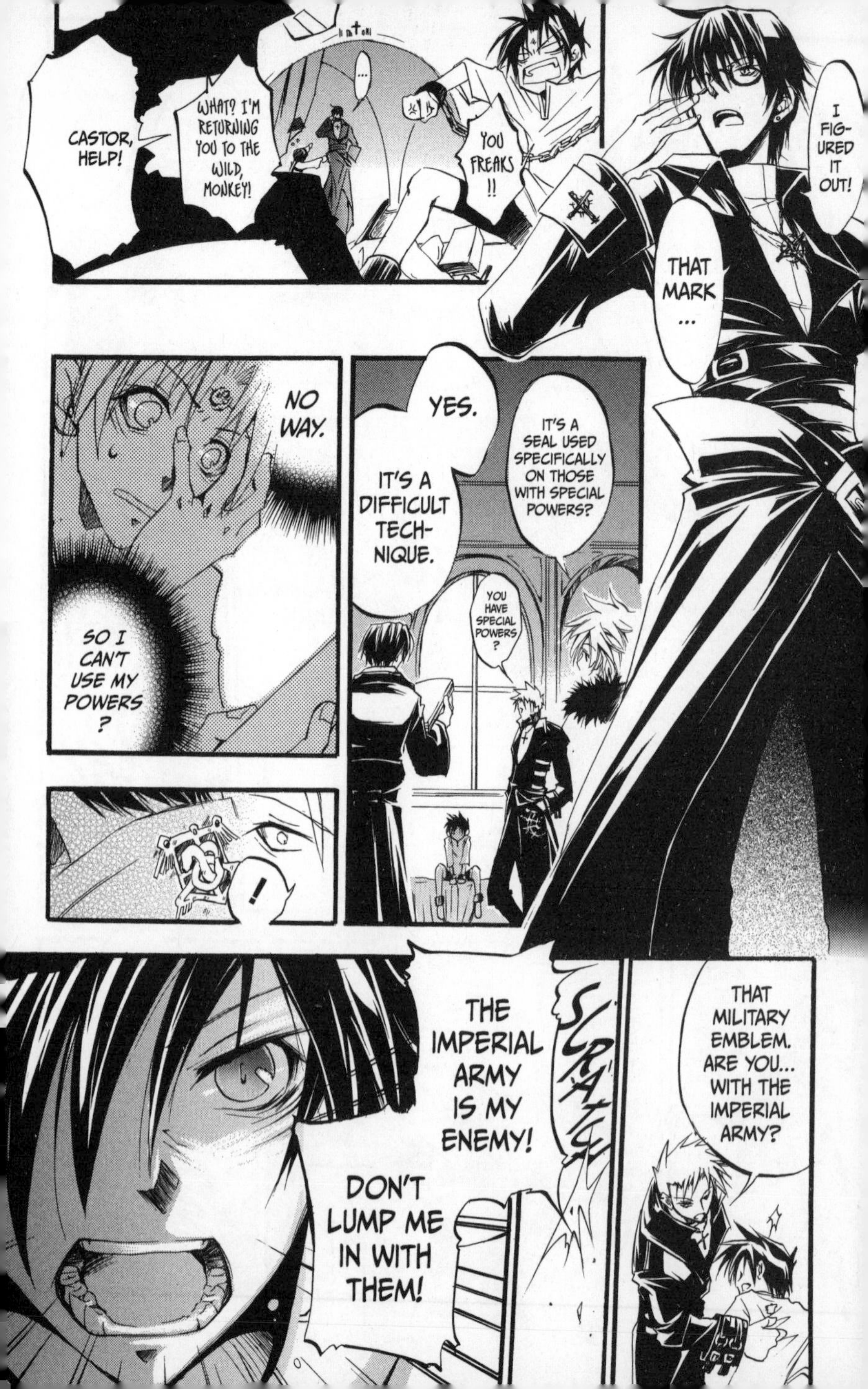
I FIGURED IT OUT!
THAT MARK...
YOU FREAKS!!
...
WHAT? I'M RETURNING YOU TO THE WILD, MONKEY!
CASTOR, HELP!
IT'S A SEAL USED SPECIFICALLY ON THOSE WITH SPECIAL POWERS?
YES.
IT'S A DIFFICULT TECHNIQUE.
YOU HAVE SPECIAL POWERS?
NO WAY.
SO I CAN'T USE MY POWERS?
!
THAT MILITARY EMBLEM. ARE YOU... WITH THE IMPERIAL ARMY?
SCRATCH
THE IMPERIAL ARMY IS MY ENEMY!
DON'T LUMP ME IN WITH THEM!

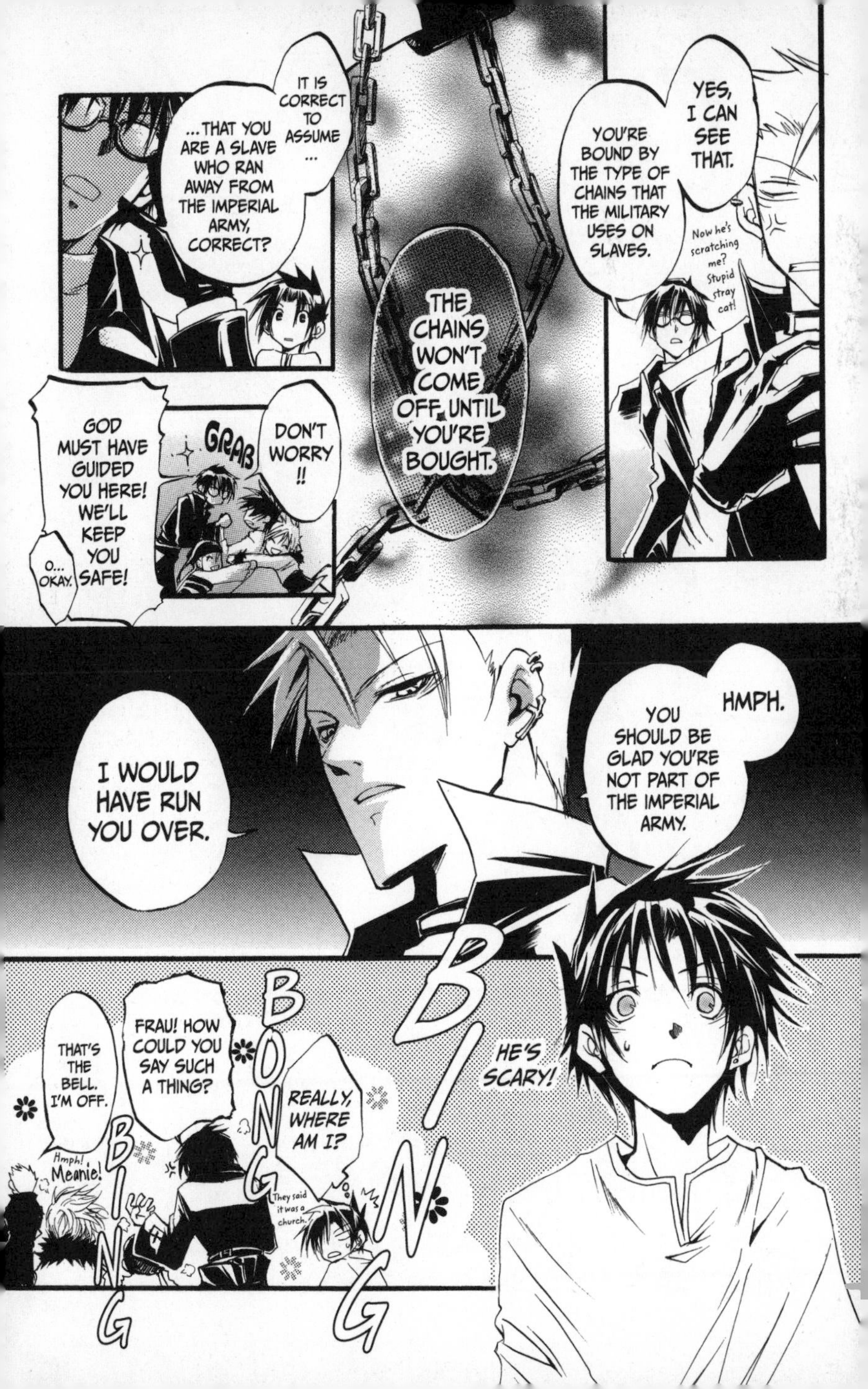
YES, I CAN SEE THAT.
YOU'RE BOUND BY THE TYPE OF CHAINS THAT THE MILITARY USES ON SLAVES.
Now he's scratching me? Stupid stray cat!
THE CHAINS WON'T COME OFF UNTIL YOU'RE BOUGHT.
IT IS CORRECT TO ASSUME...
...THAT YOU ARE A SLAVE WHO RAN AWAY FROM THE IMPERIAL ARMY, CORRECT?
DON'T WORRY!!
GRAB
GOD MUST HAVE GUIDED YOU HERE! WE'LL KEEP YOU SAFE!
O... OKAY.
HMPH.
YOU SHOULD BE GLAD YOU'RE NOT PART OF THE IMPERIAL ARMY.
I WOULD HAVE RUN YOU OVER.
BING
BONG
HE'S SCARY!
REALLY, WHERE AM I?
They said it was a church.
FRAU! HOW COULD YOU SAY SUCH A THING?
THAT'S THE BELL. I'M OFF.
Hmph! Meanie!
BONG
BING

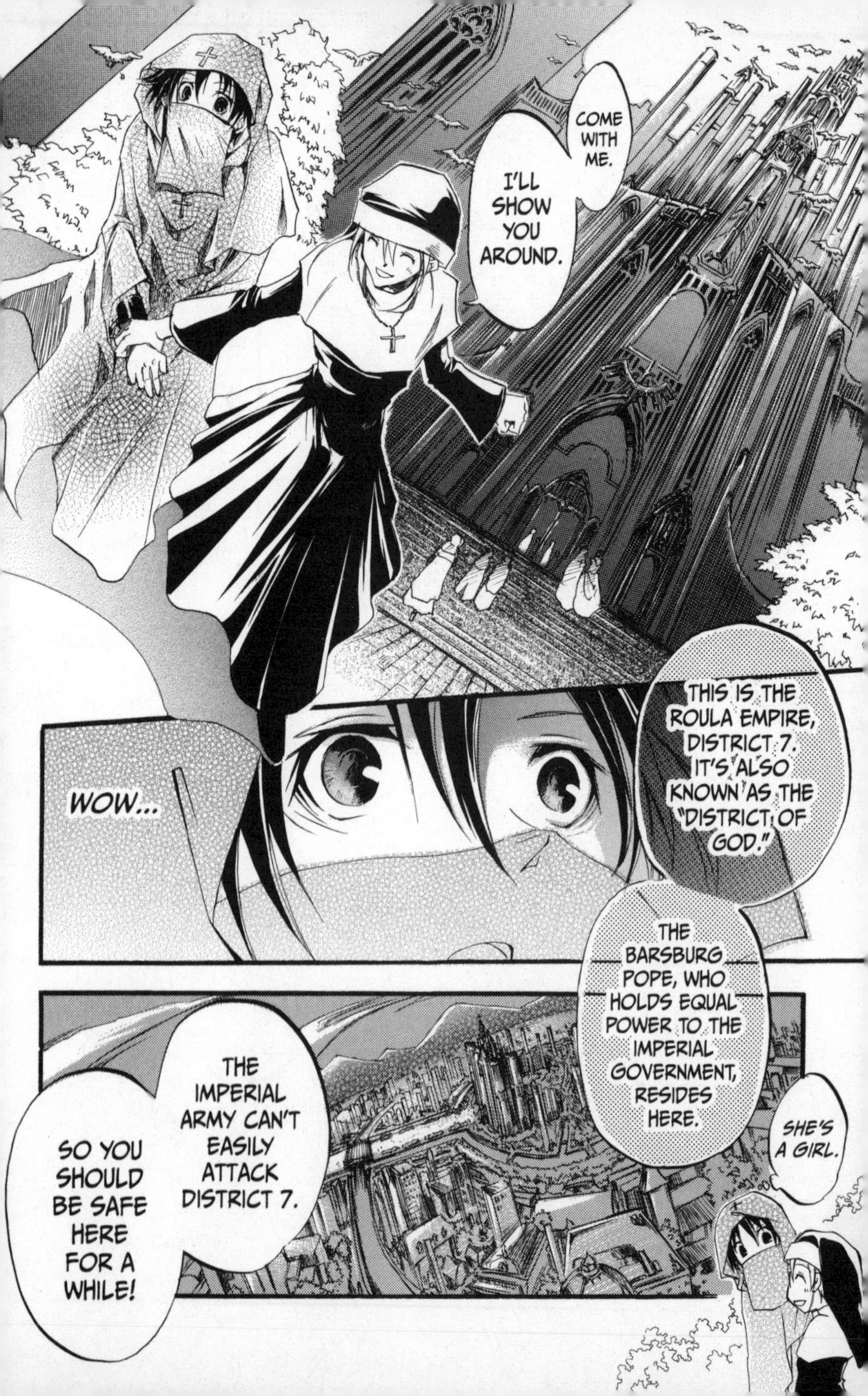
COME WITH ME.
I'LL SHOW YOU AROUND.
THIS IS THE ROULA EMPIRE, DISTRICT 7. IT'S ALSO KNOWN AS THE "DISTRICT OF GOD."
WOW...
THE BARSBURG POPE, WHO HOLDS EQUAL POWER TO THE IMPERIAL GOVERNMENT, RESIDES HERE.
THE IMPERIAL ARMY CAN'T EASILY ATTACK DISTRICT 7.
SO YOU SHOULD BE SAFE HERE FOR A WHILE!
SHE'S A GIRL.

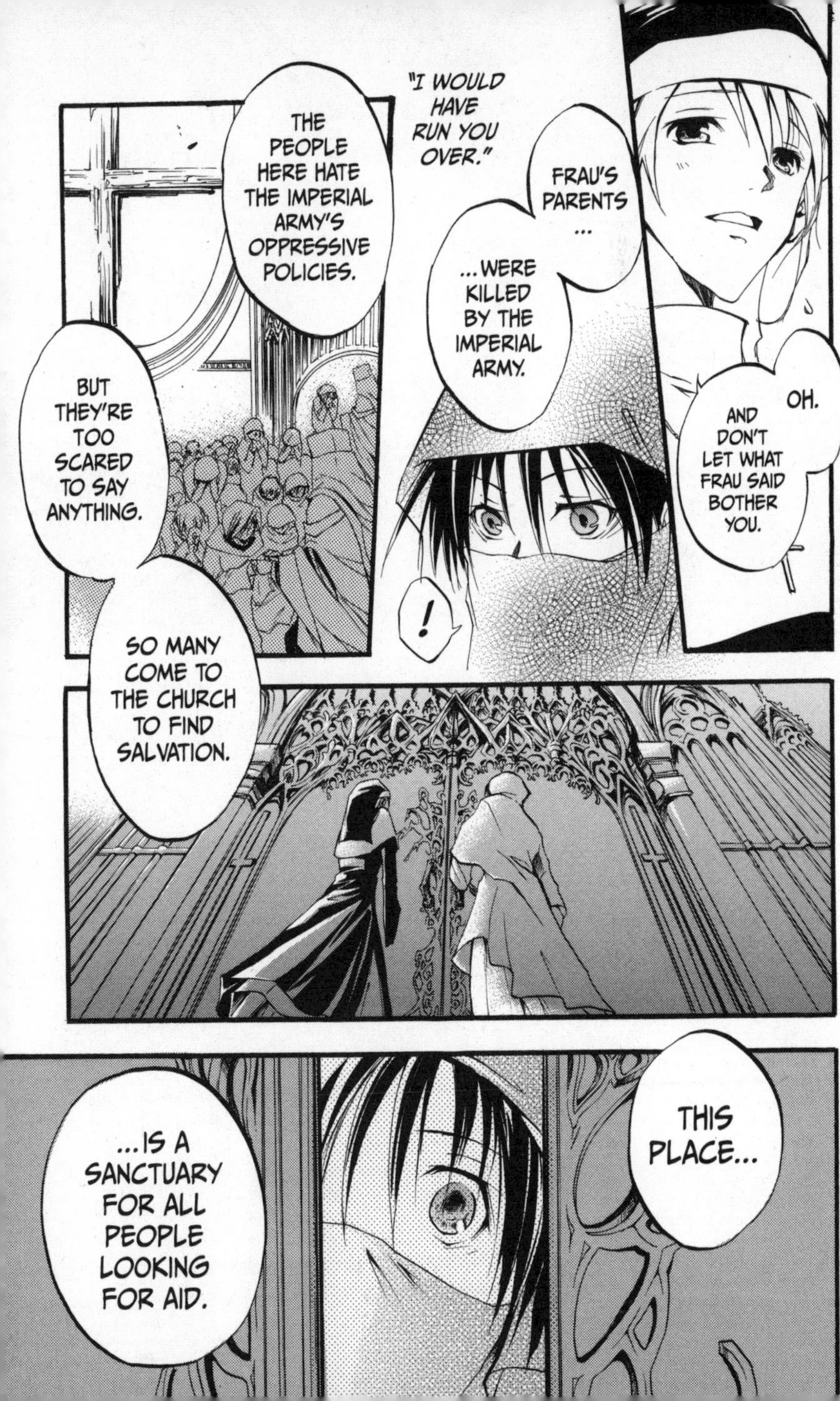
OH.
AND DON'T LET WHAT FRAU SAID BOTHER YOU.
"I WOULD HAVE RUN YOU OVER."
FRAU'S PARENTS...
...WERE KILLED BY THE IMPERIAL ARMY.
!
THE PEOPLE HERE HATE THE IMPERIAL ARMY'S OPPRESSIVE POLICIES.
BUT THEY'RE TOO SCARED TO SAY ANYTHING.
SO MANY COME TO THE CHURCH TO FIND SALVATION.
THIS PLACE...
...IS A SANCTUARY FOR ALL PEOPLE LOOKING FOR AID.

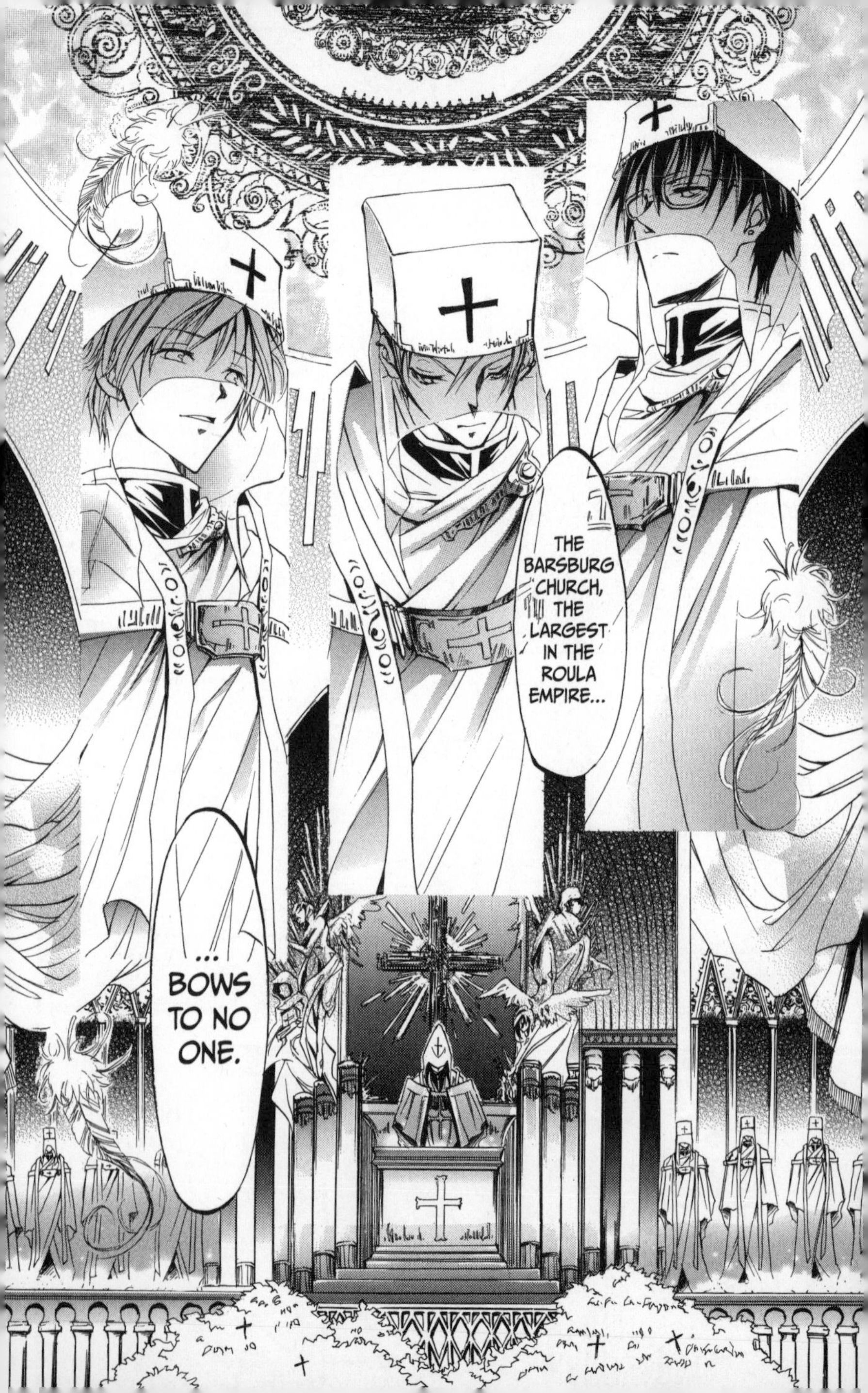
THE BARSBURG CHURCH, THE LARGEST IN THE ROULA EMPIRE...
... BOWS TO NO ONE.

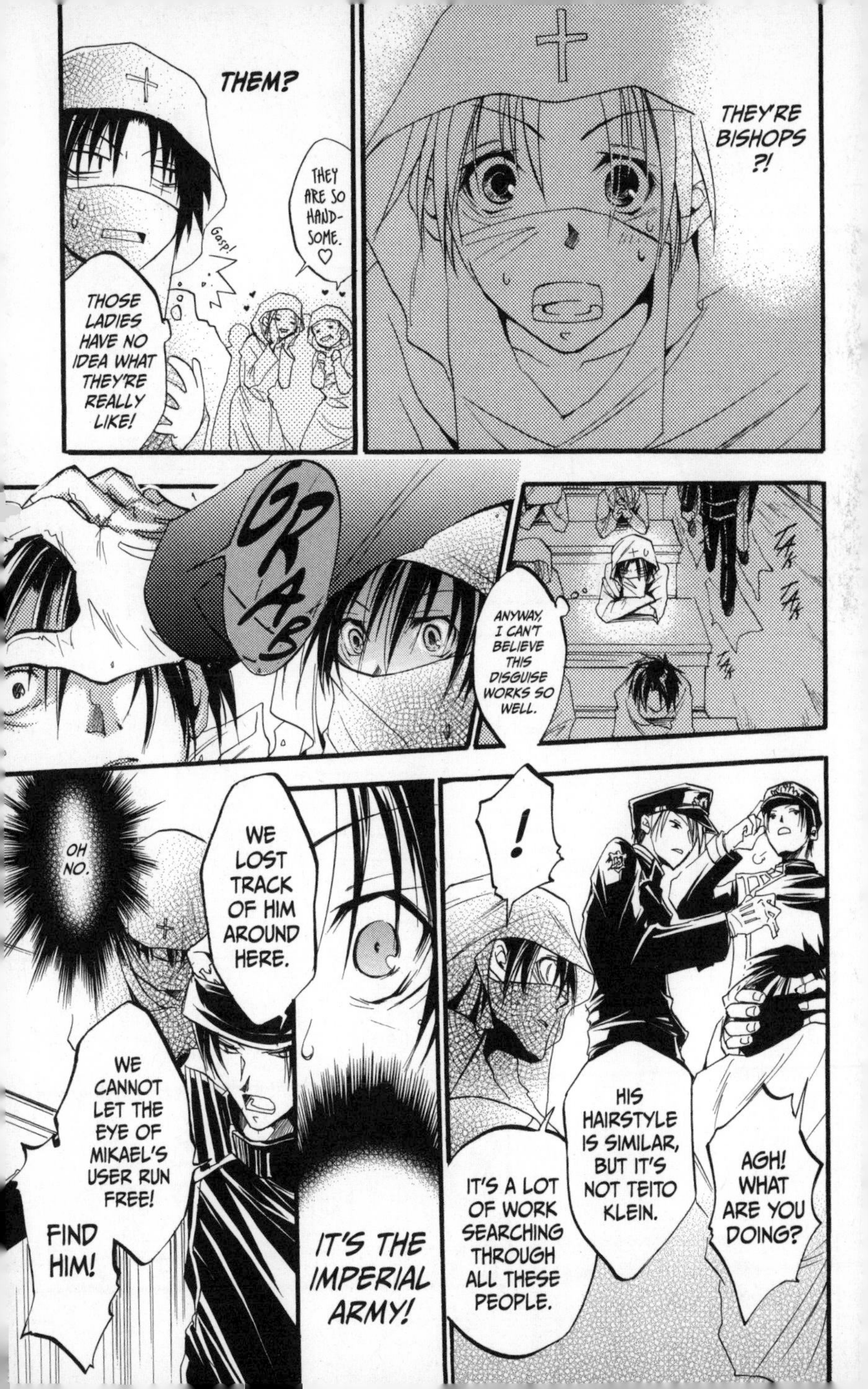
THEY'RE BISHOPS ?!
THEM?
THEY ARE SO HAND-SOME. ♡
Gasp!
THOSE LADIES HAVE NO IDEA WHAT THEY'RE REALLY LIKE!
ANYWAY, I CAN'T BELIEVE THIS DISGUISE WORKS SO WELL.
TAK TAK TAK TAK
GRAB
!
AGH! WHAT ARE YOU DOING?
HIS HAIRSTYLE IS SIMILAR, BUT IT'S NOT TEITO KLEIN.
IT'S A LOT OF WORK SEARCHING THROUGH ALL THESE PEOPLE.
WE LOST TRACK OF HIM AROUND HERE.
OH NO.
IT'S THE IMPERIAL ARMY!
WE CANNOT LET THE EYE OF MIKAEL'S USER RUN FREE!
FIND HIM!

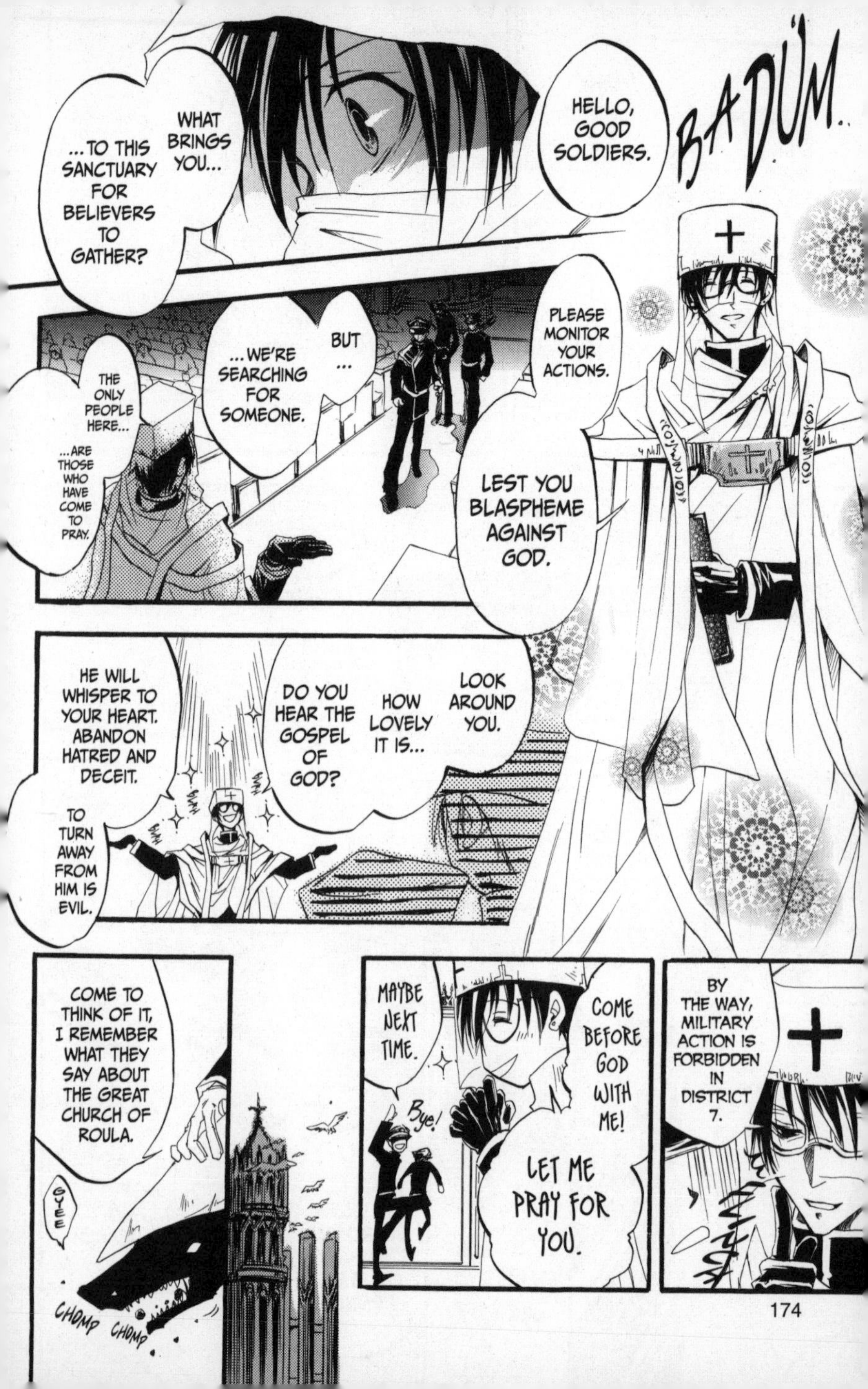
BA DUM...
HELLO, GOOD SOLDIERS.
WHAT BRINGS YOU...
...TO THIS SANCTUARY FOR BELIEVERS TO GATHER?
PLEASE MONITOR YOUR ACTIONS.
LEST YOU BLASPHEME AGAINST GOD.
BUT...
...WE'RE SEARCHING FOR SOMEONE.
THE ONLY PEOPLE HERE...
...ARE THOSE WHO HAVE COME TO PRAY.
LOOK AROUND YOU.
HOW LOVELY IT IS...
DO YOU HEAR THE GOSPEL OF GOD?
HE WILL WHISPER TO YOUR HEART. ABANDON HATRED AND DECEIT.
TO TURN AWAY FROM HIM IS EVIL.
BY THE WAY, MILITARY ACTION IS FORBIDDEN IN DISTRICT 7.
COME BEFORE GOD WITH ME!
LET ME PRAY FOR YOU.
MAYBE NEXT TIME.
Bye!
COME TO THINK OF IT, I REMEMBER WHAT THEY SAY ABOUT THE GREAT CHURCH OF ROULA.
GYEE
CHOMP CHOMP

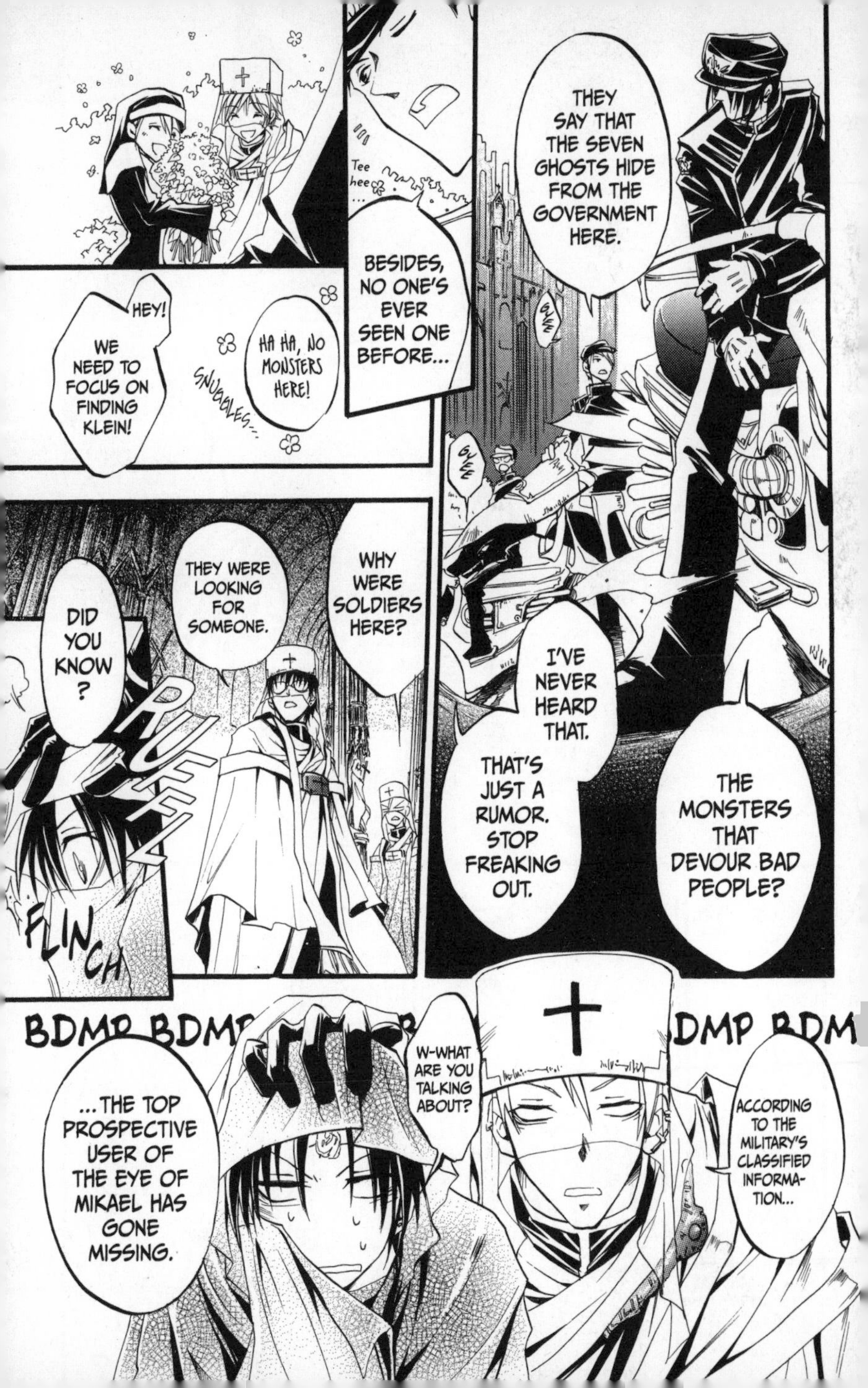

THEY SAY THAT THE SEVEN GHOSTS HIDE FROM THE GOVERNMENT HERE.
THE MONSTERS THAT DEVOUR BAD PEOPLE?
I'VE NEVER HEARD THAT.
THAT'S JUST A RUMOR. STOP FREAKING OUT.
Tee hee...
BESIDES, NO ONE'S EVER SEEN ONE BEFORE...
HA HA, NO MONSTERS HERE!
SNUGGLES
HEY!
WE NEED TO FOCUS ON FINDING KLEIN!
WHY WERE SOLDIERS HERE?
THEY WERE LOOKING FOR SOMEONE.
DID YOU KNOW?
RUFFLE
FLINCH
BDMP BDMP BDMP BDMP BDMP BDM
ACCORDING TO THE MILITARY'S CLASSIFIED INFORMATION...
W-WHAT ARE YOU TALKING ABOUT?
...THE TOP PROSPECTIVE USER OF THE EYE OF MIKAEL HAS GONE MISSING.

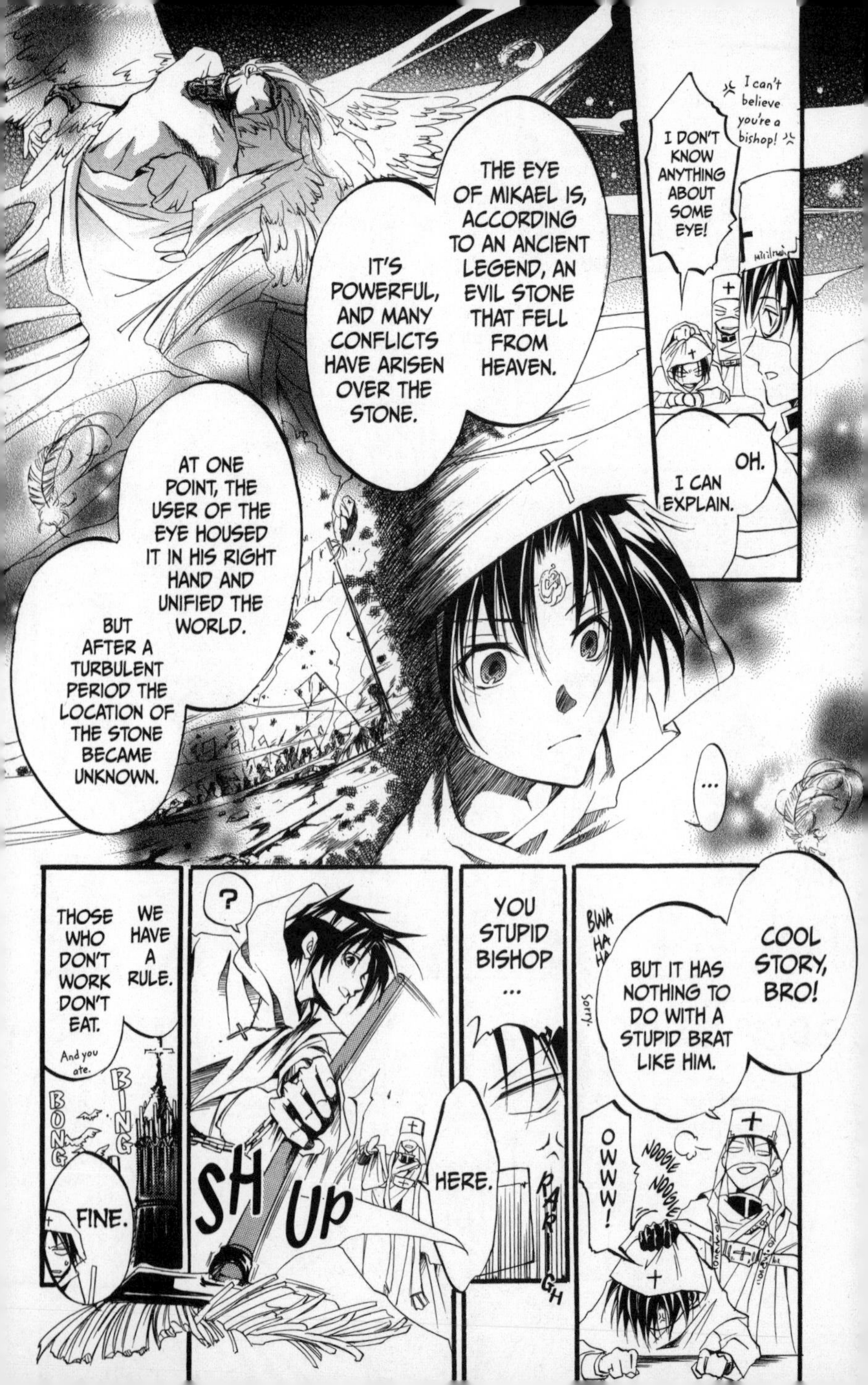
I DON'T KNOW ANYTHING ABOUT SOME EYE!
I can't believe you're a bishop!
OH.
I CAN EXPLAIN.
THE EYE OF MIKAEL IS, ACCORDING TO AN ANCIENT LEGEND, AN EVIL STONE THAT FELL FROM HEAVEN.
IT'S POWERFUL, AND MANY CONFLICTS HAVE ARISEN OVER THE STONE.
AT ONE POINT, THE USER OF THE EYE HOUSED IT IN HIS RIGHT HAND AND UNIFIED THE WORLD.
BUT AFTER A TURBULENT PERIOD THE LOCATION OF THE STONE BECAME UNKNOWN.
...
COOL STORY, BRO!
BUT IT HAS NOTHING TO DO WITH A STUPID BRAT LIKE HIM.
BWA HA HA HA
Sorry.
NOOGIE NOOGIE
OWWW!
YOU STUPID BISHOP ...
RARIGH
HERE.
?
SH UP
WE HAVE A RULE.
THOSE WHO DON'T WORK DON'T EAT.
And you ate.
BING
BONG
FINE.

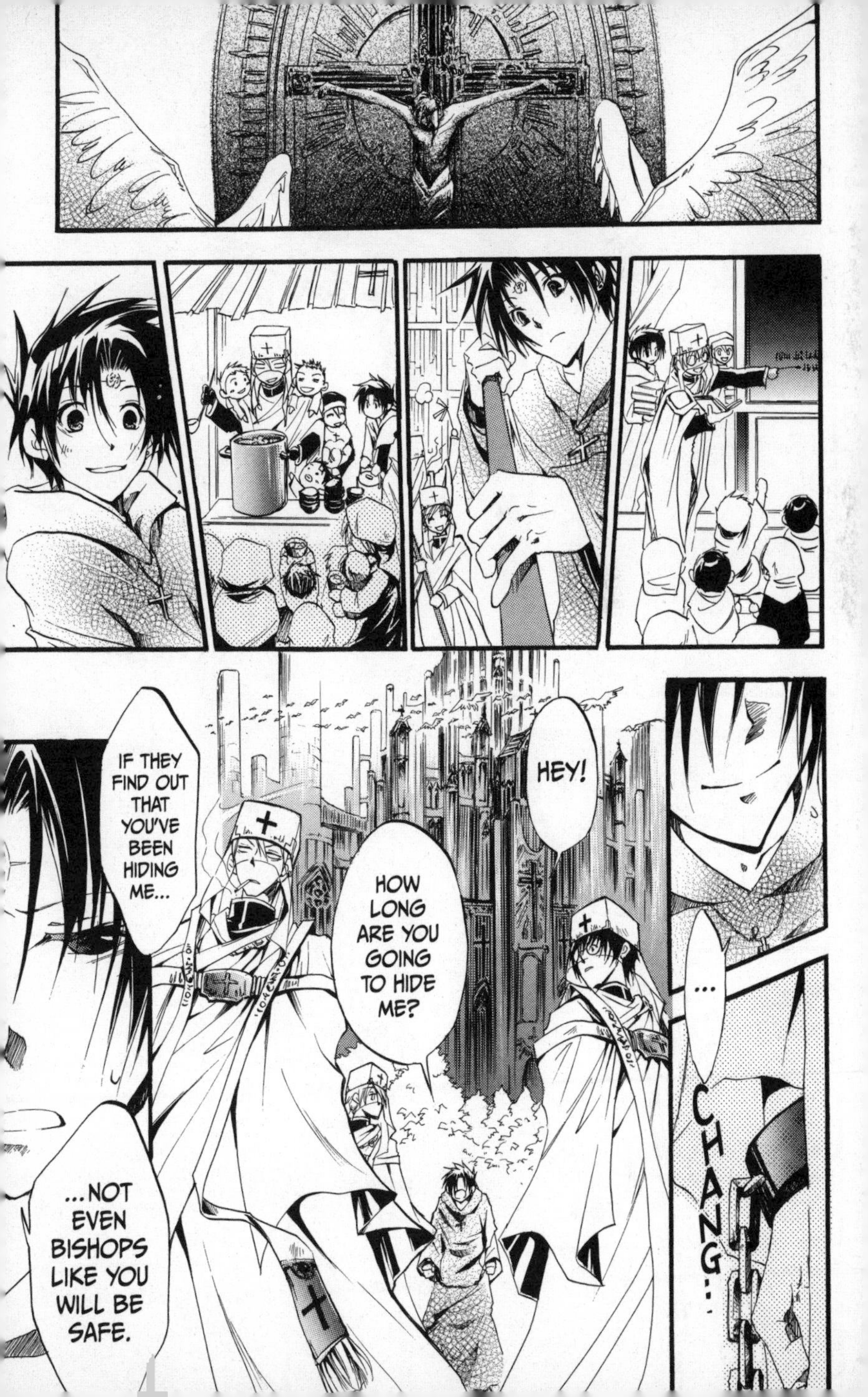
...
CHANG...
HEY!
HOW LONG ARE YOU GOING TO HIDE ME?
IF THEY FIND OUT THAT YOU'VE BEEN HIDING ME...
...NOT EVEN BISHOPS LIKE YOU WILL BE SAFE.

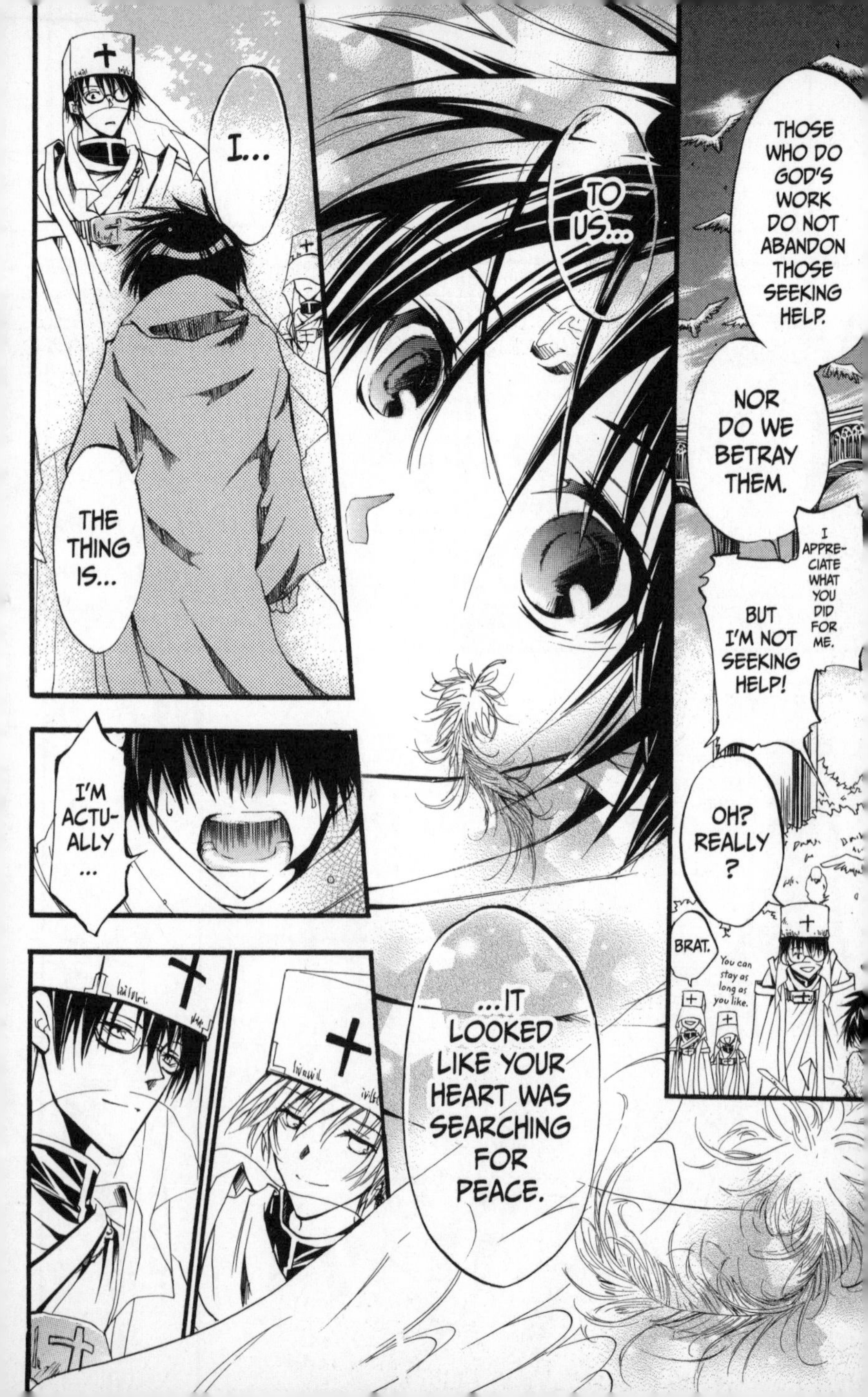
THOSE WHO DO GOD'S WORK DO NOT ABANDON THOSE SEEKING HELP.
NOR DO WE BETRAY THEM.
I APPRECIATE WHAT YOU DID FOR ME.
BUT I'M NOT SEEKING HELP!
OH? REALLY?
BRAT.
You can stay as long as you like.
TO US...
I...
THE THING IS...
I'M ACTUALLY...
...IT LOOKED LIKE YOUR HEART WAS SEARCHING FOR PEACE.

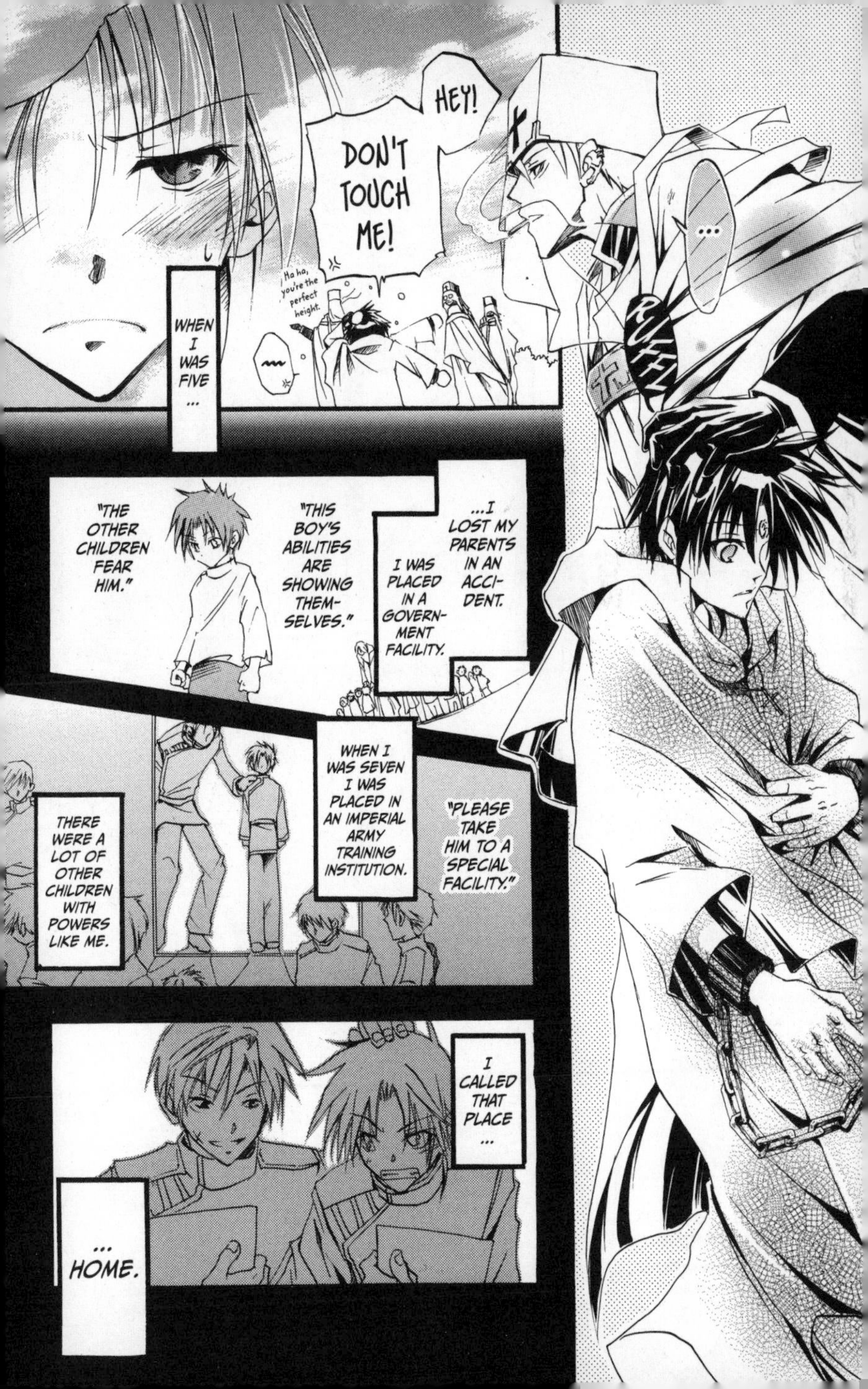
...
RUFFL
HEY!
DON'T TOUCH ME!
Ha ha, you're the perfect height.
~~
WHEN I WAS FIVE ...
...I LOST MY PARENTS IN AN ACCIDENT.
I WAS PLACED IN A GOVERNMENT FACILITY.
"THIS BOY'S ABILITIES ARE SHOWING THEMSELVES."
"THE OTHER CHILDREN FEAR HIM."
"PLEASE TAKE HIM TO A SPECIAL FACILITY."
WHEN I WAS SEVEN I WAS PLACED IN AN IMPERIAL ARMY TRAINING INSTITUTION.
THERE WERE A LOT OF OTHER CHILDREN WITH POWERS LIKE ME.
I CALLED THAT PLACE ...
... HOME.

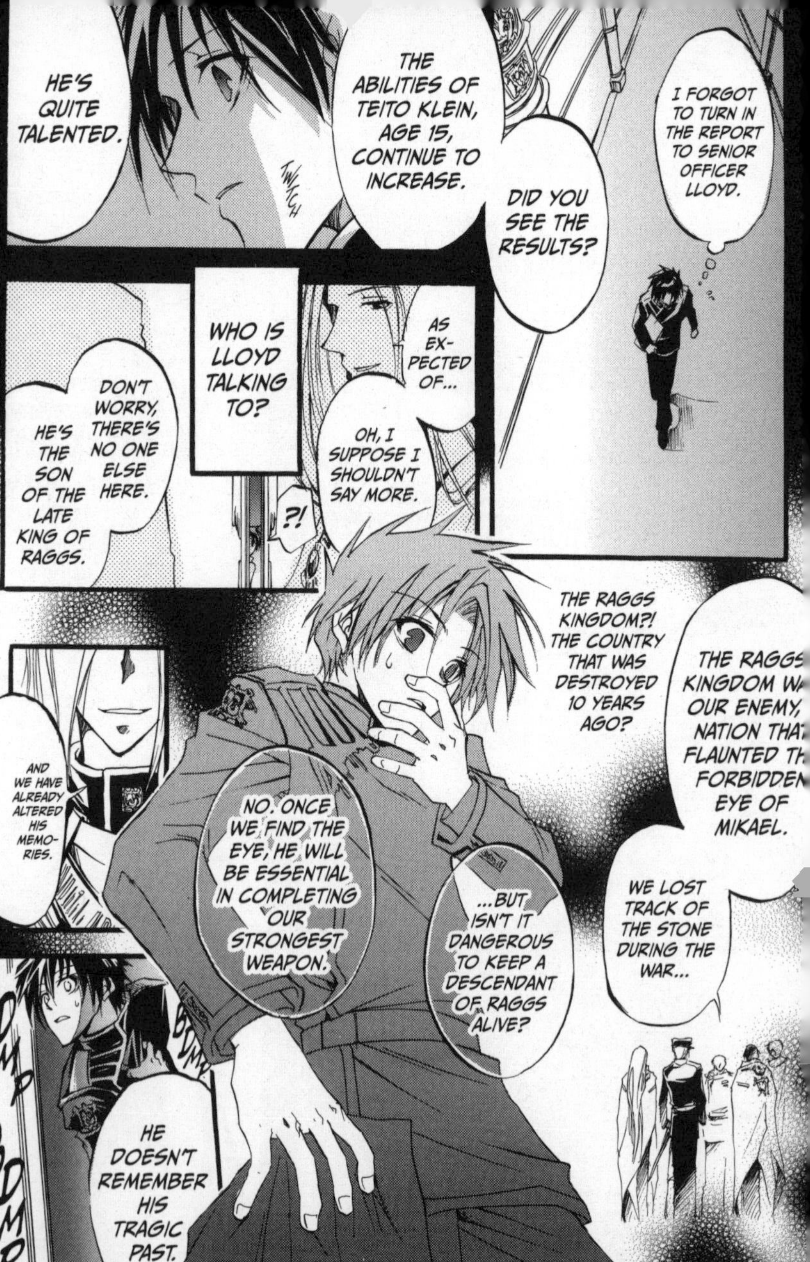
I FORGOT TO TURN IN THE REPORT TO SENIOR OFFICER LLOYD.
DID YOU SEE THE RESULTS?
THE ABILITIES OF TEITO KLEIN, AGE 15, CONTINUE TO INCREASE.
TWITCH
HE'S QUITE TALENTED.
AS EX-PECTED OF...
OH, I SUPPOSE I SHOULDN'T SAY MORE.
?!
WHO IS LLOYD TALKING TO?
DON'T WORRY, THERE'S NO ONE ELSE HERE.
HE'S THE SON OF THE LATE KING OF RAGGS.
THE RAGGS KINGDOM WA OUR ENEMY, NATION THA FLAUNTED TH FORBIDDEN EYE OF MIKAEL.
THE RAGGS KINGDOM?! THE COUNTRY THAT WAS DESTROYED 10 YEARS AGO?
WE LOST TRACK OF THE STONE DURING THE WAR...
...BUT ISN'T IT DANGEROUS TO KEEP A DESCENDANT OF RAGGS ALIVE?
NO. ONCE WE FIND THE EYE, HE WILL BE ESSENTIAL IN COMPLETING OUR STRONGEST WEAPON.
AND WE HAVE ALREADY ALTERED HIS MEMORIES.
HE DOESN'T REMEMBER HIS TRAGIC PAST.
BDMP
BDMP
BDMP

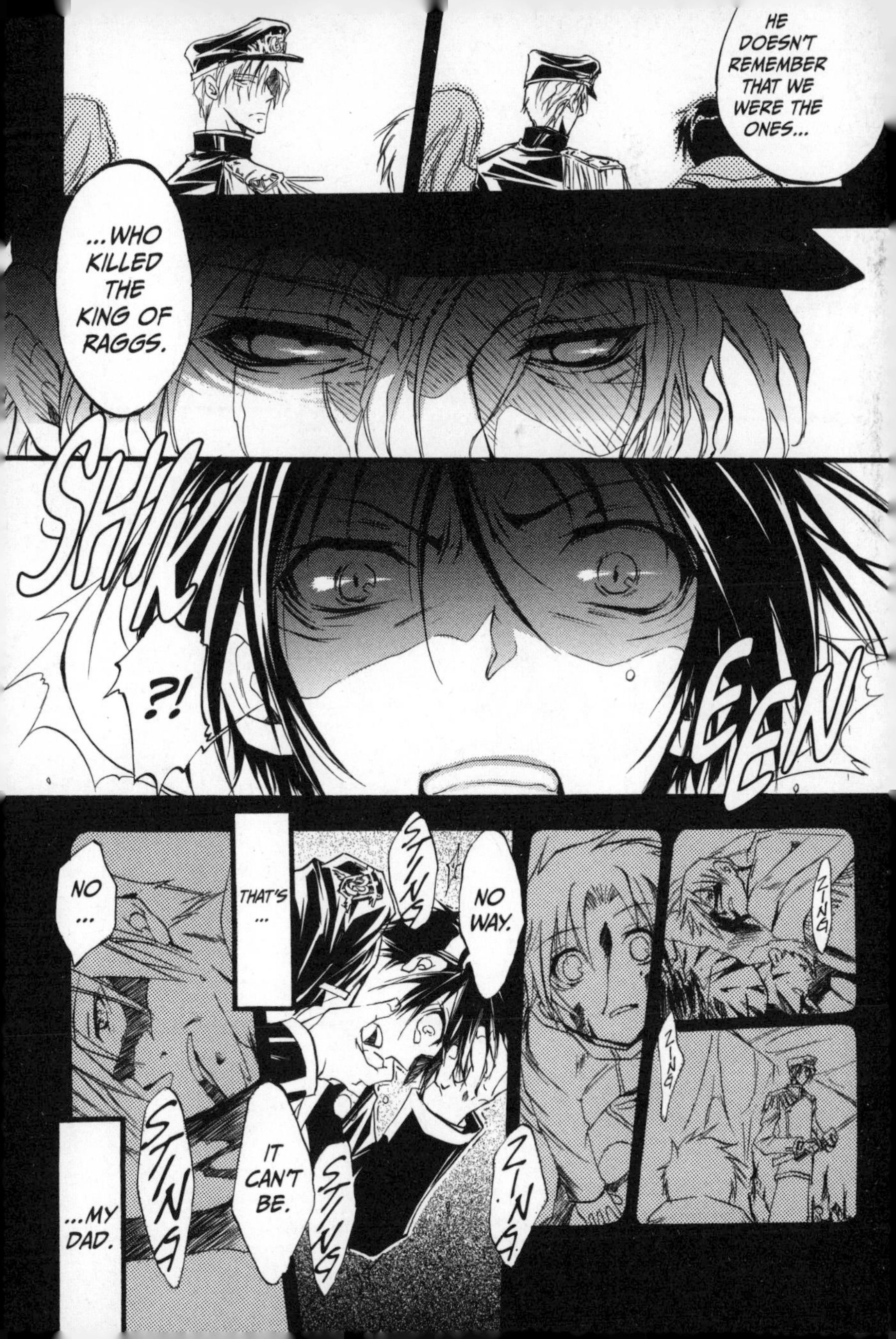
HE DOESN'T REMEMBER THAT WE WERE THE ONES...
...WHO KILLED THE KING OF RAGGS.
SHI
EEN
?!
ZING
ZING
NO WAY.
SHING
THAT'S...
ZING
SHING
IT CAN'T BE.
SHING
NO...
...MY DAD.

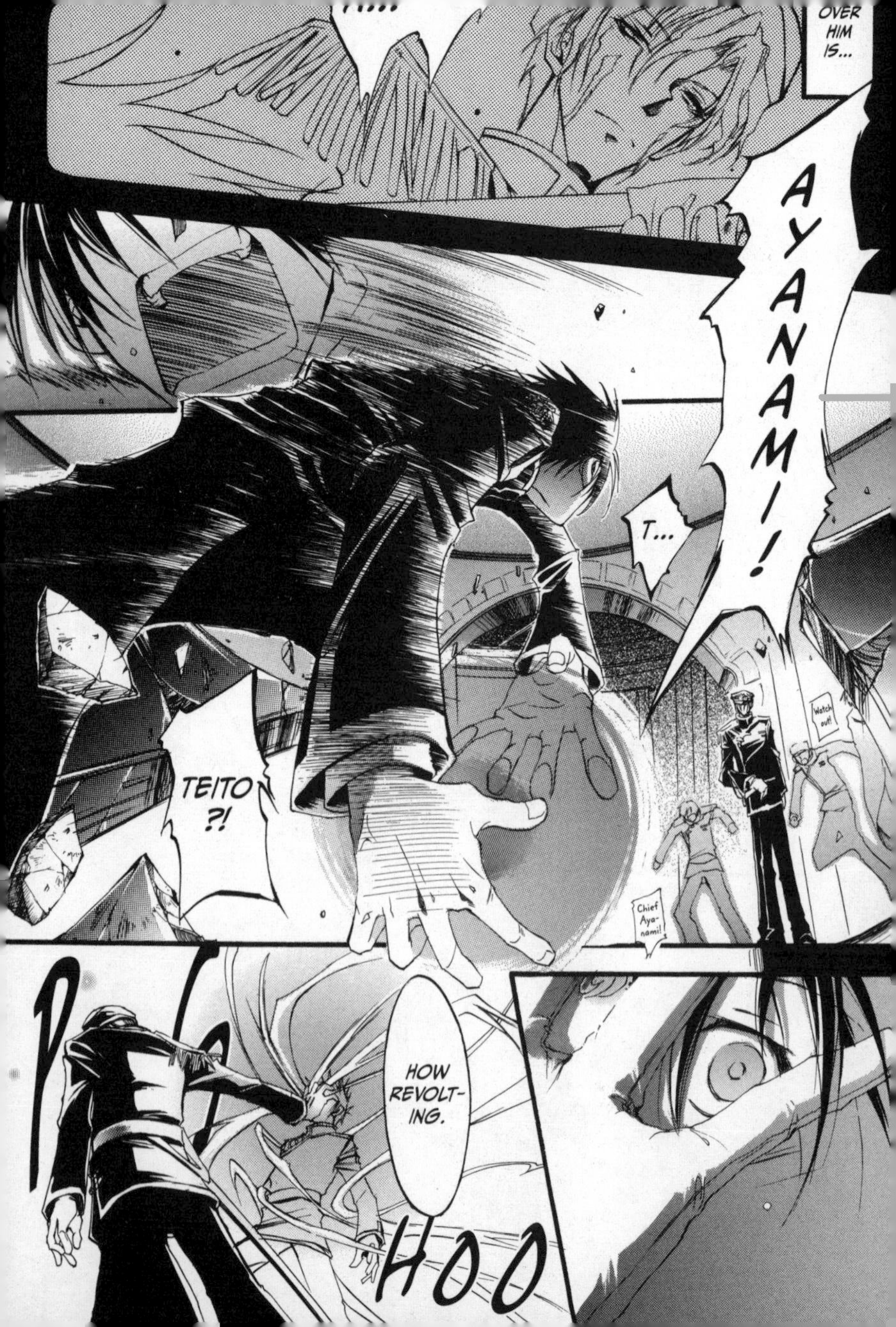
OVER HIM IS...
AYANAMI!!
T...
Watch out!
Chief Ayanami!
TEITO ?!
HOW REVOLTING.

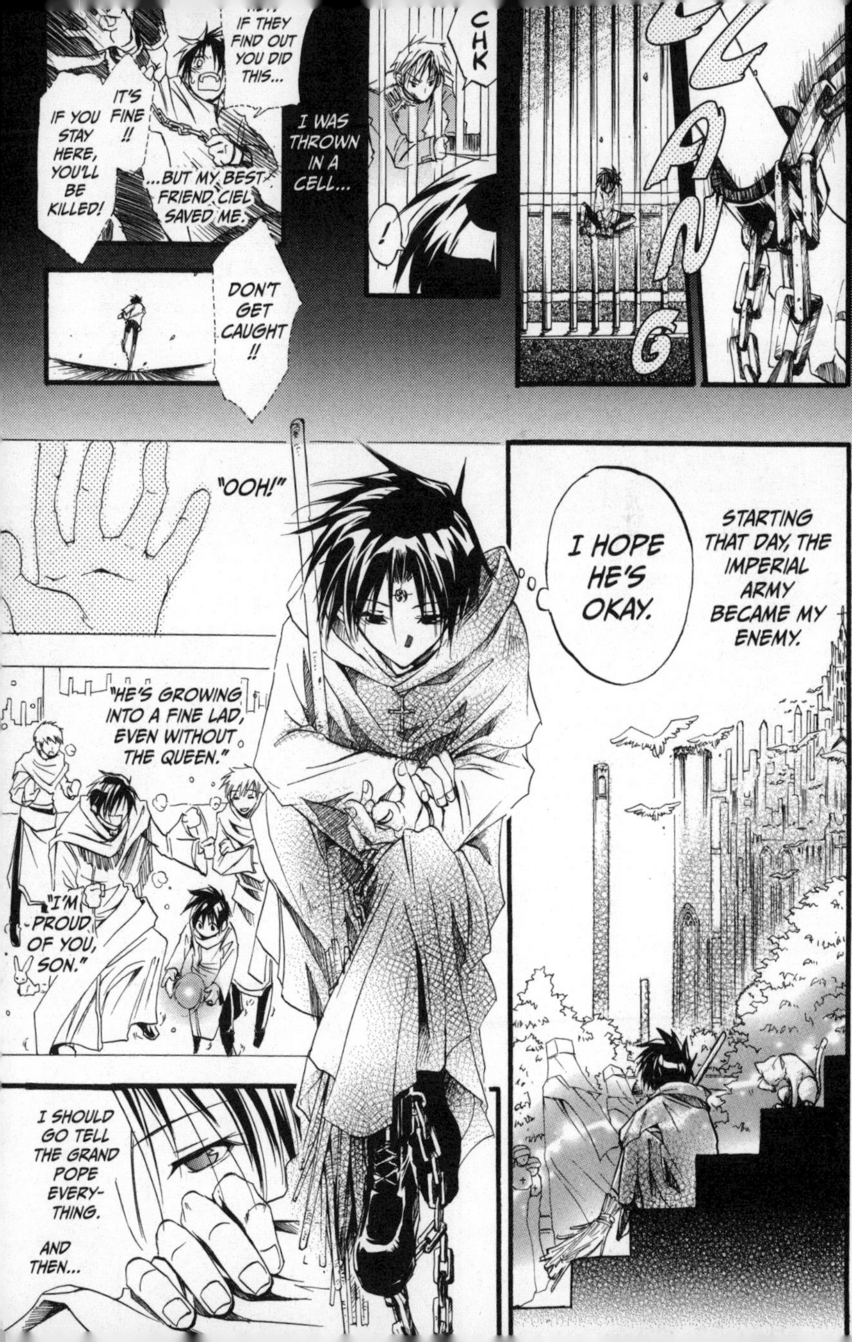
CLANG
CHK
!
I WAS THROWN IN A CELL...
IF THEY FIND OUT YOU DID THIS...
IT'S FINE !!
IF YOU STAY HERE, YOU'LL BE KILLED!
...BUT MY BEST FRIEND CIEL SAVED ME.
DON'T GET CAUGHT !!
STARTING THAT DAY, THE IMPERIAL ARMY BECAME MY ENEMY.
I HOPE HE'S OKAY.
"OOH!"
"HE'S GROWING INTO A FINE LAD, EVEN WITHOUT THE QUEEN."
"I'M PROUD OF YOU, SON."
I SHOULD GO TELL THE GRAND POPE EVERYTHING.
AND THEN...

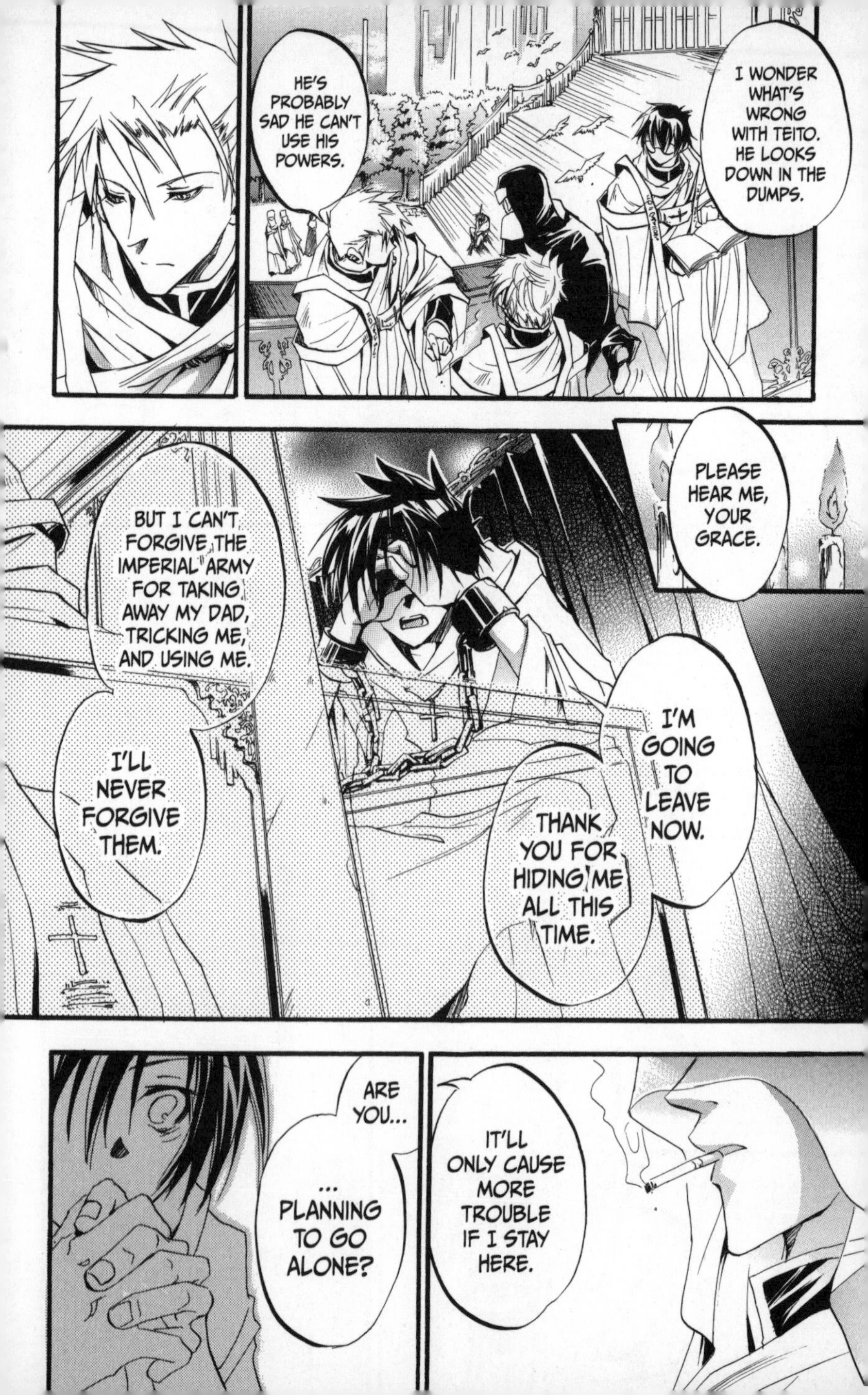
I WONDER WHAT'S WRONG WITH TEITO. HE LOOKS DOWN IN THE DUMPS.
HE'S PROBABLY SAD HE CAN'T USE HIS POWERS.
PLEASE HEAR ME, YOUR GRACE.
I'M GOING TO LEAVE NOW.
THANK YOU FOR HIDING ME ALL THIS TIME.
BUT I CAN'T FORGIVE THE IMPERIAL ARMY FOR TAKING AWAY MY DAD, TRICKING ME, AND USING ME.
I'LL NEVER FORGIVE THEM.
IT'LL ONLY CAUSE MORE TROUBLE IF I STAY HERE.
ARE YOU...
... PLANNING TO GO ALONE?

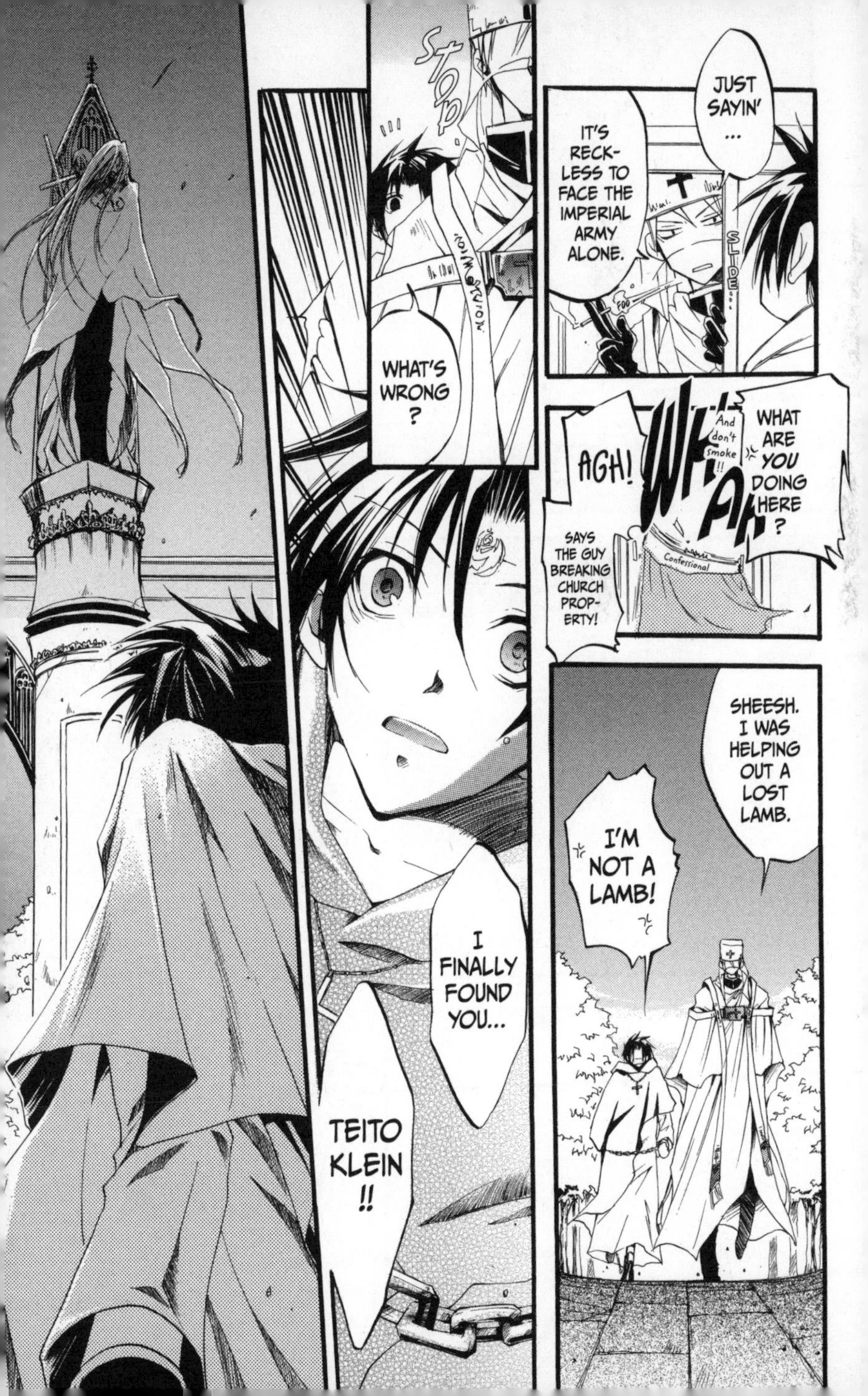
JUST SAYIN' ...
IT'S RECKLESS TO FACE THE IMPERIAL ARMY ALONE.
SLIDE...
FOO
WHAT ARE YOU DOING HERE?
And don't smoke!!
AGH!
Confessional
SAYS THE GUY BREAKING CHURCH PROPERTY!
SHEESH. I WAS HELPING OUT A LOST LAMB.
I'M NOT A LAMB!
STOP.
WHAT'S WRONG?
I FINALLY FOUND YOU...
TEITO KLEIN!!

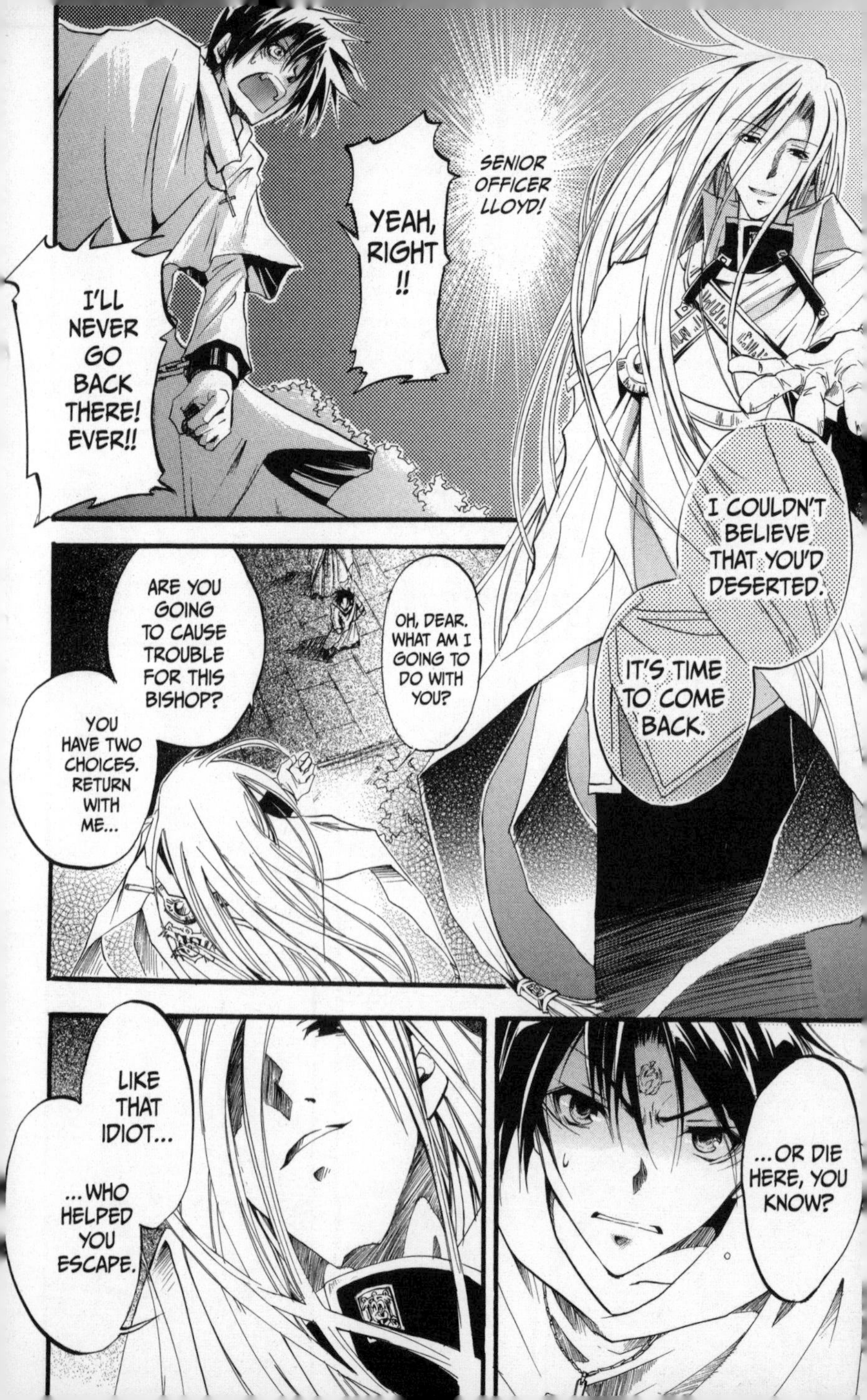

SENIOR OFFICER LLOYD!
I COULDN'T BELIEVE THAT YOU'D DESERTED.
IT'S TIME TO COME BACK.
YEAH, RIGHT !!
I'LL NEVER GO BACK THERE! EVER!!
OH, DEAR. WHAT AM I GOING TO DO WITH YOU?
ARE YOU GOING TO CAUSE TROUBLE FOR THIS BISHOP?
YOU HAVE TWO CHOICES. RETURN WITH ME...
...OR DIE HERE, YOU KNOW?
LIKE THAT IDIOT...
...WHO HELPED YOU ESCAPE.

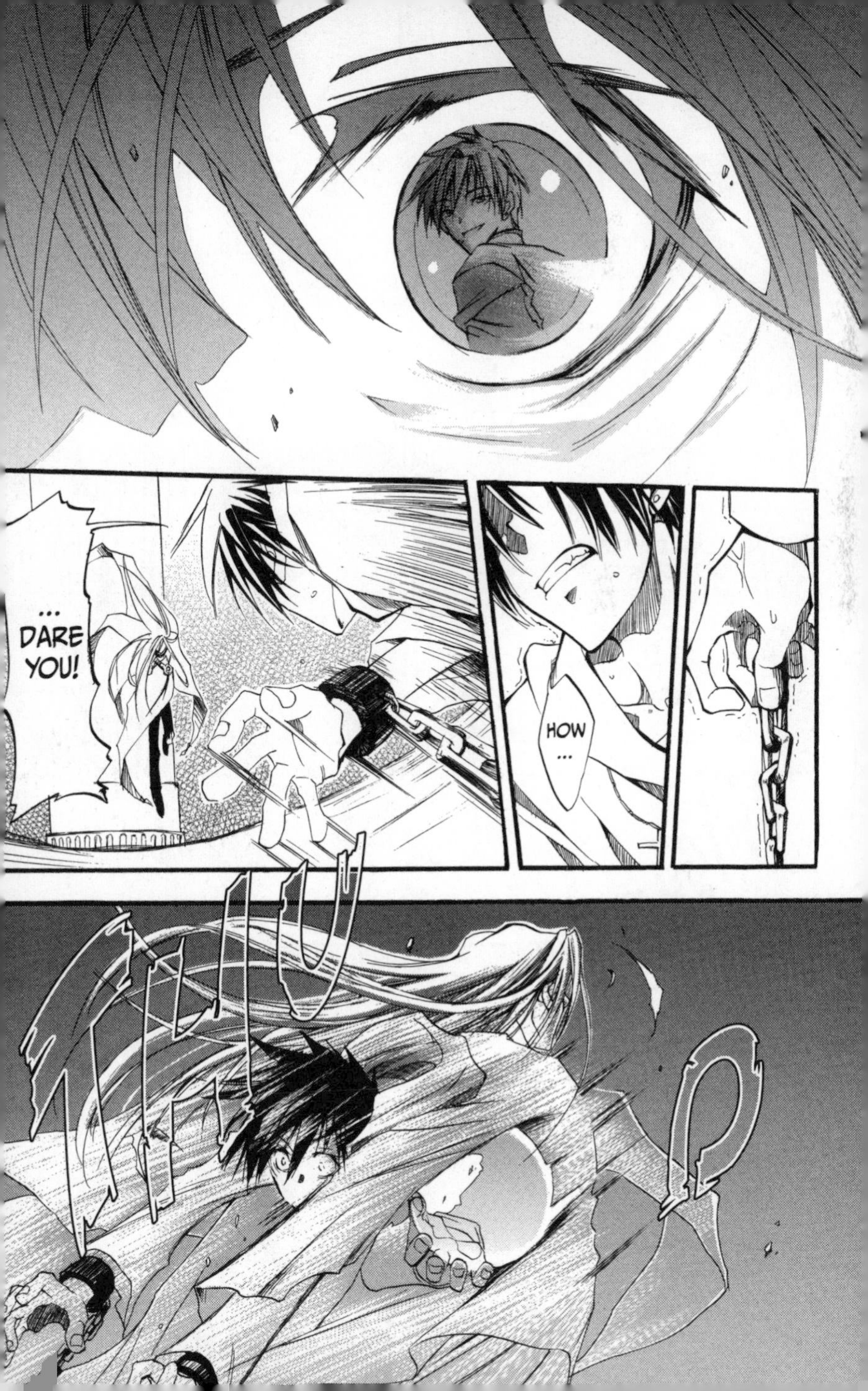
HOW ...
... DARE YOU!

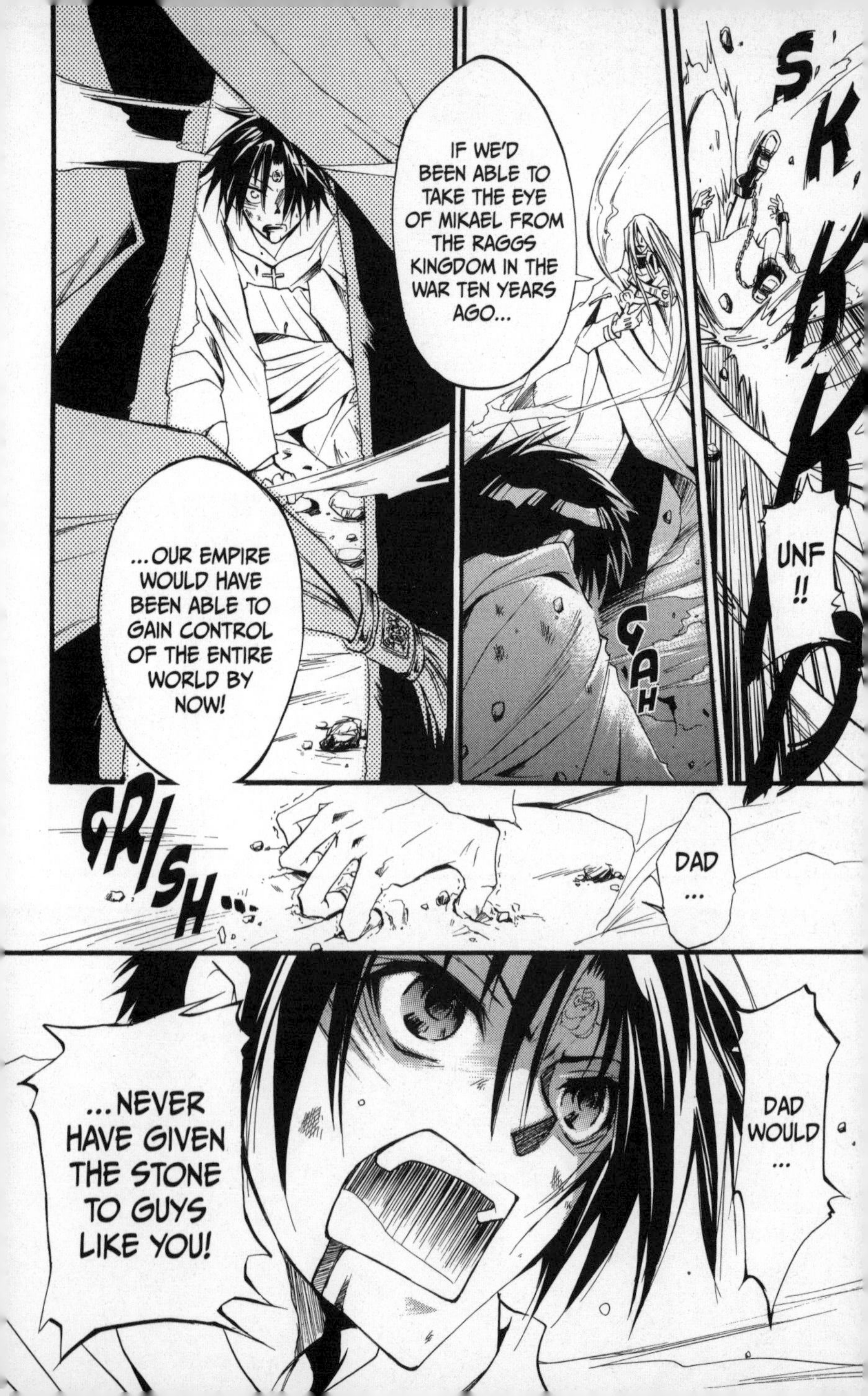
SKKKKD
UNF !!
IF WE'D BEEN ABLE TO TAKE THE EYE OF MIKAEL FROM THE RAGGS KINGDOM IN THE WAR TEN YEARS AGO...
GAH
...OUR EMPIRE WOULD HAVE BEEN ABLE TO GAIN CONTROL OF THE ENTIRE WORLD BY NOW!
DAD ...
GRISH...
DAD WOULD ...
...NEVER HAVE GIVEN THE STONE TO GUYS LIKE YOU!

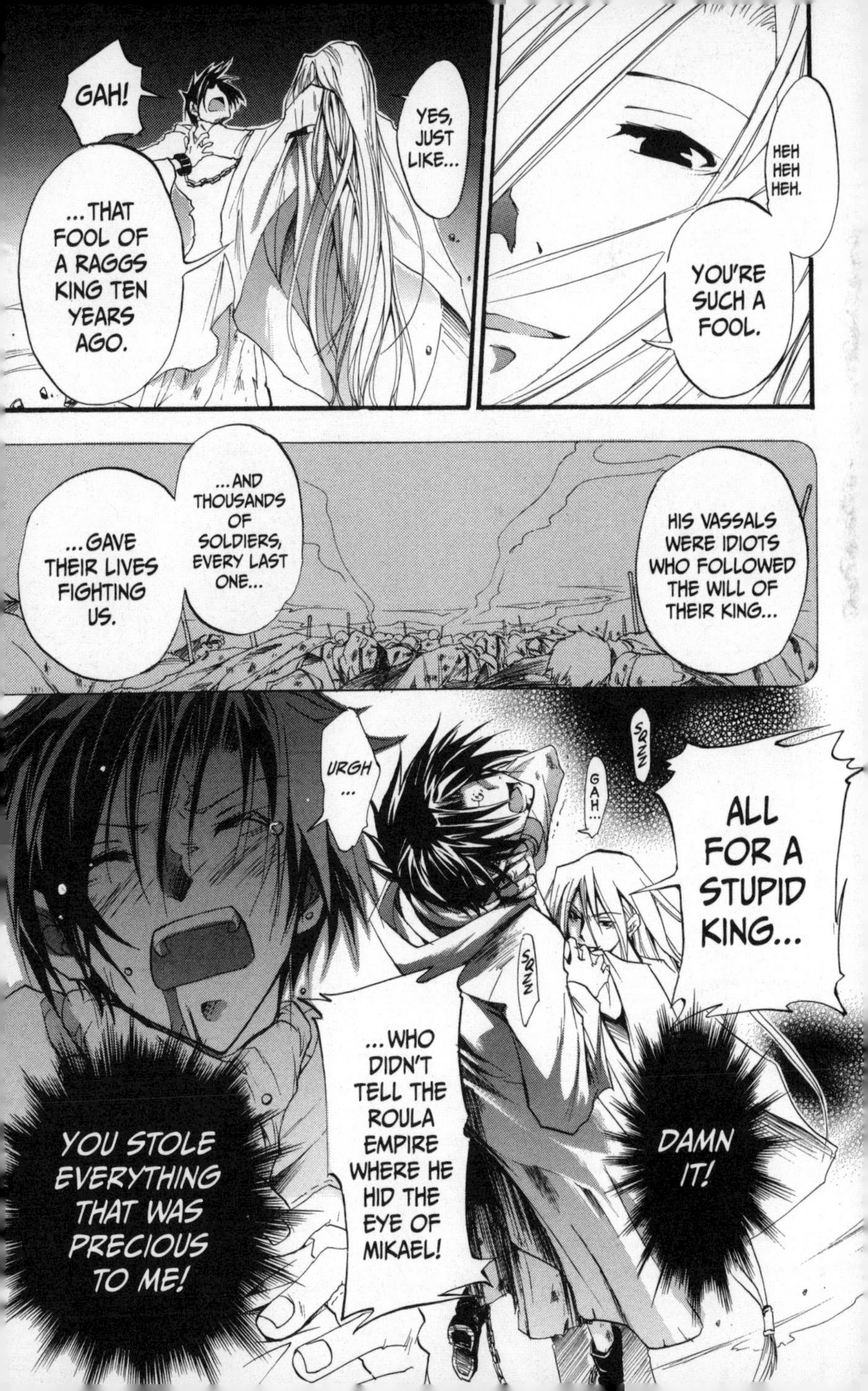
HEH HEH HEH.
YOU'RE SUCH A FOOL.
YES, JUST LIKE...
GAH!
...THAT FOOL OF A RAGGS KING TEN YEARS AGO.
HIS VASSALS WERE IDIOTS WHO FOLLOWED THE WILL OF THEIR KING...
...AND THOUSANDS OF SOLDIERS, EVERY LAST ONE...
...GAVE THEIR LIVES FIGHTING US.
SRZZ
ALL FOR A STUPID KING...
GAH...
URGH...
SRZZ
DAMN IT!
...WHO DIDN'T TELL THE ROULA EMPIRE WHERE HE HID THE EYE OF MIKAEL!
YOU STOLE EVERYTHING THAT WAS PRECIOUS TO ME!

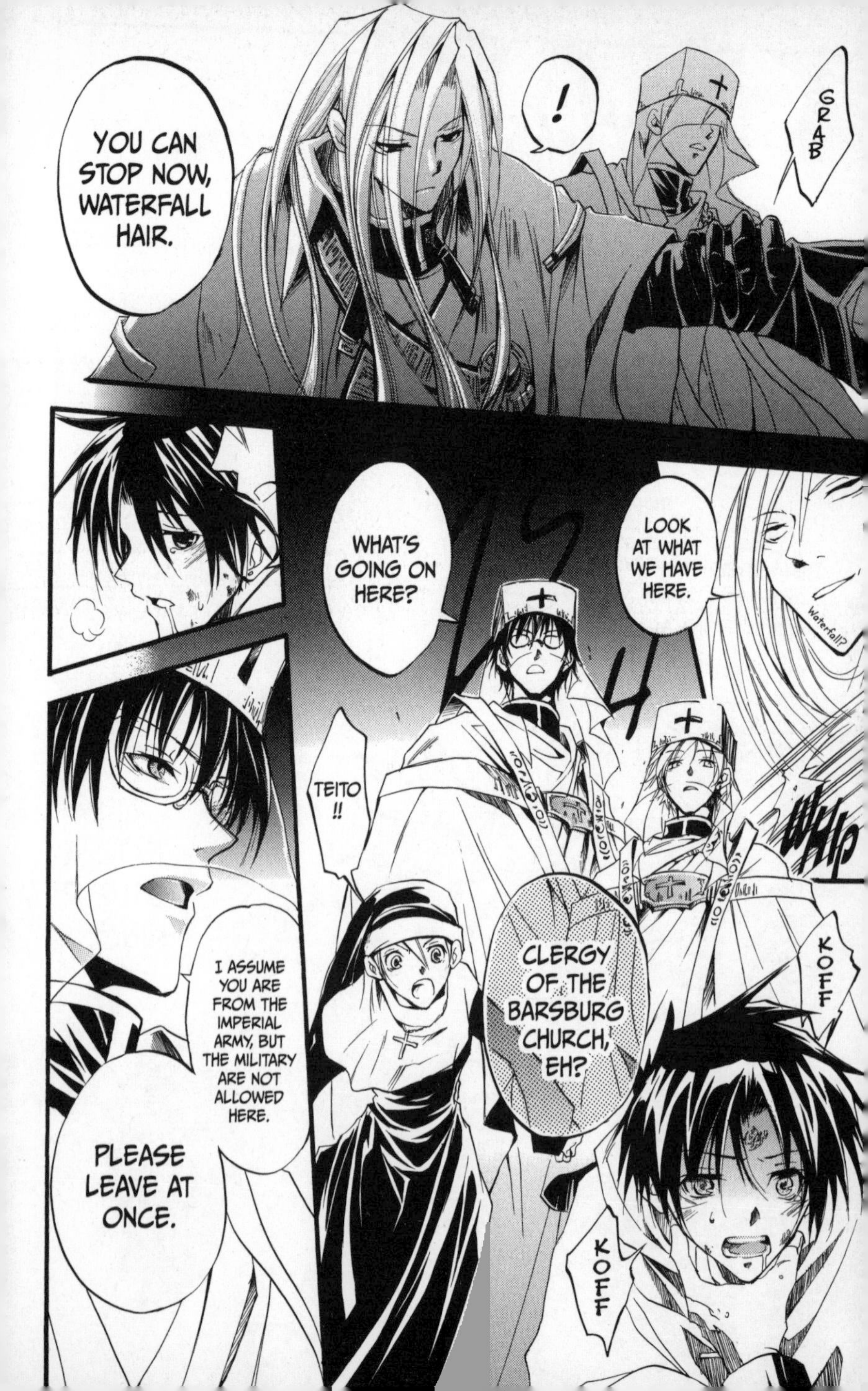
GRAB
!
YOU CAN STOP NOW, WATERFALL HAIR.
LOOK AT WHAT WE HAVE HERE.
Waterfall!?
WHAT'S GOING ON HERE?
WHIP
TEITO!!
KOFF
CLERGY OF THE BARSBURG CHURCH, EH?
KOFF
I ASSUME YOU ARE FROM THE IMPERIAL ARMY, BUT THE MILITARY ARE NOT ALLOWED HERE.
PLEASE LEAVE AT ONCE.

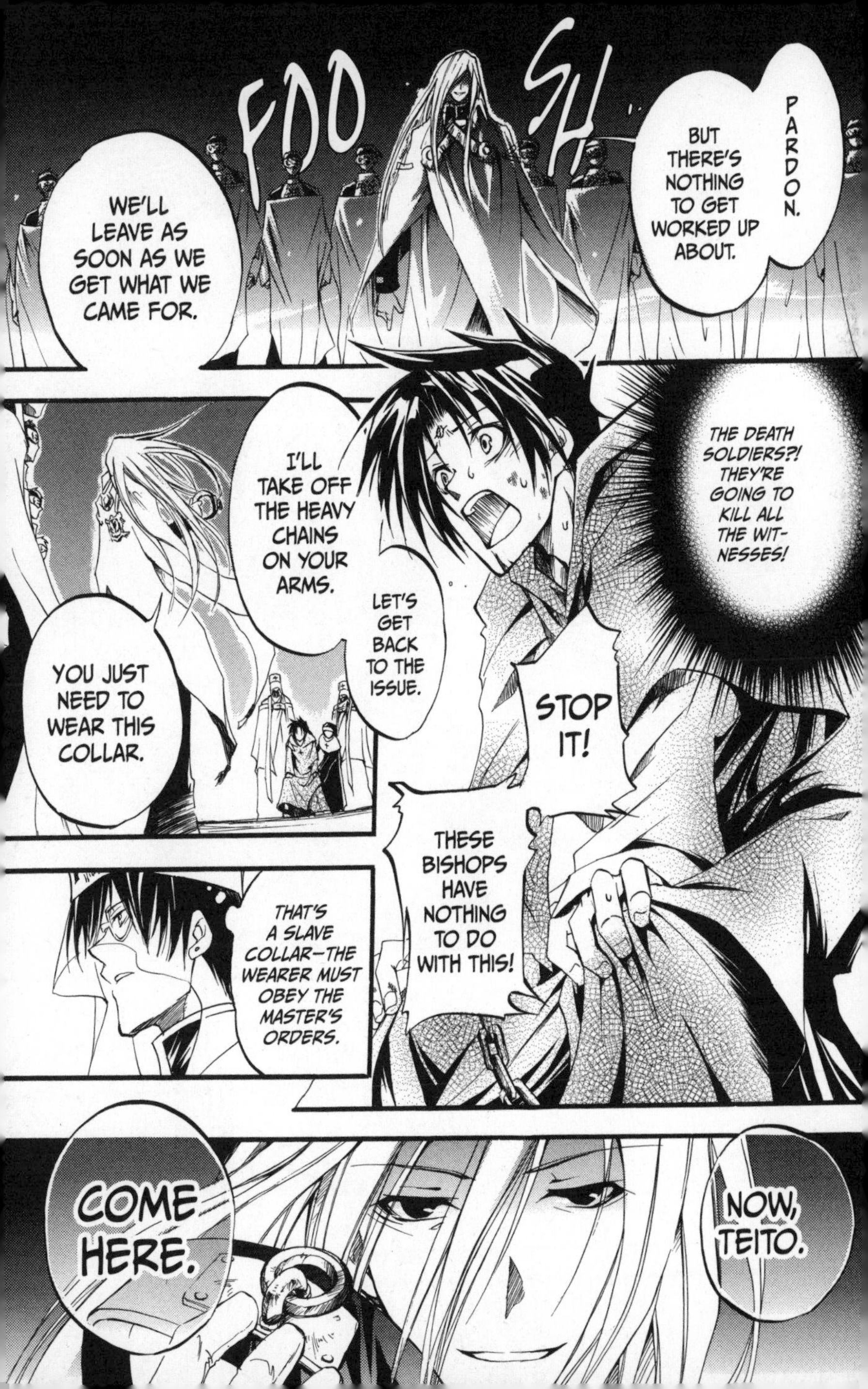
PARDON.
BUT THERE'S NOTHING TO GET WORKED UP ABOUT.
FDOSH
WE'LL LEAVE AS SOON AS WE GET WHAT WE CAME FOR.
THE DEATH SOLDIERS?! THEY'RE GOING TO KILL ALL THE WIT-NESSES!
STOP IT!
THESE BISHOPS HAVE NOTHING TO DO WITH THIS!
LET'S GET BACK TO THE ISSUE.
I'LL TAKE OFF THE HEAVY CHAINS ON YOUR ARMS.
YOU JUST NEED TO WEAR THIS COLLAR.
THAT'S A SLAVE COLLAR—THE WEARER MUST OBEY THE MASTER'S ORDERS.
NOW, TEITO.
COME HERE.

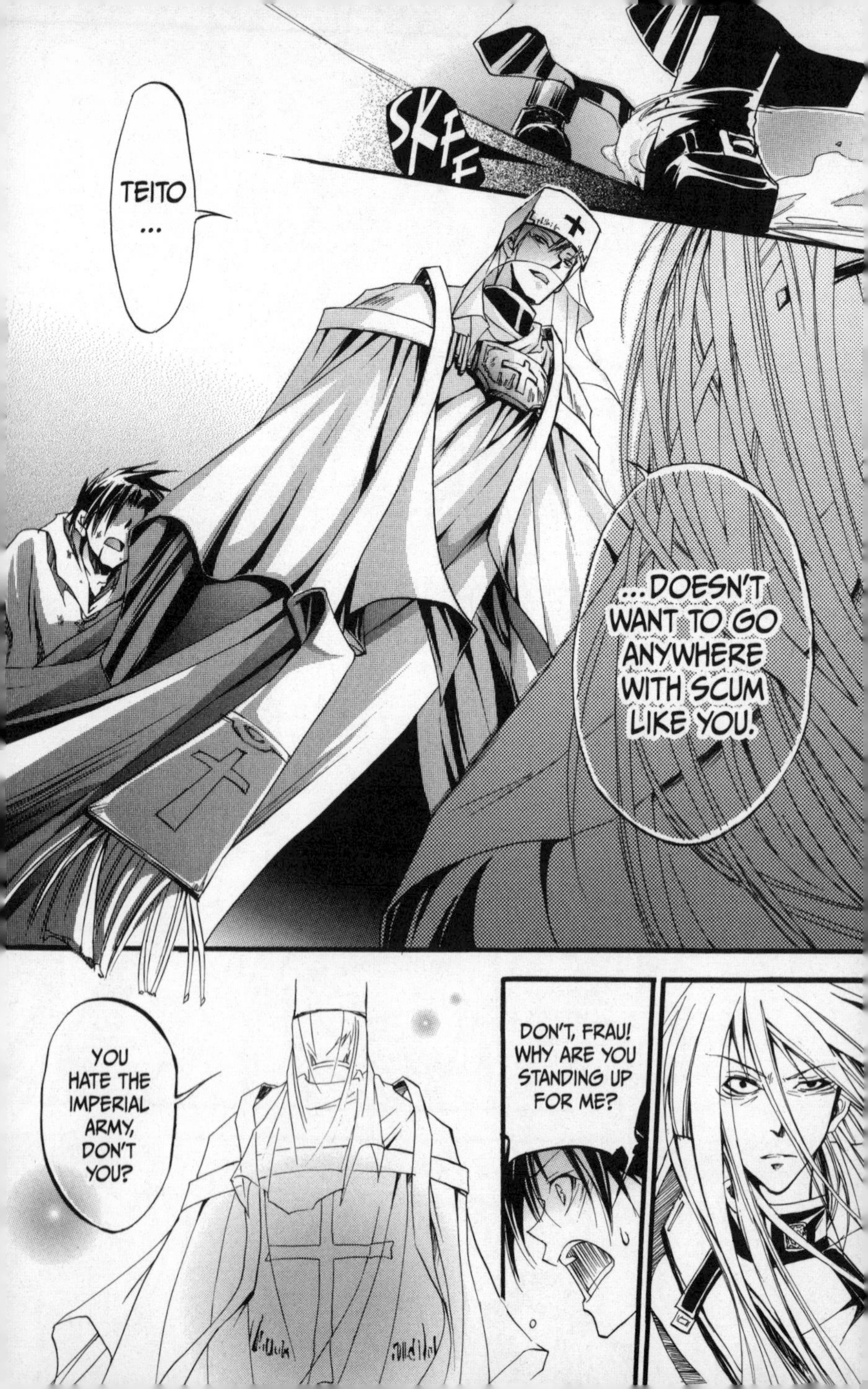
SKFF
TEITO ...
...DOESN'T WANT TO GO ANYWHERE WITH SCUM LIKE YOU.
DON'T, FRAU! WHY ARE YOU STANDING UP FOR ME?
YOU HATE THE IMPERIAL ARMY, DON'T YOU?

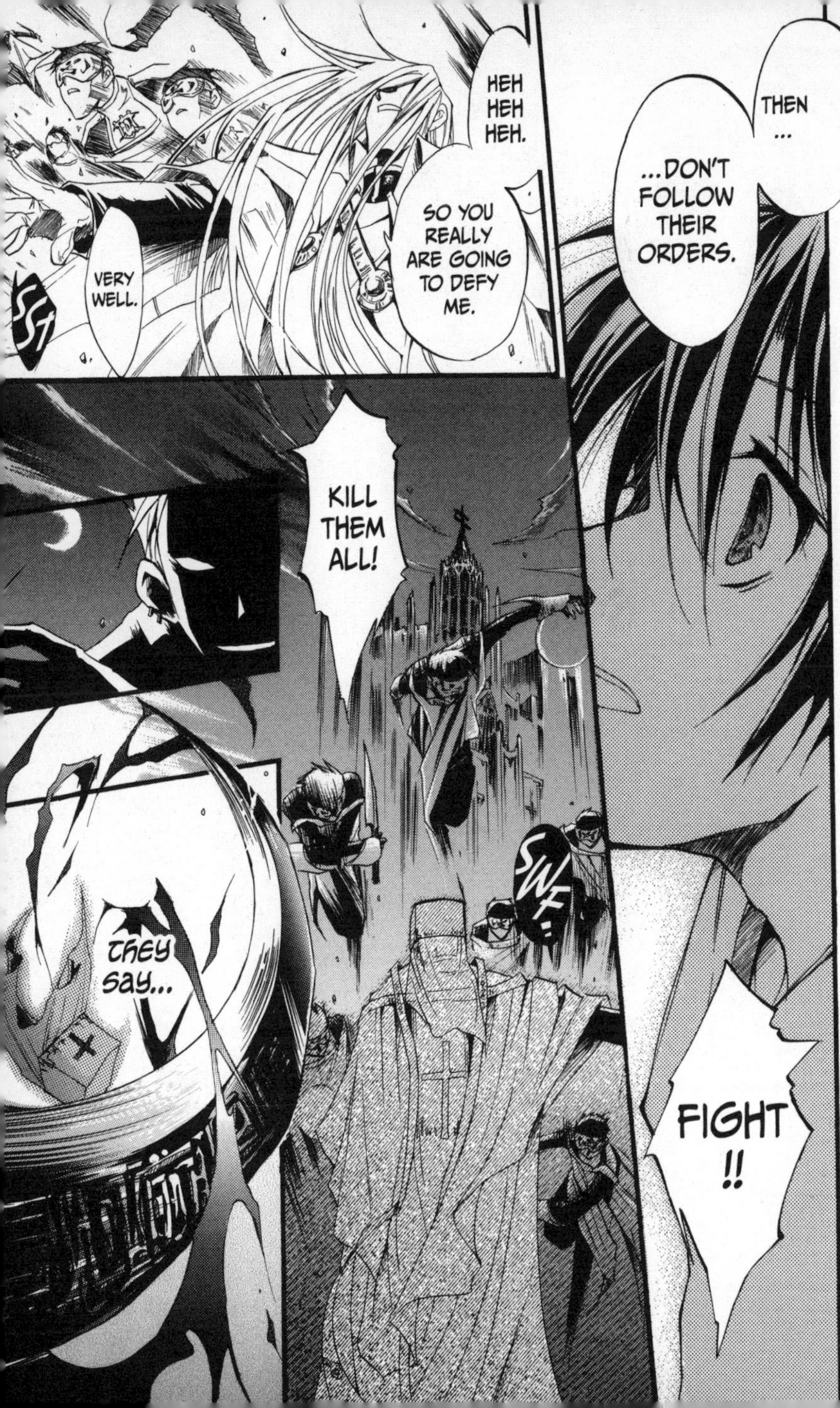
THEN ...
...DON'T FOLLOW THEIR ORDERS.
FIGHT!!
HEH HEH HEH.
SO YOU REALLY ARE GOING TO DEFY ME.
VERY WELL.
SST
KILL THEM ALL!
SWF
THEY SAY...

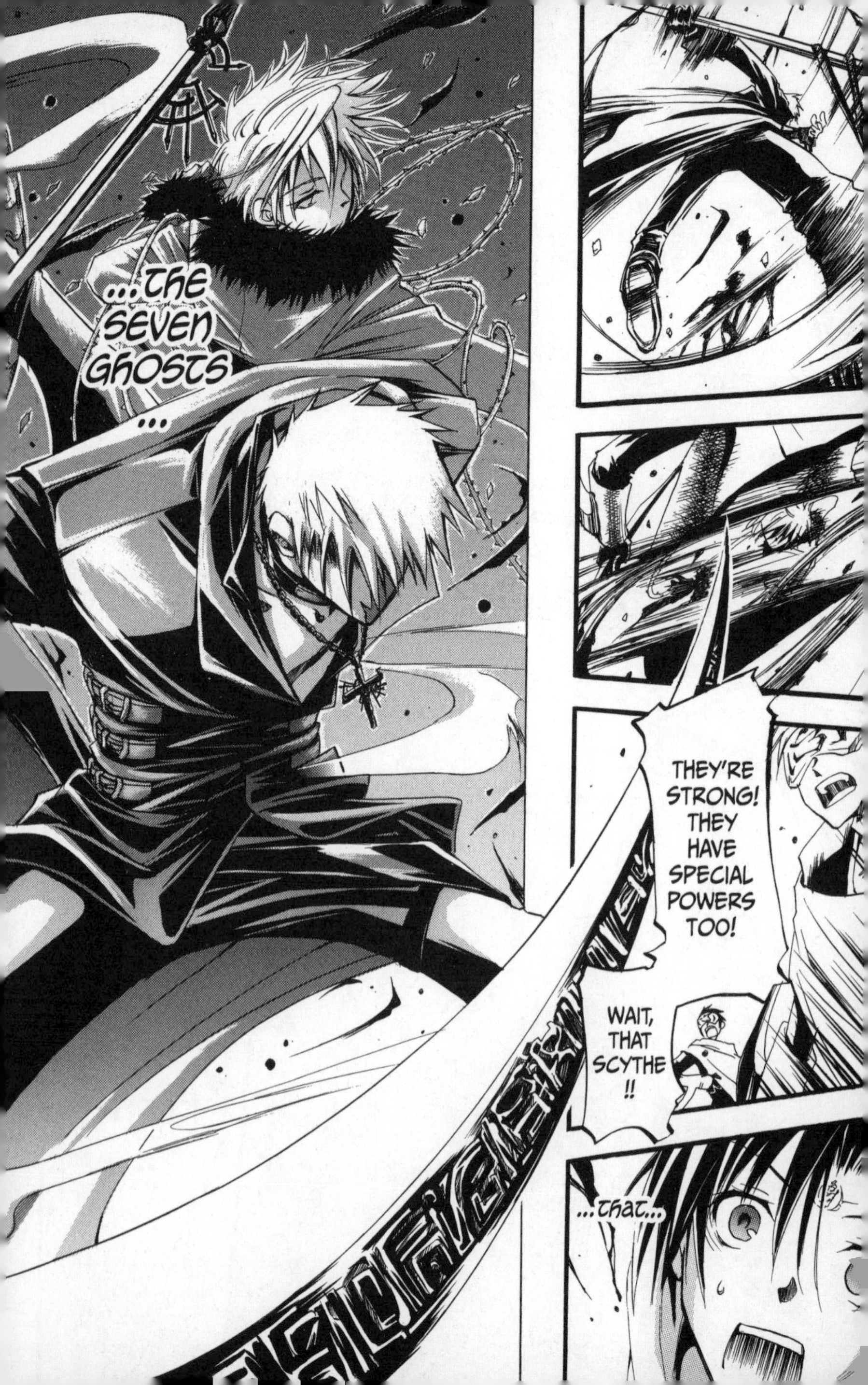
THEY'RE STRONG! THEY HAVE SPECIAL POWERS TOO!
WAIT, THAT SCYTHE !!
...that...
...THE SEVEN GHOSTS ...

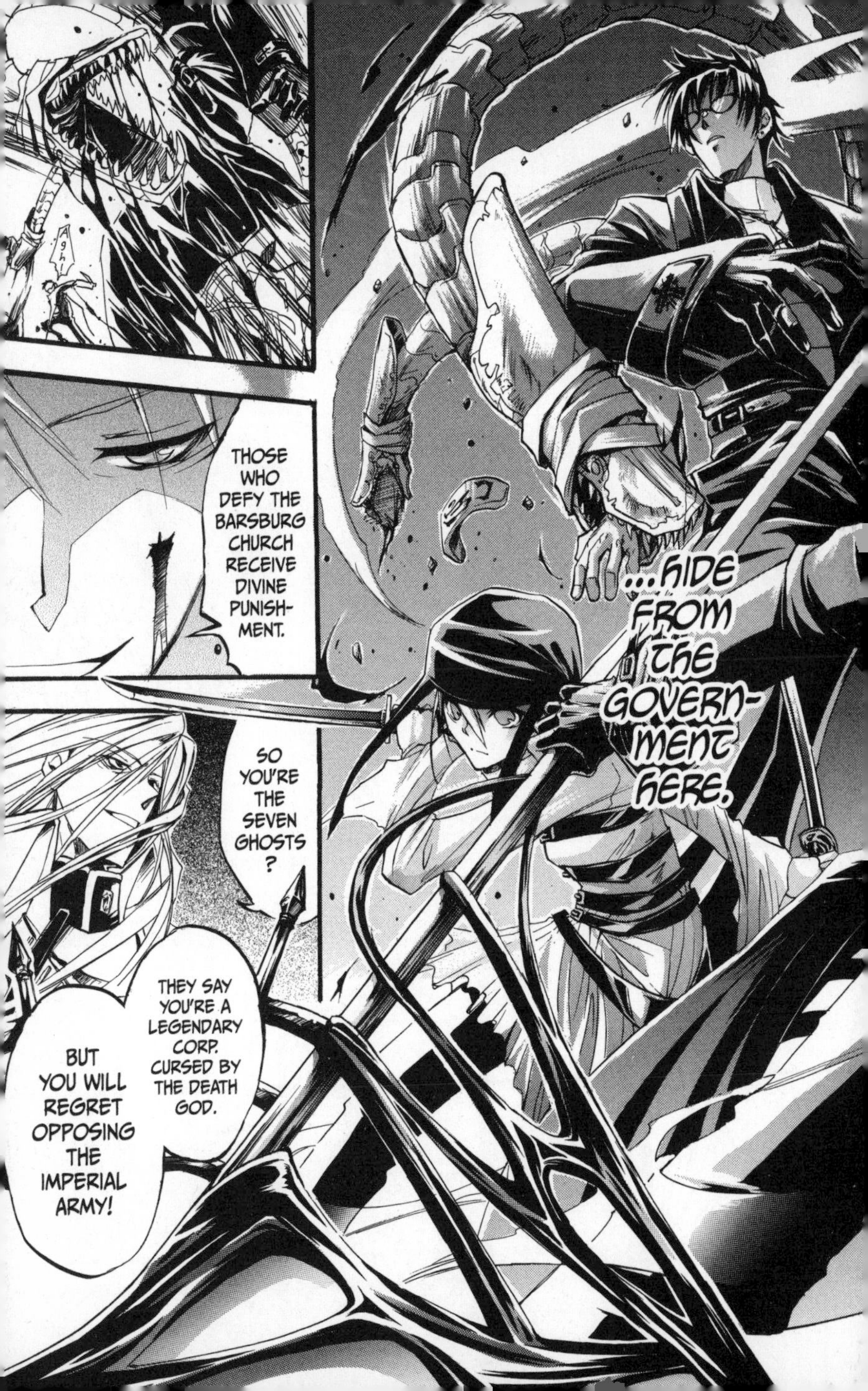
...HIDE FROM THE GOVERNMENT HERE.
Agh!
THOSE WHO DEFY THE BARSBURG CHURCH RECEIVE DIVINE PUNISHMENT.
SO YOU'RE THE SEVEN GHOSTS?
THEY SAY YOU'RE A LEGENDARY CORP. CURSED BY THE DEATH GOD.
BUT YOU WILL REGRET OPPOSING THE IMPERIAL ARMY!

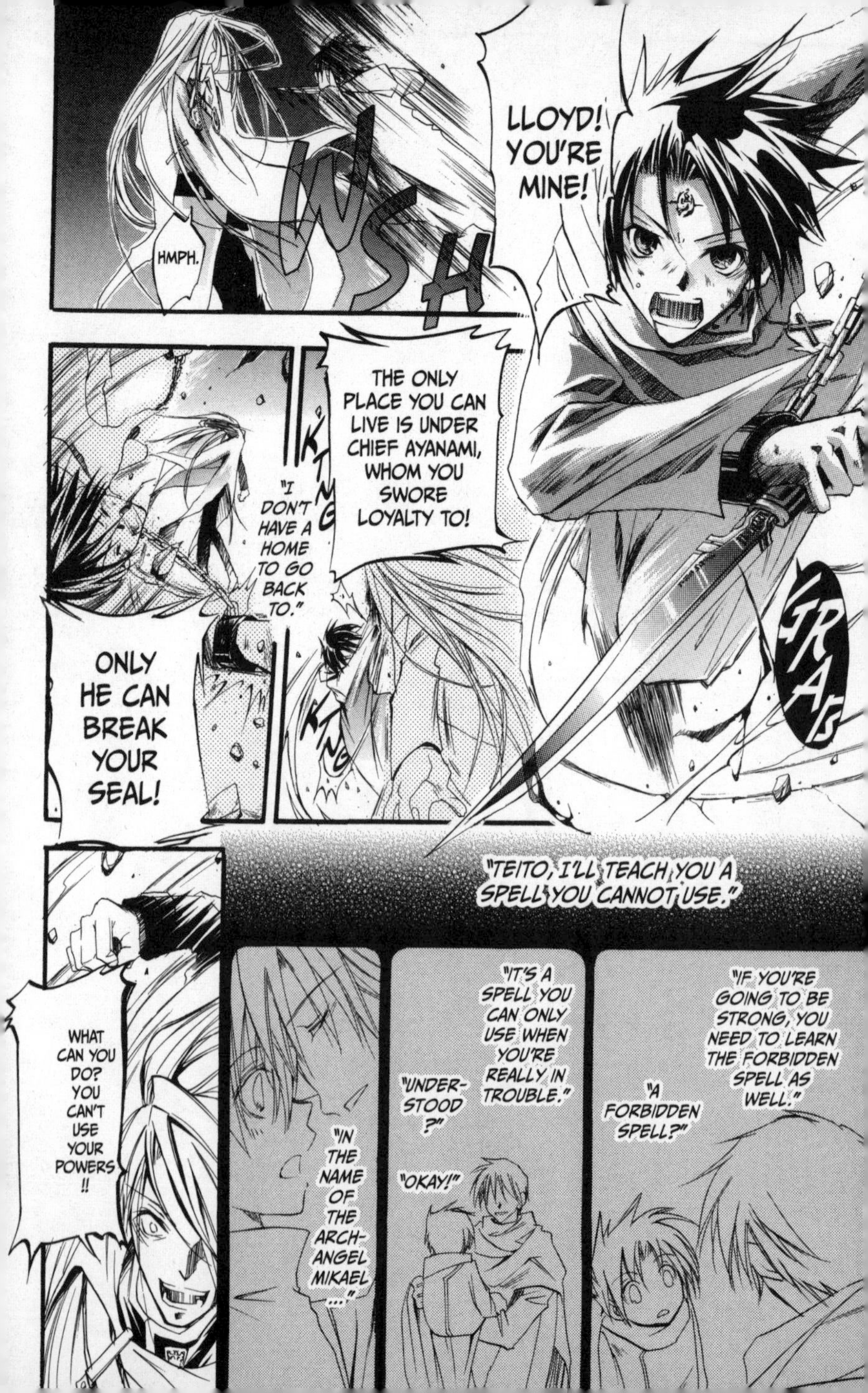
LLOYD! YOU'RE MINE!
GRAS
HMPH.
WSH
THE ONLY PLACE YOU CAN LIVE IS UNDER CHIEF AYANAMI, WHOM YOU SWORE LOYALTY TO!
"I DON'T HAVE A HOME TO GO BACK TO."
KTING
KTING
ONLY HE CAN BREAK YOUR SEAL!
"TEITO, I'LL TEACH YOU A SPELL YOU CANNOT USE."
"IF YOU'RE GOING TO BE STRONG, YOU NEED TO LEARN THE FORBIDDEN SPELL AS WELL."
"A FORBIDDEN SPELL?"
"IT'S A SPELL YOU CAN ONLY USE WHEN YOU'RE REALLY IN TROUBLE."
"UNDER-STOOD?"
"OKAY!"
"IN THE NAME OF THE ARCH-ANGEL MIKAEL..."
WHAT CAN YOU DO? YOU CAN'T USE YOUR POWERS!!

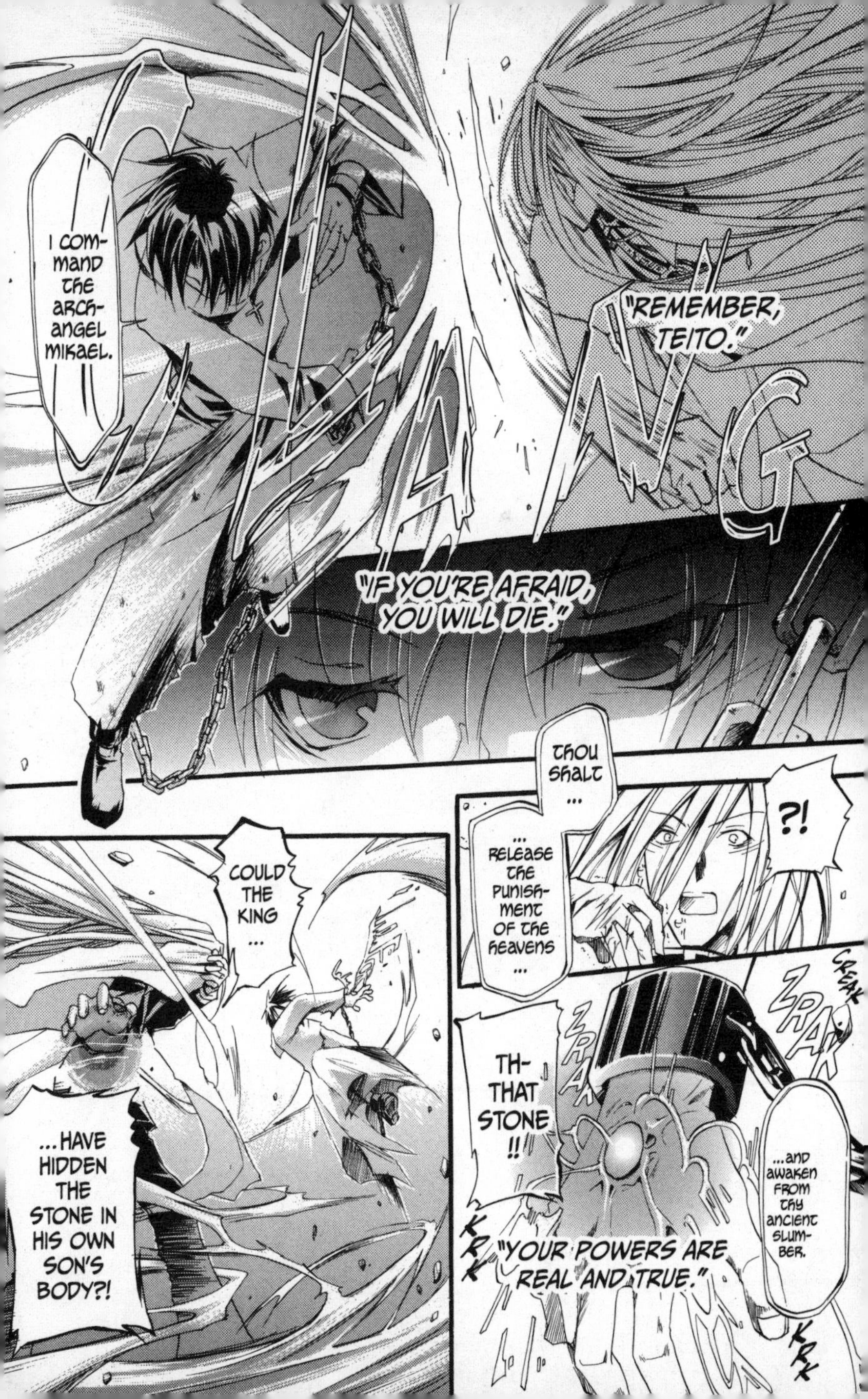
"REMEMBER, TEITO."
CLANG
I COMMAND THE ARCHANGEL MIKAEL.
"IF YOU'RE AFRAID, YOU WILL DIE."
?!
THOU SHALT ...
... RELEASE THE PUNISHMENT OF THE HEAVENS ...
CREAK
ZRAK
ZRAK
...AND AWAKEN FROM THY ANCIENT SLUMBER.
TH-THAT STONE!!
"YOUR POWERS ARE REAL AND TRUE."
KRK
KRK
COULD THE KING ...
...HAVE HIDDEN THE STONE IN HIS OWN SON'S BODY?!

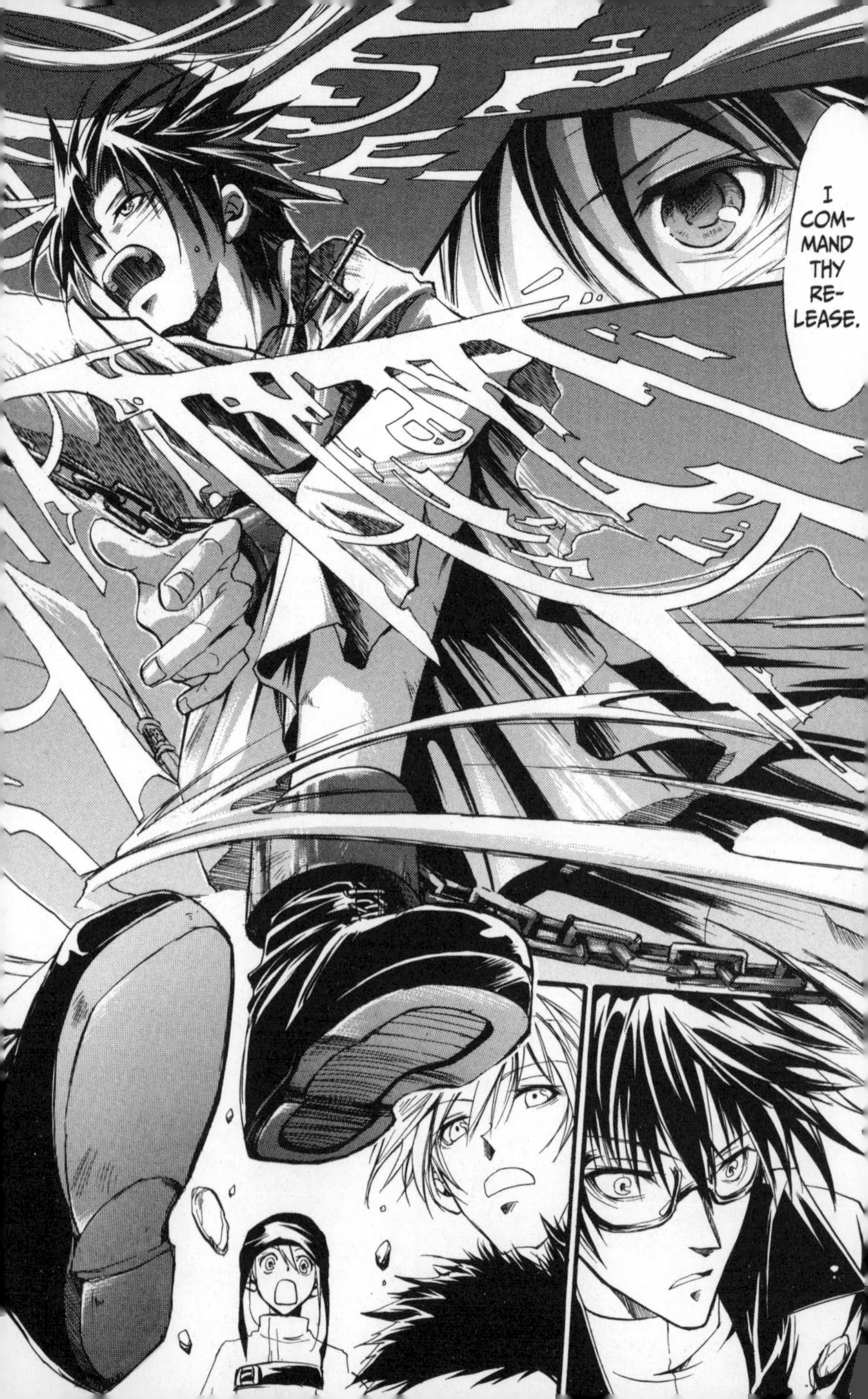
I COMMAND THY RELEASE.

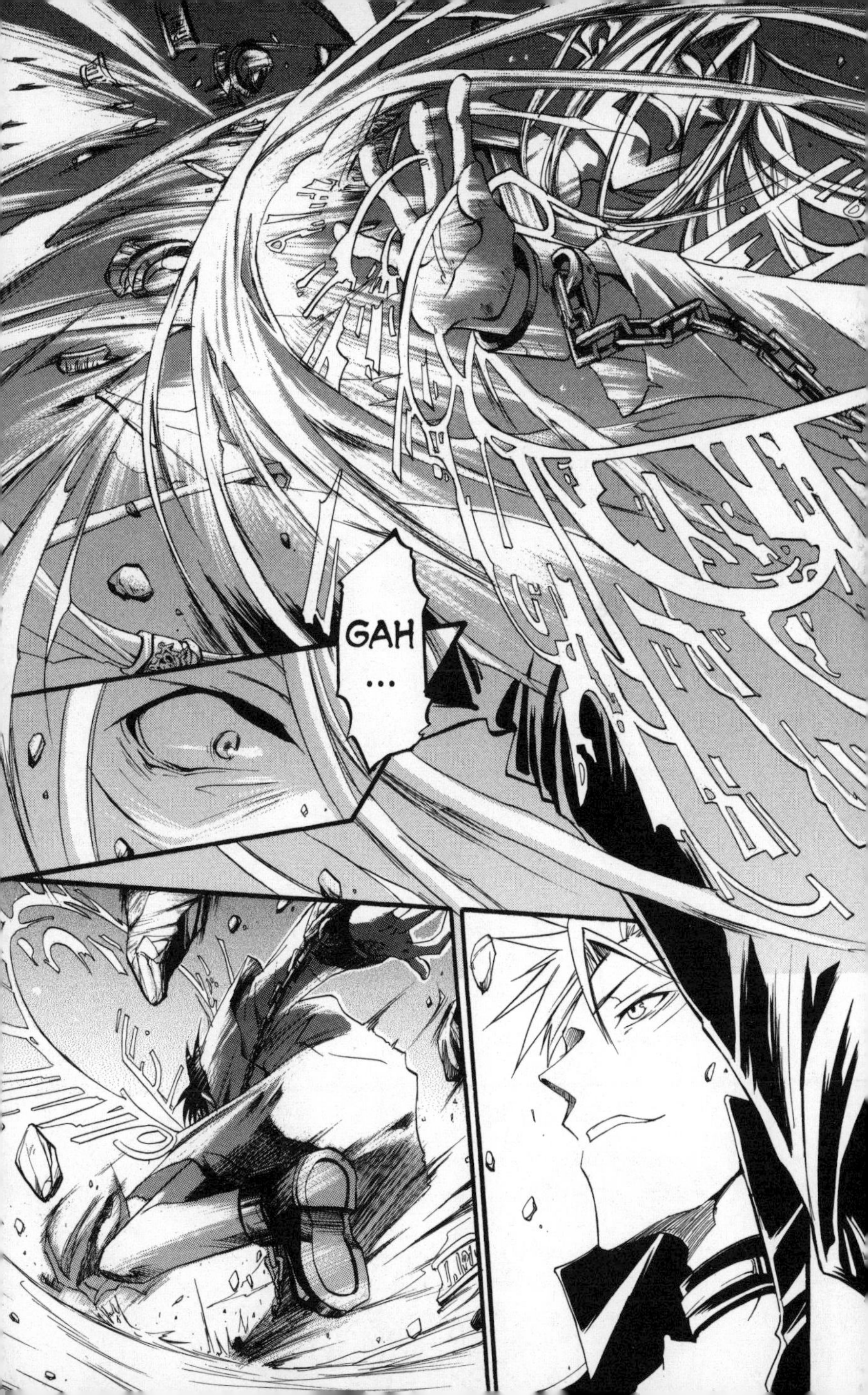
GAH ...

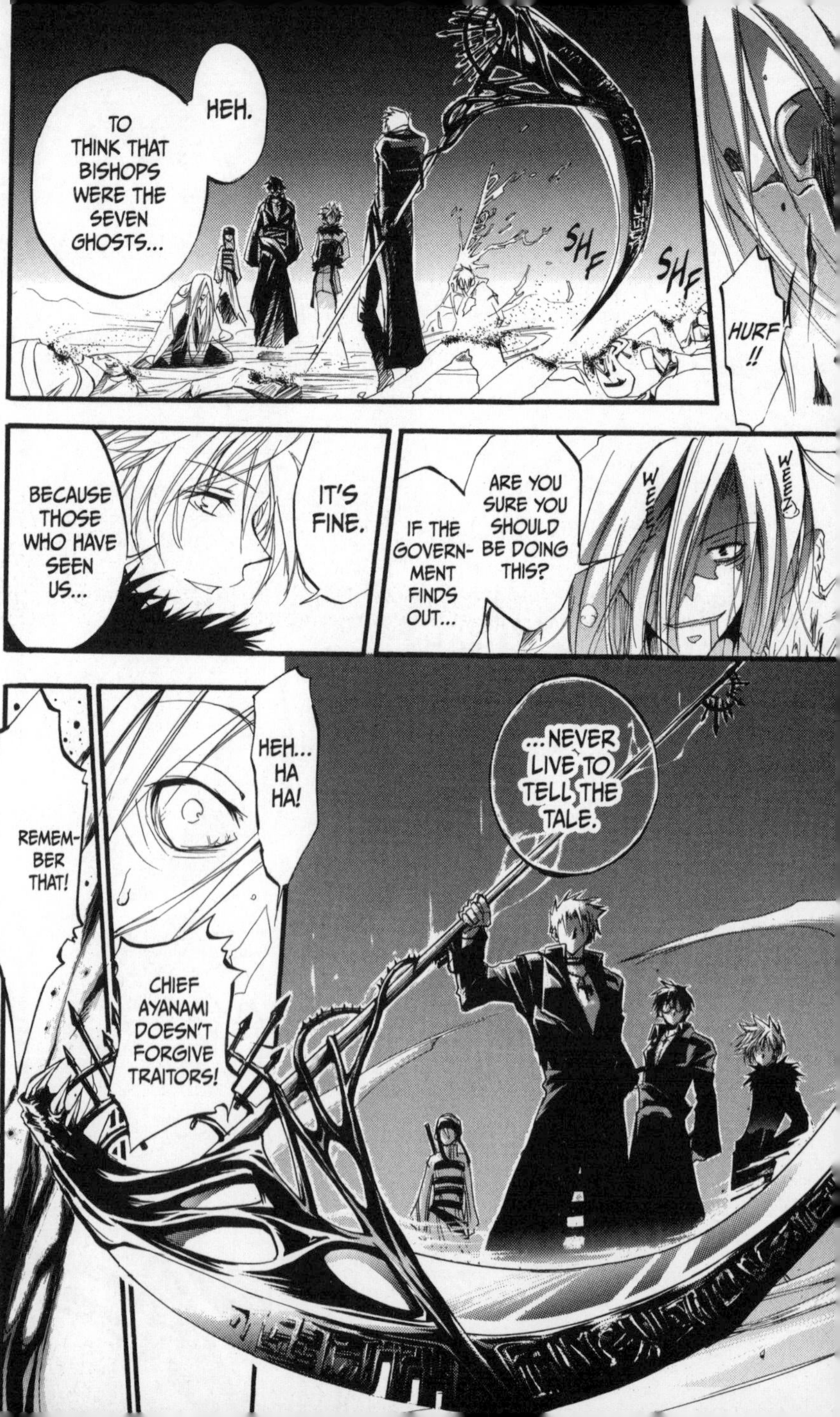
HURF !!
HEH.
TO THINK THAT BISHOPS WERE THE SEVEN GHOSTS...
SHF
SHF
WEEN
WEEN
ARE YOU SURE YOU SHOULD BE DOING THIS?
IF THE GOVERN-MENT FINDS OUT...
IT'S FINE.
BECAUSE THOSE WHO HAVE SEEN US...
...NEVER LIVE TO TELL THE TALE.
HEH... HA HA!
CHIEF AYANAMI DOESN'T FORGIVE TRAITORS!
REMEM-BER THAT!

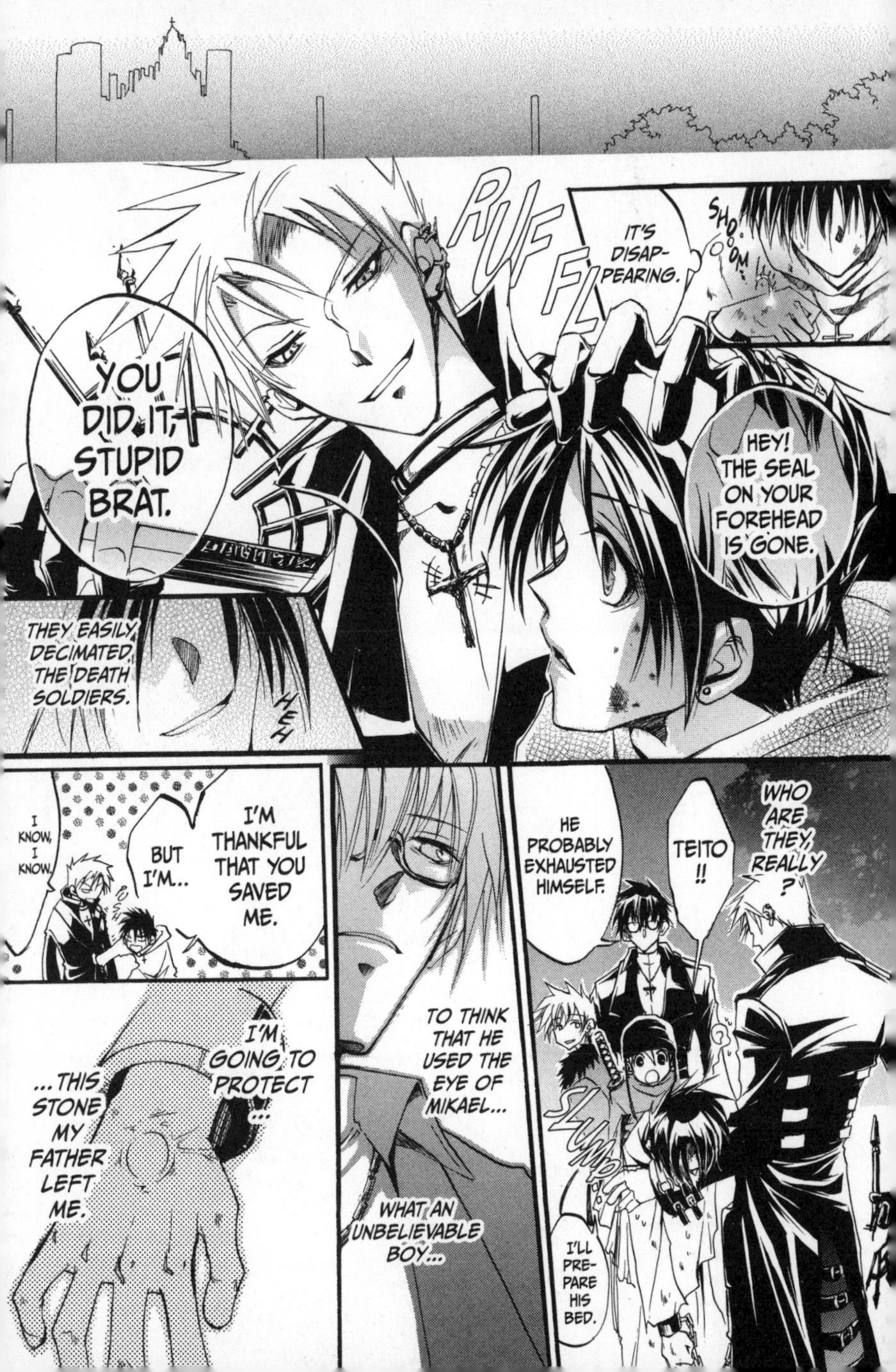

IT'S DISAPPEARING.
SHOOOOM
HEY! THE SEAL ON YOUR FOREHEAD IS GONE.
RUFFL
YOU DID IT, STUPID BRAT.
THEY EASILY DECIMATED THE DEATH SOLDIERS.
HEH
WHO ARE THEY, REALLY?
TEITO!!
HE PROBABLY EXHAUSTED HIMSELF.
SLUMP
I'LL PREPARE HIS BED.
TO THINK THAT HE USED THE EYE OF MIKAEL...
WHAT AN UNBELIEVABLE BOY...
I'M THANKFUL THAT YOU SAVED ME.
BUT I'M...
I KNOW, I KNOW.
PUSH
I'M GOING TO PROTECT...
...THIS STONE MY FATHER LEFT ME.

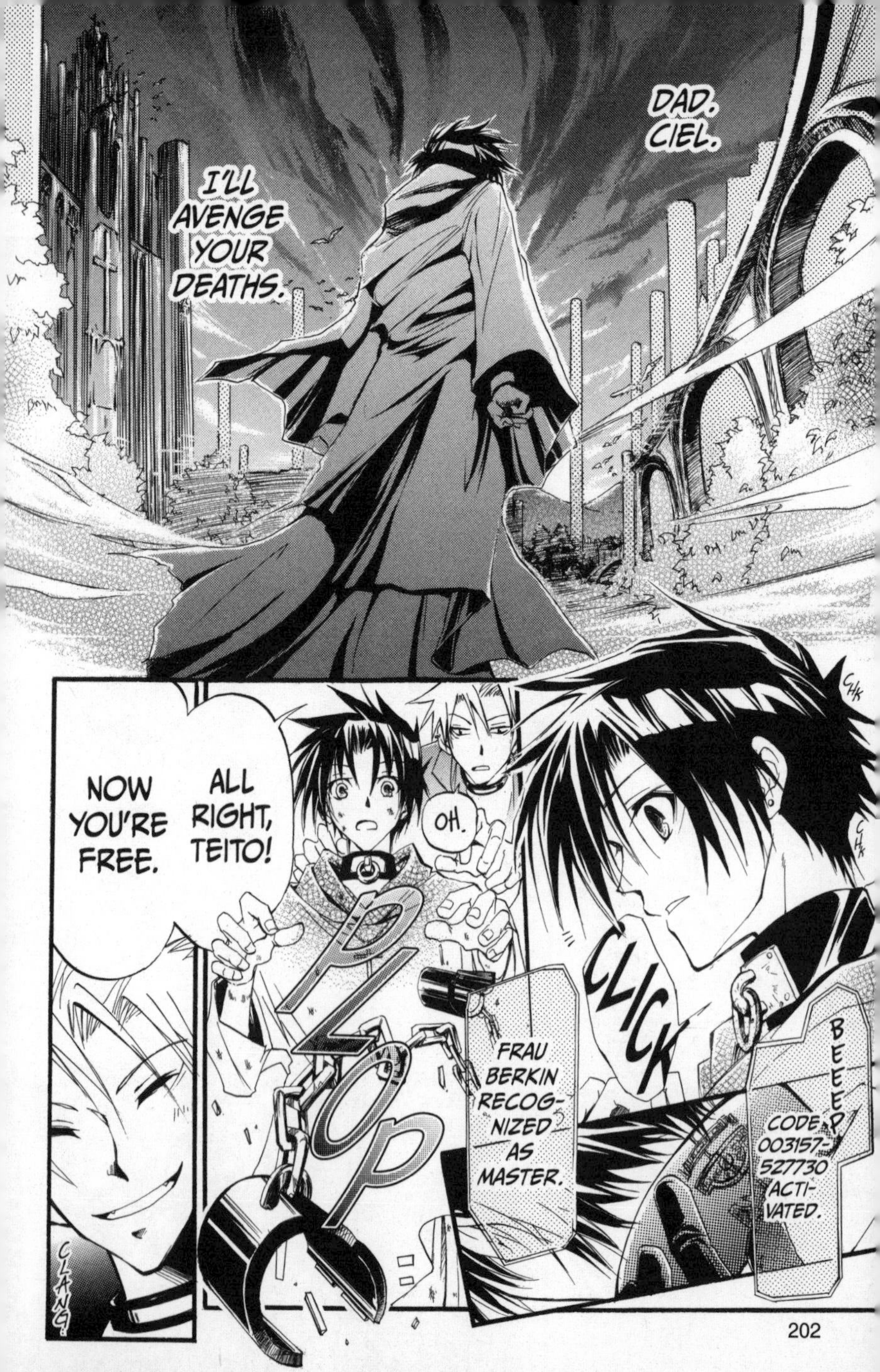
DAD. CIEL.
I'LL AVENGE YOUR DEATHS.
CHK
CHK
CLICK
BEEEP
CODE 003157-527730 ACTIVATED.
FRAU BERKIN RECOGNIZED AS MASTER.
ALL RIGHT, TEITO!
NOW YOU'RE FREE.
OH.
PLOP
CLANG

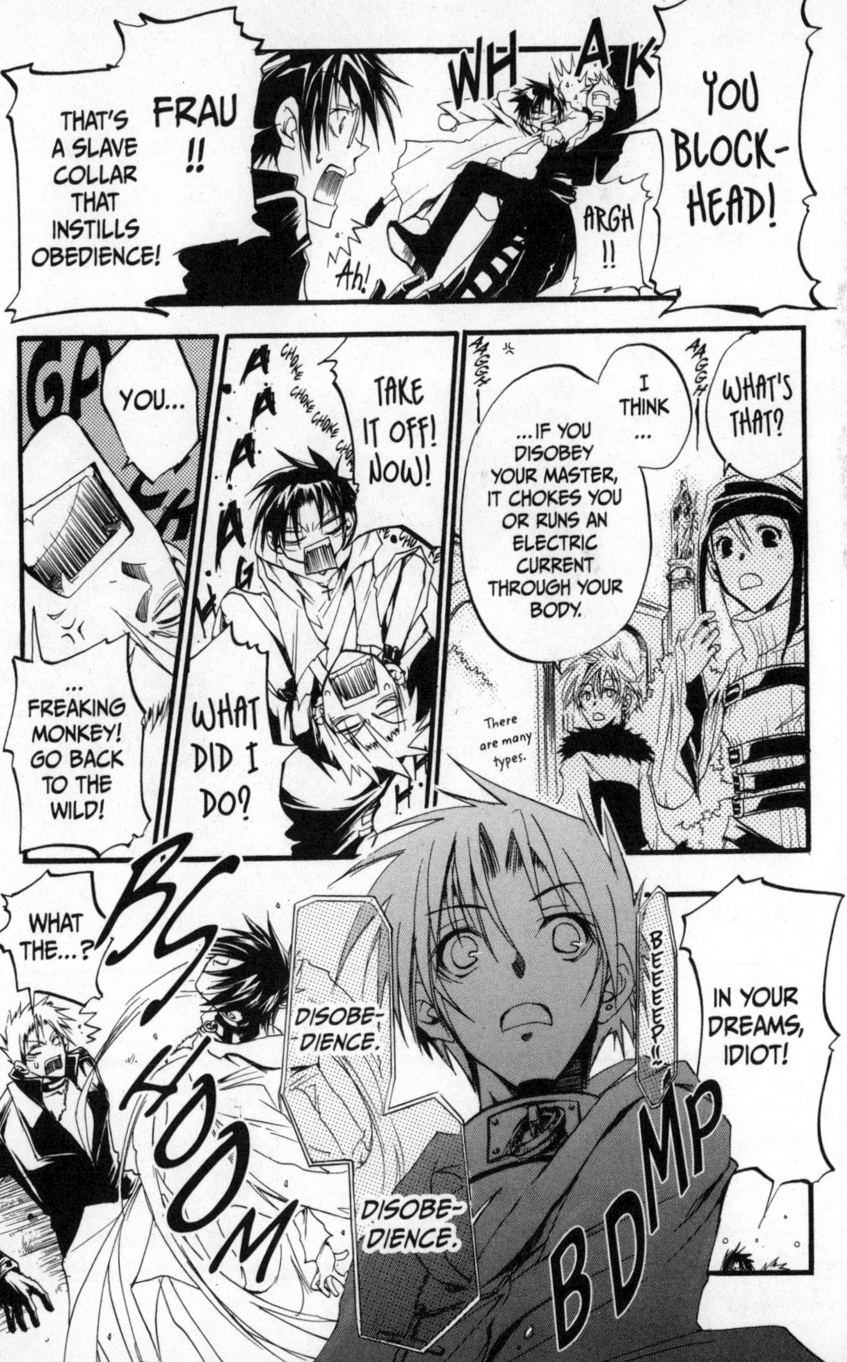
YOU BLOCK-HEAD!
WHAK
ARGH !!
FRAU !!
Ah!
THAT'S A SLAVE COLLAR THAT INSTILLS OBEDIENCE!
WHAT'S THAT?
AAGGH
I THINK ...
...IF YOU DISOBEY YOUR MASTER, IT CHOKES YOU OR RUNS AN ELECTRIC CURRENT THROUGH YOUR BODY.
AAGGH
There are many types.
TAKE IT OFF! NOW!
CHOKE CHOKE CHOKE
WHAT DID I DO?
YOU...
... FREAKING MONKEY! GO BACK TO THE WILD!
IN YOUR DREAMS, IDIOT!
BEEEEEP!!
BDMP
DISOBE-DIENCE.
DISOBE-DIENCE.
BSHOOM
WHAT THE...?

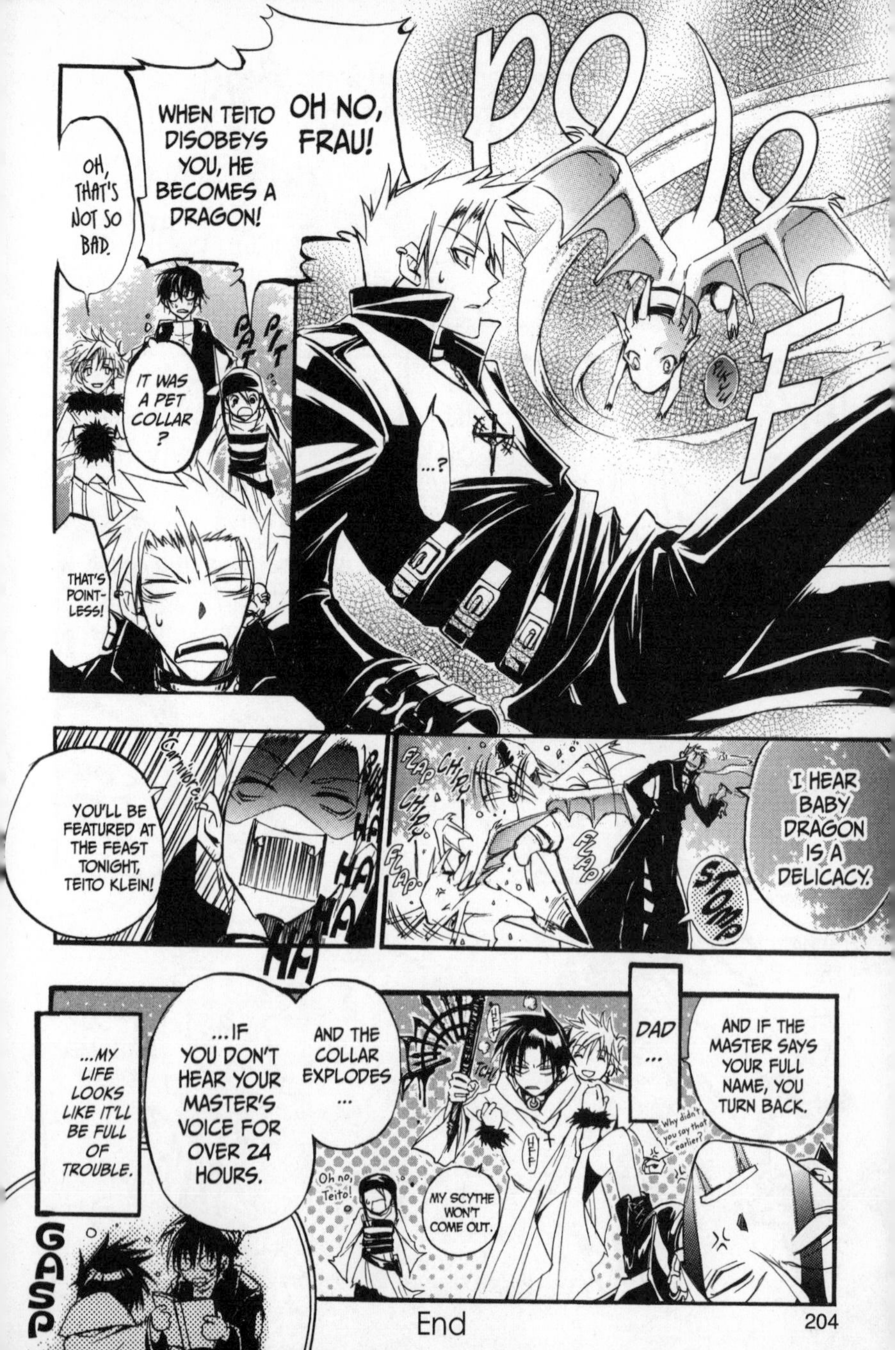
POOF
PIKU
OH NO, FRAU!
...?
WHEN TEITO DISOBEYS YOU, HE BECOMES A DRAGON!
OH, THAT'S NOT SO BAD.
PAT PIT
IT WAS A PET COLLAR?
THAT'S POINTLESS!
I HEAR BABY DRAGON IS A DELICACY.
STOMP
FLAP CHIRP CHIRP FLAP FLAP
BWAHAHAHAHA
Carnivore...
YOU'LL BE FEATURED AT THE FEAST TONIGHT, TEITO KLEIN!
AND IF THE MASTER SAYS YOUR FULL NAME, YOU TURN BACK.
DAD...
Why didn't you say that earlier?
HEF TCH HEF
MY SCYTHE WON'T COME OUT.
AND THE COLLAR EXPLODES...
...IF YOU DON'T HEAR YOUR MASTER'S VOICE FOR OVER 24 HOURS.
Oh no, Teito!
...MY LIFE LOOKS LIKE IT'LL BE FULL OF TROUBLE.
GASP

End

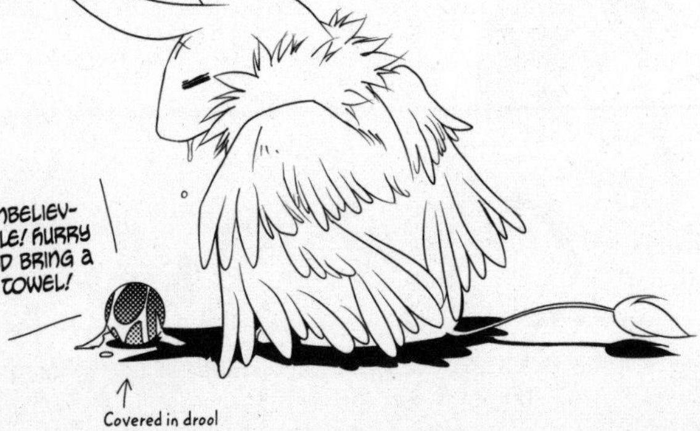
...
UNBELIEV-ABLE! HURRY AND BRING A TOWEL!
Covered in drool

Thank you for staying with us. Did you enjoy traveling to the Barsburg Empire in the company of death gods?

Special thanks to Shindosha for printing the books, our editors and the editorial department who helped us create this manga, and many other people who helped us create *07-Ghost*. And we would especially like to thank the readers who shared their feelings about this manga. Thank you very much.

We'd love to see you on our next journey.

Yuki Amemiya & Yukino Ichihara

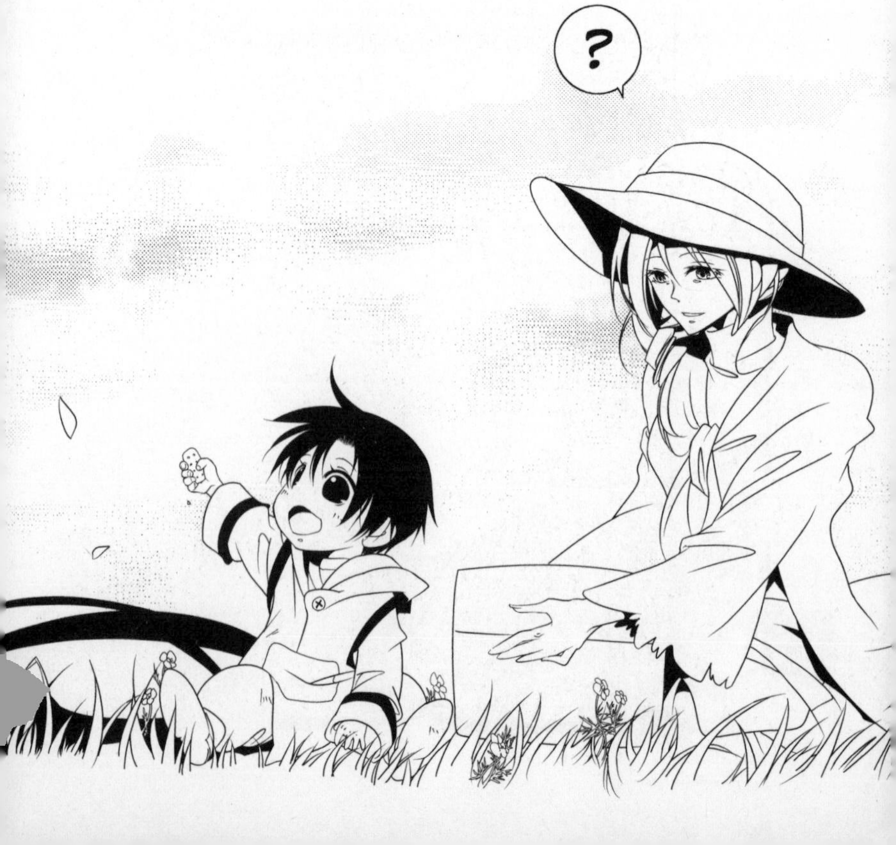
?

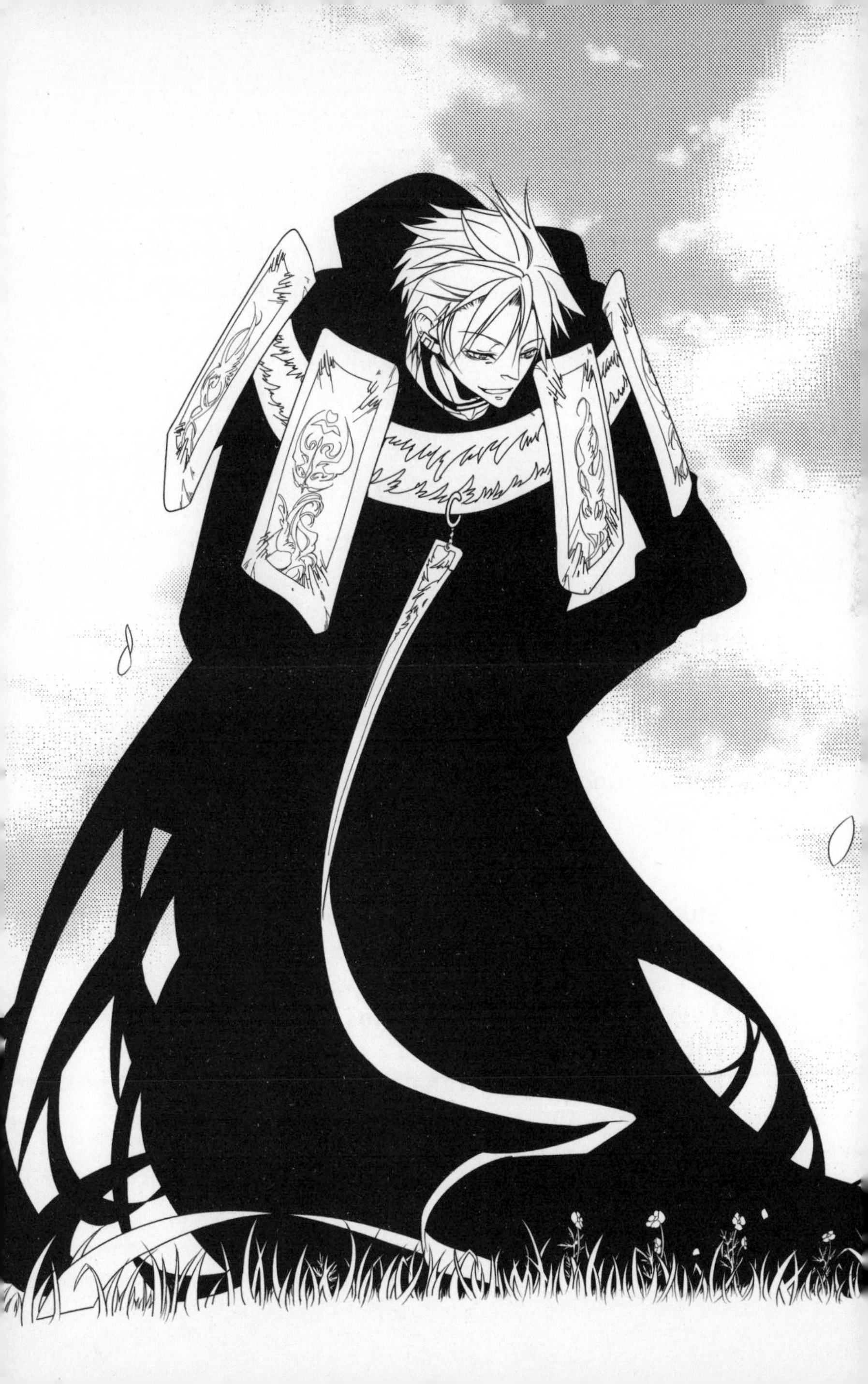

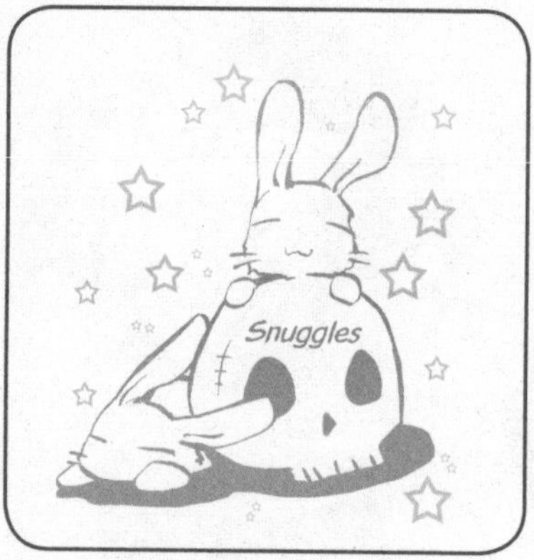
Snuggles

During the eight and a half years we worked on this series, Amemiya's Cooking Skill leveled up! Ichihara's Bathtub Cleaning Skill leveled up!

—Yuki Amemiya & Yukino Ichihara, 2013

Yuki Amemiya was born in Miyagi, Japan, on March 25. Yukino Ichihara was born in Fukushima, Japan, on November 24. Together they write and illustrate *07-Ghost*, the duo's first series. Since its debut in 2005, *07-Ghost* has been translated into a dozen languages, and in 2009 it was adapted into a TV anime series.

07-GHOST

Volume 17

STORY AND ART BY
YUKI AMEMIYA and
YUKINO ICHIHARA

Translation/Satsuki Yamashita
Touch-up Art & Lettering/Vanessa Satone
Design/Yukiko Whitley
Editor/Hope Donovan

Printed in the U.S.A.

Published by VIZ Media, LLC
P.O. Box 77010
San Francisco, CA 94107

10 9 8 7 6 5 4 3 2 1
First printing, July 2015

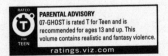

www.viz.com

Hey! You're Reading in the Wrong Direction!

This is the end of this graphic novel!

To properly enjoy this VIZ graphic novel, please turn it around and begin reading from right to left. Unlike English, Japanese is read right to left, so Japanese comics are read in reverse order from the way English comics are typically read.

This book has been printed in the original Japanese format in order to preserve the orientation of the original artwork. Have fun with it!

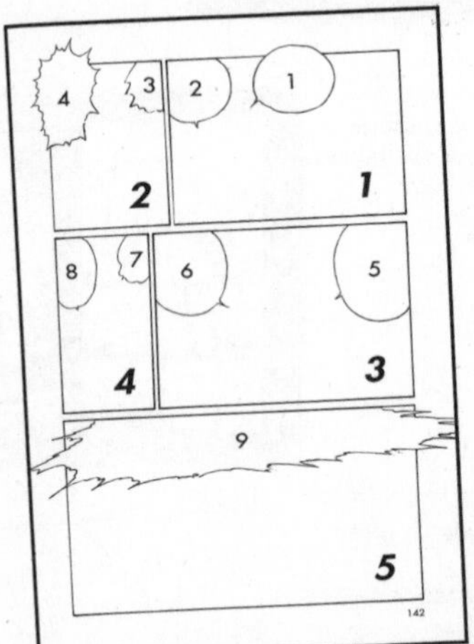

1
2
3
4
1
2
5
6
7
8
3
4
9
5
142

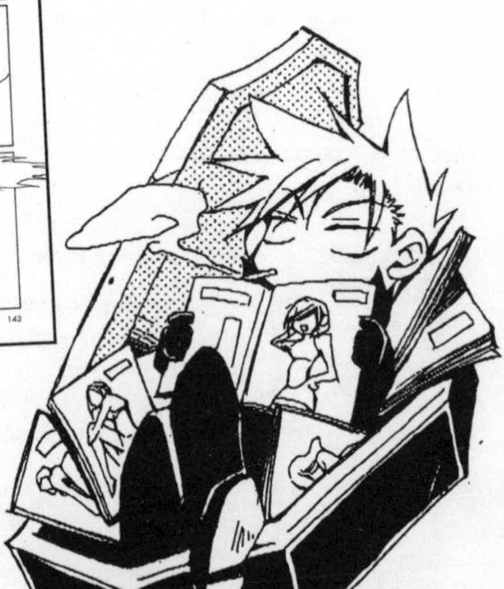